P9-APY-263

ISLAM AND THE SECULAR STATE

Abdullahi Ahmed An-Naʿim

Islam and the Secular State

Negotiating the Future of Shariʿa

HARVARD UNIVERSITY PRESS

Cambridge, Massachusetts, and London, England   2008

Copyright © 2008 by the President and Fellows of Harvard College
All rights reserved
Printed in the United States of America

Library of Congress Cataloging-in-Publication Data

Na'im, 'Abd Allah Ahmad, 1946–
Islam and the secular state : negotiating the future of Shari'a / Abdullahi Ahmed An-Na'im.
p.   cm.
Includes bibliographical references and index.
ISBN-13: 978-0-674-02776-3 (alk. paper)
1. Islam and secularism.   2. Islam and state.   3. Islamic law.   4. Religious pluralism—Islam.
I. Title.
BP190.5.S35N35 2005
297.2'72—dc22   2007034057

Contents

Preface

This book is the culmination of my life's work, the final statement I wish to make on issues I have been struggling with since I was a student at the University of Khartoum, Sudan, in the late 1960s. I speak as a Muslim in this book because I am accountable for these ideas as part of my own religion and not simply as a hypothetical academic argument. But the focus of my proposal is the public role of Shari'a, not matters of religious doctrine and ritual practice in the private, personal domain. While Muslims are my primary audience, non-Muslims should also participate in debating the public role of Shari'a, because what Muslims think and do about these issues affects all human beings everywhere. However, the ethics and rationale of cross-cultural and interreligious dialogue require all sides to strive to learn and understand one another's positions and to be respectful of and sensitive to their apprehensions and concerns. This ethos applies among Muslims as well as between Muslims and non-Muslims. Otherwise, the debate will degenerate into a futile and counterproductive confrontation.

The Islamic argument for a secular state that I am making is in terms of a paradigm or framework for thinking about the issues, and not a hermeneutical or exegetical analysis of Islamic sources which needs to be based on an agreed interpretative framework to be persuasive. A hermeneutical argument without an agreed interpretative framework can simply be countered by an opposing interpretation based on another framework. As I emphasize at various stages of this book, we always understand Islamic sources (or any other text, for that matter) as who we are, in our specific location and context. This book is about issues of self-perception, location, and context in present Islamic societies, which must first be clarified for an agreement on an interpretative framework to evolve. In addition to being premature at this stage, a hermeneutical argument would also be too technical and narrowly focused for the general audience of Muslims and non-Muslims I am seeking to engage in this debate. This broader audience is necessary for facilitating and sustaining agreement on an interpretative framework. If the proposed paradigm is accepted, it can then be further substantiated and developed through hermeneutical or exegetical arguments in support of its basic propositions or specific implications for those who wish to engage in that sort of analysis.

I should also emphasize that the general statement of the framework I am calling for in this book cannot include all the theoretical or practical aspects of the proposed theory. Starting from the premise that Shariʿa will indeed have a role in public life where Muslims are the majority or a significant minority of the population, I am primarily concerned here with clarifying and promoting the most conducive conditions for the negotiation of the future of Shariʿa in the public domain. Since that domain is shared by Muslims and non-Muslims at the local and global levels, the negotiation of the future of Shariʿa must include all human beings who are affected by it. I realize that all aspects of my proposal require further clarification and development, but it is neither possible nor desirable to attempt an exhaustive discussion of all conceivable issues. Debates will continue about the nature of the secular state, the role of religion in public life, the meaning and application of constitutionalism and human rights, the evolving and dynamic understanding of citizenship, and many other issues and concerns. The framework I am proposing is intended to facilitate and clarify the relationship of Islam, the state, and society in the hope of helping to bring about a more positive engagement of Muslims in these debates.

Many elements of what I am proposing have been presented by other Muslim scholars, which I find to be encouraging, because it indicates that my proposal can draw on that accumulation of insights and arguments. Since I am concerned about being persuasive and not about claiming exclusive original authorship, I find it helpful and reassuring that I am not alone in saying this. As I will argue in various parts of this book, the state was never Islamic, though it was not fully secular in the sense I am proposing here. In this light, I am trying to contribute to the clarification of what has been the reality of Islamic societies from the very beginning by seeing how that historical reality can evolve into a viable framework for the future. What I hope to contribute is to bring various elements together, particularly the dimensions of constitutionalism, human rights, and citizenship, in ways that facilitate the practical implementation of the proposed framework for mediating the relationship of Islam, the state, and society.

To that end, I have conceived and conducted the study presented in this book in a way that gives particular priority to presenting my tentative ideas for debate among Muslim scholars and community leaders. In this way, I have sought to address the need for persuasion in the conception and development of the theory itself, rather than simply attempting to do so only after publication. The public debate dimension of the study was therefore integral to the original plan for both its theoretical premise and its desired outcomes. On the one hand, I sought to develop my thesis and its implications out of the insights and reflections of the most current and future-oriented thinking on the subject, which may not be available in a published form. I also planned from the start to relate my analysis to public policy and actual practices as early in this process as possible. On the other hand, I sought ways of contributing to the current thinking while testing the viability and prospects of my own ideas, in addition to improving and refining my ability to communicate them effectively. In other words, I tried to emphasize the actual advocacy for change according to the proposed theory in the process of research and writing, by deliberately seeking to identify possible objections and developing appropriate responses to them, instead of attempting to produce a final statement composed in academic isolation. I am as concerned with my ability to be persuasive as I am with the theoretical integrity and cohesion of the outcome of this study.

Accordingly, I began this process by drafting an initial "concept paper," which was distributed among and discussed with many scholars and opinion leaders during my visits to Istanbul (Turkey), Cairo (Egypt), Khartoum (Sudan), Tashkent and Samarqand (Uzbekistan), New Delhi, Aligarh, Mumbai, and Cochin (India), Jakarta and Yogjakarta (Indonesia), and Abuja, Jos, Kano, and Zaria (Nigeria) between January 2004 and September 2006. With the assistance of local researchers, I was able to conduct individual interviews, roundtable discussions, and seminars. I also presented public lectures to Muslim audiences during visits to all those locations, and in various places in Europe and the United States. At several stages during this process, I revised and expanded the initial concept paper in response to the critical comments and suggestions received and developed out of those activities.

Another important aspect of this advocacy-oriented process is that a draft of the English manuscript was translated into Arabic, Bahasa Indonesia, Bengali, French, Persian, Russian, Turkish, and Urdu. All these manuscripts were gradually uploaded on a website (www.law.emory.edu/fs) launched from Emory Law School in July 2006 for the purpose of generating debate among Muslims in their own languages about the ideas presented in this study. Readers are able to access the manuscript in their own language and communicate whatever responses they may have in that language through a designated e-mail address managed by the translator, who is a native speaker of that language. This emphasis on rendering this manuscript and interaction concerning its findings and conclusions in the native languages of Islamic societies has obvious practical and symbolic significance for the objectives of the study as a whole. However, this emphasis on native languages should not be taken to diminish the value of making this manuscript available in English, which is probably read by more Muslims around the world than any other language. It is true that those who read English tend to be middle-class and professional, but those are a powerful force for change in all societies.

Throughout this process, I have been privileged to have had the assistance and collaboration of too many people and institutions to acknowledge here, but the following deserve special mention. First, I am pleased to gratefully acknowledge the generous financial support of the Ford Foundation and the technical and administrative support of the Center for the Study of Law and Religion of the Emory School of Law. The whole process of research and initial advocacy activities would not have been possible without the intellectual partnership and scholarly contributions of Rohit Chopra of Emory University, who also coordinated the seminars and lectures process in India. This process was coordinated in Indonesia by Chaider S. Bamualim, Irfan Abubakar, and Muhammad Jadul Maula; in Turkey by Recep Senturk and Somnur Vardar; and in Uzbekistan by Aizada A. Khalimbetova. I am also grateful for the rigorous efforts of numerous local researchers, especially Fazzur Rahman Siddiqe and V. A. Mohamad Ashrof in India; Hisyam Zaini and Ruhaini Dzuhayatin in Indonesia; Hani Ali Hassan and Mohamed Salah Abu Nar in Egypt; and Rasha Awad Abduallah in Sudan. I am also grateful for the research and editorial assistance of Rohit Chopra, Abbas Barzgar, and Danielle Goldstone throughout the final stages of preparation for publication.

ISLAM AND THE SECULAR STATE

CHAPTER 1

Introduction:
Why Muslims Need
a Secular State

In order to be a Muslim by conviction and free choice, which is the only way one can be a Muslim, I need a secular state. By a secular state I mean one that is neutral regarding religious doctrine, one that does not claim or pretend to enforce Shari'a—the religious law of Islam—simply because compliance with Shari'a cannot be coerced by fear of state institutions or faked to appease their officials. This is what I mean by secularism in this book, namely, a secular state that facilitates the possibility of religious piety out of honest conviction. My call for the state, and not society, to be secular is intended to enhance and promote genuine religious observance, to affirm, nurture, and regulate the role of Islam in the public life of the community. Conversely, I will argue that the claim of a so-called Islamic state to coercively enforce Shari'a repudiates the foundational role of Islam in the socialization of children and the sanctification of social institutions and relationships. When observed voluntarily, Shari'a plays a fundamental role in shaping and developing ethical norms and values that can be reflected in general legislation and public policy through the democratic political process. But I will argue in this book that Shari'a principles cannot be enacted and enforced by the state as public law and public policy solely on the grounds that they are believed to be part of Shari'a. If such enactment and enforcement is attempted, the outcome will necessarily be the political will of the state and not the religious law of Islam. The fact that ruling elites sometimes make such claims to legitimize their control of the state in the name of Islam does not mean that such claims are true.

The fact that the state is a political and not a religious institution is the historical experience and current reality of Islamic societies. From a theoretical point of view, Ali Abd al-Raziq, for instance, conclusively demonstrated the validity of this premise from a traditional Islamic perspective more than eighty years ago (Abd al-Raziq 1925). In the 1930s, Rashid Ridda strongly affirmed in *al-Manar* that Shari'a cannot be codified as state law. My purpose in this book is not only to support and substantiate this view, but also to contribute to securing its practical benefits for present and future Islamic societies. In particular, dispelling the dangerous illusion of an Islamic state that can enforce Shari'a is necessary for legitimizing and implementing the principles and institutions of constitutionalism, human rights, and citizenship in Islamic societies.

Since, as I will explain, Shari'a principles by their nature and function defy any possibility of enforcement by the state, claiming to enforce Shari'a principles as state law is a logical contradiction that cannot be rectified through repeated efforts under any conditions. In other words, it is not simply a matter of improving upon a bad experience in any country, there or elsewhere, but an objective that can never be realized anywhere. Yet this does not mean the exclusion of Islam from the formulation of public policy and legislation or from public life in general. On the contrary, the state should not attempt to enforce Shari'a precisely so that Muslims are able to live by their own belief in Islam as a matter of religious obligation, not as the outcome of coercion by the state. I will explain and discuss this view of Islam and the secular state in this first chapter, and elaborate various aspects of my argument in subsequent chapters.

An initial issue in this regard is whether the success of my proposal is contingent on substantial reform in the way Muslims understand certain aspects of Shari'a. As I will explain later, this reform is indeed necessary, and I believe that it can best be realized through the methodology proposed by Ustadh Mahmoud Mohamed Taha (Taha 1987). This does not, of course, preclude the possibility of alternative approaches that are capable of achieving the necessary degree of reform. But in this book I will not debate various approaches or elaborate on my own preference for the methodology proposed by Ustadh Mahmoud, which I have done elsewhere (An-Na'im 1990). My primary concern this time is to promote normative standards and institutional conditions for free and orderly public debate and contestation of various approaches to personal choices and responsibility for them. In this regard, the point to emphasize is that there are competing methodologies for the development of Shari'a, which will always remain the total obligation of Muslims to observe in their daily lives.

It may be helpful, however, to distinguish between Shari'a as a *concept* and the particular methodology for determining the normative *content* of

Shariʿa. As a concept, this term refers to the religious law of Islam in general, which is derived from human interpretations of the Qurʾan and Sunna of the Prophet, as briefly explained later. The methodology applied in practice will of course determine what interpretations come to be accepted as authoritative formulations of Shariʿa in a particular time and place. Since any methodology of interpretation is necessarily a human construction, the content of Shariʿa can change over time, as alternative methodologies come to be accepted and applied by Muslims. This constant process is part of what I mean by "negotiating the future of Shariʿa," namely, the elaboration and specification of the concept of Shariʿa into particular content that Muslims will voluntarily comply with in their own context. Other aspects of this process of negotiation relate to promoting the spirit of independent inquiry and supporting personal responsibility for the moral and religious choices Muslims make.

The premise of my proposal is that Muslims everywhere, whether minorities or majorities, are bound to observe Shariʿa as a matter of religious obligation, and that this can best be achieved when the state is neutral regarding all religious doctrines and does not claim to enforce Shariʿa principles as state policy or legislation. That is, people cannot truly live by their convictions according to their belief in and understanding of Islam if rulers use the extensive coercive powers of the state to impose their view of Shariʿa on the population at large, Muslims and non-Muslims alike. This does not mean that the state can or should be completely neutral, because it is a political institution that is supposed to be influenced by the interests and concerns of its citizens. Indeed, legislation and public policy should reflect the beliefs and values of citizens, including religious values, provided this is not done in the name of any specific religion, since that would necessarily favor the views of those who control the state and exclude the religious and other beliefs of other citizens. While this proposition may at one level appear obviously valid to many Muslims, they may still be ambivalent about its clear implications because of the illusion that an Islamic state is supposed to enforce Shariʿa. I am therefore concerned with challenging the core claim of an Islamic state as a postcolonial discourse that relies on European notions of the state and positive law. But I am equally concerned with mounting this challenge in ways that are persuasive to Muslims in particular.

The primary objective of this book is to promote voluntary compliance with Shariʿa among Muslims in their communities by repudiating claims that these principles can be enforced through the coercive powers of the state. By its nature and purpose, Shariʿa can only be freely observed by believers; its principles lose their religious authority and value when enforced by the state. From this fundamental religious perspective, the state must not be allowed to claim the authority of implementing Shariʿa as such. It is true that the state has its proper functions, which may include adjudication among competing claims of religious and secular institutions, but it should be seen as a politically neutral institution performing necessarily secular functions, without claiming religious authority as such. It is also true that the religious beliefs of Muslims, whether as officials of the state or as private citizens, always influence their actions and political behavior. But these are good reasons for keeping a clear distinction between Islam and the state while regulating the connectedness of Islam and politics. As I will emphasize later, Islam is the religion of human beings who believe in it, while the state signifies the continuity of institutions like the judiciary and administrative agencies. This view is fundamentally Islamic, because it insists on the religious neutrality of the state as a necessary condition for Muslims to comply with their religious obligations. Religious compliance must be completely voluntary according to personal pious intention *(niyah),* which is necessarily invalidated by coercive enforcement of those obligations. In fact, coercive enforcement promotes hypocrisy *(nifaq),* which is categorically and repeatedly condemned by the Qurʾan.

My purpose is therefore to affirm and support the institutional separation of Islam and the state, which is necessary for Shariʿa to have its proper positive and enlightening role in the lives of Muslims and Islamic societies. This view can also be called "the religious neutrality of the state," whereby state institutions neither favor nor disfavor any religious doctrine or principle. The object of such neutrality, however, is precisely the freedom of individuals in their communities to accept, object to, or modify any view of religious doctrine or principle.

This does not mean that Islam and politics should be separated; their separation is neither necessary nor desirable. Separating Islam and the state while maintaining the connection between Islam and politics allows for the implementation of Islamic principles in official policy and legislation but subjects them to the safeguards explained below. This view is premised on a difficult distinction between the state and politics, despite the obvious and permanent connection of the two, as explained in Chapter 3. It may therefore be helpful to speak of the deliberate and strategic mediation of this tension by striving to separate Islam and the state, as well as regulating the connection between Islam and politics to sustain that separation, instead of attempting to impose a categorical resolution one way or the other.

The state is a complex web of organs, institutions, and processes that are supposed to implement the policies adopted through the political process of each society. In this sense, the state should be the more settled and deliberate operational side of self-governance, while politics serves as the dynamic process of making choices among competing policy options. To fulfill that and other functions, the state must have a monopoly on the legitimate use of force: the ability to impose its will on the population at large without risking the use of counterforce by those subject to its jurisdiction. This coercive power of the state, which is now more extensive and effective than ever before in human history, will be counterproductive when exercised in an arbitrary manner or for corrupt or illegitimate ends. That is why it is critically important to keep the state as neutral as humanly possible. The establishment of this neutrality requires constant vigilance by the generality of citizens acting through a wide variety of political, legal, educational, and other strategies and mechanisms.

The distinction between the state and politics therefore assumes a constant interaction among the organs and the institutions of the state, on the one hand, and the organized political and social actors and their competing visions of the public good, on the other. This distinction is also premised on an acute awareness of the risks of abuse or corruption of the necessary coercive powers of the state. The state must not be simply a complete reflection of daily politics. For it to mediate and adjudicate among competing visions and policy proposals, it must remain relatively independent from varying political forces in society. However, since complete autonomy is not possible, because the state cannot be totally independent of those political actors who control its apparatus, it is sometimes important to recall the state's political nature. Paradoxically, this reality of connectedness makes it necessary to strive to separate the state from politics, so that those excluded by the political processes of the day can still resort to state organs and institutions for protection against excessive use or abuse of power by state officials.

Consider what happens when a single ruling party takes complete control over the state, as in Nazi Germany, the Soviet Union, and many states in Africa and the Arab world during the last decades of the twentieth century. Whether it was Arab nationalism in Egypt under Nasser or the Baaʿth Party in Iraq under Saddam Hussein and in Syria under Hafiz al-Assad, the state became the immediate agent of the ruling party, and citizens were trapped between the state and the party, without the possibility of any administrative or legal remedy from the state or of lawful political opposition outside its sphere of control. Failure to observe the distinction between the state and politics tends to severely undermine the peace, stability, and healthy development of the whole society. Such disintegration occurs when those who are denied the services and the protection of the state, or effective participation in politics, either withdraw their cooperation or resort to violent resistance in the absence of peaceful remedies.

The question should therefore be how to sustain the distinction between the state and politics, instead of ignoring the tension in the hope that it will somehow resolve itself. This necessary though difficult distinction can be mediated through the principles and institutions of constitutionalism and the protection of the equal human rights of all citizens. But as I will discuss in Chapter 3, these principles and institutions cannot succeed without the active and determined participation of all citizens, which is unlikely if people believe them to be inconsistent with the religious beliefs and cultural norms that influence their political behavior. The principles of popular sovereignty and democratic governance presuppose that citizens are sufficiently motivated and determined to participate in all aspects of self-governance, including organized political action to hold their government accountable and responsive to their wishes. This motivation and determination, which is partly influenced by the religious beliefs and cultural conditioning of the citizens of the state, must be founded on their appreciation of and commitment to the values of constitutionalism and human rights. This is why it is important to strive to justify my proposal from an Islamic perspective for Muslims, without denying the right of others to support the same position from their respective religious or philosophical positions.

Stated differently, this book is an attempt to clarify and support the necessary but difficult mediation of the paradox of institutional separation of Islam and the state, despite the unavoidable connection between Islam and politics in present Islamic societies. As a Muslim, I seek to contribute to this process in Islamic societies without implying that the issues I am discussing here are peculiar to Islam and Muslims alone. I challenge the dangerous illusion of an Islamic state that claims the right to enforce Shari'a principles through its own coercive power. But I also challenge the dangerous illusion that Islam can or should be kept out of the public life of the community of believers. The wide diversity of opinions among Muslim scholars and schools of thought *(madhahib)* in practice means that state institutions would have to select among competing views that are equally legitimate from one Islamic view or another. Since there are no generally agreed-upon standards or mechanisms for adjudicating among these competing views, whatever is imposed by the organs of the state as official policy or formal legislation will necessarily be based on the human judgment of those who control those institutions.

In other words, whatever the state enforces in the name of Shariʿa will necessarily be secular and the product of coercive political power and not superior Islamic authority, even if it is possible to ascertain what that means among Muslims at large. The categorical repudiation of the dangerous illusion of an Islamic state that can coercively enforce Shariʿa principles is necessary for the practical ability of Muslims and other citizens to live in accordance with their religious and other beliefs. The notion of an Islamic state is in fact a postcolonial innovation based on a European model of the state and a totalitarian view of law and public policy as instruments of social engineering by the ruling elites. Although the states that historically ruled over Muslims did seek Islamic legitimacy in a variety of ways, they were not claimed to be "Islamic states." The proponents of a so-called Islamic state in the modern context seek to use the institutions and powers of the state, as constituted by European colonialism and continued after independence, to regulate individual behavior and social relations in ways selected by the ruling elites. It is particularly dangerous to attempt such totalitarian initiatives in the name of Islam, because they are far more difficult for Muslims to resist than initiatives sought by an openly secular state. At the same time, the institutional separation of any religion and the state is not easy, because the state must necessarily regulate the role of religion to maintain its own religious neutrality, which is required for its role as a mediator and an adjudicator among competing social and political forces.

The separation of Islam and the state does not prevent Muslims from proposing policy or legislation stemming from their religious or other beliefs. All citizens have the right to do so, provided they should support such proposals with what I call "civic reason." The word "civic" here refers to the need for policy and legislation to be accepted by the public at large, as well as for the process of reasoning on the matter to remain open and accessible to all citizens. By civic reason, I mean that the rationale and the purpose of public policy or legislation must be based on the sort of reasoning that most citizens can accept or reject. Citizens must be able to make counterproposals through public debate without being open to charges about their religious piety. Civic reason and reasoning, and not personal beliefs and motivations, are necessary whether Muslims constitute the majority or the minority of the population of the state. Even if Muslims are the majority, they will not necessarily agree on what policy and legislation should follow from their Islamic beliefs.

The requirement of civic reason and reasoning assumes that people who control the state are not likely to be neutral. Not only is this requirement essential, but it must also be the objective of the operation of the state, precisely because people are apt to continue to act on personal beliefs or justifications. The requirement to present publicly and openly justifications that are based on reasons which the generality of the population can freely accept or reject will over time encourage and develop a broader consensus among the population at large, beyond the narrow religious or other beliefs of various individuals and groups. Since the ability to present civic reasons and debate them publicly is already present at some level in most societies, I am calling only for its further conscious and incremental development over time.

It is difficult in practice to ensure that people comply with the requirements of civic reason in making choices within the realm of inner motivation and intentions. It may be difficult to understand why people vote in a particular way or how they justify their political agenda to themselves or to their close associates. But the objective should be to promote and encourage civic reason and reasoning, which over time will diminish the exclusive influence of personal religious beliefs over public policy and legislation. This view does not apply to personal and communal religious experience outside the realm of the state, because protecting freedom of religion and belief from state intervention is in fact one of the objectives of the whole approach.

I am calling for the state to be secular, not for secularizing society. I argue for keeping the influence of the state from corrupting the genuine and independent piety of persons in their communities. Ensuring that the state is neutral regarding religious doctrine is necessary for true conviction to be the driving force of religious and social practice, without fear of those who control the state or desire for the power and wealth they may claim to bestow. This combination should address the apprehensions of Muslims about secularism as secularization of society or hostility to religion. The common negative perception of secularism is due to a failure to distinguish between the state and politics, as discussed later. By failing to recognize this distinction, many Muslims take the separation of Islam and the state to mean the total relegation of Islam to the purely private domain and its exclusion from public policy. I use the term "secular state," instead of "secularism," to avoid this negative perception. The question for me is how to transform the attitudes of Muslims regarding the inherently secular nature of the state and the critical role of the principles of constitutionalism, human rights, and citizenship in mediating the permanent tensions among Islam, the state, and society.

I am also concerned with clarifying how the constant negotiation of these relationships in present Islamic societies is shaped by profound transformations in their political, social, and economic structures and institutions as a result of European colonialism and, more recently, global capitalism. This context is also shaped by the internal political and sociological circumstances of each society, including the internalization of externally inspired changes, whereby Islamic societies have voluntarily continued to follow Western forms of state formation, education, social organization, and economic, legal, and administrative arrangements after achieving political independence. I am not suggesting that Muslims should accept these realities because they have no choice. Rather, I argue that adaptation to these realities is in fact more consistent with historical Islamic traditions than are the totalitarian post-colonial claims of an Islamic state.

Islam, Shariʿa, and the State

Since the subject of this book is the relationships among Islam, the state, and society, it is important to briefly clarify the manner in which I am using these terms to avoid any misunderstanding that might arise from false or unwarranted assumptions. This is particularly important since I am attempting to influence the attitudes of other Muslims as a Muslim, rather than in a detached or impersonal manner.

Let us begin with the general understanding of Islam as the monotheistic religion *(Din al-Tawhid)* that the Prophet Muhammad propagated between 610 and 632 CE, when he delivered the Qur'an and expounded its meaning and application through what came to be known as the Sunna of the Prophet. These two sources are therefore foundational to any sense in which the term "Islam" and its derivative concepts and adjectives are used, especially among Muslims. They provide the articles of faith and doctrine that Muslims espouse, including the ritual practices they are supposed to observe and the moral and ethical precepts they are bound to respect. The Qur'an and Sunna are also where Muslims look for guidance in developing their social and political relations, legal norms, and institutions. In this foundational sense, Islam is about realizing the liberating power of a living and proactive confession of faith in an infinitely singular, omnipotent, and omnipresent God. This is the sense of Islam that the vast majority of Muslims experience in everyday life, and from which they seek spiritual and moral guidance. My proposal should therefore be judged by its utility in enhancing the ability of Muslims to live by the dictates of their religion.

The term "Shari'a" is often used in present Islamic discourse as if it were synonymous with Islam itself, as the totality of Muslim obligations both in the private, personal religious sense and vis-à-vis social, political, and legal norms and institutions. As indicated earlier, however, it is important to distinguish between the concept of Shari'a as the totality of the duty of Muslims and any particular perception of it through a specific human methodology of interpretation of the Qur'an and Sunna. But even as a concept, Shari'a is the door or passageway into being Muslim and does not exhaust the possibilities of experiencing Islam. There is more to Islam than Shari'a, though knowing and complying with the dictates of Shari'a is the way to realize Islam as the principle of *tawhid* in the daily lives of Muslims. It should also be emphasized that Shari'a principles are always derived from human interpretation of the Qur'an and Sunna; they are what human beings can comprehend and seek to obey within their own specific historical context (Ibn Rushd 2001, 8–10). Striving to know and observe Shari'a is always the product of the "human agency" of believers—a system of meaning that is constructed out of human experience and reflection, which over time evolves into a more systematic development according to an established methodology.

The premise of an Islamic discourse is that each and every Muslim is personally responsible for knowing and complying with what is required of him or her. The fundamental principle of individual personal responsibility that can never be abdicated or delegated is one of the recurring themes of the Qur'an (for example, 6:164; 17:15; 35:18; 39:7; 52:21; 74:38). Yet when Muslims seek to know what Shari'a requires of them in any specific situation, they are more likely to ask an Islamic scholar (*alim,* plural *ulama*) or a Sufi leader they trust than to refer directly to the Qur'an and Sunna themselves. Whether done personally or, more usually, by a scholar or a Sufi leader, reference to the Qur'an and Sunna necessarily happens through the structure and methodology every Muslim has been raised to accept. This process normally occurs within the framework of a particular school *(madhhab)* and its established doctrine and methodology. But this never happens in a totally fresh and original manner, and certainly not without preconceived notions of how to identify and interpret the relevant texts of the Qur'an and Sunna. In other words, whenever Muslims consider these primary sources, they cannot avoid the layered filters of the experiences and interpretations of preceding generations of Muslims and the elaborate methodology that determines which texts are deemed to be relevant to any subject and how they should be understood. Human agency is therefore integral to any approach to the Qur'an and Sunna at multiple levels, ranging from centuries of accumulated experience and interpretation to the current context in which an Islamic frame of reference is invoked.

The state is not an entity that can feel, believe, or act by itself. It is always human beings who act in the name of the state, exercise its powers, or operate through its organs. Thus, whenever a human being makes a decision about a policy matter, or proposes or drafts legislation that is supposed to embody Islamic principles, this will necessarily reflect his or her personal perspective on the subject and never that of the state as an autonomous entity. Moreover, when these policies or legislative proposals are made in the name of a political party or organization, such positions are also taken by the human leaders speaking or acting for that entity. It is true that specific positions on matters of policy and legislation can be negotiated among many actors, but the outcome will still be the product of individual human judgment and the human choice to accept and act on a view that is agreed upon among those actors.

For instance, a decision to punish the consumption of alcoholic drinks as a *hadd* crime or to prohibit charging interest on loans *(riba)* is necessarily the view of individual political actors taken after weighing all sorts of practical considerations. Moreover, the formulation, adoption, and implementation of legislation to achieve that objective are all always matters of human judgment and choice. The whole process of formulating and implementing public policy and legislation is subject to human error and fallibility, which means that it can always be challenged or questioned without violating the direct and immediate divine will of God. This is part of the reason that matters of public policy and legislation must be supported by civic reason, even among Muslims, who can and do disagree in all such matters without violating their religious obligations.

The methodology known as *usul al-fiqh*, through which Muslims have historically understood and applied Islamic precepts as conveyed in the Qur'an and Sunna, was developed by early Muslim scholars. In its original formulations, this field of human knowledge sought to regulate the interpretation of these foundational sources in light of the historical experiences of early generations of Muslims. It also defines and regulates the operation of juridical techniques such as *ijma'* (consensus), *qiyas* (reasoning by analogy), and *ijtihad* (juridical reasoning). These techniques are commonly understood as the methods for specifying Shari'a principles rather than as substantive sources. However, *ijma'* and *ijtihad* have had more foundational roles beyond their limited technical meanings. It is that broader sense that can form the basis of a more dynamic and creative development of Shari'a now and in the future.

Islam and Shari'a

The foundational and continuing role of consensus among generations of Muslims is important not only for historical interpretation of Shari'a but for its constant reform and evolution over time. The critical role of consensus is clear from the fact that it is the basis of the acceptance of the text of the Qur'an *(al-Mushaf)* and records of Sunna as authentic content of the fundamental sources of Islam and Shari'a among countless generations of Muslims. The belief that the text we are reading today in Arabic is in fact the actual text of the Qur'an as delivered by the Prophet is based on the fact that it has been handed down from one generation to the next since the time of the Prophet. The same is true of Sunna, which most Muslims accept as the authentic report of what the Prophet said and did. The fact that some controversies continue among Muslims about the authenticity of certain texts of Sunna reflects the weakness of the consensus basis of those particular texts. But in general, our knowledge of the Qur'an and Sunna is the result of intergenerational consensus since the seventh century. Moreover, consensus is the basis of the authority and continuity of *usul al-fiqh* and all of its principles and techniques, because this interpretative structure is always dependent on its acceptance as such among the generality of Muslims from one generation to the next. In this sense, consensus is the basis of the acceptance of the Qur'an and Sunna themselves, as well as of the totality and the details of the methodology and content of their interpretation.

For Muslims, the significant difference between the Qur'an and Sunna and the techniques of *usul al-fiqh* is that there is no possibility of new additions to either of these texts. The Prophet Muhammad was the final prophet and the Qur'an is the conclusive divine revelation. In contrast, there is nothing to prevent the formation of a fresh consensus around new interpretative techniques or innovative interpretations of the Qur'an and Sunna, which would become a part of Shari'a, just as the existing methodologies and interpretations came to be a part of it in the first place. The safeguards of separating Islam from the state and regulating the political role of Islam through constitutionalism and the protection of human rights are necessary to ensure freedom and security for Muslims so that they can participate in evolving new techniques and proposing and debating fresh interpretations of the Qur'an and Sunna. As to concerns about the validity of such innovations, the safeguard is the same as it used to be with what is now "established" Shari'a, namely, acceptance by generations of Muslims. In other words, a new interpretative methodology or new substantive principles will not become part of Shari'a unless they are accepted by most Muslims over time. This is the same way any methodology or principle became part of Shari'a in the first place. The challenge is to ensure the freedom to propose and debate so that consensus can freely evolve among Muslims, either in support of or against whatever is being proposed.

Any understanding of Shari'a is always the product of *ijtihad*, in the general sense that reasoning and reflection by human beings are ways of understanding the meanings of the Qur'an and Sunna of the Prophet. But in the process of the development of Shari'a during the second and third centuries of Islam, this term was defined and limited by Muslim scholars in two ways. First, they determined that *ijtihad* can be exercised only in matters that are not governed by the categorical texts *(nass qat'i)* of the Qur'an and Sunna. This is a logical proposition, but it not only assumes that Muslims agree on which texts are relevant to a particular issue and on how to interpret those texts, but also deems that whatever consensus was achieved over these matters in the past is permanent. Second, early Muslim scholars specified detailed requirements for a person to be accepted as qualified to exercise *ijtihad (mujtahid)*, as well as the manner in which *ijtihad* can be exercised. But even the very definition of the term or qualification needed by the scholar who can exercise this role is necessarily the product of human reasoning and judgment. So why should that human process preclude subsequent reconsideration?

Determinations about whether or not any text *(nass)* of the Qur'an or Sunna applies to an issue, whether or not it is categorical *(qat'i)*, and who can exercise *ijtihad* and how are all matters that can be decided only through human reasoning and judgment. It therefore follows that imposing prior censorship on such efforts violates the premise of how Shariʿa can be derived from the Qurʾan and Sunna. It is illogical to say that *ijtihad* cannot be exercised regarding any issue or question, because that determination itself is the product of human reasoning and reflection. It is also dangerous to limit the ability to exercise *ijtihad* to a restricted group of Muslims who are supposed to have specific qualities, because in practice that will depend on those human beings who set the criteria and select a person as a qualified *mujtahid*. To concede this authority to any institution or group, whether it is official or not, is dangerous, because that power will likely be manipulated for political or other reasons. The fact that knowing and upholding Shariʿa is the permanent and inescapable responsibility of every Muslim means that no human being or institution should control this process. The power to decide who is qualified to exercise *ijtihad* and how it is to be exercised is part of the religious belief and obligation of every Muslim. Any restriction of free debate by entrusting human beings or institutions with the authority to decide which views are to be allowed or suppressed is inconsistent with the religious nature of Shariʿa itself. This reasoning is one of the main Islamic foundations I propose for safeguarding constitutionalism, human rights, and citizenship for all.

Another relevant point to note here is that the systemic development of Shariʿa began during the early Abbasid era (after 750 CE). This view of the relatively late evolution of Shariʿa as a coherent and self-contained system in Islamic history is clear from the time frame for the emergence of the major schools of thought, the systematic collection of Sunna as the second and more detailed source of Shariʿa, and the development of the juridical methodology. All these developments took place in the second and third centuries of Islam. The early Abbasid era witnessed the emergence of the main schools of Islamic jurisprudence, including those still known today. The surviving schools are attributed to Jaʿfar al-Sadiq, the founder of the main school of Shiʿa jurisprudence (died 765), Abu Hanifa (died 767), Malik (died 795), al-Shafiʿi (died 820), and Ibn Hanbal (died 855). Al-Shafiʿi is commonly acknowledged to have laid the foundations of *usul al-fiqh* to regulate the interpretation of the Qurʾan and Sunna, but the process of collection and authentication of Sunna reports continued beyond his time. The most authoritative compilations of Sunna for Sunni Muslims are attributed to Bukhari (died 870), Muslim (died 875), Ibn Majah (died 886), Abu Dawud (died 888), al-Tirmidhi (died 892), and al-Nasa'i (died 915). For the Shi'a, the most authoritative compilations also emerged during that general time frame, namely, those attributed to al-Kulayni (died 941), Ibn Babawayh (died 991), and al-Tusi (died 1067). The subsequent development and the spread of the various schools have been influenced by many political, social, and demographic factors, which have sometimes resulted in shifting schools from one region to another, thus confining them to certain parts, as is the case with Shi'a schools at present. Such factors may have also contributed to the total extinction of schools, like those of al-Thawri and al-Tabari in the Sunni tradition.

The principle of consensus apparently acted as a unifying force during the second and third centuries of Islam by drawing the substantive content of Sunni schools together, diminishing the scope of creative new thinking through *ijtihad*. The commonly held view is that there was a gradual decrease in the role of creative juridical reasoning (the so-called closing of the gate of *ijtihad*) on the assumption that Shari'a had already been fully and exhaustively elaborated. Whether there was a closing of the gate of *ijtihad* or not is the subject of debate among historians (Hallaq 1984). But it is clear that there has not been any change in the basic structure and methodology of Shari'a since the tenth century, although practical adaptations continued in limited scope and locations. That rigidity was probably necessary for maintaining the stability of the system during the decline, and sometimes breakdown, of the social and political institutions of Islamic societies. However, from an Islamic point of view, no human authority was or is entitled to declare that *ijtihad* is not permitted, though there may have been consensus on this matter among Muslims. There is nothing, therefore, to prevent the emergence of a new consensus that *ijtihad* should be freely exercised to meet the new needs and aspirations of Islamic societies. The purpose of the proposal presented here is to secure the political, social, and intellectual space for debate and reformation, not to prescribe a particular approach to that debate. The essentially religious nature of Shari'a and its focus on regulating the relationship between God and human believers mean that believers can neither abdicate nor delegate their responsibility. No human institution can be religious in this sense, even when it claims to apply or enforce principles of Shari'a. In other words, the state and all its institutions are by definition secular and not religious, regardless of claims to the contrary.

Shari'a and the State

Another aspect of the legal history of Islamic societies that is associated with the religious nature of Shari'a is the development of private legal consultation *(ifta)*. Scholars who are independent of the state can issue legal opinions *(fatwa)* at the request of provincial governors and state judges, in addition to providing advice for individual persons, as they have done from the very beginning of Islam. But the individual responsibility of each and every Muslim can be neither abdicated nor delegated through the institution of *fatwa*. The person seeking such an opinion remains responsible, from a religious point of view, for whatever action he or she takes or fails to take under the *fatwa*, while the person expressing the opinion *(mufti)* is also responsible for that opinion. The practical need for administration and adjudication will of course continue, as will the need to seek to benefit from the knowledge and views of scholars. My point is simply that such efforts are secular, since they cannot displace the religious responsibility of each individual Muslim.

This can be illustrated with reference to the Ottoman Empire, the last major state ruled by Muslims before European colonial rule and the current postcolonial era. As explained in Chapter 5, the Ottoman sultans represent one of the best examples of how worldly rulers negotiated a balance between pragmatic politics and administration, on the one hand, and invocation of religious authority to legitimize their rule, on the other. The Ottoman sultans never attempted to implement the totality of Shari'a and preferred to apply the Hanafi school in specific and limited jurisdictions. When they eventually decided to codify some Hanafi principles, by the mid-nineteenth century, that marked the first time in Islamic history in which Shari'a principles interpreted by a single school were codified and enacted as the uniform official law of the land. That innovation, which became the norm in the postcolonial Muslim world, at least on family-law matters, legitimized and institutionalized state selectivity among the competing views of Shari'a without genuinely opening the basis of family-law legislation to debate as a matter of public policy. Similar displacement of Shari'a and local customary systems by colonial codes, while isolating a so-called family-law field to be governed by Shari'a principles, occurred in Islamic parts of Asia and Africa.

However, there was a tension between the reality of state sponsorship of a particular school and the need to maintain the traditional independence of Shari'a, as rulers are supposed to safeguard and promote Shari'a without creating or controlling it. This tension has continued into the modern era, when Shari'a remains the religious law of the community of believers, independent of the authority of the state, while the state seeks to enlist the legitimizing power of Shari'a in support of its political authority.

Moreover, the concessions made by the Ottoman Empire to European powers set the model for the adoption of Western codes and systems of administration of justice. Ottoman imperial edicts justified the changes not only in the name of strengthening the state and preserving Islam but also in order to emphasize the need to ensure equality among Ottoman subjects. That rationale probably laid the foundation for the adoption of the European model of the nation-state and its legally equal citizens. A brief review is instructive, because the late Ottoman experience became the model for the whole Muslim world in the twentieth century.

The Ottoman codification of some aspects of Shari'a as represented by the Hanafi school, known as *Majallah,* acquired the position of supreme authority soon after its enactment, partly because it represented the earliest and most politically authoritative example of the authority of the state to promulgate Shari'a principles officially, thereby transforming them into positive law in the modern sense of the term. Moreover, that legislation was directly applied in a wide range of Islamic societies throughout the Ottoman Empire and continued to apply in some parts into the second half of the twentieth century. The success of the *Majallah* was also due to the fact that it included some provisions drawn from sources other than the Hanafi school, thereby expanding the possibilities of selectivity from within the broader Islamic tradition. The principle of selectivity *(takhayur)* among equally legitimate doctrines of Shari'a was already accepted in theory, as noted earlier, but was not used in practice on such a formal and general scale. By applying it through the institutions of the state, the *Majallah* opened the door for subsequent reforms, despite its initially limited purpose. At the same time, however, the codification of the views of a single school, even with some selectivity and inclusion of some other views, precluded access to other schools and scholars. The whole process was the product of the secular political authority of the state, not the religious authority of Shari'a as such.

This trend toward increased eclecticism in the selection of sources and the synthesis of Islamic and Western legal concepts and institutions not only became irreversible but was also carried further, especially through the work of the French-educated Egyptian jurist Abd al-Razziq al-Sanhuri (died 1971). The pragmatic approach of al-Sanhuri was premised on the view that Shari'a cannot be reintroduced in its totality and cannot be applied without strong adaptation to the needs of modern Islamic societies. He used this approach in drafting the Egyptian Civil Code of 1948, the Iraqi Code of 1951, the Libyan Code of 1953, and the Kuwaiti Civil Code and Commercial Law of 1960–1961. In all cases, al-Sanhuri was brought in by an autocratic ruler to draft a comprehensive code that was enacted into law without public debate. It is therefore difficult to tell whether that model could have worked if those countries had been democratic at the time. What is clear, however, is that irrespective of the alleged inclusion of Shari'a principles, the process itself was clearly one of secular legislation and not a direct enactment of the divinely ordained law of Islam.

Paradoxically, those changes also made the entire corpus of Shari'a principles more available and accessible to judges and policymakers in the process of selecting and adapting aspects to be incorporated into modern legislation. The synthesis of the Islamic and European legal traditions also exposed how impossible it was to apply Shari'a principles directly and systematically in the modern context. The main reason for that is the complexity and diversity of Shari'a itself, owing to its evolution through the centuries. In addition to the strong disagreement between and within Sunni and Shi'a communities that coexist within a single country (as in Iraq, Lebanon, Saudi Arabia, and Pakistan), various Muslim communities may follow different schools or scholarly opinions, though those schools or opinions are not formally applied in the courts. In addition, judicial practice may not necessarily be in accordance with the school that the majority of the Muslim population in the country follows. For example, state courts in Egypt and Sudan inherited the official Ottoman preference for the Hanafi school, even though the popular practice in that region adheres to the Shafi'i and Maliki schools. Since modern states can operate only on officially established principles of law of general application, Shari'a principles cannot be enacted or enforced as the positive law of any country without being subjected to selection among competing interpretations, which are all deemed to be legitimate by the traditional Shari'a doctrine. This legislative process is as unavoidable for a purported Islamic state that is supposed to enforce the totality of Shari'a as it is for secular regimes that claim to enforce Shari'a principles only in the family-law field.

The legal and political consequences of these developments were intensified by the significant impact of European colonialism and global Western influence in the fields of general education and professional training of state officials. Curricular changes in educational institutions meant that Shari'a was no longer the focus of advanced instruction in Islamic knowledge, and Shariʿa was displaced by a spectrum of secular subjects mostly derived from Western models. In legal education in particular, the first generation of law-yers and jurists undertook advanced training in European and North Ameri-can universities and returned to teach the subsequent generations or to hold senior judicial offices. Moreover, in contrast to the extremely limited degree of literacy in traditional Islamic societies of the past, in which the scholars of Shariʿa monopolized the intellectual leadership of their communities, mass basic literacy is now growing rapidly throughout the Muslim world, thereby opening the door for much more democratic access to knowledge.

Thus, not only have the *ulama* lost their historical monopoly on the knowledge of the sacred sources of Shariʿa, but the traditional interpreta-tions of those sources are gradually being questioned by ordinary Muslims. This opportunity should motivate Muslim advocates of a secular state and the protection of human rights to learn more about Islamic sources, history, and the methodology of Shariʿa in order to be more effective in challenging traditional interpretations. But this does not mean that there should be a formal certification process by an institution whereby a Muslim becomes qualified to exercise *ijtihad.* On the contrary, all Muslim men and women have the religious obligation to learn enough to decide for themselves and to express their views on matters of public concern. It is just that those with the most knowledge of the Islamic sources and methodology will be more au-thoritative and persuasive than those who lack such knowledge.

The transformation of the nature of the state itself in its local and global context is particularly significant for our purposes here. Although estab-lished under colonial auspices, the European model of the state for all Is-lamic societies has radically transformed political, economic, and social rela-tions throughout various regions. By retaining this specific form of state organization after political independence, Islamic societies have chosen to be bound by a minimum set of national and international obligations of membership in the world community of territorial states. While there are clear differences in their level of social development and political stability, Is-lamic societies today live under domestic constitutional regimes and legal systems that require respect for certain minimum rights of equality and nondiscrimination for all of their citizens. Even where national constitutions and legal systems fail to expressly acknowledge and effectively provide for these obligations, the present realities of international relations ensure a minimum degree of practical compliance. These changes are simply irrevers-

ible, though stronger and more systematic conformity with the requirements of democratic governance and human rights remains uncertain and
problematic for many countries and societies throughout the world.

In conclusion of this brief overview of Islam, Shariʿa, and the state, it is
clear that there is an urgent need to continue the process of Islamic reform
to reconcile the religious commitment of Muslims with the practical needs
of their societies today. It is also clear that the main premise of a viable reform process is that the meaning and the implementation of the Qurʾan and
Sunna in everyday life are always the product of human interpretation and
action in a specific historical context. It is simply impossible to know and apply Shariʿa in this life except through the agency of human beings. Any view
of Shariʿa known to Muslims today, even if unanimously agreed upon, had
to emerge from the opinion of human beings about the meaning of the
Qurʾan and Sunna, as accepted by many generations of Muslims and the
practice of their communities. In other words, opinions of Muslim scholars
became part of Shariʿa through the consensus of believers over many centuries, and not by the spontaneous decree of a ruler or the will of a single
group of scholars. Accordingly, as I will further clarify, what I am proposing
is in fact the true continuity of historical Islamic traditions. In contrast, the
advocate of an Islamic state to enforce Shariʿa as state law is in fact promoting a European, positivistic view of law and a totalitarian model of the state
that seeks to transform society into its own image.

The Framework and Processes of Social Transformation

One aspect of the transformation of the relationship among Islam, Shariʿa,
and the state relates to the domain of the state, while the other operates at
the civil-society level. These two dimensions of transformation through official institutional and civil-societal changes are in fact interdependent and
mutually supportive. Each objective may require different strategies and action, which may vary from one social and cultural context to another, but
the two kinds of transformations are deeply connected in that each is both
the cause and the outcome of the other. For this dynamic transformation to
happen in Islamic societies, we also have to clarify and transform the permanent and desirable relationship between Islam and politics, as suggested earlier.

The proposed approach, therefore, recognizes the multiple levels of relevance of Islam to Muslim communities across the globe: as a religion, as a

political ideology for some Muslims, and, more broadly, as a culture and the basis of social practice. This indicates a third dimension of my proposal, which is the question of how to root social change in culture or endow it with cultural legitimacy. Cultural transformation or social change cannot be achieved as a purely external initiative that is indifferent to history, culture, or social practice. Rather, social change and cultural transformation must be grounded in the culture of communities themselves to be legitimate, coherent, and sustainable. This in turn indicates the role played by the communities and their members as participants, subjects, and actors of social change—in other words, the role of human agency in the process. I will now discuss the various dimensions of this framework of social transformation in terms of the dynamics of culture and identity, the imperative of cultural legitimacy for social change, and the role of human agency.

Culture and Identity

Cultures may seem identifiable and distinguishable from each other, but each of them is characterized by internal diversity, propensity to change, and mutual influence in its relationship with other cultures. We may speak of particular local, national, and regional cultures, or communal culture defined by language, ethnicity, religion, or economic and security interests. Shared norms, customs, and histories within a group bring coherence to the notion of a common culture even when there are overlaps with other groups. While recognition of such commonality should not come at the expense of the recognition of diversity and contestation within each culture, seeing cultures as different should not lead us to believe that they defy cross-cultural or comparative analysis. Internal diversity and contestation, as well as cross-cultural dialogue and mutual influence, can in fact facilitate the development of an overlapping consensus on certain values and practice, such as constitutionalism and human rights, despite persistent differences about the foundations and rationale of such agreement.

Islamic societies are subject to the same principles of social and political life that apply to other human societies, because Muslims, like all human beings, strive to meet their basic needs for food and shelter, security, political stability, and so forth. Muslims seek to meet those needs, and also to change and adapt their culture to work under new circumstances, in ways that may be similar to or different from those of other societies, but that is not necessarily determined by Islam. While the characteristic features of Islam as a religion shape the ways in which it is understood and practiced by Muslims in different settings, that understanding is not so exceptional as to defy the principles of social and political life of human societies in general. Some Islamic communities in the Indian subcontinent may have more in common with Hindu or Sikh communities of the same region, because of shared history, colonial experiences, and present context, than with Islamic communities of sub-Saharan Africa, whose culture and practices may similarly be closely related to those of neighboring non-Muslim communities.

The term "identity" is often invoked to indicate something that is clearly defined, stable, and fixed. However, it is also clear that people organize their lives to be open and flexible enough to take advantage of alternative options, which they can justify in terms of their cultural or religious value system and meaning. We all make choices every day about which aspects of our identity to emphasize or deemphasize so as to promote or protect our short- or long-term interests. As a Muslim, I may assert an exclusive Islamic identity or emphasize Islamic tolerance and acceptance of religious differences, depending on whether I am a member of a majority or minority and the prevailing political relations among the religious communities of my country.

In other words, identity formation and transformation is a dynamic process involving deliberate choices, not an immutable or inevitable condition. Individuals construct meanings and values through cultural codes that are shared by particular groups. However, it is not uncommon for a person to switch between the codes as he or she moves among a variety of sociocultural identities. These codes include "primordial attachments," such as language and religious affiliations, which are learned or formed at an early age, as well as new codes that are learned later in life. We also sometimes switch codes in an "instrumentalist" or calculated manner, which may not necessarily be consistent with the publicly declared or assumed objectives of the original codes. Moreover, each set of processes and interactions combines elements of adjusted and/or retrieved preexisting identities, together with newly created or situation-specific identities. For example, to be a Muslim in a specific context includes what being a Muslim has meant to me in the past, which necessarily includes previous negotiation with others about that meaning as well as the purpose of Islamic identity in the situation at hand. In other words, the determination of identity at any given point or in any specific situation is a product of the actors, context, and purpose. The broader meaning or content that different actors associate with their own identity in relation to the identity of another person or community whom they are dealing with is also a relevant factor.

One aspect of the process of identity formation and transformation is the need for acceptance or recognition of the assumed or claimed identity of others. While internal self-identification is important, success even at that personal and private level is dependent on the response of the external "other" against whom an independent identity is being asserted. Since we do not have much control over how others perceive us, we need to negotiate with them about their perception of our identity and how they relate to that identity from their perspective. It is therefore misleading to speak of isolated or self-contained identities, for the nature and the outcomes of the process of defining these identities are contingent and uncertain. I may walk into a situation assuming that others will regard my identity as a Muslim with hostility, which may lead me to hide or understate this aspect of myself. However, if I realize that my identity as a Muslim may in fact be irrelevant to others, or even to my advantage, then I may reveal it, but then the question becomes what sort of Muslim I am expected to be or am accepted as—liberal or conservative, pious or not. Engaging in such tactical or instrumental expression of cultural or religious identities is so common and spontaneous that we are often unaware that we are doing it, or at least we do not wish to acknowledge it openly.

The concept of identity can be broadly or narrowly defined, depending on the actors, context, and purpose. It is often a code for moral and political discourse or a proxy for a wide variety of declared and undeclared objectives. It includes how we define ourselves—where and when, to what ends—as well as how others perceive and relate to us, and, finally, how they react to one aspect of our identity or another. Whether collective or personal, identity encompasses a range of actions, motivations, substantive commitments, and instrumental affiliations. For instance, does being an Indian Muslim presuppose or require hostility toward a Hindu Indian or acceptance of that person as an equal human being and citizen of India? How about the way a Pakistani Sunni Muslim is supposed or expected to feel about a Shiʿa or Ahmadi Muslim in Karachi, an Iranian Shiʿa Muslim about a Bahaʾi in Tehran, or a Turkish Sunni about an Alavi in Istanbul? None of these relationships is uniform or inevitably determined one way or another, since members of each community differ or change the way they perceive of or relate to each other.

It is precisely because notions of self and the other, as well as the meanings of values and construction of cultural memories, are all open to contestation and reformulation that I emphasize the critical importance of safeguarding the space in which that process can take place. The fact that proponents of the dominant interpretations of the presumed or perceived aspects of cultural or religious identity would represent them as the *only* authentic or legitimate positions of the culture on a given issue simply emphasizes the importance of ensuring every possibility for dissent and freedom to assert alternative views or practices. The existence of overlapping cultures and shared identities between persons and groups does not mean that there are homogenous or monolithic cultures or identities, or that such visions should be imposed across groups or societies. The equally true reality of diversity within cultures indicates the need for tolerance and acceptance of the differences within as well as among cultures. This perspective on the processes of cultural and identity formation and transformation emphasizes the need to protect the space and processes of contestation and reformation through which an individual can affirm his or her own identity. The process also includes the ability to contest the meaning and implications of one's identity as the individual deems necessary or desirable. Such space is necessary for internal debate and cross-cultural dialogue, for individual as well as collective self-expression.

I am arguing for a secular state, constitutionalism, human rights, and citizenship from an Islamic perspective because I believe that this approach is indispensable for protecting the freedom of each and every person to affirm, challenge, or transform his or her cultural or religious identity. My right to be myself presupposes and requires me to accept and respect the right of others to be themselves too, on their own terms. This principle of reciprocity, or the Golden Rule, is the ultimate cross-cultural foundation of the universality of human rights, as I will argue in Chapter 3. But for now I will turn to the question of why I believe it is so important to affirm these principles from an Islamic perspective.

Cultural Legitimacy for Social Change

These same realities of diversity among and within cultures and the need to secure the possibilities of contestation as well as consensus within and among them emphasize why social change needs to be culturally legitimate, comprehensible, and coherent within the existing framework. A normative system cannot be culturally neutral. Virtually everything human beings do, from mundane everyday activities and interactions to what is profoundly religious or symbolic, is culturally rooted. If we do not realize this, it is simply because our own culture has been so deeply internalized as the norm. Once we realize that our ways of being and doing things are not in fact the universal norm, sometimes not even for everyone within our own community, we will appreciate how difficult it is to speak of universal values or norms without dealing with the reality of permanent and inherent cultural diversity.

A culturally legitimate norm or value is respected and observed by the members of the particular culture because it satisfies certain needs or purposes in the lives of those individuals and their communities. The proponents of change must not only have a credible claim to being insiders in the culture but also use internally valid arguments to persuade the local population. In this way, the presentation and the adoption of alternative perspectives can be achieved through a coherent *internal discourse* in the culture. The internal criteria of validity of any initiative to secure cultural legitimacy for change will vary from issue to issue within the same society and across societies, but that too can be questioned and reformulated.

The authority and relevance deriving from internal validity for any change are crucial for several reasons that are inherent to the dynamics of social relations and social interaction. First, society may retrospectively perceive change as positive and beneficial, but such changes are likely to face initial resistance by the guardians of the previous order. Neither the proponents nor the opponents of social change are necessarily malicious or inherently oppressive people. Indeed, the proponents of change may serve the legitimate needs of their evolving society, while the opponents may serve the needs of the same society by resisting change until the case for it has been made. After all, upholding human rights and equal citizenship for all, as I argue in Chapter 3, must include the rights of those who oppose us or those we dislike. We must pay even more careful attention to respecting the rights of those who oppose us than to those of people who agree with us or whom we like, because we are more likely to violate the rights of our enemies than those of our friends. Such consistency is critical for the credibility of the human rights principle itself.

Second, since the individual is dependent on his or her society, public policy and action are more likely to accord with ideal cultural norms and patterns of behavior than private actions are. Open and systematic nonconformity gravely threatens those in authority over society—the elites who have a vested interest in the status quo. In suppressing nonconforming behavior, those elites assert the imperative of preserving the stability and the vital interests of society at large, rather than admitting the reality that it is their own interests which they seek to protect. The question thus becomes, who has the power to determine what encompasses the public good? The substance of the issue being debated becomes a proxy for that permanent struggle. These factors emphasize the desirability of seeking the support of the cultural ideal for any proposition of public policy and action, because that ideal is less likely to be successfully resisted by the self-appointed guardians of the stability and well-being of society.

My emphasis on the role of internal actors and discourse for the cultural legitimacy of social change does not preclude the role outsiders can play in promoting acceptance of change. But outsiders can best influence an internal situation by engaging in discourses within their own societies about the same values, thereby enabling participants in one culture to point to the similar processes taking place elsewhere. Outsiders can also help support the rights of the internal participants to challenge the prevailing perceptions but should avoid overt interference, which can undermine the credibility of internal actors. Advocates of change in various societies should also engage in a cross-cultural dialogue to exchange insights and strategies of internal discourse and to promote the global acceptance of their shared objectives. Cross-cultural dialogue can also seek to promote the universality of shared values at a theoretical or conceptual level by highlighting shared moral and philosophical positions.

The Role of Human Agency

As already emphasized, for any initiative of social change to become established practice, it must be interwoven with the fabric of the everyday lives and social practices of the people. The broad and far-reaching nature of this process clearly indicates that there is need for action at the state as well as the societal level, and that these two dimensions of change should be complementary and mutually reinforcing. The need to secure cultural legitimacy for social change emphasizes this dual strategy at the level of law and policy and makes those policy changes meaningful in terms of the social and cultural lives of communities. However, this approach assumes a certain type of relationship between the state and its citizens.

The state may be the agent of the desired kind of institutional change, but it should also be noted that the state is not a completely autonomous entity

that can act independently of the social and political forces within its populations or be free from the constraints of its resources or other factors. In
fact, the nature and structure of the state and its willingness and ability to
act at all are the products of primarily internal sociological, economic, and
political processes as well as external and international influences. Whatever material resources and coercive powers are available to the elites who
control the state, they depend on the willingness of the general population
to accept or at least acquiesce to the state's actions. Those in control of the
state are a tiny fraction of those who accept its authority, and their ability to
enforce their will through direct force is untenable in the face of persistent
large-scale resistance. To retain control and achieve their objectives, those
who control the state must persuade or induce the vast majority to submit to
their power and authority, which they tend to do by claiming to represent
the will of the majority or acting in their best interest. This is not to suggest
that hegemony and dominance cease to be oppressive, but only to note the
underlying need for persuasion, which opens some possibility for change.

To have any hope of success, the proponents of social change must motivate the human agency of the population at large in favor of the proposed
change. The methodology of cultural legitimacy, therefore, emphasizes the
central role of human agency by firmly locating the impetus for change
within the social and cultural lives of communities and individuals, rather
than viewing persons and communities as passive subjects of change. At
the same time, human agency operates in the context of networks of social
action and interaction, which emphasizes the need for collaboration and
cooperation. Nothing happens in human relationships except through the
agency of some persons or groups who act or fail to act. But this conception
of the role of human agency must be inclusive of all human beings, especially in today's globalized world, and cannot be limited to elites alone. Consequently, the outcome of human agency in any society is contingent on
what else is happening in the world around us and not only on what happens within our societies or communities.

Once the centrality of human agency is recognized, whether in the interpretation of Shari'a or in general social change, many creative possibilities
for reform and transformation will emerge. Times of severe crisis, as experienced by Islamic societies and communities today, should lead Muslims
to question prevalent assumptions and challenge existing institutions that
have failed to deliver on the promise of liberation and development. These
crises are opening new opportunities for people to take control of their own

lives and realize their own objectives, thereby becoming the source and cause of the sort of transformation I am hoping for. But we cannot sit back and expect desired outcomes to materialize by themselves simply because societies are experiencing a deep and profound crisis. We must also apply our human agency, through both theoretical reflection and practical implementation, to advance our initiatives for the social change we desire. A good theory is necessary to direct strategies and action, but any theory must be practical to be good. It is from this perspective that I now turn to an explanation of what I hope is a good theory that can mobilize and motivate Muslims everywhere to action in favor of positive social transformation.

Elements of a Theory of Islam, the State, and Social Relations

Various understandings of Shari'a will remain, of course, in the realm of individual and collective practice of freedom of religion and belief. What is problematic is for Shari'a principles to be enforced as a state law or policy on that basis alone, because once a principle or norm is officially identified as "decreed by God," it is extremely difficult for believers to resist or change its application in practice. Since Islamic ethical principles and social values are indeed necessary for the proper functioning of Islamic societies in general, the implementation of such principles and values is consistent with, and indeed required by, the right of Muslims to self-determination. This right however, can be realized only within the framework of constitutional and democratic governance at home and of international law abroad, since these are the legal and political bases of this right in the first place. That is, the right to self-determination presupposes a constitutional basis that is derived from the collective will of the totality of the population and can be asserted against other countries because it is accepted as a fundamental principle of international law.

The paradox of separation of religion and state despite the connection of religion and politics can only be mediated through practice over time, rather than completely resolved by theoretical analysis or stipulation. This means that the question is how to create the most conducive conditions for this mediation to continue in a constructive fashion, instead of hoping to resolve the paradox once and for all. The two poles of this necessary mediation can be clarified as follows. First, the modern territorial state should neither seek to enforce Shari'a as positive law and public policy nor claim to interpret its doctrine and general principles for Muslim citizens. Second, Shari'a principles can and should be a source of public policy and legislation, subject to the fundamental constitutional and human rights of all citizens, men and women, Muslims and non-Muslims, equally and without discrimination. In other words, Shariʿa principles must be neither privileged nor enforced, nor necessarily rejected as a source of state law and policy, simply because they are believed to be the will of God. The belief of even the vast majority of citizens that these principles are binding as a matter of Islamic religious obligation should remain the basis of individual and collective observance among believers. But that cannot be accepted as sufficient reason for their enforcement by the state, because they would then apply to citizens who may not share that belief.

Since effective governance requires the adoption of specific policies and the enactment of precise laws, the administrative and legislative organs of the state must select among competing views within the massive and complex corpus of Shariʿa principles, as noted earlier. That selection will necessarily be made by the ruling elite. When the policy or law is presented as mandated by the "divine will of God," it is difficult for the general population to oppose or resist it. For example, there is a well-established principle of Shariʿa, known as *khulʾ*, whereby a wife can pay her husband an agreed amount (or forfeit her financial entitlement) to induce him to accept the termination of their marriage. Yet this choice was not available in Egypt until the government decided to enact this Shariʿa principle into law in 2000. The fact that this principle was a part of Shariʿa did not make it applicable in Egypt until the state decided to enforce it. Moreover, although this legislation gave Egyptian women a way out of a bad marriage, they could not contest the condition that this is possible only at a significant financial cost for the wife. Such a limitation existed because the legislation was made in terms of "enacting" Shariʿa rather than simply as a matter of good social policy. Thus, the diversity of Shariʿa principles means that whatever is enacted and enforced by the state is the political will of the ruling elite, not the normative system of Islam as such. Yet such policies and legislation are difficult to resist or even debate when presented as the will of God.

To avoid such difficulties, I am proposing that the rationale of all public policy and legislation must always be based on civic reason, as explained earlier. Muslims and other believers should be able to propose policy and legislative initiatives emanating from their religious beliefs, provided that they can support them in free and open public debate by reasons that are accessible and convincing to the generality of citizens regardless of their religious or other beliefs. But since such decisions will in practice be made by majority vote in accordance with democratic principles, all state action must also conform to basic constitutional and human rights safeguards against the tyranny of the majority. This is because democratic government depends not only on the rule of the majority view but also on the fact that the will of the majority is subject to the rights of the minority, however small.

It is ultimately a question of degree and quality of implementation, of course, but these propositions are already accepted as the basis of legitimate government in the vast majority of present Islamic societies. Although practice is far from satisfactory anywhere, the theoretical acknowledgment of the need for constitutional democratic government opens the way to improving implementation, because it allows those principles to be invoked in challenging their violation. At the same time, however, the legitimacy and popular acceptance of those principles need to be reinforced by showing their consistency with Islamic doctrine. This Islamic legitimacy may not be readily or easily established in different parts of the Muslim world, but the proposal advanced in this book is intended to contribute to that process by clarifying some relevant issues, such as the nature of the state and its relationship to religion and politics.

The State Is Territorial, Not Islamic

A necessary consequence of the inevitability of human interpretation of Islamic texts, as emphasized earlier, is that alternative views of Islam and formulations of Shari'a principles are always possible and can be equally valid if accepted by Muslims. Since it is impossible to know whether or not Muslims would accept or reject any particular view until it is openly and freely expressed and debated, it is necessary to maintain complete freedom of opinion, belief, and expression for such views to emerge and be propagated. The idea of prior censorship is therefore inherently destructive and counterproductive for the development of any Islamic doctrine or principle; hence, maintaining the possibilities of dissent is the only way for the tradition to remain responsive to the needs of believers. As I will argue, the necessary space for dissent and debate is best secured now through constitutional democratic governance and protection of human rights. In other words, these modern concepts and institutions are necessary not only for the religious freedom of Muslim and non-Muslim citizens of any present territorial state but for the survival and development of Islam itself. Indeed, freedom of dissent and debate was always essential for the development of Shariʿa, because it enabled consensus to emerge freely and evolve around certain views that matured into established principles through acceptance and practice by generations of Muslims in a wide variety of settings. After all, every orthodox view that comes to prevail was a heresy to the previous view, including Islam itself in relation to the religious and social beliefs of Arabia before the Prophet. (This is not to say that every heresy should or will become the orthodox view.)

It is from this Islamic perspective that I oppose the idea of an Islamic state that can enforce Shariʿa as positive law and official state policy. To live up to this claim, a state would be required to implement traditional Shariʿa principles like the *dhimma* system because there is no Shariʿa-based justification for failing to do so. According to the *dhimma* under traditional interpretations of Shariʿa, when Muslims conquer and incorporate new territories through *jihad*, People of the Book (mainly Christians and Jews) should be allowed to live as protected communities upon submission to Muslim sovereignty but cannot enjoy equality with Muslims. Those who are deemed to be unbelievers by Shariʿa standards have not been permitted to live within the territory of the state at all, except under temporary safe conduct *(aman)*. The pretext of necessity *(darura)* is often cited to justify the failure to enforce such Shariʿa principles, but the rationale for that notion is limited and short-term. Those who claim that justification must also strive to remove whatever conditions force them to fail to observe what they believe to be Shariʿa obligations. They cannot invoke necessity as a permanent justification for their failure to enforce the *dhimma* system.

I am not, of course, suggesting that this system should be applied today, but I wish to show that it is now so untenable that even the most ardent advocates of an Islamic state do not seriously consider applying it in the present local and global realities of Islamic societies. The recent case of the Taliban in Afghanistan is perhaps the exception that proves the rule. Though even that regime did not attempt to implement the *dhimma* system to its full extent, its limited effort to apply it in the late 1990s resulted in the almost total isolation of the Taliban and its condemnation by Muslims everywhere. It should be recalled here that only four out of more than forty-four Muslim-majority countries in the world were willing to recognize the Taliban regime as the legitimate government of Afghanistan.

Any and all proposed possibilities of change or development must therefore begin with the reality that European colonialism and its aftermath have drastically transformed the basis and nature of political and social organization within and among territorial states where all Muslims live today. A return to precolonial ideas and systems is simply not an option, and any change and adaptation of the present system can be realized only through the concepts and institutions of this local and global postcolonial reality. Yet many Muslims, probably the majority in many countries, have not accepted some aspects of this transformation and its consequences. This discrepancy seems to underlie the apparent acceptance by many Muslims of the possibility of an Islamic state that can enforce Shari'a principles as positive law; it also underlies the widespread ambivalence about politically motivated violence in the name of *jihad*. Significant Islamic reform is necessary to reformulate such problematic aspects of Shari'a but should not and cannot mean the wholesale and uncritical adoption of the dominant Western theories and practices.

To illustrate the sort of internal Islamic transformation I am proposing, I will briefly review how the traditional Shari'a notions of *dhimma* should evolve into a coherent and humane principle of citizenship in view of the following considerations. First, human beings tend to seek and experience multiple and overlapping types and forms of membership in different groups. These include ethnic, religious, and cultural identity; political, social, and professional affiliation; and economic interests. Second, the meanings and implications of each type or form of membership should be determined by the purpose of belonging to the group in question, without precluding or undermining other forms of membership. That is, multiple and overlapping memberships should not be mutually exclusive, as they tend to serve different purposes for different persons and communities. Third, the term "citizenship" is used here to refer to a particular form of membership in the political community of a territorial state in the global context. It should therefore be related to this specific rationale or purpose without precluding possibilities of membership in other communities for different purposes. People are not always consciously aware of the reality of their multiple memberships, nor can they always appreciate that those memberships are mutually inclusive, each being appropriate or necessary for its unique purpose or rationale. On the contrary, it seems that there is a tendency to collapse different forms of membership, as when ethnic or religious identity is equated with political or social affiliation. This is true of the coincidence of nationality and citizenship in Western political theory that was transmitted to Muslims through European colonialism and its aftermath.

Thus, official or ideological discourse regarding the basis of citizenship as membership in the political community of a territorial state did not necessarily coincide in the past with a subjective feeling of belonging or an independent assessment of actual conditions on the ground. Such tensions used to exist in all major civilizations and continue to be experienced in various ways by different societies today. The development of the notion of citizenship in the European model of the territorial "nation-state" after the Peace Treaty of Westphalia (1648) tended to equate citizenship with nationality. This model defined citizenship in terms of a contrived and often coercive membership in a "nation" on the basis of shared ethnic and religious identity and political allegiance that was both required by and assumed to follow from residence within a particular territory. In other words, the coincidence of citizenship and nationality was not only the product of a peculiarly European and relatively recent process but was often exaggerated in that region itself at the expense of other forms of membership, especially of ethnic or religious minorities. I prefer to use the term "territorial state" to identify citizenship with territory, instead of "nation-state," as that can be misleading, if not oppressive to minorities.

The term "citizenship" is used here to denote an affirmative belonging to an inclusive, pluralistic political community that accepts and regulates the possibilities of various forms of difference among persons and communities to ensure equal rights for all, without distinction on such grounds as religion, sex, ethnicity, and political opinion. This term is intended to signify a shared cultural understanding of equal human dignity and effective political participation for all. In other words, citizenship is defined here in terms of the principle of the universality of human rights as "a common standard of achievement for all people and nations," according to the Preamble of the 1948 United Nations Universal Declaration of Human Rights. That is, human rights determine the meaning and implications of citizenship everywhere.

There is a dialectical relationship between domestic and international conceptions of citizenship, whereby the agency of subjects at each level seeks to ensure human dignity and social justice everywhere in the world, whether at home or abroad. Citizens acting politically at home participate under the fundamental understanding of universal human rights, which in turn contributes to the definition and protection of the rights of citizens at the domestic level. The relationship between citizenship and human rights is therefore inherent to both paradigms, which are mutually supportive.

The desirability of this understanding of citizenship is supported by the Islamic principle of reciprocity *(mu'awada),* also known as the Golden Rule, and is emphasized by the legal and political principles of self-determination. Persons and communities everywhere have to affirm this conception of citizenship in order to be able to claim it for themselves under international law as well as domestic constitutional law and politics. In other words, my right to citizenship is dependent on my recognition of the other's equal right to citizenship. That is, acceptance of this understanding of citizenship is the prerequisite moral, legal, and political basis for its enjoyment. Muslims should strive toward this pragmatic ideal from an Islamic point of view, regardless of what other people do or fail to do in this regard.

These reflections clearly emphasize the importance of creative Islamic reform that balances the competing demands of religious legitimacy and principled political and social practice, which can best be achieved under a secular state. Still, one should also specifically challenge the notion of an Islamic state, which seems to be so appealing to many Muslims in the current domestic and global context. For example, it is sometimes suggested that the idea of an Islamic state should stand as an ideal while citizens seek to control or manage its practice. But as long as this notion is accepted as an ideal, some Muslims will attempt to implement it according to their own understanding, with disastrous consequences for their societies and beyond. It is impossible to control or manage the practice of this ideal without challenging its core claims of religious sanctity for human views of Islam. Once the possibility of an Islamic state is conceded, resisting the next logical step—seeking to implement it in practice—would be regarded as a heretical or an "un-Islamic" position.

Maintaining this ideal is also counterproductive because it precludes debates about more viable and appropriate political theories, legal systems, and development policies. Even if one overcomes the psychological difficulty of arguing against what is presented as the divine will of God, charges of heresy may lead to severe social stigma, if not to prosecution by the state or direct violence by extremist groups. As long as the idea of an Islamic state is allowed to stand, societies will remain locked in stale debates about issues such as whether constitutionalism or democracy is "Islamic" and whether interest banking is to be allowed or not, instead of working to secure constitutional democratic governance and pursuing economic development. These fruitless debates have kept the vast majority of modern Islamic societies locked in a constant state of political instability and economic and social underdevelopment since independence. Instead, Muslims need to accept that constitutionalism and democracy are the ultimate foundation of the state itself and to engage in the process of securing them in practice. To establish authoritatively that the state will not and cannot enforce any religious view of charging or paying interest on loans *(riba)* is to ensure the freedom of all citizens to choose to practice or avoid interest banking as a matter of personal religious belief. Moreover, citizens who wish to avoid such practices can establish their own banking institutions, subject to appropriate regulation by the state and general public supervision, like any other business venture. These are examples of the real issues facing Islamic societies today, which cannot be resolved by futile debates about an incoherent and counterproductive notion of an Islamic state to enforce Shariʿa as the automatic basis of public policy and law.

Another argument in support of the notion of an Islamic state is based on the distinction between Shariʿa and *fiqh* (Islamic jurisprudence), namely, the claim that since *fiqh* is a human interpretation, it can be amended and adjusted to fit the current circumstances of Islamic societies, whereas Shariʿa should remain immutable. In fact, both Shariʿa and *fiqh* are the products of human interpretation of the Qurʾan and Sunna of the Prophet in a particular historical context. Whether a given proposition is said to be based on Shariʿa or *fiqh*, it is subject to the same risks of human error, ideological or political bias, or influence by its proponents' economic interests and social concerns. For example, a person may claim that the prohibition of *riba* is decreed by Shariʿa, but this claim cannot be meaningful without a clear definition and application of this term, which is the subject of *fiqh*. Since human interpretation of relevant texts of the Qurʾan and Sunna is unavoidable in both aspects of this issue, it is difficult to distinguish between the two.

A modified version of the same argument asserts that all that is required is to observe the basic objectives or purposes of Shariʿa *(Maqasid al-Shariʿa)*, while *fiqh* principles are subject to change from one time or place to another. But the problem with this view is that the so-called basic objectives of Shariʿa are expressed at such a high level of abstraction that they are neither distinctly Islamic nor sufficiently specific for the purposes of public policy and legislation. As soon as these principles are presented in more specific and concrete terms, they will be immediately implicated in the familiar controversies and limitations of *fiqh*. For example, "the protection of religion" is one of the objectives of Shariʿa, but this principle has no practical utility without a clear definition of what "religion" means in this context; nor is it useful without specifying the necessary conditions and limitations of the protection of religion as a matter of state policy and legislation. Does "religion" include non-theistic traditions like Buddhism and atheism? Can a Muslim adopt another religion or belief? When can freedom of religion be limited in the public interest of the state or the rights of others? Addressing such questions immediately takes the subject into the realm of *fiqh* principles, which raise a number of serious human rights and political objections, as we have seen.

If the notion of an Islamic state is incoherent and unworkable, what alternative model of the state am I proposing, and how different is it from the so-called Western secular state that many Muslims oppose? To challenge the basis of this hostility to secularism, by which I mean a secular state as defined from the beginning of this chapter, I will now attempt to show that this necessary political doctrine in fact promotes possibilities of honest piety and diminishes the risks of hypocrisy among believers.

Secularism as Mediation

The word "secular" in the English language derives from the Latin word *saeculum,* meaning "great span of time" or, more closely, "spirit of the age." In time the meaning changed to "of this world," which implies the presence of more than one world. Eventually the term came to be understood as reflecting a distinction between secular (temporal) and religious (spiritual) concepts. The term also evolved in the European context from "secularization" as the privatization of church lands to the secularization of politics and, later, art and economics.

Secularism does not mean the exclusion of religion from the public life of a society, though the misconception that it does is one of the reasons many Muslims tend to be hostile to the concept. It is of course possible to define secularism as a totally hypothetical notion of strict and systematic separation in all aspects of the relationship between religion and the state, and then to assert this narrow and unrealistic definition in rejecting any form of regulation of that relationship. That purely theoretical and polemical definition of secularism is not valid even for those Western countries commonly assumed to be secular. Instead of chasing such an illusory notion, it is more productive to discuss secularism as it is actually understood and practiced by different societies, each in its own context. All societies are in fact negotiating the relationship between religion and the state over many issues at different times, rather than applying a specific or rigid definition or model of secularism. A conception of secularism as a product of deeply contextual negotiation in each society does not mean that there are no unifying principles among these various experiences, or that the meaning and implications of this concept are totally relative to each society. It is indeed possible and useful to develop a shared understanding of the meaning of the concept and its implications through comparative analysis of different experiences. But there is no universal preconceived definition that can be imposed or transplanted from one society to another.

The ability of a mediating secularism to unite people despite religious and philosophical differences depends on its making minimal moral claims on the community and its members. It is true that secularism is not morally neutral, as it must encourage a certain civic ethos to achieve its own objective of separation of religion and state. It is also possible for minimal neutrality to evolve into stronger consensus on the values of pluralism and acceptance of difference. But the ability of secularism to unite diminishes to the degree that it is taken to require certain resolutions of some morally difficult issues. In fact, the more morally charged an issue is, the greater its impact on the credibility of secularism will be if the proponents of one position or the other attempt to impose their view on others. For example, secularism should be asserted to prevent the direct enforcement of religious doctrine about abortion or euthanasia on the sole basis that such doctrine constitutes the religious beliefs of some people. But denying those believers the right to express their views on such matters in religious terms would undermine the principle of secularism. The secular state must protect the right to express religious views on such issues while ensuring that public policy and legislation on abortion or euthanasia are based on civic reason, as discussed elsewhere in this book. This paradoxical balance is difficult to establish and maintain, but there is no alternative to striving to achieve it.

Thus asserting strict separation without accounting for the public role of religion is both unrealistic and misleading. It is unrealistic because it is a negative view of the relationship between religion and public policy, emphasizing the exclusion of religious ethics without providing an alternative, and thereby failing to take into account the moral or ethical foundations of public policy. It is misleading because it assumes a partially religious morality in the culture of every society without specifically stating it. Questions of public policy, such as whether or not to legalize abortion or how to adjudicate the custody of children after a divorce, necessarily draw on moral and ethical reasoning, which is influenced, if not significantly shaped, by religion in any society. Secularism, defined to mean only the separation of religion and state, is therefore incapable of meeting the collective requirements of public policy. Moreover, such separation by itself cannot provide sufficient guidance for individual citizens in making important personal choices in their private lives or public political participation.

In addition, secularism as simply the separation of religion and state is not sufficient for addressing any objections or reservations believers may have about specific constitutional norms and human rights standards. For example, since discrimination against women is often justified on religious grounds in Islamic societies, this source of systematic and gross violation of human rights cannot be eliminated without addressing the commonly perceived religious rationale. The mediation aspect of secularism is relevant to how to balance protection against discrimination with freedom of religion or belief. This is simply an aspect of how the scope of fundamental rights is determined by balancing competing claims, since these rights are not absolute. For instance, it is obviously reasonable to limit freedom of speech to protect the rights of others—for instance, freedom of speech does not mean that one can shout "fire" in a crowded theater—or to defame the reputation of other people.

The principle of secularism, as I am defining it here, includes a public role for religion in influencing public policy and legislation, subject to the requirement of civic reason. This acknowledgment of the public role of religion can encourage and facilitate debate and dissent within religious traditions, which can overcome religion-based objections to equality for women. When a society ensures that the state is neutral with regard to religion, the coercive power of the state cannot be used to suppress debate and dissent. But citizens need to use that safe space actively to promote religious views that support equality for women and other human rights. In fact, such views are required to promote the religious legitimacy of the doctrine of separation of religion and state itself, as well as other general principles of constitutionalism and human rights.

Allowing Shari'a principles to play a positive role in public life without permitting them to be implemented through state institutions simply because that is the belief of some citizens is a delicate balance that each society must strive to maintain for itself over time. For example, matters such as dress style will normally remain in the realm of free choice, so that women can neither be forced to wear the veil nor be prevented from doing so if they wish to wear it. But style of dress can be an issue for public debate, including constitutional litigation, to balance competing claims when, for instance, it relates to safety concerns in the workplace. Religious education should normally be a matter of private choice for parents but can involve public-policy considerations regarding the need for comparative and critical religious education to enhance religious tolerance and pluralism. I am not suggesting that the context and conditions of free choice of dress or religious education will not be controversial. In fact, such matters are likely to be complex at both the personal and the societal level. My concern is with ensuring, as far as humanly possible, fair, open, and inclusive social, political, and legal conditions for the negotiation of public policy in such matters. These conditions, for instance, are to be secured through the entrenchment of such fundamental rights of individuals and communities as the rights to education and freedom of religion and expression. Considerations of legitimate public interests or concerns are also relevant, for instance, in ensuring complete and equal access to education for girls as well as boys. There is no simple or categorical formula to be prescribed for automatic application in every case, although general principles and broader frameworks for the mediation of such issues will emerge and continue to evolve within each society. This notion of secularism as mediation will become clearer when applied to specific situations, as I will attempt to do in relation to India, Turkey, and Indonesia in later chapters.

It is critically important for Islamic societies today to invest in the rule of law and protection of human rights in their domestic politics and international relations. This is unlikely to happen if traditional interpretations of Shariʿa that support principles like male guardianship of women *(qawama)*, sovereignty of Muslims over non-Muslims *(dhimma)*, and violently aggressive *jihad* are maintained. Significant reform of such views is necessary because of their powerful influence on social relations and the political behavior of Muslims, even when Shariʿa principles are not directly enforced by the state. One premise of my approach is that Muslims are unlikely to actively support human rights principles and effectively engage in the process of constitutional democratic governance if they continue to maintain such views as part of their understanding of Shariʿa.

Religion is an important force that competes with other life philosophies in the sphere of civic reason to influence policy, whether operating through organized groups or in the domain of personal views and beliefs. This can be observed in relation to personal concerns about quality of life, educational policy, abortion and other aspects of family policy, religious freedom, immigration and naturalization policies, and so forth. The underlying notion of secularism as mediation is that such issues are debated and negotiated among social and political actors through consensus-building and compromise rather than total victory for one side and utter defeat for another. This should be as true for Muslims regarding Shari'a as it is for other societies and their religious traditions. In all cases, issues of public policy and legislation should be the subject of negotiations within the imperatives of constitutionalism, human rights, and citizenship. To be clear on the point, no state is authorized to violate constitutionalism, human rights, and citizenship; failure to comply with these principles is simply *ultra vires,* beyond the capacity of state institutions. But within those parameters, there is still room to negotiate and seek compromise among competing perspectives.

The ability of religious actors to influence public policy is influenced by historical relations of religion and state and by current conditions such as urbanization, demographic changes, level of religiosity in the society, and relations among religious communities. Since such historical and current conditions themselves tend to shift and change over time, the impact and outcome of religion on public policy must adjust to such changes. Moreover, while religion has the potential to operate as a hegemonic discourse in civic reason, nonreligious forces or ideologies can play a similar role. The separation between religion and state is compromised when the dictates of a particular religion, as interpreted by religious authorities or the ruling elite, are made into a prerequisite condition for participation in civic reason.

But this can also happen from a nationalist or so-called secular perspective. It is seen, for example, in the controversy over recent French legislation that prohibits Muslim girls from wearing headscarves in school. The decision to ban the use of the Islamic headscarf in the name of *laïcité,* the French conception of secularism, reflects the higher priority given to the assimilation of immigrants into French cultural citizenship as a policy goal than to the possibilities of ethnic or cultural identity within a national framework of multiculturalism like that which prevails in northern European countries and Canada. The French republican conception of secularism that was invoked functioned as a tool of coercive cultural uniformity among French citizens, especially among immigrant populations.

The debate over the headscarf and French secularism must be located in a wider context of postcolonial relations, including the ambivalent relationship of France with its former colonies, as well as in the context of stereotypical perceptions and anxieties about Islam and Muslims. Often the victims of racism and discrimination, Muslims are uniformly perceived and treated as outsiders in French society, although a significant number of them have French citizenship. This raises important questions about the extent to which Muslims in France have representation in and access to civic reason through French state and nonstate institutions.

The French case also illustrates how secularism can be invoked as a hegemonic idea of national culture to the exclusion of other identities, thereby violating the requirements of civic reason. The exclusion of persons and groups from the scope of civic reason is always objectionable, whether done in the name of nationalism, secular ideology, or religion. In other words, the French case illustrates how the principles of secularism itself can be violated in the name of its protection. The country's public policy regarding the headscarf is rationalized as required by *laïcité*, when in fact it is driven by irrational fear of the Muslim alien, even if legally a citizen, instead of being founded on civic reason. Ironically, the citizenship of Muslims, their right to be Muslims and citizens, is sacrificed to appease the guardians of *laïcité*, regardless of the demands of civic reason.

As noted earlier, secularism as the separation of religion and state is the basic and minimal condition for participation in the sphere of civic reason. But the relationship between secularism and religion can also have deeper significance, especially in the domain of civic reason. Religion may provide an important framework in which many social actors can present their respective claims, as long as these are formulated in the mode of publicly accessible reason. The relationship between religion and secularism can also be viewed as mutually sustaining. Secularism needs religion to provide a widely accepted source of moral guidance for the political community, as well as to help satisfy and discipline the nonpolitical needs of believers within that community. In turn, religion needs secularism to mediate relations between different communities (whether religious, antireligious, or nonreligious) that share the same political space or space of civic reason.

Secularism is able to unite diverse communities of belief and practice into one political community precisely because the moral claims it makes are minimal. It is true that all varieties of secularism prescribe a civic ethos on the basis of some specific understanding of the individual's relation to the community. Such an ethos may indeed be sufficiently complex and deeply entrenched so as to address some major moral issues facing the society in question. But the ability of secularism to achieve the degree of consensus needed to enable and sustain political stability in religiously diverse societies means that it cannot tackle fundamental ethical and moral questions on which there is serious disagreement among different communities.

To be clear on the point, secularism cannot replace religion for believers, nor provide cross-cultural foundations for universal norms of human rights. Indeed, some believers may need a religious justification for the principle of secularism itself. I am not saying that a serious engagement of religion is essential for secularism to be legitimized everywhere and always, but such engagement is necessary to obtain the consent of most religious believers, who constitute the clear majority of all human beings. In particular, secularism by itself is unable to address objections or reservations that religious believers may have about specific principles of secular governance. A purely secular discourse can be respectful of religion in general, but its ability to rebut religious justifications of certain policies is unlikely to convince believers. For example, an assertion of equal citizenship for non-Muslims is unlikely to persuade Muslims unless there is an Islamic justification for that principle. In other words, the minimal normative content that makes secularism conducive to interreligious coexistence and pluralism and supportive of a space of civic reason diminishes its capacity to legitimize itself as a universal principle without reference to some other moral source.

Secularism precludes any specific understanding of religious doctrine from being directly enforced as state policy, but that is not enough to address the need of religious believers to express the moral implications of their faith in the public domain. That is why I have emphasized that secularism as separation of religion and state is necessary but insufficient without acknowledging and regulating the political role of religion. Both elements of this broader definition of secularism can be enhanced by insisting on a contextual understanding of the rationale and functioning of secular government in each location.

And it is here that religion can play a vitally important role. The condition of secularism is likely to be seen as merely expedient and temporary by religious adherents unless they are also able to find secularism consistent with (or, preferably, implied or stipulated by) their religious doctrine. It is also clear that the dichotomy of demanding a choice between religion and secularism has already failed, as shown by the dramatic rise of religious affiliation and practice throughout the territories of the former Soviet Union after decades of state-sponsored atheism and suppression of religion. Politics and religion do not operate in distinct realms, because each continually informs and is informed by the other. The concept of the secular lacks independent motivating power for believers, who tend to understand it in a dialectical relationship to their religious beliefs rather than in isolation from the religious realm.

Shared concerns facing all human societies, which must necessarily struggle with the relationship between religion and the state, include the question of the constitutional and legal status of religion. As can be seen from the experiences of various Western countries, secularism allows a great variety of options for the constitutional status of religion. One possibility is for religious leaders to participate in state institutions and legislative bodies and attempt to promote their religious values as any other democratically elected representative would. Another possibility suggested by the European experience is the system of special bilateral agreements between the state and religious entities, as is the case in Spain and Italy today. This can be a third alternative—to theocracy and strict state neutrality—that permits flexibility in reconciling competing claims and reassuring minority religions or sects. The realities of religious diversity facing all Islamic societies can also be addressed through a variety of mechanisms to promote genuine pluralism and acceptance of religious differences. To recall the point about secularism as mediation within the parameters of constitutionalism, human rights, and citizenship, temporary or limited solutions for contentious issues may be applied while longer-term negotiations continue.

In the final analysis, there is a permanent paradox in the competing roles of religious autonomy and authority, on the one hand, and the political authority, legal powers, and material powers of the state, on the other. This paradox derives from the inherent nature and interdependence of the two types of institutions. Religious communities need the cooperation of the state in order to fulfill their own mission. However rich and well-organized a religious community may be, it cannot avoid conflict with the state, because both sides seek to influence, if not control, the behavior of the same population living in the same territory. But the state has to seek some measure of control over religious institutions in order to limit the ways in which they can influence or shape the public behavior of believers in their communities. In other words, even when the state is not required or allowed to provide material and administrative support for rich and well-organized religious communities, it cannot afford to grant them complete freedom to propagate whatever values or engage in whatever activities they wish to pursue independently in the name of freedom of religion and belief.

The framework I am proposing in this book would first acknowledge this paradox and then seek to mediate its consequences through a range of mechanisms, rather than claim to impose a categorical and final solution. To begin with, this paradox must be acknowledged through a consistent commitment to the combination of religious neutrality of the state and acceptance of the role of religion in the public life of the society. This combination is more applicable to the history of Islamic societies, and more consistent with the nature of Shari'a, than are postcolonial notions of an Islamic state that can enforce Shari'a as the official law and policy of any country today. However, this difficult combination cannot be sustained in the context of the modern territorial state without a clear legal and political framework for mediating inevitable tensions and conflicts. For this, I am proposing the principles of constitutionalism, human rights, and citizenship, which can work only when they enjoy sufficient cultural and religious legitimacy to inspire and motivate people to participate in organized and sustained political and legal action. An Islamic discourse is essential for legitimizing the necessary strategies for regulating the public role of Islam. At the same time, that discourse cannot emerge or be effective without the security and stability provided by the secular state.

CHAPTER **2**

Islam, the State, and Politics in Historical Perspective

The main purpose of this chapter is to show that my proposal for a secular state is more consistent with Islamic history than is the so-called Islamic state model proposed by some Muslims since the second quarter of the twentieth century. An overview of various states or regimes that ruled Islamic societies for many centuries should also help to dispel any romantic notions about Islamic states and pious rulers. But the point I am making is relative. I am not claiming that the historical states of Islamic societies were in fact secular states as defined in this book. Still, a clear understanding of at least the nonreligious state should help to dispel apprehension among Muslims that the secular state is a Western imposition. This perception is really the product of the propaganda of Islamist groups based on the ideological views of Abul A'la Maududi (Maududi 1980) and Sayyid Qutb (Shepherd 1996) and not on the actual history of Islamic societies. In any case, there is no uniform Western model of the secular state that can be imposed, because each Western society negotiated the relationship between religion and the state and between religion and politics in its own historical context. It is also false to assume that religion has been relegated to the purely private domain under the secular states of Western Europe and North America.

The underlying point to emphasize is that Islamic societies are not fundamentally different from Western societies regarding the relationship between religion and the state. As Ira Lapidus put it, "There is a notable differentiation of state and religious institutions in Islamic societies. The historical evidence also shows that there is no single Islamic model for state and religious institutions, but rather several competing ones. Moreover, in each of the models there are ambiguities concerning the distribution of authority, functions and relations among institutions. Finally, there are evident differences between theory and practice" (Lapidus 1996, 4). The differentiation of state and religious institutions in the histories of Islamic societies does not mean that the precolonial state was secular in the modern sense of the term, in view of the significant differences between the traditional "minimal" imperial state of the past and the centralized, hierarchical, bureaucratic state of today. But the point for our purposes is that the states under which Muslims lived in the past were never religious, regardless of occasional claims to the contrary, as highlighted later. Islamic history supports the proposal I am making in the sense that the state was never Islamic, but not in the affirmative sense of the religious neutrality of the state. To make this main point, I will begin by clarifying the sense in which I am reading or interpreting Islamic history and then contrast the ideal vision and the pragmatic reality of that history. The third section of the chapter will illustrate that overview with a more detailed examination of the Fatimid and Mamluk states in Egypt to demonstrate the implications of those historical experiences for the future of Shari'a in Islamic societies.

It may be argued that the history I am examining here is that of Muslim-majority populations, which may not necessarily be as Islamic as the ideal prescribed by Islam in its foundational sources. Such arguments have been common among Muslims, both past and present, who insist that the failure to live up to the ideal of Islam should not be taken to imply that the problem is with Islam itself. The fallacy of this view is that Islam in the abstract is not at issue here. There is always a dimension of Islam that is beyond human comprehension and experience, at least in the collective communal sense that is relevant to the social and political organization of societies (Qur'an 43:3, 4). But our concern is with Islam as understood and practiced by Muslims, not in its ideal, abstract form.

To begin with, whenever someone mentions verses of the Qur'an, he or she is providing a personal understanding, not the totality of all possible meanings or the only and exclusively valid meaning. The inescapability of diverse interpretations of the Qur'an was discussed by the leading Muslim philosopher and judge Ibn Rushd (died 1198), who distinguished between three levels of interpretations of the Qur'an and Sunna. He associated the first level of interpretation with jurists, who are mainly concerned with the literal, strictly linguistic sense of the verses. The second level of interpretation is that of the theologians, who are interested in arriving at a more rigorous and widely accepted view through debate and disputation. The third level of interpretation, according to Ibn Rushd, is that of the philosophers, whose interpretation is based on rational principles that are incontestable by any human in his capacity as a rational being. The point for our purposes here is that the diversity of interpretations follows from both human nature and the textual nature of the Qur'an and Sunna. Ibn Rushd's consideration of varieties of interpretation also reflects the impact of contextual factors, training, orientation, and experience (Ibn Rushd 2001, 8–10).

Even when there is wide consensus on a particular meaning among many generations, that meaning is still a claim about a human understanding of the Qur'an. Indeed, any claim of consensus is itself a human judgment, which may be difficult to prove empirically—what Ibn Rushd calls suppositional *(zanian)* and not certain:

> What may indicate to you that consensus is not to be determined with certainty about theoretical matters, as it is possible for it to be determined about practical matters, is that it is not possible for consensus to be determined about a particular question at a particular epoch unless: that epoch is delimited by us; all the learned men existing in that epoch are known to us, I mean, known as individuals and in their total number; the doctrine of each one of them on the question is transmitted to us by means of an uninterrupted transmission; and in addition to all this it has been certified to us that the learned men existing at that time agreed that there is not an apparent and an inner sense to the Law that it is obligatory that knowledge of every question be concealed from no one and that there is only one method for people to know the law (al-Shari'a). (10–11)

In this light, not only are conditions of establishing *ijma'* (consensus) very difficult to fulfill, but even if the necessary conditions are satisfied on a particular view, it cannot be exclusive or final, because such consensus depends on the context and the method of interpretation employed. Any attempt to identify and describe *to other human beings* the Islamic ideal is inherently constrained by all the limitations and fallibilities of the human beings who are making the claim. It is true that people vary in their level of experience and understanding of the meaning of the Qur'an, but no human being can completely transcend his or her humanity, especially when dealing with other human beings. In this light, how can we determine the quality of being Islamic in this general collective sense that can apply to the state as a whole? Given the realities of inevitable individual variations in the comprehension and realization of Islamic values, why should some of them constitute the Islamic basis of the state to the exclusion of others?

It is from this perspective that I am attempting to show the inherent contradictions in the conflation or convergence of religious and political authority and the unavoidable dangers of attempting to implement a fusion of the
two. These contradictions exist whether conflation or convergence is explicitly claimed, implied, or just attempted selectively without openly asserting
the claim as such. The objective of this chapter is attempted through an
overview rather than a comprehensive history of any of the locations and
periods reviewed or a full discussion of the specific aspects or incidents mentioned.

History and Authority

The history of any society contains various types of events and dimensions
of human relations. Different perceptions of that history tend to emphasize
one element or another in order to support specific views of social institutions, economic relations, or political organizations. For instance, different
perceptions of history may emphasize a tradition of tolerance or intolerance
of the diversity of religious or political opinion and practice within society.
Since such divergent perceptions of history are intended to influence the
views and behaviors of present-day Muslims, policymakers and participants
in the public debate tend to emphasize those perceptions that are consistent
with their own positions. Each side in a struggle or a debate probably emphasizes its vision of history in good faith and genuine belief in its validity,
but that does not mean that that vision is necessarily true or valid. It is therefore true that the framing and interpretation of the history of some Islamic
societies that follows here is one among various competing perceptions of
those events and dimensions of human relationships, and not the only possible or valid view. But this is true of every approach to examining history, as
no one can deal with Islamic or any other history in a neutral or objective
manner.

It is also true that the case study of the Fatimid and Mamluk regimes in
Egypt which I present is far from being representative of all past Islamic societies, even within the same general region and time frame, let alone of other
regions, like central Asia or sub-Saharan Africa. Although this region is not
representative of the generality of the Muslim world, it has been particularly
influential in shaping political thinking and social institutions, especially
during the first few centuries of Islam. Consequently, Muslim elites in other
regions have tended to identify the experiences of Middle Eastern societies

as the only legitimate or authoritative framework of Islamic discourse. The general population in other regions has also accepted the subordination of its religious and social experiences when Middle Eastern experiences have been presented as a religious imperative. This is perhaps understandable, because the texts of the Qur'an and Sunna were rendered in the Arabic language and understood in terms of the specific local experiences of that region and time.

The historical relationship among Islam, the state, and politics clearly reflects the permanent tension between claims of the conflation of Islam and the state and the need of religious leaders to maintain their autonomy from state institutions in the interest of their own moral authority over both state and society. The basic framework for the constant mediation of that tension was the expectation of Muslims that the state should uphold Islamic principles in fulfilling its obligations, on the one hand, and the inherently political and secular nature of the state, on the other. The first part was based on the Muslim belief that Islam provides a comprehensive model for individual and communal life, in the public as well as the private domain. However, the state was inherently political and not religious because of differences between the nature of religious authority and political authority. While religious leaders can and should insist on the ideals of justice and fidelity to Shari'a in theory, they have neither the power nor the obligation to confront practical questions of maintaining the peace among local communities, regulating economic and social relations, or defending the realm against external threats. Such pragmatic functions of the state require the possession of effective control over the territory and population and the ability to use coercive force to ensure compliance, which is more likely to be exercised by political than religious leaders.

This view of the pragmatic functions of the state and their reliance on skill rather than religious piety was supported by the leading Islamic traditionalist scholar Ibn Taymiyyah (died 1328), who asserted that the selection of each public officer or magistrate should be based on the pragmatic requirements and the individual's capacity to comply with the ethical and professional code of the job being assigned, not considerations of religious piety. He cited in this context the example of how the Prophet repeatedly appointed Khalid Ibn al-Walid as commander of Muslim armies, despite his frustration and dissatisfaction with Khalid's attitudes and behavior from a religious point of view (Ibn Taymiyyah 1983, 9–26). He cited other examples, and concluded that the Prophet "appointed men based on pragmatic interest even if there are men around that commander who are better than him in knowledge and faith" (18). Ibn al-Qaym al-Jawziyyah (died 1350) also emphasized that intelligence and practical wisdom should be the foundations of ruling (government), and argued that it was only through misunderstanding the political dimension of Islam that rulers "misconceived the relation between Shari'a and the actuality of experience" and through that made serious mistakes under the rubric of applying Shari'a (Ibn Qaym 1985, 14–15). Thus, these two traditional scholars, who are often cited by the advocates of an Islamic state, were clearly aware of the importance and indeed the necessity of separating the religious dimension of any individual from his function or role in the state, which must be entrusted to those who are best qualified to accomplish the task. The same view was strongly stated by al-Ghazali (died 1111), one of the most authoritative Sunni scholars of all time (Ghazali 1968, 67–83).

This is not to say that religious leaders cannot achieve political authority over their followers, but rather to call for two distinct *types* of authority, even when exercised by the same person. For instance, the authority held by a religious leader derives from personal relationships with his or her followers and their confidence in his or her piety. This sort of subjective value judgment can best be made through local routine interactions, which are difficult for large numbers of people to have with a single religious leader, especially in urban centers or at great distances. In contrast, political authority tends to be based on more "objectively" assessed qualities regarding the ability to exercise coercive power and execute effective administration for the general good of the community. I hope that this distinction will become clearer in light of the following remarks.

Every society needs a state to perform essential functions, such as defending the realm against external threats, keeping peace and public safety within its territories, adjudicating disputes among its subjects, and providing whatever services it can for the well-being of its citizens. For the state to perform these functions, it has to make a choice among competing policy options and enjoy an effective monopoly over the legitimate use of force in order to impose its will in implementing those policies. It should be emphasized that we are talking here about public policy on a large scale and not the personal confidence and trust a person may have in his or her religious leaders in voluntarily complying with the advice they give in temporal as well as spiritual matters. The need to enforce general public policy, as distinguished from voluntary compliance by individual persons, requires that rulers be granted authority (whether by selection, election, or other means) on the basis of their actual or presumed political skills and their ability to perform state functions and exercise coercive powers. The qualities of effective political leadership must therefore be determined on a large and public scale, in a decisive and settled manner, to minimize the risks of civil strife and violent conflict. Uncertainty about political leaders and their authority raises the risk of civil war, chaos, and strife, or at least stalemate and confusion in government.

In contrast, religious leaders achieve recognition among believers because of their piety and their knowledge, which can be determined only by the private judgment of individual persons, who need to get to know potential religious leaders through daily interactions. The identity and authority of religious leaders can be settled only in a gradual and tentative manner through interpersonal relations with their followers. Among Shiʿa Muslims and some large Sufi brotherhoods, some degree or form of institutionalized religious leadership can evolve without interpersonal interaction. But even in such settings, the source of authority is personal relationships and piety, whereby daily interactions at a local level are imbued with the authenticity of the chain of command in the particular community. This is different from public assessment of political skill for political leaders. The difference between political and religious authority I am emphasizing can also be expressed in terms of the distinction between the *coercive* and exclusive powers of political leaders over a specific territory and population and the *moral* authority of religious leaders, even when it is exercised over a large number of followers across great distances.

There is therefore a fundamental difference between the qualities of political and religious leadership, the manner in which leaders are identified or selected, and the scope and nature of their authority over people. It is possible for some political leaders also to have religious piety and learning, as it is possible for some religious leaders to have political skills and the ability to exercise coercive powers. Indeed, Muslims may find it desirable for each type of leader to have some of the qualities of the other, as rulers should be restrained by piety and learning, while religious leaders need political skills to fulfill their role in society. However, rulers will not permit independent assessment of their piety and learning, especially when it is linked to the legitimacy of their claim to rule. Conversely, the political skills of religious leaders can be assessed only in peaceful, nonviolent interpersonal interactions. It is as unrealistic to expect rulers to relinquish their coercive powers because their subjects find them lacking in piety and learning as it is to expect religious leaders to give up their moral authority because of the inadequacy of their political qualities and skills. Allowing the same persons to assert both types of authority is dangerous and counterproductive, because that makes it much harder to dislodge them without the risk of serious civil strife and violence.

Since it has always been highly desirable for rulers to have a measure of Islamic legitimacy to sustain their political authority over Muslims, various types of rulers have claimed religious authority. Such claims did not make past rulers superior Muslims or the state they controlled Islamic, and it may in fact be that they tended to assert religious legitimacy most strongly when their claims were least likely to be valid. From a religious perspective, it is a contradiction for a leader actively to assert piety—it is impious to claim piety. Since this would undermine the basis of religious authority, those aspiring to religious leadership would need to assert autonomy from rulers. Conversely, rulers needed to concede the autonomy of the scholars precisely in order to gain Islamic legitimacy from those scholars' endorsement of the state. In other words, rulers needed to balance their control of religious leaders by conceding their autonomy from the state, which is the source of the ability of religious leaders to legitimize the authority of the rulers. At the same time, rulers could not afford to leave religious leaders completely free, because the religious leaders might use that independence to undermine the political authority of the state. In other words, the distinction between state and religious institutions was historically both necessary and difficult to maintain in practice for both sides.

This deep and complex paradox, which is also true in the historical experience of other religious communities, is inherent to the relationship between the two types of authority. Religious leaders tended to enjoy political influence in proportion to their ability to check the excesses of political leaders and hold them accountable to Shari'a principles. Since religious leaders lacked institutional means to enforce the accountability of rulers, one of the most vexing questions facing Islamic political thought has always been how to make rulers accountable without at least the threat of rebellion. Once religious authorities threaten or resort to rebellion, as many have done through the centuries, rulers naturally have sought to suppress them, violently if necessary, which has often led to civil wars or drastic civil strife and chaos. This is the dilemma that has led religious leaders to tolerate an oppressive or illegitimate ruler as the lesser of two evils. This problem was not peculiar to Islamic societies in the past but remains a serious challenge to Muslims unless they can establish alternative forms of effective political and legal accountability. With the European model of the state under which all Muslims live today, that alternative requires the establishment of constitutionalism, human rights, and citizenship (as explained in Chapter 3). But these resources were totally lacking among all societies everywhere until the modern era.

From this perspective, Islamic history can be read according to the relationship between the state and religious institutions that different regimes have experienced and/or cultivated. The first of the two polar models of this relationship is that of complete conflation or convergence, based on the prototype of the Prophet in Medina, and assumes that political and military leadership must necessarily accompany religious leadership. In such a model, there should be no separation between state and religious institutions; society is oriented toward the figurehead, who combines the two types of leadership, and there is a strong sense of hierarchy and centralization. The other polar model, complete separation between religious and political authorities, may have been the dominant view in practice, although it was rarely, if ever, openly acknowledged because of the perceived need for rulers to enjoy Islamic legitimacy. This ambivalence meant that most political regimes in Islamic history fell in between these two polar models. They never achieved the complete conflation or convergence model according to the ideal of the Prophet, yet they always claimed or sought to be closer to it than to its polar opposite, complete separation of religious and political authority. The point I am emphasizing in this chapter is that it is better for Muslims to recognize the impossibility of achieving the complete conflation or convergence model in order to better organize and regulate the more pragmatic model of separation. This point can be explained as follows, subject to further clarification later in this chapter.

The conflation/convergence ideal has been impossible to achieve since the time of the Prophet because no other human being can enjoy the Prophet's combination of religious and political authority. As the ultimate embodiment of this model, the Prophet was accepted by Muslims to be their sole legislator, judge, and commander. That experience was unique and cannot be replicated, because Muslims do not accept the possibility of prophets after the Prophet Muhammad. All rulers since Abu Bakr, the first caliph (632–634), have had to negotiate or mediate the permanent tension between religious and political authority, because none of those rulers has been accepted by all Muslims as capable of holding the supreme position of the Prophet, who defined Islam and determined how it could be implemented.

It is true, of course, that all political leaders face opposition, which can be very strong, even violent sometimes. But the significant difference between the conflation and separation models is that opposition to political authorities can only claim to be based on human judgment, which can be assessed by other human beings, while religious leadership necessarily invokes divine authority, which is supposed to transcend human challenge. Since the basis of political leadership is representation of the views and interests of the whole population, even when it is in fact authoritarian or despotic, it can be challenged on that ground. In contrast, the basis of religious leadership is a claim of superior moral authority, which is judged by transcendental criteria. While an individual is free to accept or reject the message of Islam itself, there was no question of political opposition to the Prophet among Muslims, who accepted him as the final and conclusive prophet. In contrast, for example, when Abu Bakr asserted his authority to fight the Arab tribes who refused to pay *zakat* to the state, many of the leading Companions of the Prophet, including Umar, who succeeded Abu Bakr as caliph two years later, opposed him. (*Zakat* is the alms Muslims who own a specified amount of property are required to pay annually to certain categories of beneficiaries who are identified in the Qur'an, as in verse 9:60. Whether it is to be paid by believers privately or through the state treasury—that is, as a tax—was exactly the issue in that early conflict.)

This instance remains controversial among Muslim scholars, as explained in the next section, because Abu Bakr asserted a religious rationale for fighting the rebels. I believe that Abu Bakr made the right decision, but it is also clear to me that his view prevailed because he was the political leader of the community and not because the other Companions accepted it as a matter of religious authority. It is true, of course, that for the Companions at that time, as for many Muslims of subsequent generations, submission to the legitimate ruler of the community was a religious obligation, as stipulated in such verses of the Qur'an as 4:59. That verse is commonly understood to require Muslims to obey God, His Messenger, and the rulers of the community. But submission to the will of a ruler may be necessary for political stability and peace regardless of acceptance of the religious validity of that ruler's view, in which case a believer would be submitting to political and not religious authority. If Umar had been the caliph at the time, his view— not to fight the Arab tribes who refused to pay *zakat*—would have prevailed and the subsequent wars of apostasy would not have happened. From this perspective, the whole situation was clearly political and not religious, because a religious outcome should not depend on who controls political authority. Still, the campaign against the renegade Arabs probably had a religious as well as a political rationale for various actors at the time. This overlap between the religious and the political is one of the reasons such issues are to be mediated, instead of resolved through an attempt to apply a rigid formula.

The reading or view of Islamic histories I am proposing is the differentiation between religious and political authorities that can be traced back to the time when Abu Bakr became the first caliph of the Medina state. The fact that this view is not prevalent among Muslims today does not by itself mean that it is wrong. On the contrary, the deep crisis Muslims everywhere are experiencing regarding the relationship of Islam to the state and politics indicates the need for a fresh reading of history for guidance about the future of Shari'a in Islamic societies. Old, familiar modes of thinking are not working. Of course, this does not mean that the view I am presenting here is necessarily correct, but only that it should be seriously considered as an alternative to the currently prevalent view, instead of being dismissed simply because it is unfamiliar to Muslims today. As noted earlier, this differentiation should not be seen as secularism in the modern sense, but it was certainly the functional equivalent for the sort of state Muslims lived with in the past.

Early Mediations of Ideal Vision and Pragmatic Reality

Since, as indicated earlier, the model of the Prophet in Medina is too exceptional to be replicated, I will first focus in the following overview on clarifying the significance of the caliphate of Medina (Abu Bakr, Umar, Uthman, and Ali) of 632–661, through the Umayyad era (661–750) (Hodgson 1974, I: 187–230; Madelung 1997; Lapidus 2002). I will confine my consideration of that early history to the two competing models of conflation and separation of Islam and the state. In the second subsection I will briefly examine the events and consequences of the inquisition (al-Mihna) initiated by the caliph al-Ma'mun in 833.

Like the vast majority of Muslims, I find it very difficult to offer analytical reflections on these early periods of Islamic history because of the high reverence associated with the Companions of the Prophet (sahaba) involved in the events. How can I presume to judge whether Abu Bakr, the highest-ranking Companion among Sunni Muslims, was right or wrong in waging what is commonly known as the wars of apostasy *(hurub al-ridda)*, or in how he is reported to have dealt with the charges against Khalid ibn al-Walid, another Companion, for his conduct during that campaign? In fact, my apprehension about engaging in critical reflection on the political actions of such religious personalities is part of the reason for insisting on the religious neutrality of the state, as I am proposing here. The separation of Islam and the state is necessary to enable Muslims to uphold their genuine religious beliefs and to live accordingly, without abandoning their responsibility for or participation in the public affairs of their societies. Historically, religious leaders were either enticed to cooperate with the political agenda of rulers or coerced to do so to avoid facing harsh consequences, as illustrated by the inquisition. Instead of presenting Muslims with similar difficult choices today, I am calling for the separation of Islam from the state, which means that those who control the state cannot use its coercive powers to enforce their own beliefs. The purpose of my reflection on the relevance and significance of those early and highly contested events is to see what they tell us today about Islam and the state, without judging what was right or wrong or who was good or bad.

The Wars of Apostasy and the Nature of the State

The succession of the Prophet has remained highly contested throughout the history of Islamic societies because of its implications for the nature of the state and its relationship to Islam. The commonly accepted sequence of events is that the claim of the group of Muslims who migrated with the Prophet from Mecca *(al-Muharajun)* prevailed over that of those who welcomed and supported him in Medina *(al-Ansar)*. Reports that the latter group suggested that there should be a ruler *(amir)* from each of the two communities indicate that they were worried about the risks of consolidated governance, rather than that they opposed Abu Bakr as such. This fact is relevant to understanding the reasons for the rebellion of other Arab tribes, who were suppressed through the wars of apostasy. Abu Bakr finally prevailed over all other contenders in what Umar called a "fortuitous coincident" *(falta)*, which confirms the political nature of the whole process. One critical aspect of the enduring controversy over that process is that some Muslims, who came to be known as Shi'at Ali (partisans of Ali; hence the term "Shi'a"), continued to challenge the validity of the selection of Abu

Bakr over Ali. Another aspect, which is even more significant for our purposes here, is that differing opinions on the rationale for the selection of any successor to the Prophet and the criteria for such selection have had profound consequences on the nature of the state and the position of the caliphate as institutions. I will now address this underlying question through an analysis of the wars of apostasy and what they signify for the nature of the state as a political institution.

The wars of apostasy were the first crisis that the emerging polity faced immediately after the death of the Prophet Muhammad. Abu Bakr had to assert the authority of the state over a number of Arabian tribes that apparently resisted that authority. The conventional position held by Muslims is that Abu Bakr executed those wars because the tribes had apostatized by following false prophets or by refusing to pay the *zakat,* and that either type of action warranted their suppression by force in the name of Islam. This episode came to be highly revered in the Sunni discourse as the great achievement that confirmed the validity of the selection of Abu Bakr as the first caliph. After all, it was that consolidation of political power throughout the Arabian Peninsula that propelled Muslim expansion into the Byzantine and Sassanian empires.

I am not concerned here with the validity of that dominant view, or with whether Abu Bakr was right or wrong in waging that war, but only with the meaning or significance of that major episode for the *nature of the state* at that phase. Abu Bakr's determination to fight those tribes until they submitted to his authority as the caliph is emphasized in his well-known statement about their withholding *zakat:* "I swear by God if they withheld only a hobbling-cord [of a camel] of what they used to give to the Prophet, I would fight them for it." What was the rationale for that position, and how or why should it be interpreted to mean that Abu Bakr was asserting his succession to the Prophet in a religious and not a political sense? That is, the Prophet exercised political as well as religious authority, and it was obviously necessary to select a political head for the community, but why or how could that person succeed the Prophet in his religious role? In terms of the analysis I am proposing, did the way in which the decision to fight those Arab tribes was made, its rationale or reasons, and the events associated with those wars indicate a conflation model of fused religious and political Islamic leadership? If those events did indicate that model, what do they tell us about the inherent difficulties and contradictions of that view?

For instance, a distinction can be made between the two major categories of those against whom Abu Bakr waged war: those who refused to pay the caliphate of Medina the annual *zakat* and those who abandoned Islam by following self-proclaimed prophets. It could also be argued that Abu Bakr regarded the refusal to pay *zakat* to the treasury of the state in Medina as tantamount to apostasy, which is punishable by death. Alternatively, that refusal could be seen as a rebellion against the authority of the state as a political institution, which warranted an effective assertion of that authority by military force. It is not possible, of course, to discuss in detail those protracted and complex controversies that continued to rage into the second century of Islamic history. My limited objective here is to reflect on the implications of those controversies for the nature of the state at that formative time, regardless of what one may think of what Abu Bakr did. For example, whether in enforcing the collection of *zakat* or punishing for apostasy, was Abu Bakr exercising a purely political authority as the caliph, or was he the caliph because of his religious authority over the community?

Many of the underlying questions remain undecided to the present day, such as whether *zakat* was voluntary during the life of the Prophet and whether it was collected and sent to Medina or spent locally. There is also evidence that during the life of the Prophet, paying *zakat* was not a universal requirement for becoming a Muslim, and that the Prophet accepted conversion to Islam even with the stipulation of nonpayment. It has been suggested that the fixed rates of *zakat* collection were not codified until the caliphate of Abu Bakr. The available evidence indicates that the Prophet did not use force in the collection of *zakat* (Madelung 1997, 46–47). The prominent Companions of the Prophet, such as Umar and Abu Ubayda, urged Abu Bakr to "rescind the tax for the year and to treat the tribes loyal to Islam leniently in order to enlist their support for those who had abandoned Islam" (Madelung 1997, 48; Berkey 2004, 261–264). Others, like Ali, never participated in the campaign. The existence of such disagreement on this issue among Muslims is itself significant for understanding the basis of Abu Bakr's decision and its implications for the nature of the state at that time.

Another aspect that was controversial at the time was Abu Bakr's appointment of the elite members of the Mecca aristocracy as commanders in the military campaigns, though they had only recently converted to Islam after years of fierce and adamant opposition to the Prophet (Donner 1981, 86–87). On one level, that was part of the political nature of the campaigns, because "the alms-tax potentially meant the surrender of tribal autonomy and the acceptance of tax officials with the right to force recalcitrant subjects [in addition to] the subjection of the tribes to a ruler or government, something the tribes had previously most vigorously resisted" (Madelung 1997, 47). An appreciation for the apprehensions of the Arab tribes, who were facing a drastic transformation of their social and political institutions and relations, was probably the reason that the Prophet never resorted to force in collecting *zakat*. In fact, when the leaders of the rebellious tribes were captured and taken before Abu Bakr, they rejected the charge of apostasy by affirming that they were Muslims who were only unwilling to pay *zakat* to the state (Kister 1986, 61–96).

An incident that generated a lot of controversy at the time was Abu Bakr's command to Khalid ibn al-Walid to kill Malik ibn Nuwayra of the Banu Yarbu, a tribe of the larger federation of Banu Tamim. This command came after Malik ibn Nuwayra withheld from Abu Bakr a number of camels that he had amassed to give the Prophet as *zakat* on behalf of his tribe. The withholding of the *zakat* was based on his belief that he owed allegiance only to the Prophet and remained within his rights as a Muslim to return the *zakat* to his tribe. Although he reaffirmed his allegiance to Islam, Malik was killed by Khalid, along with other men of his tribe, and Khalid took Malik's wife away after killing him, presumably treating her as part of "the spoils of war."

Leading Companions strongly objected to Khalid's behavior. Umar demanded that Khalid be reprimanded for his actions, and Ali called for imposing the *hadd* punishment on Khalid, presumably for *zina* (by taking the wife of Malik) (Madelung 1997, 50; Sanders 1994, 43–44), but Abu Bakr as the caliph rejected both demands (Jafri 2000, 58–79). Such demands would have been inconceivable if Abu Bakr had been exercising the religious authority of the Prophet, because Companions of that high standing would not have disputed any aspect of Abu Bakr's decisions if they accepted them as expressing the religiously binding precepts of Islam. Yet despite the Companions' disagreement with Abu Bakr, they did not attempt to act on their own in implementing what they thought was the correct view, presumably out of respect for Abu Bakr's political authority as the caliph. Subsequent early scholars, like al-Shafi'i, Ahmed ibn Hanbal, and Ibn Rajab (died 1396), dealt with the ambiguities of that situation in various ways, ranging from textual analyses of early Sunna reports *(hadith)* to simple apologetics (Kister 1986, 36–37). The view that came to prevail among Sunni Muslims is that Abu Bakr had no choice but to fight the rebels to maintain the authority of the state.

I am not presuming to decide who was right or wrong; the point for our purposes here is the inherent ambiguity in and the risks of claiming to implement a religious view through the coercive authority of the state. That ambiguity may be clarified if we understand the issues in terms of Abu Bakr's role as the political leader of the community, not as a religious one. This reading is not inconsistent with the view that Abu Bakr's own motivations may have been religious, in the sense that he believed that he was defending Islam as well as upholding the integrity of the state as a political institution.Conversely, he may not have been aware of the idea of the state in this sense. Moreover, the willingness of the leading Companions to abide by Abu Bakr's decisions though they believed them to be wrong may have been motivated by political factors, especially the need to consolidate and secure the community during that critical period. But religious rationales were also cited for such factors, including verse 4:59 of the Qur'an, cited earlier. In addition to this obligation to obey the ruler, Muslims have the obligation to enjoin justice and oppose injustice (al-amr bil ma'ruf wa l-nahy an al-munkar). There is a Sunna report (or maxim) that no human being should obey what constitutes disobedience to God (la ta'ata li makhluq fi ma'siayat al-Khliq). This "right to rebel" has been asserted by various factions throughout Islamic history, as we will see in the context of the inquisition.

Thus, whatever justification is considered, it is difficult to separate the religious aspects from the political ones: Muslims will always disagree on both counts, and religious reasoning includes political considerations and vice versa. Regarding the wars of apostasy, it is possible that Abu Bakr's actions were valid from an Islamic point of view. For instance, he decided to wage war on the Arab tribes either as apostates or as rebels against the state, which warrants the punishment of death under what came to be known as the capital crime of waging war against the community (hadd al-haraba under verse 5:33–34). Whatever may have been the rationale, Abu Bakr was able to enforce his view over the objections of the leading Companions because he was the caliph, not because he was "right" or "correct" from an Islamic point of view. This is not to say that Abu Bakr was right or wrong, because both are possible, but there was no possibility of an independent authority that could have adjudicated or arbitrated his disagreement with the other Companions. Conversely, as noted earlier, if Umar or Ali, for instance, had been the caliph instead of Abu Bakr, the wars of apostasy would not have occurred.

The conclusion I am drawing here for our purposes is that it may be helpful to distinguish between Abu Bakr's religious views and his political decisions and actions as the caliph. Similarly, some leading Companions disagreed with Abu Bakr, probably on religious grounds as well as political ones. This distinction should be maintained regardless of the religious motivation of Abu Bakr and the other Companions, because the nature of the action should not be determined by the motivation of the actor. Such a distinction may still be difficult for Muslims to see regarding the Medina period because of the very personal nature of political authority at the time, when the state hardly existed as a political institution. That was due to many factors, including the recent example of the Prophet and the lack of prior state formations in Arabia, as well as the ways in which the first four caliphs were selected and ruled. The point is that whatever view may be taken of those events in that historical context, such confusion is neither justified nor acceptable in the present context of the postcolonial state.

In fact, confusing the political authority of the caliph with his religious authority was already untenable after the assassination of Ali and the beginning of the Umayyad state. Although it was a total and complete monarchy in every way, the Umayyad dynasty still sought to maintain the fiction that the authority of their caliphs was an extension of the authority of the Prophet. The various grand titles of the Umayyad caliphs, like *khalifat Allah* (vice-regent of God), *amin Allah* (guardian of God), and *na'ib Allah* (deputy of God), which were proclaimed in the formal sermon of the weekly Friday congregational prayer throughout the territories they ruled, were intended to assert direct and supreme religious authority. Yet there was no doubt among Muslims that the state established by Mu'awiya after the assassination of Ali, who is historically accepted as the legitimate caliph of the time, had no religious legitimacy. This view is usually confirmed by the fact that Mu'awiya established a monarchy by ensuring the succession of his son, Yazid, who lacked any of the commonly accepted qualifications for being a caliph. As Yazid faced increasing rebellions and insurgencies that directly targeted his authority and legitimacy as a Muslim ruler, he resorted to such violent repression of dissent that he further diminished his religious authority. In suppressing those rebellions, he ordered the killing of Husayn ibn Ali, the Prophet's grandson, and his small band of followers and family at Karbala. Abdullahi ibn al-Zubayr, the grandson of Abu Bakr and the son of another leading Companion of the Prophet, raised another revolt and claimed to be the caliph around the same time, in 681, with followers in the holy cities of Mecca and Medina. That revolt was crushed by the Umayyad armies within a decade, and the holy cities of Mecca and Medina, even the Ka'ba itself, were desecrated in the process. This crisis in Islamic legitimacy persisted throughout the eight decades of Umayyad rule and beyond (Crone and Hinds 1986, 12).

The permanent paradox of the Umayyad and all subsequent regimes that ruled over Muslims is that they sought to satisfy their need for genuine religious legitimacy by making the impossible claim of replicating the model of the Prophet or at least that of the first four caliphs of Medina. Ironically, that problem was often exacerbated by the rulers' drive to consolidate their control over the population, which undermined their Islamic legitimacy. The Abbasid revolution based its successful challenge on the Umayyads' lack of Islamic legitimacy and claimed to (re)establish the ideal of the proper Muslim social order. However, it quickly became clear that the caliphate was already institutionalized as a royal dynasty, with rulers proceeding through lines of heredity—nothing more than an adaptation of the Sassanian and Byzantine models of monarchical rule (Lapidus 1996, 58–66).

The emergent Arab empire was spectacularly successful in destroying those much more developed empires, but adopted their structures and often kept the officials of the previous regime in the same positions. Ironically, the early Abbasid caliphs sought to create or enhance their legitimacy by founding their claim to rule on shared lineage with the Prophet, thereby implying that they were qualified to reenact his model. They attempted to uphold the unity of religious and political leadership through their appointments of Islamic scholars as judges *(qadis)* and through patronage of religious sciences and institutions, as well as in their role as military defenders of the Islamic empire (Zaman 1997, 129–166). But the inherent contradiction of these two claims was conclusively exposed by what came to be known as the inquisition.

Implications of the Inquisition for the Conflation Myth

The obvious rupture between the Islamic ideal of conflated religious and political leadership and the empirical reality of Muslim history became apparent even before the rebellions of the Kharijites and the various Shi'a. The political troubles that all of the caliphs of Medina faced from their fellow Muslims were clear proof that the ideal office the Prophet so masterfully commanded was not suitable for replication. The proliferation of early Islamic sects such as the Qadirriya, Murjiyya, and others also challenged the myth of Islamic unity. Moreover, the drastic events of what came to be known as the inquisition *(al-Mihna)* should be considered from the perspective of social history. The conflicts between the authority of the caliph and the *ulama* should be seen in the context of the social relations among the Arab elites, who represented the caliph's court and its imperial administrative apparatus, a variety of religious leaders, and the descendants of Khorasani rebels who initiated the successful Abbasid revolution.

What came to be known as *al-Mihna* was primarily a theological inquisition aimed at making members of the *ulama*, which was by no means a unified group at the time, conform to the philosophical position that the Qur'an was a creation of God and not the uncreated word (thus an attribute) of the Creator. This issue was part of a long-standing debate between those who favored a more allegorical and rational approach to Islamic sources (Mu'tazilites) and others *(ahl-hadith,* or Ash'arites) who adhered to a strictly textual, literalist approach. In that context, the Abbasid caliph al-Ma'mun instigated an inquisition in 833 (218 of the Islamic era) to force certain *ulama* to adopt the Mu'tazilites' view. Although al-Ma'mun died shortly thereafter, the inquisition was continued by his three successors for another sixteen years. The caliph al-Mutawakkil ended the persecution by releasing the noncomplying *ulama* from prison and at times placing some of them in positions of authority. But the episode should also be understood in the political and security context of Baghdad, the Abbasid capital, at the time. By the time al-Ma'mun returned to Baghdad after the civil war he waged against his own brother, al-Amin, the city was in great chaos. He attempted to impose a brand of theology on the public, and this probably contributed to the total and final loss of the caliphate's Islamic authority, instead of enhancing it. The conditions of extreme chaos that engulfed Baghdad as a result of having various factions competing for power and a disgruntled army, complicated by bands of criminals and thugs, resulted in the emergence of several movements that are particularly significant for emphasizing that the conflated model of religious and political leadership was simply untenable in practice.

For example, Sahl ibn Salama al-Ansari, a resident of Baghdad who "wore a copy of the Qur'an around his neck and called on the people to 'command the good and forbid the evil,'" drew followers with various backgrounds from all corners of the city and called upon them not only to defend their neighborhoods by providing security and stability for their own quarters, but also to commit themselves to implementing the Qur'an and Sunna of the Prophet: "Sahl envisaged allegiance to a higher principle which justified opposing even the Caliph and the state authorities if they failed to uphold Islam . . . [He] preached that allegiance to the Qur'an and *sunna* superseded obedience to authorities who were compromised by the failure to uphold Islam" (Lapidus 1975, 372). He adopted the slogan that there should be no obedience to any human being if that would be in disobedience to God *(la ta'at lil-makhluq fi ma'siyat al-khaliq)*. His followers in various quarters of Baghdad "built *burj* (towers) in front of their houses, fortifying themselves within the city" (Lapidus 1975, 373). Thus, Sahl's community-based organization represented the spontaneous emergence of a religious polity that openly and militantly defied the authority of the caliph.

The vigilante movement embodied a revolutionary conception of the structure of Muslim society by employing religious language to appeal to an essentially communal idea of Islam, which reached beyond the boundaries of caliphate government (Lapidus 1975, 376). "Commanding the good and forbidding the evil" was originally regarded as the duty of caliphs, but Sahl's movement sided with many *ulama* who believed that it was a duty incumbent on all Muslims, thereby drawing upon a powerful symbol of religious authority and duty left vacant by incompetent rulers. One of the most prominent of those *ulama* was Ahmed ibn Hanbal, who, incidentally, was a resident of one of the quarters of Baghdad whose residents undertook to provide security and stability for themselves (Lapidus 1975, 375–377). Thus, the social force represented by Sahl and others coincided with the theological independence of the scholar Ahmed ibn Hanbal and his followers, such as Ahmad ibn Nasr ibn Malik, who were residents of some of the quarters of Baghdad represented by Sahl and other opponents of the caliph. It is significant for our purposes to note that Sahl was tried for his "religious views" instead of sedition, and that his head was displayed in public to warn others of the fate of those who defied the caliph (Lapidus 1975, 381–382).

The protracted inquisition represented a confrontation between the *ulama* and the caliphs over religious authority. The refusal of Ibn Hanbal to accept the caliph's religious claims, which led to his imprisonment until his death, confirmed the rejection of the ideal notion of a unified religious and state authority. As Lapidus rightly said,

> The struggle over the createdness of the Qur'an confirmed the institutional separation of the caliphate and the community, the division of authority between them, and the separate roles for each as bearers of part of what had been the legacy of the Prophet. Henceforth, the caliphate would evolve,

contrary to the Muslim ideal, as a largely military and imperial institution legitimated in neo-Byzantine and neo-Sassanian terms, while the religious elites would develop a more complete authority over the communal, personal, religious, and doctrinal aspects of Islam. (1996, 12)

Although the differentiation of state and religious institutions has never been recognized in popular Muslim discourse, this separation did win indirect, tacit acceptance through the work of subsequent scholars like al-Baqillani (died 1013), al-Mawardi (died 1058), and Ibn Taymiyyah. "The upshot of their theorizing was that the state was not a direct expression of Islam, but a secular institution whose duty it was to uphold Islam; the real community of Muslims was the community of scholars and holy men who carried on the legacy of the Prophet in daily life" (Lapidus 1996, 19). This view is consistent with my call for accepting and understanding secularism as the religious neutrality of the state that retains the inherent connectedness between Islam and politics.

The differentiation between Islam and the state was firmly consolidated through the emergence of military control over the caliphate itself around the same time. The difficulties the Abbasid caliphs had in managing the internal problems of the empire led to deterioration in loyalty and allegiance to the caliphate in Baghdad. In response to continued Shi'a and Khariji rebellions throughout the empire, the Abbasid caliphate employed mercenary/slave soldiers (Mamluks) to consolidate its rule. Reliance on Mamluks as soldiers began during the reign of Caliph al-Mu'tasim (833–842), which immediately followed the chaos that marked al-Ma'mun's tenure as the caliph (Petry 1981, 15). The non-Arab soldiers and military commanders had little genuine allegiance to the caliphate as an institution and tended to regard it as a source of political power and economic gain.

The *ulama* deferred political and military authority to foreign military regimes, whether Seljuk, Ayyubid, Mamluk, or Ottoman, while they retained authority over matters of religious practice, doctrine, and institutions. What I call the "negotiative" model was thus solidified with the two broad institutions working together; the *ulama* supported the military state, while the military state protected the Muslim lands. The military elites and the prominent civilian administrators secured their ties with the religious communities by endowing religious colleges, mosques, and other institutions of the Muslim community. This model continued throughout the precolonial era, and remnants are still in effect today, as seen in the predominance of military cultures in some parts of the Muslim world.

While that became the model in Baghdad and the surrounding regions, a drastically different type of political or religious model of governance arose in North Africa. The Fatimid dynasty began in 909 in Tunisia, when Ubayd Allah al-Mahdi, an Isma'ili Shi'a, claimed legitimacy as the sole heir of all the descendents of the Prophet through Ali and Fatima *(ahl al-bayt)*. That movement, as discussed later, sought to reassert the old notion of fusing religious and political leadership. However, the Fatimids were only a part of a wider North African tendency toward such models of leadership, which dominated its history after the decline of the Umayyad dynasty. Muslim rulers of various regimes in North Africa, like the Idrisid, Fatimid, Almoravid, and Almohad, claimed divine authority to rule on the basis of their personal qualifications and descent from the Prophet. It is clear that the models of relations between religious and state authorities "vary across a wide spectrum from a high degree of state control over a centrally managed religious establishment, to a more independent but co-operative relationship (as in the Saljuq case), to full autonomy and even open opposition to state policies" (Lapidus 1996, 24). I will attempt to clarify and illustrate this view with reference to the historical experience of Egypt from the ninth to the fourteenth century.

The Fatimid and Mamluk States in Egypt

I do not intend to provide a general history of the Fatimid and Mamluk periods in Egypt, only an overview of each period. I will then highlight certain aspects to illustrate the practical impossibility of the conflation of Islam and the state. It is not that the conflation claim was not made in the past, because the Fatimids clearly asserted a "divine right to rule," but such an assertion does not mean that the claim was valid or realistic. The point for us is that the claim not only failed in practice but could not possibly have succeeded, because of the fundamental differences between religious and state authority. As this section will show, the dangers of conflation were realized both when the Fatimid state explicitly claimed religious authority and when the Mamluk state did so implicitly.

Overview of the Fatimid State in Egypt

The Fatimid dynasty was founded around 909 in North Africa (present-day Tunisia) by Ubayd Allah, who was regarded as the Mahdi by one branch of Isma'ili Shi'a. The Fatimid period in Egypt began when Jawhar, the chief military commander of al-Mu'izz, Fatimid imam from 953 to 975, conquered Egypt in 969. Al-Mu'izz himself entered Egypt four years later. (Instead of "caliph" and "caliphate," "imam" and "imamate" are more appropriate for the Fatimids as a Shi'a state.) Al-Aziz ibn al-Mu'izz reigned from 975 to 996 and was followed by al-Hakim, who ruled for a quarter of a century (996–1021). Upon al-Hakim's disappearance, or possible murder on the order of his sister Sitt al-Mulk, his son al-Zahir reigned for another fifteen years (1021–1036), followed by al-Mustansir. The exceptionally long reign of al-Mustansir (1036–1094) witnessed an extensive civil war, which eventually led to the consolidation of the regime's power in the hands of the military. From that period onward, attempts were made by viziers, judges, military commanders, and provincial governors to expand their own power bases at the expense of that of the Fatimid imamate. The following seventy-five years saw the rise of six different imams, with diminishing authority under conditions of sectarian division, military coup, and overall disintegration. The dynasty ended when Saladin, the Ayyubid commander, seized the vizierate of the Fatimids and declared loyalty to the Abbasid caliph in Baghdad in 1171.

The Fatimid self-image as an imamate categorically asserted the continuation of the spiritual and political authority of the Prophet. Both main sects of Shi'a, the Imamis (Twelvers) and the Isma'ilis, identified "the legitimate head of state as [the] deputy of God on earth" (Crone and Hinds 1986, 99). By this, they declared the total convergence of political and spiritual dimensions of leadership. The extent to which the imam was considered a divinely inspired authority cannot be understated. For example, the imams were understood to be "imams of justice who guide people away from perdition"; "beacons of truth and guidance . . . shining suns, guiding stars"; and "the pillars of religion, rain and life to mankind" (Crone and Hinds 1986, 100–101). In this view, the imam was "the completion of the prayer, zakat, fasting, pilgrimage and jihad, the augmentation of the booty and the alms taxes, the execution of the hudud . . . he is superior to all other people, ranking below prophets only" (Crone and Hinds 1986, 102). That special place of knowledge was believed to require that the imam also be a curator of religious discourse. His special status of infallibility essentially made him the most just and perfect of all rulers and guaranteed that guidance would be available to Muslims. The imam was also said to share the quality of mufahham, instructed by God, as Solomon is described in the Qu'ran (Crone and Hinds 1986, 103).

In practice, however, such assertions of the Prophet's model of leadership did not reflect even remotely similar humility and aversion to materialism by Fatimid imams in their public image. Beginning in 990, the then reigning caliph, al-Aziz, implemented a procession for the festival prayer (most likely Id al-Fitr) in which "the caliph rode with his troops, who wore costumes of ornamented brocade and were girded with swords and belts of gold. Horses led by the hand during the parade had jeweled saddles of gold and amber. Elephants, ridden by soldiers bearing arms, paraded in front of him. The caliph himself rode under a parasol ornamented with jewels" (Sanders 1994, 49). Such displays of wealth and power in the midst of often starving Muslims were apparently used to reinforce the imam's religious authority. For example, in the Id al-Fitr procession, the imam and his top administrators and judges would proceed in a paradelike fashion from the palace quarters to the open-air courtyard where the congregational prayer would be held. Throughout the procession, recitation of "God is most great" *(takbir)* would continue until the imam entered the site of prayer. As a historian of the period observed, since the congregational prayer of those festivals *(salat al-idyan:* Adha and Fitr) requires not the traditional call to prayer *(adhan)* but only the *takbir,* "we might say that the festival prayer began at the start of the caliph's procession and that the procession itself was now part of the prayer" (Sanders 1994, 49–50). This association of such extravagant spectacles with Isma'ili doctrine was designed to assert in the minds of the Muslim public a connection between the Friday prayer and that of the two festivals, on the one hand, and the role of the imam in the overall mission of Islam, on the other.

The practical dangers of the alleged conflation model can be seen in the administration of justice. The main Fatimid institutions for the administration of justice included the judiciary *(qada),* private complaints *(mazalim),* public complaints *(hisba),* and the police *(shurta),* all supposedly subsumed under the jurisdiction of the chief judge *(qadi al-qudat).* The Fatimid *qadi al-qudat* had jurisdiction over all of the provinces in general, though at the imam's discretion; some areas were covered under different spheres of influence. This was the case of Palestine under the reign of al-Hakim, who excluded it from the jurisdiction of the Hanbali *qadi al-qudat* Abi al-Awwam. The army was also less subject to the authority of the chief judge and either subjected to the jurisdiction of complaints or left completely unaccountable (Haji 1988, 198–200). In addition to these normal responsibilities, "the *qadi's* competence [could] be extended to include religious attributions such as leadership of prayers and administration of mosques and sanctuaries, as well as extraordinary attributions such as directorship of the mint *(dar al-darb)*, inspectorate of the standard of weights and measures *(mi'yar)* and the supervision of the administration of the Treasury, *bayt al-mal*" (Haji 1988, 200; Lev 1991, 135). That conflation of judicial and fiscal duties facilitated the abuse of power by officials, such as the hoarding of food commodities or the manipulation of prices.

Another institution that was considered administrative, judicial, and religious in nature was that of *al-muhtasib,* or jurisdiction of the *hisba,* which existed under the Fatimid state in Egypt and throughout the wider region under various regimes. Regardless of differing opinions about its pre-Islamic origins or development, it is clear that the role or the office of *al-muhtasib* (one who exercises the jurisdiction of *hisba*) was well established by the end of the fourth century of Islam, not only as the censor and the market inspector but also as the protector of public morals in terms of the Islamic mandate of "commanding the good and forbidding the wrong" (Lev 1991, 160–176; Berkey 2004). The *muhtasib* became a central figure in the public life of Muslim societies, wielding enormous institutional authority as an official of the state, as well as religious authority as the agent for maintaining public interest and morality. The marketplace *(suq)* over which the *muhtasib* exercised authority was broadly conceived to constitute the totality of commerce and social life (Berkey 2004, 247; Zaman 1997, 129–166). What makes this role peculiar is that the *muhtasib* was an arbiter of trade while being an agent of the ruling regime, which was an active participant in the activities he arbitrated (often to the point of monopolization in the commercial life of Egyptian society) (Lev 1991, 162). The regime obtained grain by purchasing it on the free market, by cultivating it on the private estates of the imam, and sometimes by taking possession of commodities against the will of the merchants carrying them (Shoshan 1981, 182). This made it difficult to differentiate between private property and the interests of the ruler and the public domain. For instance, the grain-trading practices of the ruling elite during the Fatimid period were mainly self-interested and ignored the demands of the dependent and impoverished subjects (Lev 1991, 162, 163, 176).

The potential problems associated with blending religious institutions with those of the state often entail hypocrisy and corruption, as illustrated by the additional functions of the *muhtasib* as a tax collector and a guardian of public morality. Islamic scholars, like al-Mawardi in *al-Akham al-sultaniyya,* described the responsibilities of the *muhtasib* as including the enforcement of prayer, fasting, and payment of *zakat* in addition to public morality concerns about public mixing of men and women, displays of drunkenness, and the use of musical instruments. These functions were coercively enforced in the streets of Cairo and other cities (Berkey 2004, 261–264). Dealing with *dhimmis* (Christians and Jews granted protection in exchange for submission to Muslim sovereignty and payment of a special tax, *jizya*) was also within the jurisdiction of the office. This included enforcing rules prohibiting the *dhimmis* from riding on horses or donkeys within the city limits and prescribing that they wear distinctive clothing in public and bells around their necks when visiting public bathing facilities (Berkey 2004, 262–263).

Influence of the Fatimid State over Judicial and Religious Institutions

The preceding brief overview of the Fatimid state and its institutions is intended to provide background information and context for our primary concern with the consequences of the conflation of religious and political authority. Although the Fatimid dynasty ruled Egypt for two centuries, the Shi'ism of the state never actually filtered down to the general populace, and the Muslims of Egypt remained predominantly Sunni throughout this period. So what were the consequences of the regime's patronage of Shi'a practices and beliefs, and what are the implications for the model of conflation of religious and political authority it represented?

Upon conquering Egypt, Jawhar, the Fatimid military governor, offered a letter of security *(aman)* to the notables of Fustat (then the capital) and set forth the political program of the new regime, including the way in which religious life would be governed (Lev 1988, 315). On the first Friday of the conquest, the ceremonial sermon *(khutba)* was read in the name of the Fatimid imam al-Mu'izz (then still in Tunisia) at the central mosque of Fustat. It included goals of the new regime, which alluded to the reestablishment of Islamic prestige by recovering the holy cities of Mecca and Medina from the Qarmatians, another Isma'ili sect, and restoring justice throughout Islamic lands (Daftary 1990, 161–165). The proclamation of the names of Fatimid imams at every Friday congregational prayer, though not new, was a powerful symbol of Fatimid claims to religious as well as political authority and legitimacy over and above the Abbasid counterparts in Baghdad. The legitimacy of the Fatimid imams was also promoted through charitable works and promises to redress all injustice (Lev 1988, 315–316).

There was also a high level of conflation between state and religious institutions. While the two main mosques combined administrative, religious, and civic functions, the palace of the imam was seen as the appropriate place for the dissemination of knowledge. "The chief *qadi* Muhammad b. al-Nuʿman lectured there on the sciences of the Family of the Prophet. The chief missionary *(daʿi)* also delivered lectures there, as well as at the Azhar [Islamic university in Cairo]" (Sanders 1994, 43–44). The imam was often the curator and patron of various religious activities and institutions, endowing mosques, libraries, and schools in addition to hosting lectures and debates. His viziers (civilian ministers or high officials) engaged in similar activities (Lev 1991, 71).

In debates and disputation sessions *(munazarat)*, "opponents were summoned before an authority of the state for interrogation, or at the least, for a session of questions and answers on issues of religious understanding and interpretation" (Walker 1997, 180–181). The prestige of the state itself was at stake in such events and their outcomes. There were also sessions of wisdom and learning *(majlis al-hikma* or *majlis al-ʿilm)*, which were the primary tools of mass-based Ismaʿili religious education, by which the Ismaʿili *madhhab* was cultivated, developed, and taught (Walker 1997, 184–185). The House of Wisdom *(dar al-hikma* or *dar al-ʿilm)* was established in 1005, possessing "a large library and [serving] as a school where a wide variety of subjects, including theology, philosophy, medicine, astronomy, and even Sunni law were taught. It was also the training academy for Ismaʿili missionaries. The lectures were aimed at both Ismaʿilis and non-Ismaʿilis" (Sanders 1994, 56). This institution was funded as a *waqf* (religious endowment, plural *awqaf*) five years after its creation, which may have given it a measure of autonomy for the benefit of both Shiʿa and Sunni scholars. A century later, however, when two scholars began to teach Ashʿarite theology and al-Hallaj-inspired beliefs, "the wazir al-Afdal ordered these people arrested and the *dar al-ʿilm* closed" (Walker 1997, 192). From that point, *dar al-ʿilm* came to be supervised by the Ismaʿili head propagandist *(daʿi)*, and it was eventually destroyed by Saladin when he ended the Fatimid dynasty in Egypt (Walker 1997, 193).

The gradual adjustments the Fatimids made to transform religious practice and belief included the introduction of the Shiʿa formula of the call to prayer *(adhan)* (Lev 1988, 317). But there was resistance from and negotiation by Sunnis from the start. For example, in the *khutba* of the Jummʿa prayer, a Sunni imam announced the name of Jawhar, the military ruler of the Fatimid army, but not the name of al-Muʿizz, the Fatimid imam. The resident imam (of the mosque) thus declared allegiance to the military rule of the Fatimids as the de facto authority, as usually done by Sunni *ulama*, while denying the Fatimids religious authority. Another example of the constant pressure to promote Isma'ili Shi'a doctrine among Sunni Muslims of Egypt included the imposition of the Fatimid practice of calculating the end of Ramadan astronomically, as opposed to witnessing the rise of the new moon (Lev 1988, 316; Sanders 1994, 45). It is reported that a man was executed because of the performance of the *qunut*, probably in the sense of *tarawih* prayers (performed by Sunni Muslims in the evenings of Ramadan, the month of fasting) (Lev 1991, 143, 161; Berkey 2004, 249; Lapidus 1996, 24). But such measures are not reported to have been carried out in Egypt, presumably because of political expediency in dealing with the Sunni majority.

Other Shi'a practices, such as the celebration of Id al-Ghadir and the mourning of al-Hussain (Ashura), which were more public and more provocative to the Sunni majority, also took strong hold under Fatimid tutelage. It seems that in 973, Id al-Ghadir was officially sanctioned, as it was in the Buyyid lands to the east sometime earlier (Lev 1988, 317; Sanders 1994, 124–125). The institutionalization of Ashura became official in 970, though it initially led to violent clashes with Sunnis (Lev 1988, 318). During Ashura of 1005, mourners of the death of al-Hussain gathered at the Mosque of al-Amr and, after Friday prayer, poured into the streets cursing the Companions of the Prophet for opposing the appointment of Ali as caliph. To curb such disturbances, officials arrested and executed a man and announced that the same fate awaited anyone who cursed Aisha or Abu Bakr (Sanders 1994, 125–126). Although Ashura processions were ordered out of the city by the Isma'ili *qadi*, they continued to cause disruptions in the city (Lev 1988, 318). In 1009, al-Hakim prohibited Ashura and later appointed a popular Hanbali *alim* to the post of chief judge in an effort to diminish Sunni opposition. Yet the state sponsored the inauguration of a number of Shi'a festivals, such as festivals during the nights of Sha'ban and Rajab, as well as the birthdays of the Prophet and that of the Shi'a imams Ali, al-Hassan, and al-Husain. Such innovations in the religious calendar could only be accomplished with the help of a powerful state infrastructure that utilized its resources both to implement and to manipulate them. Such uses of power were regularly resisted and reviled by Sunni *ulama*.

The judiciary was also used to gradually impose Isma'ili doctrine on the country, and Sunni judges were forced to reconcile their positions with the Fatimid policies. For example, Abu Tahir was the chief judge of the Maliki school in Egypt prior to the Fatimid conquest and tried to appease the new regime. Although Jawhar immediately sought to impose the Ismaʿili law in cases of divorce and inheritance, Abu Tahir was allowed to continue as the judge of Fustat, because he was cordial to Jawhar and imam al-Muʿizz when they came to Egypt. The incoming *qadi,* Ali ibn al-Nuʿman, had jurisdiction over the Fatimid army and the *mazalim* cases. However, al-Nuʿman, with the help of the now Fatimid imam al-Aziz, effectively ousted the elderly Abu Tahir so that the entire realm of his jurisdiction was subsumed under al-Nuʿman's leadership as *qadi.* Ali ibn al-Nuʿman appointed his brother Muhammad as deputy, and together they imposed the Fatimid law in both Cairo and Fustat and in other cities. Muhammad ibn al-Nuʿman appointed an Ismaʿili jurist in the main mosque to give legal opinions according to the Fatimid law and suppressed opposition by Sunni jurists (Lev 1988, 320–323). Thus, even though the Fatimids were initially reluctant to offend indigenous religious elites, they began to consolidate their powers when they became better established. For our purposes, the point is that the Fatimid approach to such issues was primarily political.

The Bahri Mamluk State in Egypt

The Mamluk corps of slave soldiers enjoyed considerable prestige for centuries under the Fatimid and Ayyubid dynasties without ever claiming the supreme position of caliph or imam for themselves. The height of their prestige came in 1260, when they defeated the Mongols at Ayn Jalut, south of Damascus (Hodgson 1974, II: 292). Since they owed their status and power entirely to the ruler or the dominant oligarchy responsible for their purchase, training, and maintenance, the Mamluks were an efficient military machine that was used by several imperial states to suppress rebellions and defend against external attack. But the peculiar slave status of those regiments also led to social, political, and economic tensions (Petry 1981, 16).

The Mamluk soldiers, who were staunch supporters of the Sunni orthodoxy, owed titular allegiance to the office of the Sunni caliph, which became more of a symbol of Sunni unity than an independent political position. The caliphs preserved their self-image as servants or custodians of Sunni Islam, when in fact they were simply rulers. Turkish soldiers were used by the Seljuks to uphold Sunni Islam in the face of an increasing Shiʿa threat from the Buyyids, Hamanids, Fatimids, and Qarmatians. The combination of staunch support for Sunni institutions and far superior military capability ultimately led to the violent suppression of non-Sunni elements in Muslim society. However, in 1517, the entire Mamluk sultanate was brought to an end by the advanced military capability of the Ottomans (Hodgson 1974, II: 419). In this section, I will review the institutions of leadership, administration, and religion of the Bahri Mamluks in Egypt to highlight the tension in the relationship between religious and political authorities and institutions in that period of Islamic history.

The Mamluk sultanate consisted of an exclusive oligarchy of commanders *(amirs)*, each with his own substantial political or military base, which was founded upon the strength of his personal imported Mamluk regiments. Not only were all the elites of the regime, including the sultan, slaves or former slaves, but the entire military elite was of foreign origin, purchased and raised as slaves and trained to be soldiers and administrators. Having no family or local ties, every official, commander, and solider was totally dedicated to his master and to the service of the military caste. This regime was financed by an adaptation of the *iqta* system, under which the Mamluk *amirs* had the revenues of lands without actually having governmental authority over them (Lapidus 2002, 291–292). Like the Ayyubids and the Seljuks before them, the Mamluks had no justification for rule other than superior military capability; therefore, their legitimacy rested on their self-assertion as guardians of Islam.

Military campaigns against crusaders, the protection of Muslim lands, and the endowments of religious institutions were public symbols designed to emphasize the Mamluk service to Islam. Thousands of religious scholars lived and were taught or trained in these institutions, earning their livelihood from the *awqaf* (religious endowments) established by the Mamluks. Although these *amirs* had their pious intentions, there was also the obvious political motivation of such endowments in conferring religious legitimacy on the ruling elite and their officials (Little 1986b, 169–172). In addition to endowing institutions of religious learning, Mamluk rulers emphasized their presence in the holy cities of Mecca and Medina by patronizing the annual *hajj* festivities and assuming the role as chief guardians of what is known as the Holy House of God (the Kaʿba). In 1281, for instance, Sultan Qalawun exacted an oath from the Qatada tribe, which was in charge of Mecca, not only to use the cloth sent every year from Egypt to cover the Kaʿba but also to display the banners of the Mamluks in front of the banners of all other Muslim rulers (Little 1986b, 171).

Since the Mamluks could not have an independent claim to rule, they controlled the state under a figurehead. After the fall of Baghdad to the Mongols in 1258, the Mamluk sultan al-Zahir Baybars supported the claim of al-Mustansir to the Abbasid caliphate and took him to Cairo to set him up as caliph in 1261. In return, the caliph recognized Baybars as the sultan (Irwin 1986, 43). The sultan then sent the caliph to Baghdad to confront the Mongol presence in the historic Islamic capital. When al-Mustansir was killed in that doomed expedition, the sultan replaced him within a year, in a similar fashion, with al-Hakim, whose caliphate was reduced to ceremonial showcasing and house arrest. Although the Mamluk sultans generally kept the caliph under strict watch, reserving him mostly for public ceremonial displays, they were clearly aware of the potential political power of the office and the inherent threat such a figure posed. As they lacked any title to rule and possessed only force as a means of control, the Mamluks used the religious symbolism of the caliph for political gain (Little 1986b, 173–174).

The complex relationship between the *ulama* and the Mamluks was highlighted by the reliance of the *ulama* in their continuing internal competition on the political authority of the Mamluks. The hierarchical judiciary was composed of two major categories of judges, principals and deputies. The principals authorized the rulings of deputies before they could be recorded in the judicial register *(diwan al-hukm)* and thereby be made enforceable by the state (Jackson 1995, 61; Irwin 1986, 43). If the deputy was not of the same school as the principal judge, the principal was still supposed to implement the deputy's ruling. But a minority view within the Shafi'i school would not permit such a procedure, because it would amount to a violation of one's own school of law. Thus, if a Shafi'i judge sat at the top of the judicial hierarchy, he simply would not implement judicial decisions based on the views of other schools. Since the chief judge when Baybars rose to power belonged to the Shafi'i school, Baybars decided to gradually appoint other chief judges to represent other Sunni schools (Jackson 1995, 54). The obvious political advantages for the Mamluk rulers included the gratitude and loyalty of judges in an expanded judiciary that ensured legal decisions favoring state interests, as well as influence that led the Muslim public to accept foreign slave soldiers as rulers (Little 1986b, 174). In times of war, the Mamluk regime relied on the *ulama* to authorize new taxes and the diversion of funds from *awqaf* for military purposes (Lapidus 1967, 135).

Under the Mamluks, the *muhtasibs* functioned in many ways like the *muhtasibs* during the Fatimid period had, acting along the spectrum from public guardians of morals to trade regulators and tax collectors. The position also reflected similar negotiation between religious and political institutions. Initially, for nearly 150 years at the inception of the Mamluk period, the post of *muhtasib* was popularly seen as a religious one *(wazifa diniyya)*, which was mainly occupied by jurists, *ulama*, scholars, and other practitioners of the Islamic sciences. Subsequently, however, the feuding Mamluks increasingly secured the office for their own protégés and ultimately themselves, with destructive economic consequences (Berkey 2004, 252–253).

Another example of Mamluk state intervention in the affairs of Islamic discourse is the case of Ibn Taymiyyah, who was imprisoned no fewer than six times throughout his life for allegations that his religious beliefs had "no support from the *Salaf,* that they contradict the consensus of the *ulama* and the rulers *(hukkam)* including his contemporaries, and that his *fatwas* disquieted the minds of the common people" (Little 1986a, 321). His views included the segregation of the *dhimmis* from the Muslim populations and the use of regime forces against "internal enemies," such as the various Shi'a populations of the empire. Regardless of the official state policy toward Ibn Taymiyyah, the Mamluks dealt with him in a shrewd political fashion because of his large and influential role with the Muslim public and a number of high-ranking Syrian Mamluk *amirs.*

In contrast, the *ulama,* especially those of Damascus, most often simply declared allegiance to whatever military commander entered the city. They did this on the assumption that this would restore order as quickly as possible and that even an oppressive ruler is better than civil war *(fitna).* Ironically, the promises of peace and amnesty the *ulama* thought they secured from the Mongols from 1299 to 1300 proved false when the Mongols pillaged the city (Lapidus 1967, 131–134). The same sequence occurred a century later, in 1400, when Tamerlane invaded Syria. While some *ulama* were willing to stay and fight and therefore prepared for siege, the leading Hanbali jurist Ibn Muflih urged surrender, placing Damascus at the mercy of the invader. Tamerlane was declared sultan after a two-day siege of the city, and Ibn Muflih became *qadi* and the agent of Tamerlane, but the city was destroyed soon after.

There were four chief *qadi* positions in each of the major Mamluk towns, each with his network of deputies, who possessed a collective degree of political power owing to their intermediate position between the *ulama* and the Mamluk state. *Qadis* and the *ulama* often bent the rules of Shari'a to authorize loans or gifts from *awqaf* sources to the sultan in order to finance the Mamluks' military needs (Lapidus 1967, 135). It was also difficult to understand the parameters of judicial authority and jurisdiction when any notion of separation of powers was totally unknown, though there were supposed to be different judicial or administrative institutions and officials. The *mazalim* authority provided the state's subjects with a channel for complaining against official oppression but also offered officials and influential persons a means of advancing their own interests or hampering those of their rivals (Nielson 1985, 123). Personal property and *awqaf* cases were often the subject of *mazalim* proceedings during the Mamluk era, as it was fairly common practice for Mamluk *amirs* to use their personal entourage of soldiers simply to confiscate land.

The Fatimid and Mamluk states, like those of Medina, the Umayyads, and the Abbasids before them, illustrate the variety of states that ruled over Islamic societies. As emphasized from the beginning of this chapter, history is always contested and interpreted in various ways to support different, sometimes opposing views. With due regard for the possibility of opposing interpretations of that history, it is clear that none of those states was Islamic in any coherent and systematic sense that can be determined and reapplied. However, it is also clear that those experiences did not fit a neat classification of separation or conflation of religion and the state. A more accurate analysis indicates a model of negotiation between political and religious authorities, as briefly explained next.

Negotiation among Differentiated Institutions

This chapter opens by quoting with approval the view of Ira Lapidus that there is historical differentiation of state and religious institutions in Islamic societies. In the rest of the chapter, I have attempted to support and illustrate the validity of this most significant insight in relation to the proposed institutional separation of Islam and the state, coupled with acknowledgment and regulation of the connectedness of Islam and politics in all Islamic societies. In other words, the critical need for differentiating state and religious authorities can be appreciated in theory as well as confirmed by historical analysis. The desirability of such differentiation can be supported from a theoretical point of view by the inherent difference between religious and political authority, as explained earlier. The basic point here is that the state has to be inherently secular and political, because the nature of its powers and institutions requires a form and a degree of continuity and predictability that religious authority cannot provide. While religious leaders can and should

insist on the ideals of justice and fidelity to Shari'a in theory, they have neither the power nor the obligation to confront the practical questions of
maintaining peace among local communities, regulating economic and social relations, and defending the realm against external threats. Such pragmatic functions require the possession of effective control over territory and
population and the ability to use coercion to enforce compliance, which
would be appropriate from state officials, not from religious leaders.

As also indicated earlier, some religious leaders can enjoy political authority over their followers, and some political leaders may have religious legitimacy for segments of the general population. But the point for us here is
that these are two different *types* of authority, even when exercised by the
same person. This point can also be appreciated in terms of the *criteria* for
achieving each type of authority or the *manner* in which other people identify the nature of the person's authority. Religious authority is based on the
personal knowledge and piety of a scholar, as judged by those who accept it
through their own personal and subjective judgment and their routine interpersonal interaction with that scholar. The political authority of state officials, in contrast, is based on the more objectively assessed qualities of the
ability to exercise coercive power and their effective performance of their
functions for the general good of the community. The fact that some persons
can combine religious and political authority does not mean that these are
the same type of authority, or that this combination should be assumed or
required from other persons who are supposed to perform a religious or political function.

The desirability of differentiation can also be appreciated from the drastic
consequences of insisting on what I call the conflation model, as clearly illustrated by the early example of the wars of apostasy during the reign of
Abu Bakr, the first caliph of Medina. The conclusion I drew from the earlier
discussion of the issue of the apostasy wars is that whatever the rationale
may have been, Abu Bakr was able to enforce his view over the objections of
the leading Companions because he was the caliph, not because he was
"right" or "correct" from an Islamic point of view. This is not to say that Abu
Bakr was right or wrong, and Muslims will continue to disagree on this
point without any legitimate possibility of an independent conclusion that
would be acceptable to all. Rather, my point is that it is logical to distinguish
between Abu Bakr's religious views and his political decisions and actions as
the caliph. The fact that Abu Bakr, as well as the Companions (like Umar
and Ali) who disagreed with him, had religious justifications for their posi-

tions does not mean that the decision to fight the rebel Arab tribes was religious and not political. The nature of the action should not be determined by the motivation of the actor. This distinction may still be difficult for Muslims to accept regarding the Medina period because of the very personal nature of political authority at the time, when the state hardly existed as a political institution. Whatever view may be taken of those events in that historical context, confusion in distinguishing between the nature of the action and the actor's motivation is neither justified nor acceptable in the present context of the European model of the postcolonial state, under which all Muslims live today.

The usefulness of the differentiation of state and religious authority in Islamic societies can also be appreciated from the drastic consequences of the inquisition *(al-Mihna)*, which was initiated by the Abbasid caliph al-Ma'mun in 833, exactly two hundred years after the apostasy wars. This tragic episode in Islamic history is particularly instructive for our purposes because it shows the obvious dangers of the conflated model of Islam and the state, while marking a clear break in that model, when the *ulama* successfully asserted their autonomy from the state, though at great personal cost to some. That experience confirms the need for the protection of the autonomy of actors in civil society, including religious authorities, which is critical for the proposed approach of the separation of Islam and the state and the simultaneous regulation of the relationship between Islam and politics. The possibility of this delicate negotiated balance requires some institutional base and financial resources, so as to support religious leaders in their negotiations with the state. It is from this perspective that I will now briefly highlight the important role of *awqaf* in that historical context.

From the earliest periods in Islamic history, Muslims with available means have sought to establish *awqaf* (endowments) of real estate holdings or other property to support mosques, colleges, and almost anything that might be of benefit to the community. The religious rationale is that this public service provides the person who creates a *waqf* with rewards and blessings in this life as well as after death. *Awqaf* have played a far more prominent and complex role in Islamic societies than might initially have been assumed. *Waqf* regulations quickly became one of the most complex areas of Islamic jurisprudence, as they dealt with vital matters such as inheritance, including wills, testaments, and the designation of beneficiaries, and with ethical financial responsibility. Jurists were also concerned with the subject because the institution of the *waqf* was vulnerable to manipulation by those seeking to circumvent Shari'a regulations regarding inheritance and *zakat*. As can be expected, however, this combination of religious and practical importance, far-reaching social and political consequences, and technical complexity rendered *awqaf* particularly vulnerable to manipulation by rules and state officials and thus serves as another indication of the dangers of conflating religious and political authorities in Islamic societies.

Moreover, social and political implications were engendered by such donations, which were, at least in theory, intended for the benefit of the needy, the public, or some other designated group. For our purposes here, *awqaf* played an active part in the public sphere of Muslim societies by designating a space for the cultivation of Islamic norms and ethics expressed in formal and informal institutions of learning and worship and in the provision of social services. "While the act of creating an endowment was that of a private individual, the beneficiaries of the endowment were always located in the public sphere," and "by endowing his property . . . [the founder of a *waqf* expressed] his sense of belonging to the community of believers and his identification with its values" (Hoexter 2002, 121).

Shafi'i scholars defined *waqf* as "the alienation of revenue-generating property with the principal remaining inalienable, while its revenues are disbursed for a pious purpose, in order to seek God's favor" (Sabra 2000, 70). Accordingly, entities that were not intended to actually produce revenue, such as religious schools and colleges, mosques, Sufi sites, and other religious institutions, were normally funded by the surplus funds of revenue-generating *awqaf*, including farmland, apartment homes, or some other kind of business. The founder of a *waqf* would in return receive regular and continual prayers from those who benefited from the institution where they studied, worshipped, or received charity. These prayers were often public ceremonies. As to be expected, powerful rulers, sultans, merchants, and civic leaders eagerly sought to establish *awqaf* to enhance their reputations as pious leaders of their communities. But it is also reasonable to assume that such patrons were also motivated by the desire to obtain the religious rewards guaranteed by such endowments for eternity. The *waqf* was primarily a place of remembrance and continual prayer for the founder, out of which grew auxiliary yet indispensable services to the community (Sabra 2000, 95–100).

The paramount social and religious role of *awqaf* in Muslim societies has its obvious political implications. A founder could virtually guarantee loyalty from the beneficiaries of the *waqf* and, by extension, from their circle

of networks and social relations. It is not surprising that *awqaf* began to appear as religious institutions, such as colleges and mosques, when political
stakes were at their highest (Fernandes 1987, 87–98). For example, the
Fatimid imam al-Hakim's endowment of the religious school *dar al-ʿilm* was
intended primarily to serve the needs of the Sunni community at a time of
sectarian violence in Ismaʿili Cairo; likewise, Nizam al-Mulk established colleges of law at an equally turbulent time in Baghdad.

Ultimately, *waqf* was the institutional base of or space for negotiating
and mediating relationships between rulers and *ulama*. Rulers simply could
not function without the consent of their subjects, which rested upon an
unyielding demand that they implement and uphold Islamic orthodoxy, a
tradition that was defined by the *ulama*, as explained earlier. At the same
time, the *ulama* and their institutions could not function without the support of the state apparatus, which not only protected the borders of the Islamic lands and domestic peace and stability but also endowed religious institutions and enforced the regulations of *awqaf*. However, as noted earlier,
the rulers needed to respect the autonomy of the *ulama* for the latter to be
credible enough to confer religious legitimacy on the state. In other words,
the institutional and financial independence of the *ulama* was mutually
beneficial to them and their followers and to the rulers. *Awqaf* provided the
legal and social mechanisms for maintaining that precarious balance of mutual autonomy and interdependence. As the space wherein religious leaders
would publicly and privately pray for their benefactors as well as implement
their decrees, *waqf* was one of the main public representations of the tacit
yet constant relationship between the rulers and the ruled.

The regulation of *waqf* gave particular attention to the position of the
founder *(waqif)*, who often held the right to appoint himself, or persons of
his choice, as the administrator of the property and could also benefit, in
part but not exclusively, from its yield or revenue. This seemed to follow
from the notion that the founder retained some sort of title to the property
and benefited for eternity from its being vested in the *waqf*. As a general
principle, the founder had the power to set the terms and stipulations of the
waqf, as emphasized in the notion that the stipulations set by the founder of
a *waqf* are as binding as those of Shariʿa itself (Makdisi 1981, 35).

The principle of owner retention of *awqaf* estates was maintained in all
Sunni legal schools except the Maliki school, which insisted that the founder
must relinquish any rights of control over the property. This characteristic of
Maliki law apparently discouraged the founding of *awqaf* under this school,

which resulted in the "decline of this school in Baghdad in the Middle Ages at a time when the other schools were benefiting," to the extent that "the Malikis . . . never had any *madrasas* in Baghdad, nor are they known to have had any elsewhere in Eastern Islam" (Makdisi 1981, 38). At the same time, however, this feature of the Maliki school ensured a high level of autonomy for Maliki institutions. By not allowing founder interference in the functioning of the *waqf* (for example, a college or mosque), Maliki institutions may have reduced opportunities for systematic exploitation of religious institutions for political ends.

Still, founders may have had different motives for establishing *awqaf* under one or more schools. Saladin, for instance, endowed both Maliki and Shafi'i colleges while embarking on a takeover of Egypt, though he himself was of the Hanafi persuasion (Frenkel 1999, 1–20). Presumably the Maliki college was intended to appease local inhabitants who suffered under the Fatimid rule, while the establishment of the Shafi'i college catered to Saladin's ambition to tie himself and his rule to the caliph's court at Baghdad, which held this school in highest esteem. Saladin also often built colleges on top of sites that had symbolized the power of the Fatimids, such as a former palace or a police station (Fernandes 1987, 87; Lev 1991, 153n5). These examples reflect the dynamic politics of *awqaf*, which can also be understood in light of the following comments.

The degree of autonomy of a *waqf* played a significant role in the negotiation of the relationship between the *ulama* and rulers. By being designated for a particular purpose and community, *awqaf* allowed for an "autonomous group," which owned a degree of influence and participation in the public sphere. Those institutions that played a direct social and religious role, such as hosting Sufi litanies, enriching and maintaining sites of public worship, or promoting a local school of law, provided their founders and beneficiaries with a considerable degree of public prominence. The *awqaf* were "one of the important tools whereby local families secured themselves a power base independent of the ruling authorities, a leading position within the local community, and the necessary backing to stand up to the rulers in protection of community interests" (Hoexter 2002, 129).

Genuine autonomy, however, cannot be assumed, and may have been compromised by various factors. For example, if the founder was a prominent statesman, the institution would be more likely to support state policy than an institution endowed by a merchant or civic leader. The autonomy of an institution may have enhanced its credibility on one level while undermining its popular appeal on another. The Hanbali school (of Ibn Hanbal, who successfully resisted the demands of the Abbasid caliphs during the inquisition) had the reputation of being reluctant to accept patronage from state institutions or, for that matter, to get involved to any degree in state affairs. This actual or perceived position may have led to a higher degree of autonomy and arguably more leverage over state institutions than that which was achieved by the more "compliant" schools or scholars. Yet the outcome may not necessarily have been favorable for the more pluralistic or tolerant policies, as the Hanbali influence tended to be more conservative or orthodox. This combination of factors may also explain the minority standing of this school, in comparison to the three much more popular Sunni schools (Hanafi, Shafiʿi, and Maliki).

Thus the colleges of eleventh-century Baghdad were founded on the large *awqaf* of Seljuk viziers and sultans, who "paid the salaries of teachers and stipends for students" (Ephrat 2002, 32–33). That period immediately followed the Buyyid control of Baghdad, wherein Buyyid rulers, who were themselves Shiʿas and extended state support to popular Shiʿa rituals, provoked the Sunni masses of Baghdad and the surrounding areas. In other words, the rise of Seljuk patronage systems, alongside Seljuk persecution of Shiʿa scholars and the demolition of Shiʿa shrines, highlights an added dimension of the interplay between state and religious institutions, namely, the role of sectarianism. The patterns of patronage did not function exclusively between a dichotomous set of institutions but more along a continuous spectrum, with competing state actors and their interests at one end and religious institutions, composed of varied, competing, and sometimes conflicting subgroups, at the other end. In the context of the inquisition and its aftermath, as outlined earlier, the Shiʿa were the victims of Sunni dominance that benefited from the prevalent patterns of patronage at that time.

It is therefore clear that numerous lessons and implications can be drawn from various stages of Islamic history. The aspects I have explained and discussed are intended to highlight the ways in which that history supports the main propositions I am seeking to advance in this book. But it is too early at this stage in my argument to offer appropriate conclusions from this chapter for the main propositions of this book. Both of the possibilities presented by this historical dimension and the challenges it raises for the future of Shariʿa in present Islamic societies can better be understood in light of the subsequent chapters.

CHAPTER 3

Constitutionalism, Human Rights, and Citizenship

In this chapter I will discuss constitutionalism, human rights, and citizenship as an integrated framework for regulating the practical way secularism works to negotiate the tension between the religious neutrality of the state and the connectedness of Islam and public policy. Constitutionalism provides a legal and political framework for realizing and safeguarding equal dignity, human rights, and the well-being of all citizens. The standards of human rights, while authoritatively defined in international and regional treaties and customary international law, can be applied in practice only through national constitutions, legal systems, and institutions. However, the effectiveness of national and international systems is dependent on the active participation of citizens acting individually and collectively to protect their own rights. At the same time, constitutional and human rights norms enable citizens to exchange information, organize and act publicly to promote their own vision of the social good, and protect their rights. In other words, constitutionalism and human rights are the necessary means to the end of upholding the dignity and rights of citizens, but that purpose can be realized only through the agency of citizens. Thus, these concepts and their related institutions are dependent on and must interact with each other in order for the purpose of each concept to be achieved.

By attempting to clarify this integrated framework from an Islamic point of view, I hope to contribute to promoting its legitimacy among Muslims, who must accept these principles if they are to be effectively applied within Muslim societies. The relationship between Islam and these principles is unavoidable, because Islam directly affects the legitimacy and the efficacy of these principles and institutions in present Islamic societies. At the same time, this relationship will be confused and counterproductive if Islam is taken to be synonymous with the historical understandings of Shariʿa, which include certain principles that are incompatible with constitutionalism, human rights, and citizenship. To be clear on the point, I am not suggesting that any conception of Shari'a is inherently or necessarily incompatible with these modern principles. Rather, I am referring specifically to certain aspects of the traditional interpretations of Shari'a, especially those regarding women and non-Muslims, as discussed below, and not to matters of belief *(aqida)* and worship practices *(ibadat)*.

It is critically important to maintain the religious neutrality of the state precisely because human beings tend to favor their own views, including their religious beliefs, over the views of others. For this reason, the state cannot just be a reflection of the views of those human beings in power as the government of the day. But the objective of religious neutrality should not be sought through efforts to control religion or relegate it to the purely private domain, because this is neither possible nor desirable. Believers will always assert their religious convictions politically, and it is better to acknowledge and regulate this reality than to deny it and force such political expression of religious beliefs to go underground. Instead, the effort should be to separate Islam from the state while acknowledging the public role of Islam, including its influences on the formulation of public policy and legislation. This permanent tension should be mediated through the requirements of civic reason within the framework of constitutionalism, human rights, and citizenship, as discussed in this chapter. By "civic reason," I mean reasons that can be publicly debated and contested by any citizen, individually or in community with others, in accordance with norms of civility and mutual respect. Civic reasons and reasoning processes are required for the adoption of public policy and legislation in a democratic state because they are publicly accessible to and publicly contestable by all citizens.

I will begin with some clarification of the distinctions I am making between the state and politics in relation to the requirements of civic reason, as discussed later. The principles of constitutionalism, human rights, and citizenship are discussed in the subsequent three sections, and the chapter concludes with an overview of how these principles can provide the framework for the operation of civic reason in regulating the relationship between Islam and politics, on the one hand, and Islam and the state, on the other.

The State, Politics, and Civic Reason

I should first note that the following is not intended to be a comprehensive or definitive discussion of the concepts of the state, politics, and civic reason in general, or even in a particular context. Indeed, such a claim would be inconsistent with my whole thesis about the need to facilitate public debate and inclusive engagement on these issues rather than being prescriptive or definitive about what such concepts must mean. My modest and limited objective here is simply to highlight some aspects of the state, politics, and civic reason only for the purposes of clarifying my thesis and argument about the future of Shari'a among Muslims.

The Features of the Modern State

All Muslims today live under what is commonly referred to as the nation-state, which is based on European models that have been established around the world through colonialism, even in regions that were not formally colonized. This model of the state is characterized by "a centralized and bureaucratically organized administrative and legal order run by an administrative staff, binding authority over what occurs within its area of jurisdiction, a territorial basis and a monopoly of the use of force" (Gill 2003, 2–3). For our purposes here, the main features of this model of the territorial state can be summarized as follows:

- The state is a bureaucratic organization that is centralized, hierarchical, and differentiated into separate institutions and organs with their own specialized functions. But all the institutions of the state operate according to formal rules and a clearly defined hierarchical structure of accountability to central authorities.
- The hierarchical yet interconnected state institutions are distinguished from other kinds of social organizations, like political parties, civic organizations, and business associations. The scope and functions of the state require its institutions to be distinct from nonstate organizations because state officials and organs should regulate nonstate entities and may have to adjudicate differences among them. This complex relationship of theoretical distinctiveness and practical interconnectedness between state and nonstate institutions or organizations is one aspect of the distinction between *state* and *politics*.
- The expansive and far-reaching domain of the modern state—extending now to every aspect of social, economic, and political life, including the provision of education, health care, and other services—is far more extensive than that of any other kind of organization. This comprehensive range of function also emphasizes the uniqueness, autonomy, and independence of the state from all other kinds of organizations.

- To fulfill its multiple functions and roles, the state must have sovereignty, both internal and external. It must be the highest authority within its territorial borders. The state must also be the authoritative representative of its citizens and of entities within its territory to all entities and actors outside that territorial domain.
- For the reasons just cited, the state must also have monopoly over the *legitimate* use of force and coercion. This capability is essential for the state to be able to enforce its authority in order to protect its sovereignty, maintain law and order, and regulate and adjudicate disputes.
- Conversely, the state is territorially defined and limited, because it normally possesses no authority beyond its borders. Other kinds of organizations, like religious groups and Sufi orders, can operate across political boundaries of states because they are defined by their functional scope rather than their geographical reach.
- Citizens often have a sentimental attachment to and identification with their state, but this is not an essential characteristic of a state. The concept of the nation-state assumes common features, such as ethnicity or language, among groups that may identify with the state in this manner. But this can be misleading, because there is hardly ever a complete correspondence between a territory and the ethnic, religious, or other unity of its population. Such unity can be true of several groups within the territory of a state and may be shared by others living within the territory of another state. The fact that most states seek to cultivate feelings of uniform national identity is not a defining characteristic of the modern state. (Gill 2003, 3–7)

These characteristic features of the modern state are usually discussed in relation to the experiences of Western countries, whose models have also come to apply to African and Asian states where Muslims live. The following elaboration by one author, for instance (Poggi 1990, 19–33), may help clarify the features of the state for our purposes here.

As the ultimate source of power and authority over a territory, with the necessary monopoly over the legitimate use of force, the state is the final institutional actor. This power and authority derive from a combination of sovereignty and territorial integrity, which are vested in the state, and can therefore be undermined by the loss or diminishment of either quality. Territorial sovereignty means that the exclusive control of the state over its population and territory cannot be legitimately shared with any other entity, except with the consent and cooperation of the state itself. The central authority of the state means that it is autonomous, which includes its possession of the sole original authority to make rules governing its operations as well as its role as the original source of all political authority, even when such functions are delegated to other organizations or entities. This centrality of the state also requires that it coordinate the functions and activities of all its organs and institutions, which emphasizes and entrenches the power of the state as a whole (22).

Although democratic governance itself is not required for a state to qualify as such in domestic and international law and relations, the people of the country are generally assumed to be the ultimate source of power and authority of the state, which in turn exists to serve its people. This assumption seems to be true even of authoritarian dictatorships or monarchies, which tend to justify their authority in terms of the collective will and the best interests of their populations. Citizenship flows from this underlying basis of legitimacy of the state to ensure that all of the inhabitants of the territory have "general and equal obligations and entitlements" in their relation to the state (28). This combination of democratic legitimacy and citizenship should also be embodied in the nature and function of law in relation to the state. Whatever view Muslims had of the law and its sources and norms in the past, the state has increasingly taken over the function of *making* law and not just enforcing it. Historically, the autonomy of the law may have been grounded in the religion, tradition, or culture of the community. Now law is widely regarded as both the product and the instrument of state policy (29).

Finally, the modern state can be viewed as an institutional representation of political power that is no longer derived from the personal authority of the ruler or from those to whom the ruler delegates certain functions and powers. The institutionalized and centralized political power of the state is reflected in its organizational and bureaucratic structure. The state also enables the formalization of the exercise of political power through legal standards and procedures, which tend to increase the importance of citizenship as the principle regulating the relationship between state and society (33).

The Distinction between the State and Politics

The distinction between the state and politics proposed in Chapter 1 is difficult to imagine in an abstract sense, but it is necessary to maintain it in practice as much as possible. The difficulty derives from the obvious fact that the state is not an autonomous entity that can act independently of the human beings who are the real actors behind the veil of institutional authority. Yet precisely because of the state's political nature, it is necessary to maintain the paradoxical distinction between the state and politics in order to ensure that institutional actors do not abuse the powers and authority of the state to impose their views on others or promote their narrow self-interest. For example, judges are supposed to enforce the officially promulgated law of the land rather than their own personal views or the will of the government of the day. Yet personal views and government policy will probably influence the way judges interpret and apply the law to the facts of the case at hand. In this regard, the distinction between the state and politics is intended to ensure that judges do in fact apply the law despite the influence of their views and government policy. This paradox is further complicated by the fact that in democratic states, the views and beliefs of judges are taken into account in their appointment, and government policy may indeed reflect the wishes of the majority of citizens. In any case, is it humanly possible for judges to act with complete neutrality and impartiality, and how can that be verified in practice?

To clarify the proposed model for mediating this complex paradox, I will continue to speak of the state without discounting the reality of human agency behind the state's institutional authority. The features outlined above clearly indicate a distinction between the domain of the state and the domain of politics at large, whereby the state determines which issues are to be debated and negotiated in the political sphere, at varying degrees of formality or process. The state is also supposed to set and enforce the limits for negotiations between different actors who may seek to have their views represented and formulated as a policy. The reach of the modern state is also expansive, and has progressively been extended to include more aspects of social existence, such as welfare and environmental concerns. Despite its primacy as the fundamental political structure in society and despite its vast reach, the state is still limited in its scope and operations with regard to the dynamics of social relations. Because of its formalized structure, its chief duties, and its character as an autonomous entity, the state does not, and cannot, exhaust the domain of politics in society at large. The necessarily bureaucratic and institutional nature of state action also means that it cannot interact with human beings and their communities in the way that other human beings can.

The organization of the state as a highly complex set of institutions and organs can be divided vertically by function and horizontally by geography (Gill 2003, 16). Vertical divisions correspond to the "major spheres" within which many social actors are engaged with each other and with the state: "within the state, these are viewed as policy areas (and constituencies), and are signified by the presence in states of civil service departments devoted to particular policy areas, such as health, transport, education, law and order and consumer affairs" (Gill 2003, 16–17). Horizontal divisions refer to matters such as whether the polity is a federal or a unitary state. Vertical divisions by function may also be divided horizontally by region or administrative units. In vertical divisions, corresponding to the groups that address particular policy areas, the state is deeply engaged with social actors. Relationships develop between these segments of the state and political actors within the broader social spheres and policy constituencies.

The stability and autonomy of the state are relative to the degree to which it is rooted in the diverse segments of society, as that makes it more difficult for a particular group or set of groups to take control. The more normal the politics of negotiations among different interest groups and perspectives is, the less likely it is that groups will be tempted or able to join forces to seize control of the state. As more groups stake their claims and seek to pressure state institutions, no one group can take control of those institutions, and the autonomy of the state is preserved. Conversely, if some groups are excluded from the realm of normal daily politics, they will have more to gain and less to lose by challenging the premise and the operation of the state itself. This dynamic relationship between state and social actors is mutual, as the state also seeks to influence various constituencies. "In order to carry out its functions, to make and implement policy and to conduct the rule-making which is the state's role in society, it needs the cooperation of these relevant constituencies and the organizations of which they consist. In exchange, state bodies must allow their own partial penetration by these constituencies" (Gill 2003, 17).

The mechanisms for such exchange among state and other social/political actors can be formal and institutional, such as bargaining with trade unions and professional associations, representing nonstate organizations in state bodies, and involving representatives of nonstate organizations in formulating or implementing policy. Exchange can also happen through informal, personal connections and influence. Whatever the means, it does not make the state merely the representative of a particular interest group or a set of interest groups, as its autonomy is still maintained by its multiple interactions with so many groups. In other words, competition among various groups seeking to influence official policy is a safeguard against any of them succeeding in gaining complete control over the state. Moreover, the size, complexity, and centralization of the state mean that no group or small number of groups of social actors can challenge the state's authority or diminish its autonomy by manipulating any state institution or organ (Gill 2003, 18). Since particular organs or offices of the state are themselves dependent on the state's central authority and subject to rules that apply to the entire state apparatus, the autonomy of the state as a whole cannot be compromised through disproportionate influence by a nonstate institution. Thus "the state can be seen as an arena within which these actors can compete for the achievement of their aims, but the very diversity of those actors ensures the state's autonomy" (Gill 2003, 18–19).

The ways in which states are embedded in groups or segments of their society can be seen in economic as well as social and cultural fields through the class or regional affiliation of officials and the election of representatives to participate on their behalf in the decision-making process of the state. It may be interesting to note here the difference in the relationship that unelected state officials may have with their class, social, or ethnic group and that of elected representatives. Unelected state officials are not supposed to favor their social or ethnic constituencies, whereas the continuity of those ties is presumed and necessary for those who are elected to act on behalf of their constituencies (Gill 2003, 20). But the proper functioning of both elected and unelected officials requires the constant vigilance and engagement of citizens to ensure the transparency of those officials' actions and their accountability for those actions. For instance, transparency in and accountability for what elected or unelected officials do or refrain from doing is necessary to ensure that both groups behave within the appropriate boundaries of their office and role in government. This is one aspect of the rationale for the integrated framework of constitutionalism, human rights, and citizenship presented in this chapter.

To summarize, the legitimacy and the efficacy of the state depend on balancing its connectedness to social/political actors against the need to maintain its autonomy from the undue influences of those actors. Although it may seem surprising, the more entrenched the state is in society, the lower is the risk that its autonomy will diminish, since a wide variety of competing interest groups will help maintain a balance in terms of the respective degree of influence possessed by each group. The autonomy of the state is also less likely to be threatened by one group or a small number of groups when the state structures are centralized, complex, and governed by clear rules among specialized organs. These safeguards already emphasize the need for constitutionalism, human rights, and an inclusive sphere of public deliberation or civic reason, as I will elaborate shortly. While it is not possible to provide further detail here on these theories of state and politics, I hope to draw on the preceding features and dynamics of relationships to consider the main question for us: how state-society or state-politics relations can be mediated through civic reason.

Civic Reason for Mediating Policy Conflicts

The preceding discussion clearly indicates that the legitimacy of the state derives from its deep and organic links with various nonstate actors in the political field across society at large. But the state's autonomy will be lost or diminished if one group is allowed to capture any organ of the state, or the state as a whole, for its own purposes. To facilitate the realization of this necessary combination of legitimacy and autonomy, it is necessary to secure the public arena where nonstate actors can compete on free and fair footing to influence state policy, while ensuring the most inclusive participation by all segments of the population in this arena. The rationale for this proposition is that a greater diversity of groups, freely and fairly competing to secure and advance their interests and concerns, decreases the risk that the state or any of its institutions will be compromised by falling under the control of any one group or small set of groups.

These imperatives of an inclusive, accessible, and fair public space are aspects of what I call civic reason, where different social actors can seek to influence public policy and/or legislation, but in a manner that does not place the autonomy of the state at serious risk. Other elements of this concept include effective procedural safeguards for free and fair access and participation, guidelines for the content and manner of public debate, and educational and other measures to enhance the legitimacy and the effectiveness of such requirements. But the ultimate safeguard for securing public space and facilitating participation, as well as realizing its objectives, lies in the legitimacy and relevance of the process to the totality of the population. That is, the public at large must accept the concept of civic reason in principle and appreciate its various elements and how they work for this process to be effective in realizing its objectives of securing the legitimacy and autonomy of the state. For the purposes of this book in particular, these requirements of civic reason must be acceptable to Muslims from an Islamic perspective, as I argue in this chapter.

The concept of civic reason refers to the combination of civic reasons and civic reasoning, whereby any citizen can publicly express views about matters of public concern, with due regard for norms of civility and mutual respect. The concept of civic reason entitles all citizens to publicly debate any matter that pertains to or reflects on public policy and governmental or state action, including the views of other citizens about such matters. For our purposes here, the objective of civic reason is to diminish the impact of claims of religious exclusivity on the ability to debate issues of public policy. For instance, if a Muslim proposes a legal prohibition on charging or paying interest on loans *(riba)* or that a state organ should collect and disburse Islamic alms *(zakat)*, the issue becomes a legitimate subject of civic reason. This will mean not only that all citizens, Muslims and non-Muslims alike, are entitled and encouraged to join the debate, but also that the reasons given in support of the proposal are not dependent on religious belief. Muslims are of course free to observe the ban on *riba* personally or to organize *zakat* through civic associations, all through an entirely internal Islamic discourse. But if they wish to involve state institutions in the process, then they must provide civic reasons through a civic reasoning process in which all citizens can participate without reference to religion. Believers may have private religious motivation for making a proposal for public policy or legislation, but they cannot expect it to be adopted on the basis of their own religiously based rationale. In this way, matters of public policy must be supported and countered by reasons and reasoning processes that are open to all citizens, in public civic and civil discourse.

The following remarks may help further clarify the meaning and operation of this key concept.

- The domain of civic reason must be secured as a matter of state policy so that its very structure makes it difficult for any particular government or regime to overturn it easily or any social group to control it. To be accepted as legitimate by *all* citizens and segments of society, the domain of civic reason must be identified with the state itself and not with any particular government.
- Accordingly, the domain or the arena for civic reason should be secured through constitutionalism, human rights, and citizenship, as discussed

in this chapter. However, these elements are necessary but not sufficient, because they are themselves subject to political manipulation or challenge. The political and legal system of the state should also allow for extraordinary measures in times of severe emergency, but subject to safeguards against the abuses of this exception. It is therefore necessary constantly to explore ways of ensuring that various elements do in fact serve the objective of making it difficult to change the terms and conditions of civic reason to suit the wishes of a government or a small segment of the population.

• The role of the state is to empower the largest possible number of citizens, whether as individuals or as groups, to represent and debate issues of public policy through the domain of civic reason. The greater the participation of the widest cross-section of society in processes of civic deliberation and reasoning, the more legitimate the sphere of civic reason and the more balance of power in state institutions, to prevent particular groups from taking over the state to the exclusion of others.

• While the state should regulate the sphere of civic reason, the domain should not itself be a state institution. The state should be the guardian of the space of civic reason but not attempt to own it, control it, or dictate its functioning. This arrangement will affirm the autonomy of the state in addition to fostering diversity among social/political actors and enabling processes of debates, negotiations, and consensus-building among these actors on policy objectives.

An important question may be raised here: Does this model of founding public policy and legislation on civic reason unfairly deny those Muslims who believe in the unity of Islam and the state (the Islamic state model) the right to live by their convictions? Since this is the core issue I am concerned with, this whole book is really a response to that question. The basic answer is that since no person or group has the right to violate the rights of others, the issue is one of balancing competing claims. In my view, a successful mediation of this basic paradox of all social life would seek to create a process of negotiation, whereby each side to an issue would find the process sufficiently beneficial to want to work with others in protecting and implementing it. This is true, I believe, of the proposed model of civic reason, in view of the following factors.

First, the most fundamental rationale for the separation of Islam and state, and for related safeguards, including the civic-reason requirement, is that it is necessary for the very possibility of religious belief. Even those who insist that Islam and the state should be unified need the freedom to be able to make this claim without fear of reprisal from the state or any individual, group, or institution. In contrast, the proponents of a so-called Islamic state would not permit each other the freedom to disagree on what such a state means in practice.

Second, Muslims who wish to have Shari'a principles applied as state policy or enforced as state law are not denied that possibility altogether, but are denied the ability to impose their own religious beliefs on others without their consent. This is reasonable, because those Muslims would demand the same protection and must therefore ensure this for others, in accordance with the universal principle of reciprocity, or the Golden Rule. With that freedom secured for all citizens, Muslims can comply with Shari'a requirements, and non-Muslims are not compelled to follow the religious dictates of Islam against their own free choice. Moreover, Muslims, like all other citizens, have the right to propose public policy and/or legislation, provided that they can support their proposals in ways that are open to public and inclusive debate.

For example, if all I can say in support of the prohibition of interest on loans is that it is prohibited for me as a Muslim *(haram)*, then there is nothing to discuss with other citizens, who must either reject or accept my proposal only on the strength of my religious belief. Since I would not accept having others do this to me, I should not put them in that position. It is also better for my own faith as a Muslim to reflect on the social rationale for the dictates of Shari'a and try to persuade others of the general good of those commandments. The safeguards of constitutionalism, human rights, and citizenship would guarantee me the freedom to comply with the dictates of my own religion without imposing them on others. In other words, the secular state has no authority to require me to violate my own religious obligations. Moreover, voluntary compliance can be organized through collective civic associations. For instance, a group of Muslims can establish a civic association to collect and distribute *zakat* according to the religious beliefs of members of the group. Since they are not implicating a state organ or institution, this endeavor is not a matter of public policy, to be subjected to the requirements of civic reason, and it can therefore rely on an exclusively religious rationale shared by the organizers.

But what about the religious obligations of those who believe that they are religiously required to prevent certain things when others attempt to do them? Is a Christian who believes that he has a religious obligation to prevent abortion as murder entitled to physically restrain a doctor from performing an abortion by direct action when the courts refuse to grant an injunction? Can a Muslim intervene directly to prevent someone from drinking alcohol or require women to dress modestly in public when official authorities fail to act to uphold what he believes to be important Islamic precepts? This is part of the broader issue of how to determine the proper scope of various human rights, like freedom of religion and freedom *from* religion in these examples. At an elementary level, a believer should be entitled to engage in conversation or seek to persuade others to refrain voluntarily from the conduct or action he finds objectionable, but he cannot be allowed to physically intervene to prevent what he finds objectionable. The believer may also resort to the courts to obtain an injunction against the conduct or action he is opposing, but he must abide by whatever decision the court adopts. The believer may also engage in educational, political, and other activities that seek to change public attitudes about the conduct he finds objectionable, or to change the law, but whatever happens must be in accordance with the requirements of constitutionalism, human rights, and citizenship. In public discourse, in the media, before the courts, at the legislative level, and elsewhere, the debate should always be in terms of civic reason.

To insist that the rationale for public policy and legislation should be accessible to all citizens to accept or reject does not assume that participants would agree on the rationale for specific proposals. The point is that the rationales to be considered are accessible to all to debate freely and are not dependent on the religious beliefs of some citizens, which are beyond debate by others. Agreeing on one or more rationales for public policy is a process of continuing conversation about what is acceptable, a means of evolving an overlapping consensus on the issue, whereby people agree on the outcome despite their disagreement as to why they agree on that outcome. Agreement can also be the result of tactical and strategic alliances to facilitate pragmatic solutions to public issues and problems. The main point to emphasize is that the whole process is about persuasion and compromise, a negotiation, and not mutual assertion of absolute religious dogma that does not permit negotiation and compromise.

Of course, it is not possible, or even desirable in my view, to resolve all possible ambiguities and tensions in the proposed process of civic reason. For instance, the mechanisms and processes of the practical working of state regulation of civic reason, without owning or controlling it, as noted earlier, should evolve over time through trial and error rather than be prescribed in detail for all situations and issues. One of the general principles that we can imagine in this regard is that popular legitimacy of the cause the state wishes to advance cannot be the basis for the state's intervention in the domain of civic reason, since that may lead to unfair treatment of minorities at the hands of majorities. The state cannot set the rules of participation in the sphere of civic reason and then allow itself the right to be exempt from those rules. It is precisely for this reason that the distinction between *state* and *politics* is both necessary and difficult to maintain in practice.

In general, it is clear that the idea of civic reason is profoundly linked to questions of constitutionalism, human rights, and citizenship. These requirements are warranted by the necessity to set limits to admissible civic reasons and to ensure that the state is not captured by a particular interest group. They are also warranted by the need for limits and checks on the power of the state, which cannot be assumed even with the best of governments in power. The principle of civic reason is also premised on the critical need to protect freedom of dissent, whether political, social, or religious, especially when it is most at risk from social and psychological pressures on dissidents. As noted earlier, the possibility of heresy is necessary for the future development of every religious, cultural, artistic, or other tradition.

Civic Reason and Public Reason

I will now briefly compare my concept of civic reason with that of "public reason," as proposed by Western thinkers like John Rawls and Jurgen Habermas, in view of the following considerations. To begin with, there are such obvious overlaps between the two concepts that readers may wonder about the relationship between them. In fact, I debated whether to use the term "public reason" but decided against it because there are also significant differences between Rawls's concept and my own. This is one of those situations in which one wonders whether to try to redefine a familiar term: Will readers be too used to the established meaning to notice the difference? But I should emphasize that I am not concerned here about avoiding a "Western" term because my Muslim readers may be offended by it. Part of my effort is to deemphasize dichotomies between so-called Western and Islamic concepts and institutions. Contextual factors and political differences are extremely important but should not be allowed to override the commonalities of the human condition. It is also as misleading to speak of a politically or philosophically monolithic "West" as it is to do so about a monolithic Muslim world. Indeed, early Islamic scholars were not preoccupied with such concerns and freely interacted with, adopted, and adapted ideas from Hellenic, Indian, Persian, and Roman traditions. This interaction continues into the present; many Muslim readers may be more familiar with and appreciative of Western political thought than its Islamic counterpart. From this perspective, I will consider any concept or institution in terms of its relevance and utility for the argument I am trying to make, regardless of the presumed origin or alleged pedigree.

Rawls views public reason as an essential feature of the relationship between people and the state in a democratic constitutional order (2003, 212–254, 435–490). To him,

> the idea of public reason specifies at the deepest level the basic moral and political values that are to determine a constitutional democratic government's relations to its citizens and their relation to one another . . . Such reason is public in three ways: as the reason of free and equal citizens, it is the reason of the public; its subject is the public good concerning questions of fundamental political justice, which questions are of two kinds, constitutional essentials and matters of basic justice; and its nature and content are public, being expressed in public reasoning by a family of reasonable conceptions of political justice reasonably thought to satisfy the criterion of reciprocity. (441–442)

He distinguishes between the scope of public reason and what he calls the "background culture" of civil society, which includes such associations as churches, universities, and the like (443). He also excludes the media from the realm of public reason (444). The proper domain of public reason according to Rawls is the "public political forum," which provides for three different discourses to take place: "the discourse of judges in their decisions, and especially of the judges of a supreme court; the discourse of government officials, especially chief executives and legislators; and finally, the discourse of candidates for public office and their campaign managers, especially in their public oratory, party platforms, and political statements" (442–443). In these realms, the application of public reason takes a specific and particular form. Although "the requirements of public justification for that reason are always the same" in all three domains, they apply more strictly to judges, particularly at the Supreme Court level (231–240).

Rawls's view of public reason presumes a well-developed constitutional democracy supported by the rule of law. Citizens have the right to ground their views in what he calls "comprehensive doctrines" or broad world-views, like religion, morality, or philosophy, but such doctrines should not be presented as public reason (441). While public reasons should not "criticize or attack" any such comprehensive doctrines, whether religious or non-religious, they must be articulated in terms of fundamental political conceptions or values. "The basic requirement is that a reasonable doctrine accepts a constitutional democratic regime and its companion idea of legitimate law" (441).

Nevertheless, Rawls seems to accept the possibility of invoking comprehensive doctrines in public reason for particular situations, if one follows the inclusive as opposed to the exclusive view on the matter. In the exclusive view, any comprehensive doctrine (like religion) should never be introduced into public reason, even when the doctrine supports public reason. If one takes an inclusive view, citizens may provide "what they regard as the basis of political values rooted in their comprehensive doctrine, provided that they do this in ways that strengthen the ideal of public reason itself" (247). The exclusive view should be upheld in a "more or less well ordered society," where justice and basic rights are secure, so that political values allow for the expression of public reason without reference to any comprehensive doctrine. Rawls distinguishes this from situations where "there is a serious dispute in a nearly well-ordered society in applying one of its principles of justice" (248)—for example, between different groups on the issue of government support for religious education. In such a situation, an explanation in the public forum of "how one's comprehensive doctrine affirms the political values" can help affirm and further legitimize the notion of public reason itself (248–249). Rawls cites the example of the religious advocates of the abolition of slavery in the nineteenth century in the United States, where "the nonpublic reason of certain Christian churches supported the clear conclusions of public reason" (249–250). Another example he gives is the civil rights movement, although Martin Luther King, Jr. also had recourse to appeal to the political values articulated in the Constitution. In both of these cases, not only did abolitionists and civil rights movement leaders affirm the ideal of public reason, but the historical context made it necessary for them to mobilize comprehensive doctrine toward strengthening political values. Their actions strengthened the ideal of public reason in accordance with the inclusive view of this principle. Thus, "the appropriate limits of public reason vary depending on historical and social conditions" (251).

It is not possible here to review the various debates over these views among Western scholars, but it may be useful for my purposes to note Habermas's reservations regarding Rawls's distinction between comprehensive doctrines and political values (1995, 118–119). He also questions Rawls's definition of the term "political" and his distinction between public and private domains of social life. In Habermas's analysis, "Rawls treats the political value-sphere, which is distinguished in modern societies from other cultural value-spheres, as something given" and divides the person into a public political identity and a nonpublic prepolitical identity of liberties beyond "the reach of democratic self-legislation" (129). This view, according to Habermas, challenges the historical fact of shifting boundaries between public and private realms. Another point, which is particularly helpful in clarifying the idea of civic reason for my purposes here, is Habermas's emphasis on independent and nongovernmental spaces as important arenas where public (and civic) reason can develop and be expressed. As McCarthy summarized:

> Independent public forums, distinct from both the economic system and the state administration, having their locus rather in voluntary associations, social movements, and other networks and processes of communication in civil society—including the mass media—are for Habermas the basis of popular sovereignty. Ideally, the public use of reason in nongovernmental arenas is translated via legally institutionalized decision-making procedures—for example, electoral and legislative procedures—into the legitimate administrative power of the state. In Habermas' words, "the power available to the administration emerges from a public use of reason . . . Public opinion worked up via democratic procedures cannot itself 'rule,' but it can point the use of administrative power in specific directions." (1994, 49)

I am in general agreement with Rawls's thinking, as clarified by Habermas, subject to an overriding concern about the risks of transplanting those ideas to Islamic societies at large. To briefly explain, let me first recall my definition of civic reason as the requirement that the rationale and purpose of public policy or legislation be based on the sort of reasoning that most citizens can accept or reject and use to make counterproposals through public debate without reference to religious belief as such. This view can probably be supported by those of Rawls and Habermas, but their focus on the experiences of Western societies may not necessarily be relevant to my concerns. For example, Rawls's distinction between political conceptions and comprehensive doctrines may be helpful in suggesting a framework for civic reason as well. However, the distinction assumes a developed and stable constitutional order and a stable society where these concepts are rich enough to support debate around public policy issues. In fact, Rawls's conception and its application are so specific to the United States that they may not easily resonate with other societies, especially postcolonial Islamic societies in Africa and Asia. This is not a critique of Rawls's approach, as indeed, as he said, "the appropriate limits of public reason vary depending on historical and social conditions." Similarly, the precise concept and application of civic reason should also vary according to local histories and sociological conditions.

In conclusion of this section of the chapter, I emphasize that my conception of civic reason is tentative and evolving, and I take it as an advantage not to be too invested in a particular or detailed view on the subject. For our purposes here, I believe it is sufficient to affirm that the concept of civic reason should be rooted in civil society and marked by contestation among different actors seeking to influence policy through the agency of the state. With reference to the characteristics of the state described earlier, the exercise of civic reason in the nonstate sphere can further entrench the legitimacy as well as the autonomy of the state in providing citizens with a forum and mechanisms to address the state regarding their concerns. Moreover, civic reason as an inclusive and egalitarian forum where all citizens have the right to participate enhances popular perceptions of the state as impartial and accessible to all citizens and civic organizations. Constitutionalism, human rights, and citizenship can secure and regulate the operation of civic reason, but these principles themselves need to be legitimated through this domain as well. I will return to this underlying concern at the end of this chapter, after discussing each of these principles in relation to my thesis as a whole.

Constitutionalism in the Islamic Perspective

Constitutional governance refers to the set of principles that limit and control the powers of government in accordance with the fundamental rights of citizens and communities, as well as the rule of law to ensure that the relationship between individuals and the state is regulated by definite legal principles of general application rather than the despotic will of a ruling elite

(McHugh 2002, 2–3). I use the term "constitutionalism" to include the network of institutions, processes, and broader culture that is necessary for the effective and sustainable operation of this principle (Rosenbaum 1988, 4–5; Henkin 1994, 39–53; Pennock and Chapman 1979). In other words, I am more concerned with a comprehensive and dynamic set of values, and with social and political institutions and processes, than with the formal application of abstract general principles and specific rules of constitutional law. Constitutional and legal principles are relevant and important, but the effective and sustainable implementation of these principles can be realized only through the broader and more dynamic concept of constitutionalism.

As I have discussed in detail elsewhere (An-Na'im 2006), the basic understanding of constitutionalism I am working with is premised on two propositions. First, various conceptions of this principle and its institutions should be seen as complementary approaches to a desirable model of accountable and responsive government as adapted to different conditions of time and place, rather than as indicating sharp dichotomies or categorical choices. Since any definition of this concept is necessarily the product of the experiences of certain societies in their various settings, it is neither reasonable nor desirable, in my view, to insist on a single approach to its definition or implementation, to the exclusion of all others. Whether based on a written document or not, the objective must always be to uphold the rule of law, enforce effective limitations on government powers, and protect human rights. A more universally accepted understanding of constitutionalism may evolve over time, but that should be the outcome of comparative analysis of practical experiences instead of an attempt to impose an exclusive definition based on any one ideological or philosophical tradition.

Second, I strongly believe that such principles can be realized and improved through practice and experience. Thus, popular sovereignty and social justice, for instance, can be achieved through actually practicing them within a framework that is conducive to the correction of theory and modification of practice, rather than by postponing them until "ideal" conditions for success are established by the ruling elite. At the same time, the practical pursuit of popular sovereignty and social justice will provide opportunities to promote conditions that are more conducive to successful and sustainable constitutionalism. That is, the end of constitutional governance is realized through the means of practical experience of constitutional principles in the specific context of each society, which will in turn influence future theoretical reflections on the principles and improve their practice.

Broadly speaking, constitutionalism is a particular response to a basic paradox in the practical experience of every human society. On the one hand, it is clear that equal participation by all members of a community in the conduct of their public affairs is not practically possible. It is also clear, on the other hand, that people tend to have different views and conflicting interests regarding the operation of political power, the development and allocation of economic resources, social policy, and services. The state is the agency charged with mediating these differences in opinion and conflicts of interests. In practice, however, this function will be performed by those persons who control the apparatus of the state. Since these organs are not autonomous or neutral entities that can act as such, the basic function of constitutionalism is to enable those who have no direct control over the apparatus of the state to ensure that their views and interests are well served by those who are in control of the state. All aspects of constitutionalism, whether regarding the structures and organs of the state or their operation in the formation and implementation of public policy, administration of justice, and so forth, follow from this basic reality of all human societies today.

Thus, constitutional governance requires respect for and protection of collective as well as individual rights, because the two sets of rights are interdependent in their meaning and implementation. For example, respecting the freedoms of opinion, belief, and association of individual persons is the only way in which the collective freedoms of ethnic or religious groups can be protected. Yet those freedoms of the individual are meaningful and effectively exercised only within the context of the relevant group. Moreover, since rights are ultimately the tools for realizing the objectives of social justice, political stability, and economic development for all segments of the population, they should be perceived as dynamic processes rather than as abstract legal rules. Rights are not useful without the institutional means for exercising them, including the ability to form and act on judgments about the actions of government officials and to hold them accountable. Therefore, officials must not be able to obscure their activities or hide their excessive use or abuse of power; there is a general need for the transparency of official action. This can be achieved through legislation and administrative regulation, as well as through measures like protection of the freedom of the press, or the media in general, and effective remedies against those who violate the obligations of their office or contrive to evade responsibility. Administrative and financial transparency is unlikely to lead to effective legal and political accountability without competent and independent institutions that can investigate possible violations and adjudicate on disputed issues and questions. This aspect of the process relates to various matters that cannot be discussed in detail here, ranging from technical questions of administrative law and tribunals to practical arrangements for securing the independence of the judiciary or the political accountability of elected or appointed officials.

The most critical aspect of constitutionalism relates to the psychological motivation and sociological ability of citizens to participate in collective civic activities to promote and protect rights and freedoms. The whole principle of constitutionalism and its various institutions and processes is dependent on the willingness and the ability of citizens to uphold this principle for the public good of all rather than for the narrow self-interest of one segment of the population. The various aspects of constitutionalism are difficult to quantify or verify, but they certainly include the motivation of citizens to keep themselves well informed in public affairs and act collectively. Public officials and the agencies and institutions they operate must not only enjoy the confidence of local communities but also be accessible, friendly, and responsive when approached. This is the practical and most foundational meaning of popular sovereignty, whereby people can govern themselves through their own public officials and elected representatives. Constitutionalism is ultimately about realizing and regulating this ideal in the most sustainable yet dynamic way, balancing the present requirements of stability and predictability with the need for adaptation and development in the future.

The principle of constitutionalism includes general principles, such as representative government, transparency, and accountability, the separation of legislative, executive, and judicial powers, and the independence of the judiciary. However, this is not to suggest that such features must all be present in particular forms all at once for constitutionalism to be successfully implemented in a country. In fact, such principles and conditions can only emerge and develop, in a variety of models, through a process of trial and error over time (Franklin and Baun 1995, 184–217). The rationale for and purpose of a representative government, transparency, and accountability can be realized through different models, such as the parliamentary system of the United Kingdom and the presidential system in the French or American style. Such models are not only specific to each society but can and indeed do change and adapt to changing circumstances in the same country over time (McHugh 2002, 50–54, 57–58, 147, 149–150). Each successful constitutional model works in its totality and over time, whereby when some branch or official violates the principles of the rule of law, for instance, the judicial or legislative organs may take some time to respond. Eventually the proper balance and functioning of the state may be restored. But like all human institutions, every constitution will have some problems or difficulties and is transformed or adapted in its own ways in times of crisis. This can be clearly seen in the collapse and restoration of constitutionalism in France and Germany during the twentieth century (Safran 1990, 91–109).

For instance, separation of powers and independence of the judiciary can be secured either through structural and institutional arrangements, as in the United States (McHugh 2002, 35–36), or by means of deeply entrenched political "conventions" and traditions of practice in the political culture of a country, as in the United Kingdom (47–63). A sharp distinction between conventions and traditions in this sense, on the one hand, and structures and institutions, on the other, can be misleading, because each model requires or presupposes some degree or form of the other for its proper functioning. Such differences are normally the product of the historical experience and context of the country rather than the result of a single deliberate choice that was made at a specific point in time (McHugh 2002, 3–38). What is important is the ability of the system to achieve its desired constitutional objectives despite the differences in the manner in which it is realized in practice.

But to say that we should not insist on particular models of successful implementation from one country or another does not mean that all conceivable systems are equally conducive to the sustained realization of the objectives of certain constitutional principles, such as the separation of powers or the independence of the judiciary. This is usually a matter of degree, but some methods are too inadequate to be acceptable if the principle in question is to be upheld at all. For instance, while some executive discretion in the appointment and tenure of judges is unavoidable, total reliance on the "good faith" of those responsible for such determinations without external checks or safeguards will defeat the principle of the independence of the judiciary. A system that denies some segments of the population certain basic rights of citizenship, such as equality before the law or equal access to public office, on the grounds of religion or gender would amount to the total repudiation of the principle of constitutionalism.

Nevertheless, it does not follow that unacceptable models can easily and quickly be replaced by better ones. As clearly illustrated by the post-independence experiences of many African and Asian countries, the transplantation of structures, institutions, and processes that are found to be successful in some countries is a profoundly difficult task that requires extensive adaptation and careful development (Akiba 2004, 7–16). The emergence of consensus on certain features of constitutionalism and the way they are detailed and applied in each country reflect the particular experiences of that country in its global and local context. In other words, the meaning and implications of constitutionalism for a given country are the product of the interaction between the broad universal principles and specific local factors and processes. But the universal principles themselves are extrapolated from the specific experiences of various countries, which were in turn produced by a similar interaction between the universal and the local in their respective contexts.

Islam, Shari'a, and Constitutionalism

My concern with the Islamic legitimacy of constitutionalism does not mean that Islam completely or exclusively determines the constitutional behavior of Muslims, who are in fact influenced by a wide variety of political, economic, and other factors. Indeed, the understanding and practice of Islam by Muslims is itself influenced by such factors. Still, I believe that Muslims are unlikely to take constitutionalism seriously if they hold a negative view of the concept or think that some of its principles are inconsistent with their religious obligation to observe Shari'a. But as already emphasized, any human knowledge and practice of Shari'a is always the product of the understanding and experience of Muslims, which does not exhaust the totality of Islam as such.

The traditional Islamic constitutional frame of reference is commonly taken to be the experience of the original Muslim community established by the Prophet in Medina after his migration from Mecca in 622, believed to have been continued by the first generation of his followers (Faruki 1971). Patterns of individual and collective behavior, as well as models of political and social relationships and institutions, commonly ascribed to or associated with that period continue to be held as the Islamic ideal by Sunni Muslims today. But for Muslims who believe the Prophet Muhammad to be the final prophet, the model of the state he established in Medina cannot be replicated after his death. For Muslims who make this claim, those who govern will always be ordinary human beings who do not have the exclusively divine authority that the Prophet had.

Moreover, there is no agreement among Muslims about what the Medina model means or how it can be applied today. To the Sunni majority, the reign of the Prophet and of the four "rightly guided" caliphs of Medina represents the most authoritative model of Islamic constitutional theory. Shi'a communities have their own ideal models of the rightful imamate since Ali, the last of the caliphs of Medina, depending on their respective doctrine and history (whether Jafari, Isma'ili, Zaidi, and so forth) (see, for example, Arjomand 1984; Daftary 1990). Thus Sunni and Shi'a Muslims uphold their respective models as the ideal while constantly decrying deviations by the subsequent generations, often justified as coerced by compelling circumstances, such as internal strife or external invasion. "It seemed preferable to continue to pay lip-service to an inviolate Shari'a, as the only law of fundamental authority, and to excuse departure from much of it in practice by appealing to the doctrine of necessity *(darura)*, rather than to make any attempt to adapt that law to the circumstances and needs of contemporary life" (Anderson 1976, 36).

I am therefore trying to promote an understanding of Shari'a that Muslims can actually live by, instead of maintaining an unrealistic ideal that is honored only in theory but never in practice. Thus the question should be about translating the essential justice and practical implications of historical models, not about replicating them under radically different circumstances. For example, the notion of "consultation in public affairs" *(shura)* was neither binding nor practiced in a systematic and inclusive manner. Verse 3:159 of the Qur'an instructs the Prophet to consult *(shawirhum)* with the believers, but once he makes up his mind, the verse says, he should implement his decision. Another verse often cited in this context is verse 42:38, which describes the believers as a community who decide matters in consultation. But the Qur'an does not explain how such consultation might be done in practice or what happens in case of a disagreement (Coulson 1957, 55–56). This is not to blame the Qur'an, as it is not its function to cover such highly specific matters, nor the founding scholars of Shari'a, who responded wisely and appropriately to the needs of their communities. The point is simply to note the lack of such mechanisms in existing Islamic jurisprudence, where the dominant view remains that *shura* in this context indicates a requirement to seek advice without necessarily being bound by it. The actual practice of the Prophet and of the caliphs of Medina confirmed this understanding, which became the norm for the monarchies of the Umayyad and Abbasid empires and other states throughout the premodern history of Islamic societies.

This understanding of the concept of *shura* does not mean that it cannot be used today as a basis for institutionalized constitutional principles that include the population at large, as advocated by some Muslim scholars since the mid-twentieth century (Asad 1961, 51–58). In fact, that is the sort of evolution and development of Islamic principles that I am calling for. However, this possibility must begin with a clear understanding of the preexisting meanings of *shura* and its historical practice. To pretend that this notion has already been understood and practiced as "constitutional government" in the modern sense would be counterproductive, because it would falsely affirm unconstitutional practices. In any case, that claim still has to account for the lack of practical institutional arrangements for peaceful political dissent and orderly transfer of power to freely selected leaders throughout Islamic history. This weakness of institutional implementation was of course true throughout the world until the eighteenth century, when effective mechanisms began to evolve in Western Europe and North America. But the fact that institutional mechanisms were lacking everywhere hardly justifies ignoring the need for them in making the historically false claim that Muslims have already known and practiced constitutional governance.

A similar approach should also be applied to developing and evolving traditional interpretations of Shariʿa regarding equality for women and non-Muslims and freedom of religion. The fact that such traditional views were common among all human societies in the past does not justify their continuation by Muslims today. Instead, we should be clear about the rationale or justification for such practices in the various local cultures of Islamic societies of the past and how that justification was legitimated as the authoritative interpretations of Shariʿa, and then seek alternative interpretations that are more consistent with the evolving cultures and the context of Islamic societies today (An-Naʿim 1996).

I should emphasize that the general rule of Shariʿa is that people are guaranteed freedom of action or omission unless it contravenes Islamic precepts. In theory, there are no limitations on constitutional rights in general under Shariʿa, except in the specific instances to be highlighted below. In practice, however, the subject is complicated by the diffused nature of Shariʿa in a wide range of schools of jurisprudence and the strong disagreements among Islamic scholars on almost every conceivable subject (Hallaq 2004, 26–36). Muslims therefore are often uncertain about whether they have the right to act or refrain from action from a Shariʿa point of view, and this uncertainty opens the door to manipulation by elites or leaders. These ambiguities may also have serious consequences for constitutional rights, like the regulation of women's dress and the segregation of the sexes, which can encroach on personal freedoms and the ability to participate in public life.

Whatever view one may take on such issues, it is beyond dispute that women and non-Muslims are subjected to specific restrictions of their constitutional rights under the traditional interpretations of Shari'a. For example, verse 4:34 of the Qur'an has been taken to establish a general principle of men's guardianship *(qawama)* of women, thereby denying women the right to hold any public office involving the exercise of authority over men (Ali 2000, 256–263). While jurists differ on a range of relevant issues, none of them would grant women equality with men in this regard. This general principle is applied in interpreting, and is reinforced by, various specific verses that apparently grant women unequal rights compared to those of men regarding marriage, divorce, inheritance, and related matters (Maududi 1979, 141–158). The same principles of interpretation are applied to other verses, like verse 24:31 and verses 33:33, 53, and 59, to restrict the right of women to appear and speak in public or to associate with men, which thereby limits their ability to participate in government (Mernissi 1991, 152–153). Thus, although Muslim women have the same freedom of belief and opinion as men, their opportunity to exercise this right is greatly inhibited by restrictions on their access to the public domain.

A similar combination of general and specific verses has traditionally been used to restrict the rights of non-Muslims, whether accepted as People of the Book (mainly Christians and Jews) or deemed to be unbelievers (Gibb and Kramers 1991, 76). I will provide more details on this in the section on citizenship later. For now, my point is that despite theoretical differences among Muslim scholars and variation between theory and practice, it is beyond dispute that non-Muslims are not equal to Muslims under the traditional interpretations of Shari'a. It is possible to develop alternative interpretations of Shari'a that would completely eliminate discrimination on grounds of religion, but that does not justify denying that existing views in fact require such discrimination. It is relevant to note here that the prohibition of discrimination on the grounds of sex and religion is now provided for in the national constitutions of most countries where Muslims are the clear majority. Those countries are also parties to international human rights treaties, which require equality and nondiscrimination. Such constitutional and international commitments clearly indicate that these norms enjoy wide acceptance among Muslim populations (Brems 2001, 194–206; Khan 2003). It is true that the governments of those countries rarely live up to their constitutional and human rights obligations, but that is a common problem among all countries around the world. The need to understand and combat the underlying causes of this common failure does not negate the empirical reality of wide acceptance of human rights values among Muslims everywhere.

The Islamic reforms I am calling for are intended to encourage and support efforts to require complete equality for women and non-Muslims from a Shariʻa point of view and not simply for political expediency. Such reforms will also contribute to the process of legitimizing the values of political participation, accountability, and equality before the law, thereby enhancing the prospects for constitutionalism in Islamic societies. To avoid confusion here, my point is that while the underlying moral and social norms of the Medina society remain the ideal for which all Muslims should always strive, the actual structure and operation of that state cannot be reenacted today. Instead of continuing to pay lip service to the ideal of the Medina state and society without applying it, Muslims should reaffirm the underlying values of that ideal and the rationale for its social and political institutions through more workable systems of government, administration of justice, and international relations. The principles of constitutionalism, human rights, and citizenship are in fact more appropriate for realizing the ideal of the Prophet's community of Medina in the concrete context of present Islamic societies than unrealistic adherence to earlier models that are no longer workable.

For instance, the traditional oath of allegiance *(bayʻa)* should now be seen as an authoritative basis for a mutual contract between the government and the population at large, whereby the former assumes responsibility for the protection of the rights and general well-being of the latter in exchange for their acceptance of the authority of the state and compliance with its laws and public policy (Lambton 1985, 18). However, any modern constitutional theory, whether founded on Islamic principles or not, must develop adequate mechanisms and institutions for the election and accountability of government and for the safeguarding of fundamental rights like freedoms of expression and association for that notion of mutual allegiance to be meaningful today. This can be done by developing the idea of *shura* into a binding principle of representative government rather than merely discretionary consultation. Human rights and equal citizenship principles are necessary, not only for evolving this modern concept of *shura*, but also for the proper implementation of the ensuing constitutional theory, which must be inclusive of all men and women, as well as Muslims and non-Muslims alike, as equal citizens of the state.

Islam and Human Rights

Speaking of Islam is really speaking about how Muslims understand and practice their religion rather than about religion in the abstract. Moreover, this discussion of the relationship between Islam and human rights does not mean that Islam, or any other religion, is the sole "cause" of or explanation for the attitudes and behavior of believers. Muslims may accept or reject the idea of human rights or any of its norms regardless of what they believe to be the orthodox view of their religion on the subject. In fact, various levels of acceptance or compliance with human rights norms are more likely to be associated with the political, economic, social, and/or cultural conditions of present Islamic societies than with Islam as such. Consequently, whatever the role of Islam may be, it cannot be understood in isolation from other factors that influence the way Muslims interpret and attempt to comply with their own tradition. It is therefore misleading to attempt to predict or explain the degree or quality of human rights compliance by Islamic societies as the logical consequence of the relationship between Islam and human rights in an abstract theoretical sense. Still, this relationship is important enough for most Muslims that their motivation to uphold human rights norms is likely to diminish if they perceive those norms to be inconsistent with Islamic precepts. Conversely, their commitment and motivation to protect those rights will increase if they believe them to be at least consistent with, if not required by, their belief in Islam.

A second general point to emphasize here is that Shariʿa principles are basically consistent with most human rights norms, with the exception of some specific and very serious aspects of the rights of women and non-Muslims and the freedom of religion and belief, as highlighted below. While appreciating the seriousness of these issues and seeking to address them through Islamic reform, I am calling for mediation rather than confrontation in this regard, because I know that if I, as a Muslim, am faced with a stark choice between Islam and human rights, I will certainly opt for Islam. Instead of presenting Muslims with this choice, I am proposing that we as Muslims consider transforming our understanding of Shariʿa in the present context of Islamic societies. I believe that this approach is required as a matter of principle and is desirable in pragmatic tactical terms.

I am therefore calling for framing the issue in terms of the contextual nature of human understandings and practice of Islam, on the one hand, and the universality of human rights, on the other. This approach is more realistic and constructive than simplistic assertions of compatibility or incompatibility of Islam and human rights that take both sides of this relationship in static, absolute terms. This view does not uphold human rights as the standard by which Islam itself should be judged, but only proposes that these rights constitute an appropriate framework for *human* understanding of Islam and interpretation of Shariʿa. As emphasized earlier, the real issue is always about human understanding and practice and not about Islam in the abstract. Since traditional interpretations of Shariʿa are human and not divine, they can change through the process of reinterpretation and consensus-building outlined in Chapter 1. What I am proposing here is that human rights provide an appropriate framework for that unavoidably human process. But what do I mean by human rights, where do these rights come from, and how are they defined in practice?

The Universality of Human Rights

The idea of human rights emerged in the aftermath of the Second World War as an attempt to achieve the benefits of strong entrenchment of certain fundamental rights beyond the contingencies of national politics. The founding vision was that these rights are so fundamental that they must be safeguarded through international consensus and cooperation in order to ensure their protection under national constitutional and legal systems (Brems 2001, 5–7). In other words, the object of creating international legal obligations to respect and protect human rights, whether through customary law principles or treaties, is to supplement the provision for these rights under domestic systems, to the extent that it is lacking or insufficient, and to promote their practical implementation.

The essential purpose of human rights is to ensure the effective protection of certain key entitlements of all human beings everywhere, including in countries where these entitlements are not guaranteed as fundamental constitutional rights. This does not mean, however, that human rights are different from or superior to fundamental constitutional rights. In fact, human rights are usually respected and protected through their inclusion in a constitutional bill of rights or through their incorporation in the constitutional organization and regulation of state institutions. The purpose of this idea, like that of constitutional rights, is to entrench and safeguard these key entitlements from the contingencies of political and administrative processes. In other words, human rights, like fundamental constitutional rights, should not normally be subject to the will of the majority, at least not by a simple majority vote. However, this does not mean that these rights are absolute, because many of them are qualified in various ways, and some can be suspended in times of drastic emergency, for example. The idea, therefore, is to make it harder to encroach on human rights, like fundamental constitutional rights, except under specific circumstances or conditions (Brems 2001, 305).

In view of the tension between this idea and the principle and practice of national sovereignty, however, it is critical for human rights standards to be acknowledged as the product of international agreement. The challenge that these rights pose to a strict view of sovereignty would not be plausible or credible without the promise of international cooperation in the protection of human rights (Brems 2001, 309). The claim of the international community to act as arbiter in safeguarding certain minimum standards in this regard is not credible without the corresponding commitment of its members to encourage and support each other in the process. That role is also more likely to be accepted by a state when it is the collective effort of all other states and not simply the foreign-policy objective of another single state or group of states. The consistent and sustainable protection of human rights cannot be realized through military intervention or external imposition, because such measures are necessarily arbitrary and temporary. In other words, the practical protection of human rights can happen only through the agency of the states who are the primary violators of those rights. Here is another paradox (self-regulation by the state) that needs to be mediated over time rather than conclusively resolved.

The concept of human rights can be a powerful instrument for the protection of human dignity and the promotion of the well-being of persons everywhere precisely because of the universality of these rights, as demonstrated by their powerful moral and political force. The fact that these rights provide a "common standard of achievement for all peoples and nations," as stated in the Preamble of the Universal Declaration of Human Rights of 1948, means that every national constitutional or legal regime must constantly strive to protect them. However, the quality of being a universal norm can be achieved only through a global consensus-building process, instead of being assumed or imposed. Since all human societies adhere to their own normative systems, which are necessarily shaped by their own context and experiences, any universal concept cannot be simply proclaimed or taken for granted. In other words, human beings know and experience the world as themselves—men or women, African or European, rich or poor, religious believers or not. For human beings everywhere, our consciousness, values, and behavior are shaped by our own cultural and religious traditions. The question is therefore how to generate, promote, and sustain consensus on universal human rights norms, which requires a clear understanding of the nature and implications of differentials in power relations between different participants in these consensus-building processes, *within as well as among cultures.*

This view of the human rights framework as the product of a consensus-building process should not be seen as defending or justifying the claims of some governments or leaders that their societies should be exempt or excused from observing these standards. In fact, those claims are made by the ruling elites because of perceptions that human rights are "Western" and therefore alien to African and Asian societies in general (Bauer and Bell 1999). My purpose is to challenge such claims by emphasizing that all societies are struggling with how to achieve and sustain a genuine commitment to the universality of human rights and their underlying premise of the rule of law in international relations. In particular, I reject the notion that the only valid model for the universality of human rights is set by Western or any other group of societies for the rest of the world to follow if they wish to be considered a part of "civilized humanity." If human rights are to be at all universal (which they have to be, since they are the rights of all human beings everywhere), they must be integral to the culture and experience of all societies and not only of so-called Western societies that are "transplanting" them elsewhere. The following points can be noted in support of this proposition.

First, it is clear that the present formulation of international human rights standards strongly reflects Western political philosophy and experience, with many of the articles of the Universal Declaration apparently copying the language of the Bill of Rights of the United States in particular (Brems 2001, 17). But this does not make these norms alien or irrelevant to African and Asian societies, which can indeed appreciate the need to protect these rights in their own contexts. The present formulation of these standards is premised on the nature of Western models of the territorial state and international relations, which are now part of the realities of all Islamic societies, as noted earlier. Since Muslims now have to live with these Western institutions, they need to benefit from the safeguards developed by Western societies for protecting the rights of persons and communities under these systems (Baehr, Flintermand, and Senders 1999, 2). Conversely, those Muslims who claim to be rejecting human rights because they are Western should also reject territorial states, international trade and financial institutions, and economic and other relations that are premised on Western models. If they are unable or unwilling to do that, then they should accept human rights as necessary as an effective way of minimizing abuses and redressing harm that might happen under these Western models.

A second point to emphasize is that the advocates of human rights and international legality must insist on these essential foundations of civilized humanity, rather than abandon them because of the failure of some governments to uphold them. Otherwise, human rights advocates would be conceding that offending governments are the sole authors of these principles, which stand or fall on their willingness or ability to uphold them. Principles of human rights and international legality must be upheld and promoted in the face of any challenge, from whatever source, precisely because they are the joint effort of the totality of humanity everywhere. It is also important to note that, like any other human initiative, the protection of human rights can be achieved only through a process of trial and error, through practice that includes difficulties and starts, setbacks as well as progress. All people and societies must cooperate and collaborate in this process for these rights to be truly universal. For my purposes here, Muslims in particular must be active participants in this process, instead of complaining about being helpless victims of oppression by their own governments at home and subjects of Western hegemony in international relations.

A related point to note is that the framers of the Universal Declaration of Human Rights avoided identifying religious justifications for this basic idea in an effort to find common ground among believers and nonbelievers. However, this does not mean that human rights can only be founded on secular justifications, because that does not address the question of how to make human rights equally valid and legitimate from the perspectives of the wide variety of believers around the world. The underlying rationale for the human rights doctrine itself entitles believers to seek to base their commitment to these norms on their own religious beliefs, in the same way that others may seek to affirm them on the basis of a secular philosophy. All human beings are entitled to require equal commitment to the human rights doctrine by others, but they cannot prescribe the grounds on which others may wish to found their commitment.

The proposed approach is presented here with due consideration for the difficulties that have been mounting since the end of the cold war, as old rivals of the so-called Western and Eastern blocs have become collaborators in facilitating their narrower foreign-policy objectives with diminishing reference to human rights considerations. Several examples of this can be found throughout the 1990s, from Somalia to Rwanda, and from Bosnia to Chechnya, and finally to the colonization of Iraq by the United States and the United Kingdom in March 2003. Colonialism is seizing sovereignty over territory and its population by military conquest without legal justification, which is exactly what the United States and the United Kingdom and their allies did in Iraq, regardless of the alleged justification or consequences. Illegal conduct cannot be legalized by the motivation of the violator or the consequences of his conduct. When two permanent members of the Security Council violate the charter of the United Nations with impunity, it is difficult to hold other states accountable for their violations of human rights treaties.

It is true that some of the old foreign policies upholding international law and human rights continue, because such a fundamental shift in foreign policy is unlikely to occur completely and all at once. But it is also clear to me that there has been a gradual erosion and decline of the old policy, as offending governments watch carefully to see how much they can get away with, and those motivated to include human rights in their foreign policies consider how much they can risk to lose in the cause of protecting the human rights of people in faraway places. As the human rights movement concedes more of its traditional demands in appreciation of the weakness of its bargaining power in national and regional politics, governments become bolder in their assertion of the narrowly defined national interest over human rights concerns. This gradual erosion of the importance of human rights in foreign policy also tends to be legitimized through democratic processes, as illustrated in my view by the reelection of President George W. Bush in the United States in 2004.

I do not mean to discredit the human rights idea itself, or to predict its demise in domestic settings and international relations. My object is to shift the focus of human rights advocacy to a more "people-centered" approach that is less dependent on the ambiguities and contingencies of intergovernmental relations. This does not mean the termination of the strategies of international advocacy, because that is still necessary for the practical protection of human rights at present (Drinan 2001). Rather, the purpose is gradually to diminish reliance on international advocacy by progressively reducing the need for it through the development of the capacity of local communities to protect their own rights as the most effective and sustainable way (An-Naʿim 2001, 701–732; An-Naʿim 2003, 1–28). This shift to local efforts and away from international intervention is not easily made or secured against regression where it is already taking place, but it is the only way forward.

In the case of Islamic societies, this involves persuading and motivating Muslims to accept and implement human rights. It is also clear that human rights are not an automatic solution for all of the problems of any society, but these norms and institutions can empower people to engage in political and legal struggles for human dignity and social justice. However, this possibility cannot be realized without creating the necessary conditions for debate and reinterpretation to transform traditional perceptions of Shariʿa, as emphasized in Chapter 1. In view of the obvious relevance of this process to the validity of my belief and religious experience as a Muslim, the rationale for insisting on the separation of Islam and the state can be briefly illustrated as follows.

Islam, Shariʿa, and the Freedom of Religion and Belief

The earlier discussion of conflicts between Shariʿa and constitutionalism, as well as the possibilities of mediating them through a broader reference to Islam at large, is also applicable to human rights. I am therefore calling for the clarification of the nature of tensions between some aspects of Shariʿa and human rights, as well as exploring ways to address them through Islamic reform. It is necessary first to acknowledge that there is a conflict and to understand its nature before we can hope to resolve or mediate it. Conflicts between Shariʿa and human rights include issues of the rights of women and non-Muslims. I will now examine the third main area of conflict, namely, the freedom of religion and belief, by first clarifying the human rights issues and then exploring the possibilities for mediating the conflict through Islamic reform. To avoid confusion, I do believe that it is possible, indeed necessary, to reinterpret Islamic sources in order to affirm and protect the freedom of religion and belief. This is my position as a Muslim, speaking from an Islamic perspective, and not simply because the freedom of religion and belief is a universal human rights norm that is binding upon Muslims from the point of view of international law.

It is important to put the following discussion in perspective in at least two ways. First, the conflict between religious law and freedom of religion is not peculiar to Islam, as it can be found in relation to other religions and ideologies. For example, traditional understandings of Jewish and Christian texts imposed the death penalty and other drastic consequences for apostasy and related offenses (Bible, Deuteronomy 13:6–9 and Leviticus 24:16; Saeed and Saeed 2004, 35). Indeed, it can be argued that the enforcement of religious conformity by such measures is simply the equivalent of modern notions of treason, which remains a capital crime under most legal systems today. The prohibition of apostasy and related matters under Shariʻa, therefore, was neither unique among religious traditions nor a phenomenon limited to religion, as similar penal and other measures continue to be applied to the so-called secular ideologies. Nonconformity with Marxist ideology, for example, was probably punished more harshly in the former Soviet Union for much of the twentieth century than apostasy and related crimes were ever punished under Shariʻa.

Another important point to emphasize is that the relevant Shariʻa principles have rarely been strictly and systematically applied in the past and are even less so today. Nevertheless, the existence of these principles constitutes a fundamental conflict with the premise of the universality of human rights and is a source of serious violations of the freedom of religion and belief in practice. It is therefore necessary for me as a Muslim to confront this issue in order to uphold the moral integrity of my religious beliefs and to challenge the practical violation of this human right, however unlikely or infrequent that may be today.

I will briefly discuss apostasy and related matters under Shariʻa to clarify the inconsistency of those principles with religious freedom from an Islamic perspective, even without reference to modern human rights norms. The proper application of the principle of the religious neutrality of the state will eliminate any possibility of negative legal consequences for apostasy and related concepts. But that will not eliminate the negative social implications of traditional Shariʻa principles. That aspect should be addressed through educational and other measures over time to promote genuine and sustainable pluralism. The following discussion applies to both legal and social aspects by showing that those Shariʻa principles are so untenable from a moral and political point of view today that they should neither be enforced by the state nor be accepted by Islamic societies at large.

The Arabic term *ridda*, commonly translated as "apostasy," literally means "to turn back," and *murtad* is the person who turns back (al-Samarʿi 1968; Rahman 1972). Under the traditional understandings of Shariʿa, *ridda* is reverting from the religion of Islam to *kufr* (unbelief), whether intentionally or by necessary implication (Saeed and Saeed 2004, 36, 42). In other words, once a person becomes a Muslim by his or her free choice, there is no means by which he or she can change religion. According to Shariʿa scholars, the ways in which *ridda* can occur include denying the existence or attributes of God; denying a particular messenger of God or that a messenger is truly a messenger of God; denying a principle that is established as a matter of religion, such as the obligation to pray five times a day or fast during the month of Ramadan; and declaring prohibited what is manifestly permitted *(halal)* or declaring permitted what is manifestly prohibited *(haram)*. Apostasy is traditionally held to apply to any Muslim who is deemed to have reverted from Islam by an intentional or blasphemous act or utterance, even when said mockingly or out of stubbornness (Saeed and Saeed 2004, 36–37).

The view that apostasy is a crime or a legal wrong for which an apostate should suffer punishment or other legal consequences is inconsistent with the dominant theme in the Qur'an, as in verses 2:217, 4:90, 5:54, 59, 16:108, and 47:25, which condemn apostasy but do not specify any legal consequences for it in this life (Saeed and Saeed 2004, 57). In fact, the Qur'an clearly contemplates situations in which an apostate continues to live among the Muslim community. For example, verse 4:137 of the Qur'an can be translated as follows: "Those who believed, then disbelieved, then believed, and then disbelieved [once more] and became more so, God will not forgive them or guide them to the righteous pathway." This verse clearly confirms that the Qur'an envisions the apostate continuing to live among Muslims, even to engage in repeated apostasy, and still face no consequences in this life. Past Shariʿa scholars relied on some Sunna reports in imposing the death penalty on an apostate, in addition to implementing other negative legal consequences, such as barring inheritance by or from a *murtad* (Saeed and Saeed 2004, 413–414). Moreover, there are two problematic aspects of the notion of apostasy in traditional Islamic jurisprudence itself, namely, the vagueness and fluidity of the concept and the ambiguity of the basis for its legal consequences as a capital crime.

Scholars of the four main Sunni schools classified apostasy into three categories: beliefs, actions, and utterances, with further subdivisions for each of them. But each of these categories can be controversial. For instance, the first category is supposed to include doubts about the existence or eternity of

God or about the message of the Prophet Muhammad or any other prophet, and doubts about the Qur'an, the Day of Judgment, the existence of paradise and hell, or any other matter of belief on which there is consensus *(ijma')* among Muslims, such as the attributes of God. It would therefore logically follow that where there is no consensus on an issue, apostasy is not possible on that count. Yet as a matter of fact there is no consensus among Muslims on many of the issues included in the list of various scholars and schools. For example, since there is significant disagreement among Muslim scholars on the attributes of God, a person can be condemned as an apostate for rejecting an attribute of God according to the views of one scholar that is disputed by other scholars (Saeed and Saeed 2004, 37, 189). Moreover, Muslim scholars did not generally discriminate among the various associated concepts and tended to use the broader category of apostasy as subsuming all of them. This makes this term dangerously broad and vague and confuses the legal basis for an alleged crime and its punishment among different types of conduct. I will now simply illustrate this point, without attempting a comprehensive discussion of the subject.

Since apostasy means openly reverting to disbelief in Islam after having freely embraced it, an obvious association is with disbelief *(kufr)*, that is, open and complete rejection of the message of Islam itself (Saeed and Saeed 2004, 42). Although the Qur'an repeatedly speaks of disbelief and belief, it does not provide clear guidance on what these terms mean beyond the basic sense of confession of the faith: "There is no god but God, and Muhammad is his messenger." For example, the Qur'an frequently links belief to performing worship rituals such as prayer and fasting during the month of Ramadan and doing good deeds, but it does not say what should happen to those who fail to live up to these obligations, other than punishment in the afterlife.

The Qur'an does not expressly state the consequences of questioning the meaning of the confession of the faith itself. For instance, what does it mean to affirm the Muslim confession of faith that "there is no god but God"? What do believers know, or what should they know, about God? What are the imperative consequences of belief in the unity of God for the personal practice or behavior of Muslims, whether at the private, personal level or in relation to public socioeconomic and political institutions and processes? Who has the authority to adjudicate the inevitable disagreements about these and other matters after the death of the Prophet, and how? Instead of providing any answers to such questions, the Qur'an leaves Muslims free to struggle with all these issues for themselves. It is true that they have the additional practical guidance of the Sunna, and the life-model *(siyra)* of the Prophet, but that also has its uncertainties and ambiguities. It is therefore not surprising to find major differences among Muslims on the role that actions or deeds *(a'mal)* play within the definition of belief *(iman)*. Whereas some Muslim scholars were willing to accept an apparent confession of the faith as sufficient for a person to be considered a Muslim, others insisted that the professed belief must be expressed in specific actions or deeds. For those who require action according to belief, the question becomes what to do about the people who claim to be Muslims but fail to act accordingly. But then, who decides whether or not a person has acted according to the requirements of the faith, and by which criteria? These debates and their manifestations ranged from the views and actions of the Kharijites during the civil wars of the seventh century, to the status of the Ahmadiyya in Pakistan since the 1950s, to the present cults of murder and terrorism (Abou El Fadl 2001).

Such profound uncertainties are further complicated by ambiguities and disagreements about other concepts, such as blasphemy. Blasphemy is the use of foul language primarily about the Prophet Muhammad, known as insulting the Prophet *(sabb al-rasul)*, God, or any of the angels or prophets; it is held by traditional Islamic scholars to be punishable by death (Saeed and Saeed 2004, 37–38). At a later stage, this offense was extended to cover using foul language against the Companions of the Prophet. While for some scholars this is a special category of blasphemy in which the person remains a Muslim but can be killed as a punishment for this offense, others maintain that committing such a sin automatically removes the person from the fold of Islam. If the act is committed by a non-Muslim, then the question of apostasy does not arise, but the person can still be punished by death for blasphemy. As with apostasy, the punishment for blasphemy appears to be based on certain incidents in the lifetime of the Prophet, as there is no clear Qur'anic instruction on the matter. Even when the Qur'an uses the term *sabb*, as in verse 6:108, it only commands Muslims to refrain from reviling the deities of non-Muslims lest they revile God, but without any reference to punishment in this life. While scholars cite incidents in early Islamic history in support of imposing the death penalty for blasphemy, it is clear that neither the Qur'an nor the Sunna declare the existence of an offense called "blasphemy" or a specific punishment for it (Saeed and Saeed 2004, 38–39).

Similar problems exist with the jurisprudence regarding heresy. The term "heresy" *(zandaqa)* is applied in Shariʿa sources to a heretic whose teachings become a danger to the Islamic community, thereby rendering him liable to the death penalty. However, the term and its derivatives do not appear in the Qurʾan at all and seem to have come into Arabic from Persian. This term was apparently used for the first time in connection with the execution of Jaʿd bin Dirham in 742—more than a century after the Prophet's death. "In practice, the polemics of the conservatives describe as a *zindik* (one who is guilty of *zandaqa*) anyone whose external profession of Islam seems to them to be not sufficiently sincere" (Gibb and Kramers 1991, 659). However, there is no agreed definition of what that means, and a variety of views exist about the type of conduct that constitutes *zandaqa* or makes a person a *zindiq*, such as those who outwardly show that they are Muslims while retaining their former religion. But how is that to be known, or proved, in specific cases? Without a clear and specific definition of the term, it is not surprising that some scholars were prepared to infer *zandaqa* because a person advocated indulgence in various acts that are prohibited in Islam, such as *zina* or drinking wine (Saeed and Saeed 2004, 40). The need for a clear definition is also apparent when we consider that some scholars, of the Hanafi and Maliki schools in particular, deny a *zindiq* the chance to repent, while an apostate is afforded that opportunity (Saeed and Saeed 2004, 41, 54–55).

As this brief review clearly shows, there has always been substantial confusion and fluidity in these concepts and how they have been defined, as well as uncertainty about the basis of their criminal punishment. Since the Qurʾan neither defined these concepts nor imposed a punishment for any of them in this life, present Islamic societies can and should reconsider this aspect of Shariʿa in terms of the freedom of religion and belief. In fact, more texts of the Qurʾan and Sunna can be cited for this view than in support of imposing any penal or other legal consequences on such conduct (Saeed and Saeed 2004, 69–87). In other words, there should be no penal or other negative legal consequences for apostasy and all of the related concepts from an Islamic perspective, because belief in Islam presupposes and requires the freedom of choice and can never be valid under coercion or intimidation. The possibility of belief in anything logically requires choice in the matter, as one cannot believe in anything without the freedom and ability to disbelieve in it.

The inherent vagueness and ambiguity of these Shariʿa principles encourage their manipulation and abuse for political or polemical ends. Many of the leading historical Muslim scholars who are now widely accepted as among the most respected and authoritative, like Abu Hanifa, Ibn Hanbal, al-Ghazali, Ibn Hazm, and Ibn Taymiyyah, were accused of apostasy in their own lifetime (Saeed and Saeed 2004, 30–31). These risks of manipulation and abuse also tend to diminish the possibilities for legitimate theological and jurisprudential reflection and development within any Islamic society or global community of believers *(Umma)*. These are compelling reasons for abolishing apostasy and all related notions in the best interests of Islam as a religion and of Islamic societies themselves, without any reference to international human rights norms. The best way to promote freedom of religion, and by extension other human rights, is to present an internal Islamic argument for protecting these rights among Muslims (An-Na'im 1996).

A dilemma facing those who support such reform in Islamic societies today is whether to seek their objectives through the existing corpus and methodology of traditional Shari'a or to attempt to avoid the limitations of that approach through purely secular legislation. In my view, both approaches have their drawbacks. On the one hand, reform within the traditional framework of Shari'a cannot achieve the complete abolition of the notion of apostasy and related concepts, because that would not be allowed by the existing methodology *(usul al-fiqh)* as formulated by Muslim scholars like al-Shafi'i 1,200 years ago. Traditional *usul al-fiqh* would support imposing the death penalty, or at least other legal restrictions, on an apostate because those penalties are believed to be based on the categorical texts of Sunna, though not of the Qur'an. At the same time, apostasy and related notions cannot simply be abolished through purely secular legislation without sufficient Islamic justification because of the paramount moral and social authority of Shari'a among Muslims. The effective and sustainable abolition of these notions as a matter of reinterpretation of Shari'a must therefore address their traditional Islamic rationale instead of simply relying on the authority of the secular state to abstain from imposing legal consequences.

Achieving the necessary degree of Islamic reform also requires the reformation of *usul al-fiqh*, because traditional as well as alternative interpretations of the Qur'an and Sunna are necessarily the product of the historical context of the Muslim society of a specific time and place. Thus, given the radical transformation of the political, social, and economic context of Islamic societies today, as compared with what prevailed when traditional understandings of Shari'a were developed, the methodology of interpretation must reflect present realities if it is to produce appropriate formulations of Shariʿa. This can be done, for example, by reexamining the rationale for enacting certain verses of the Qurʾan and texts of Sunna into Shariʿa principles and deemphasizing others as inapplicable in the context of early Islamic societies. Once it is appreciated that this selection was made by human beings, rather than decreed by direct divine command, it becomes possible to reconsider the question of which texts are to be enacted today and which are to be reemphasized in the present context.

There is also a political or contextual dimension to this internal theological debate. A reformer's ability to gain the confidence of a community and authority among its members not only depends on the theoretical coherence of his proposal but also is contingent on a variety of factors. This makes it difficult to tell in the short term whether a particular proposal has succeeded or failed. For instance, Ustadh Mahmoud Mohamed Taha presented what I believe to be a coherent and viable methodology for Islamic reform and advocated his views in Sudan for thirty-five years, from 1951 until his execution in January 1985 (An-Naʿim 1986, 197–223). In view of the long time it has often taken for significant ideas to take hold and social transformation to occur, it may be premature to declare this particular initiative dead and gone. In any case, the more important question is what I, as a Muslim, should do about such initiatives, instead of speculating about their survival or demise. I recall several occasions when someone said to Ustadh Mahmoud, "Your ideas are good, but when will people come to accept them?" He would respond, "You *are* the people—when are you going to accept these ideas?" But in deciding what to do about such initiatives, we must take into consideration political, economic, social, and cultural factors as well as the coherence and theoretical viability of the ideas.

Deciding what to do and how to do it includes a clear understanding of the nature of the state in question and its role in the particular society. The state has a critical role in these processes, not only in refraining from purporting to enforce Shariʿa as positive law but also by fostering the educational system, promoting critical thinking in the media, and generally securing the political and social space for dissent and free debate. But the state itself, and the international community at large, can also be part of the problem. The required political and social liberalization may appear to be, or in fact be, threatening for the elite who control the state, even when they claim to be secular in their political orientation. Other states may also be supportive of oppressive regimes in Islamic countries, or pursue hostile foreign-policy objectives that provoke conservatism and defensiveness in Islamic societies instead of the confidence and sense of security that would encourage internal political and social liberalization. Accordingly, while the primary responsibility for securing religious liberty in Islamic societies lies with Muslims themselves, the international community also has a critical role to play in creating the most conducive conditions for that effort to succeed. This brings me to the final issue, namely, the relevance of the idea of citizenship in this process, again from an Islamic perspective.

Citizenship

Whatever we may think of its legacy, European colonialism and its aftermath have drastically transformed the basis and the nature of political and social organization within and among territorial states where all Muslims live today (Piscatori 1986). This transformation is so profound and deeply entrenched, permeating all aspects of economic activities, political processes, social life, and communal relations, including the provision of education, health care, and other services, that a return to precolonial political philosophies and systems is practically impossible. Any change and adaptation of the present system can be sought or realized only through the concepts and institutions of this domestic and global postcolonial reality. Yet many Muslims, probably the majority in many countries, have not fully accepted some aspects of this transformation and its consequences. To contribute to clarifying and redressing this discrepancy, I will now focus on the question of citizenship, which has far-reaching implications for political stability, constitutional governance, and development at home and international relations abroad. In particular, I will argue for human rights as a framework for assessing and mediating the tension underlying the discrepancy regarding citizenship in present Islamic societies.

Human beings tend to seek and experience multiple and overlapping types and forms of membership in different groups on grounds such as ethnic, religious, or cultural identity as well as political, social, or professional affiliation and/or economic interests. The motivation to belong and the meaning of membership tend to be related to the rationale for or purpose of the group, without precluding or undermining other forms of membership. That is, multiple and overlapping memberships should not be mutually exclusive, as they tend to serve different purposes for persons and communities. This model is obviously a simplified ideal type, because such bases of membership are unlikely to be clearly defined, their interaction is complex and contingent on other factors, and people may not necessarily be consciously aware of them or consistently act accordingly. But the main point is that people tend consciously or unconsciously to belong to or identify with various groups for different purposes, and often not only with one group.

The term "citizenship" is used here to refer to a particular form of membership in the political community of a territorial state in its global context and should therefore be related to this specific rationale or purpose without precluding other possibilities of membership. This is not to suggest that people are always consciously aware of this form or type of membership or that they appreciate that it can be mutually inclusive of other forms of membership, each being appropriate for its specific purpose or rationale. In fact, this part of the chapter assumes that there is confusion among Muslims about the meaning and implications of citizenship in a territorial state, as distinguished from, but not exclusive of, other forms or types of membership.

It is important to note here that such confusion is not peculiar to Muslims or necessarily due to Islam. For instance, there is a general human tendency to conflate different forms of membership, as when ethnic or religious identity is equated with political or social affiliation. The development of the European model of the territorial nation-state beginning in the eighteenth century not only tended to equate citizenship with nationality but has also continued to struggle with the genuine practical equality of citizens up to the present time (Heater 2004). Considering citizenship to be synonymous with nationality is misleading, because membership in the political community of a territorial state does not necessarily coincide with a subjective feeling of belonging, nor show any regard for how people feel about being identified as "belonging" to one conception of the nation or another. The rights of citizens are also subjected to a variety of legal limitations in theory and serious restrictions in practice, as recently seen in the controversy over headscarf issues in France and other West European countries, noted earlier. The conception and practice of citizenship in a territorial state as nationalism has become the undisputed norm in domestic politics and international relations throughout the world, including all Islamic societies. Even the notions of identity and sovereignty that underlie claims of self-determination are now founded on these same European models. Fortunately, these conceptions have continued to evolve and reflect the experiences of other societies, especially through the decolonization process and the development of universal human rights norms since the mid-twentieth century.

It is this evolving conception of citizenship, sovereignty, and self-determination that I am proposing that Muslims accept and work with as a matter of principle and not merely as a pragmatic concession to postcolonial realities. It is true that Muslims everywhere have already accepted a basic concept of citizenship as the foundation of the domestic constitutional and political systems of their countries, as well as of the relations of those countries with the rest of the world. Indeed, citizenship is the basis of relations among Muslims, such that I would need a visa issued by the government of Saudi Arabia to be able to go to *hajj* there and could not expect to be admitted into that country simply because I am a Muslim wishing to perform my religious obligation. While citizenship is accepted in general terms, we again must take the next step. My objective, therefore, is to develop and promote the principle of citizenship among Muslims in such a way that they can uphold and strive to realize a positive and proactive understanding of equal citizenship for *all*, without distinction on the grounds of religion, sex, ethnicity, language, or political opinion. Citizenship should signify a shared understanding of equal human dignity for all and a fully inclusive and effective political participation to ensure the government accountability for respecting and protecting human rights for all.

The desirability of this understanding of citizenship throughout the world can no doubt be founded on a variety of considerations, including purely pragmatic realities of power relations within and among societies, as indicated earlier. However, it also requires the development of multiple religious, philosophical, and/or moral foundations for a definition of citizenship that is consistent with universal human rights norms. This combination of moral and pragmatic foundations can be seen in what is known as the Golden Rule, or the principle of reciprocity *(muʿawada)* in Islamic discourse (An-Naʿim 1990). Treating each other with mutual respect and empathy is required by a shared moral sensibility among different religious and philosophical traditions, and is a prerequisite for realistic expectations of reciprocal treatment. Thus persons and communities everywhere should affirm a shared conception of equal citizenship in order to be able to claim it for themselves at home and abroad. That is, acceptance of this understanding of citizenship on the basis of universal human rights is the prerequisite for the moral, legal, and political basis of its enjoyment.

Muslims are already working with these ideas under domestic constitutional law and international law, as well as through cooperation with other people in the broader processes of defining and implementing universal human rights. These international standards and processes are in turn contributing to the process of defining and protecting the rights of citizens at the domestic level. The relationship between human rights and citizenship is therefore inherent to these two mutually supportive concepts. When citizenship is defined from a human rights point of view, it enables Muslims as citizens to participate more effectively in defining and implementing human rights. That in turn will improve their enjoyment of citizenship. This view of the relationship of these two concepts assumes that governments that are bound by international law and human rights treaties are representative of their citizens. Unfortunately, this is obviously not true of some parts of the world, especially in Africa and Asia, where the majority of Muslims live.

The challenge, therefore, is how to apply this human rights approach effectively to citizenship, which will in turn contribute to realizing the assumption of democratic governance and accountability. The question is how to use existing resources, including the already accepted concepts of citizenship and human rights, in order to promote those same resources. This process of mutual development of citizenship and human rights is subject to a large and complex web of factors and actors that are local, domestic, and international. Those negative perceptions and hegemonic power relations that diminish the effectiveness and relevance of constitutionalism and human rights noted earlier also apply to the field of citizenship and its relationship to human rights. It is therefore with a clear understanding of the complexity of the process and its unpredictable outcomes that I am focusing in the following discussion on the traditional Shari'a notion of *dhimma* in accordance with the objective of this book. As explained below, the concept of *dhimma* signified the protection of some basic rights and limited communal autonomy for specific groups of non-Muslims *(ahl al-dhimma)* in exchange for their submission to Muslim sovereignty (Gibb and Kramers 1991, 75–76; Ayoub 2004, 25–26). While that system is simply untenable as the basis of citizenship in the territorial states where all Muslims live today, it continues to have a strong influence on the attitudes and behavior of Muslims.

The Dhimma *System in Historical Perspectives*

The following review of the traditional *dhimma* system requires clarification of two elements of methodological confusion, which underlie some apologetic Islamic discourse that misrepresents Shari'a principles or subjects them to immediate and arbitrary reformulation (see, for example, Doi 1981; Khan

2003). First, our focus here is on how the founding scholars of Shari'a actually understood the relevant texts of the Qur'an and Sunna in a systematic manner. We must be clear on the existing Shari'a principles of *dhimma* before we can examine possibilities of reform. Second, any proposed reform must follow a clear and systematic methodology instead of arbitrary selectivity among different sources, because such claims can be repudiated simply by citing countersources. It is not helpful to cite texts of the Qur'an and Sunna that apparently support equality for non-Muslims without addressing those that can be cited in support of the opposite view.

The traditional system of *dhimma* as it was actually developed by Muslim scholars was part of a worldview that determined political allegiance on the basis of religious affiliation, in contrast to present notions of allegiance to a territorial state (Morony 2004, 1–23). As such, this view sought to shift political allegiance from tribal ties to Islam, thereby making membership in the political community accessible to all human beings who accepted that religious belief. As early Muslims believed themselves to be the recipients of the final and conclusive divine revelation, they assumed that they had a paramount and permanent obligation to propagate Islam through *jihad*, which included but was not limited to military conquest (Khadduri 1955, 56–57; Khadduri 1966, 15).

Accordingly, the founding scholars of Shari'a maintained that Muslims should initially offer Islam peacefully. If that offer was rejected, then they should fight unbelievers into submission and impose on them what Muslims believed were the imperative precepts of Islam (Lambton 1985, 147–150). That system was therefore premised on a sharp distinction between the territories of Islam *(dar al-Islam)*, where Muslims ruled and Shari'a was supposed to prevail, and the territories of those at war with Muslims *(dar al-harb)* (Parvin and Sommer 1980, 3). The underlying vision was that the obligation to propagate Islam through military as well as peaceful means remains until the whole world becomes *dar al-Islam*. That view was no doubt encouraged by the remarkable initial success of Muslim conquests from North Africa and southern Spain in the west to Persia, central Asia, and northern India in the east within decades of the Prophet's death. However, as the practical limitations of indefinite expansion became clearer over time, Muslim rulers had to conclude peace treaties *(sulh)* with unbelievers, which scholars acknowledged as legitimate, thereby accepting the inviolability of the territory of those at peace with Muslims *(dar al-sulh)* (Hamidullah 1968, 158–179; Khadduri 1955, 162–169, 243–244, 245–246).

According to the original model of Muslim/non-Muslim relations, which developed during the seventh and eighth centuries, Shari'a classified all human beings into three main religious categories: Muslims, People of the Book *(ahl al-kitab,* those who are accepted by Muslims as having a revealed scripture—mainly Christians and Jews), and unbelievers. For example, the status of People of the Book was extended by some Muslim scholars to Magians on the assumption that they had a revealed scripture (Yusuf 1963, 128–130). But the basic scheme that remained was not changed or modified from a Shari'a point of view, thereby making Muslims the only full members of the political community; People of the Book were partial members. Unbelievers *(kufar)* did not qualify for any legal recognition or protection as such, unless granted temporary safe conduct *(aman)* for practical reasons, such as trade and diplomatic representation (Gibb and Kramers 1991, 206; see "Kafir").

The term *dhimma* referred to a compact between the state ruled by Muslims and a community of People of the Book, whereby members of that community were granted security of their persons and property, the freedom to practice their religion in private, and communal autonomy to govern their internal affairs. In exchange, the community of People of the Book undertook to pay a poll tax *(jizya)* and observe the terms of their compact with the state (Gibb and Kramers 1991, 91; Ali 1978, 22–23). Those granted *dhimma* status were encouraged to embrace Islam but not allowed to propagate their own faith. Common features of *dhimma* compacts included restriction on participation in the public affairs of the state and on holding public office where it entailed exercising authority over Muslims (Doi 1981, 115–116). However, the actual terms of these compacts varied over time, and their practical application was not always consistent with their theory for a variety of pragmatic reasons, as illustrated below. However, the members of *dhimma* communities were by definition not entitled to equality with Muslims, who themselves did not have full citizenship in the modern sense of the term. Unbelievers were presumed to be at war with Muslims (owing allegiance to *dar al-harb),* unless they were granted temporary safe conduct to travel through or reside in territories ruled by Muslims *(dar al-Islam)* (Ali 2000, 236). The status and rights of those people who belonged to the territories that had a peace treaty with Muslims *(dar al-sulh)* were determined in accordance with the terms of that agreement (Newby 2002, 51). When considered in its proper historical context, however, the *dhimma* system not only reflected the prevalent standards of governance and intercommunal relations throughout the world at the time but also compared favorably to other systems. This system is now obviously completely untenable, as illustrated by the case of Sudan, where the failure to acknowledge this reality has resulted in decades of destructive civil war in the southern part of the country (An-Na'im and Deng 1997, 199–223; Deng 1995).

In my view, there is no alternative to the rule of law in international relations and the protection of human rights in domestic settings. International legality and human rights can be upheld only when each society upholds the values of equality and the rule of law in its own domestic and foreign policies and thereby has the moral and political standing to demand the same from other societies. For our purposes here, this means not only the formal abolition of the *dhimma* system from a Shari'a point of view but also the repudiation of its underlying values by Muslims so that they can more fully internalize and implement modern notions of citizenship as defined above. Once again, this trend has already begun among Muslims, and the question is how to develop it further and secure it against regression.

From the Dhimma *System to Human Rights–based Citizenship*

A human rights–based view of citizenship means that the substantive norms, procedures, and processes of this status should be derived from, or at least be consistent with, present universal human rights standards. As discussed above, the essential purpose of human rights is to ensure the effective protection of certain key entitlements of all human beings everywhere, regardless of whether or not these rights are protected by the constitutional system of a country. International human rights treaties do not define citizenship as such, but several of the principles enshrined in the treaties are relevant or applicable. These include the fundamental principles of self-determination, equality, and nondiscrimination on various grounds, including religion, provided for by Article 1(2) and (3) of the Charter of the United Nations of 1945, which is a treaty that is legally binding on all countries where Muslims live today. These same principles are reaffirmed in the subsequent human rights treaties, like Articles 1 and 2 of both the International Covenant on Economic, Social, and Cultural Rights and the International Covenant on Civil and Political Rights, both of 1966. These two covenants and other human rights treaties also provide for specific human rights, such as equality before the law and freedom of religion, to which non-Muslim citizens of Islamic countries are equally entitled (Cassese 1995).

The realization of the proposed human rights–based concept of citizenship among Muslims can be achieved through a combination of three elements. The first element is the actual transition from the *dhimma* system to formal citizenship in the postcolonial era. The second element is the means to sustain and develop that transition through methodologically sound and politically sustainable Islamic reform in order to root constitutional and human rights values in Islamic doctrine. The third is the consolidation of these two elements into an indigenous discourse that transcends the present limitations and weaknesses of the concept of citizenship and its practice in Islamic societies. These elements can be seen in the transitions of India and Turkey from the last imperial states into European-model territorial states by the early twentieth century. However, as further explained and evaluated in Chapters 4 and 5, the transformation of citizenship in those countries was ambivalent and contested and remains vulnerable to regression and setbacks to the present day.

Islam was first taken to the Indian subcontinent within decades of the Prophet's death, but it took several centuries for Muslims to become a minority ruling class in various parts of India (Qureshi 1970, 3–34). Despite their diverse ethnic and cultural origins (immigrant Turkic, Afghan, Persian, and Arab people as well as native converts of various backgrounds), the Muslims of India gradually evolved traditions of toleration and coexistence that facilitated their interaction and assimilation with other religious communities of the subcontinent. However, this coexistence was more in terms of mutual accommodation with Hindu feudal lords and other elite groups than of broad acceptance of the citizenship of the population at large (Rizvi 1970, 67). This is not a criticism, since this concept was unknown anywhere in the world at that time and for many centuries to come.

As discussed in Chapter 4, the system of state employment and administration developed by Akbar (1542–1605) incorporated all interests and groups in the same graded hierarchy. But a combination of technological and administrative stagnation, civil wars, and regional invasions slowly resulted in the disintegration of the Mogul Empire during the eighteenth century (Qureshi 1970, 52–57). Efforts to halt the advance of British colonialism, like those of Shah Wali Allah (1703–1772) to revive the notion of a Shari'a state and the *jihad* movement of Sayyid Ahmad Barelwi (1786–1831), Hajji Shari'at Allah (1781–1840), and Hajji Muhsin (1819–1862), all failed (Rizvi 1970, 71–74). Economic dislocations flowing from the expanding influence of the East India Company, coupled with changes in revenue and judicial administration introduced by British administrators in the late eighteenth century, contributed to the decline of the power and authority of Muslims (Rizvi 1970, 77).

Through a range of political, military, and economic strategies designed to expand its influence, the British crown finally assumed control of the government throughout India by the mid-nineteenth century. Some Muslim leaders, like Sayyid Ahmad Khan (1817–1898), adopted a positive attitude to the British and general Western influence, but he was also ambivalent about the concept and the scope of citizenship in India. He combined commitment to the modernization of India as a united nation with elitist suspicion of popular democratic institutions. His effort to mobilize Muslim opposition to the Indian National Congress also represented a precursor to the politics of the struggle for independence that culminated in the partition of India and Pakistan by 1947 (Rizvi 1970, 67–96). It is not possible to review these developments here, except to note that they reflect both Hindu resentment of earlier Muslim hegemony, including elements of the *dhimma* system, and Muslim apprehensions of Hindu domination. Ironically, while so many Muslims remained citizens of India, partition did not achieve the benefits of citizenship for the Muslims of Pakistan. In both countries, the concept of citizenship needs to be developed and protected against the risk of divisions between Muslims and non-Muslims (Ahmad 1970, 97–119).

As explained in Chapter 5, a similar evolution of citizenship occurred during the transformation of the late Ottoman Empire into the Republic of Turkey. The flexibility and fluidity of the Ottoman *millet* system in west Asia and North Africa already represented a far-reaching and irreversible retreat from traditional notions of the *dhimma* system in response to the pragmatic economic, military, and social realities. Those preexisting realities probably facilitated and were in turn enhanced by the processes of Western penetration and Ottoman capitulation that eventually transformed the empire and set the scene for the transition of Turkey into a secular republic by the 1920s. Another factor to note in that process is the rise of nationalist movements among Muslims (such as Arabs and Albanians), as well as among Christian minorities, which resulted in the establishment of territorial states based on the modern principle of citizenship. While protracted and gradual, the most significant shift in the Ottoman policy and practice started with the Tanzimat decree of 1839, which began the process of officially affirming the legal equality of all non-Muslim and Muslim subjects of the sultan (Küçük 1986, 1007–1024). While the Tanzimat decree did acknowledge Shariʿa as the law of the empire, the Ottoman decree of 1856 simply asserted the equal status of non-Muslims, abolished the *jizya*, and prohibited derogatory treatment of or reference to *dhimma* communities and their members, without any reference to Islamic principles. Various aspects of the modern principles of equality before the law and nondiscrimination on the grounds of religion were enacted in Articles 8 to 22 of the Ottoman Constitution of 1876. Those principles were consolidated by the subsequent constitutional development during the rest of the Ottoman years and further entrenched during the republican era after 1926.

Processes of transition similar to those of India and the Ottoman Empire evolved throughout the Muslim world during the twentieth century and came to be formally established during the decolonization processes after the Second World War. As a result, the *dhimma* system is neither practiced nor advocated anywhere in the Muslim world today, which has been fully integrated into the modern international system of territorial states (Saeed and Saeed 2004, 13–14). Although these transformations have been formally instituted by European colonialism, all Islamic societies have voluntarily continued the same system since independence. Far from expressing any reservations or attempting to modify this system at either the domestic or the international level, governments ruling Islamic societies are now actively engaged in the operation of this system at home and abroad (Piscatori 1986). But the tension with the traditional notions of *dhimma* and its underlying values persists, as illustrated by controversies in Indonesia about whether it is permissible for Muslims to extend Christmas greetings to Christians or to enter into interfaith marriage (Aqsha, van der Meij, and Meuleman 1995, 470–473); civil war in southern Sudan (Jok 2001); and lethal riots over the enforcement of Shari'a in northern Nigerian states since 2001 (Ilesanmi 2001, 529–554). This tension calls for the support of transitions to citizenship through methodologically sound and politically sustainable Islamic reform.

To recall the earlier discussion of this subject, the main premise of a viable Islamic reform process is that Muslim belief that the Qur'an and Sunna are the divine sources of Islam does not imply that their meaning and implementation in everyday life are independent of human interpretation and action in specific historical contexts. In fact, it is simply impossible to know and apply Shari'a in this life except through the agency of human beings, since the Qur'an is expressed in Arabic (human language) and relates to specific historical experiences of actual societies. Any view accepted by Muslims as being a part of Shariʿa today or at any other time, even if unanimously agreed to, necessarily emerged from the opinion of human beings about the meanings of the Qurʾan and Sunna or the practices of Islamic communities. Such opinions and practices became a part of Shariʿa through the consensus of believers over many centuries and not by the spontaneous decree of a ruler or will of a single group of scholars. It therefore follows that alternative formulations of Shariʿa principles are always possible and can be equally valid if accepted as such by Muslims. Moreover, a sound reform methodology should also address the two concerns indicated at the beginning of the preceding section. First, those undertaking reform efforts must be clear about the preexisting principles of Shariʿa as established by Muslim scholars and not confuse them with possible reinterpretations. Second, we must avoid arbitrary selectivity among competing Qurʾan and Sunna texts without addressing texts that can be cited in support of the opposite view.

An Islamic reform methodology that is based on the premise cited above and that meets the noted requirements was proposed by Ustadh Mahmoud Mohamed Taha, who argued for a shift in the basis of social and political aspects of Shariʿa from verses included in the Medina phase of the revelation of the Qurʾan (622–632) to those revealed during the Mecca period (610–622). To simplify and summarize, the rationale for this proposed shift is that earlier revelations represented the universal message of Islam, while the later ones were specific responses to the historical context of human societies at the time. Ustadh Mahmoud also demonstrated the temporary rationale for the notions of aggressive *jihad,* subordination of women to men, and subordination of non-Muslims to Muslims that underlie the *dhimma* system, as revealed during the Medina phase. The basic point here is that Islam was offered first through the peaceful propagation of its universal message during the Mecca period. But when that was shown to be unrealistic in the context of seventh-century Arabia, a more historically appropriate message was advanced during the Medina period, which sanctioned the use of aggressive *jihad* and subordination of non-Muslims. Thus the chronologically later message of Medina came to be implemented first as Shariʿa after the seventh century. Asserting that it is now possible to implement the earlier message of peaceful propagation and nondiscrimination, Ustadh Mahmoud calls for that shift to be achieved through a fresh concept and methodology of juridical reasoning *(ijtihad).*

In this way, the methodology proposed by Ustadh Mahmoud is able explicitly to set aside those verses underlying the *dhimma* system as a matter of Shari'a, although they remain part of the Qur'an. Since the process of selecting which verses of the Qur'an are applicable and which are not was always the work of Muslim jurists, earlier choices can be replaced by new ones simply as a revision of what Muslims did in the past, not of the Qur'an and Sunna themselves. This framework provides a coherent and systematic methodology of interpretation of the Qur'an and Sunna, instead of the arbitrary selectivity of other modern scholars, who fail to explain what happens to the verses they choose to overlook. Relevant revelations from the Mecca period can support the development of a modern concept of citizenship from an Islamic point of view (Taha 1987; An-Na'im 1990). While I find this approach very convincing, I remain open to another, similarly sound methodology that is capable of achieving the necessary degree of reform.

But assuming that this or another reform methodology is sound and applicable from an Islamic perspective, why should it be deployed to abolish the traditional *dhimma* system? One reason, emphasized earlier, is the Golden Rule, or the Islamic principle of reciprocity: Muslims must affirm equality for others in order to be entitled to the same. A second Islamic view is that it is hypocritical to uphold the *dhimma* system in theory while fully realizing that it has not been observed in practice nor is it likely to be workable in the future. Maintaining such unrealistic interpretations of Shari'a in theory while discarding them in practice seriously undermines the credibility and coherence of Islam as a religion. In response to claims that the proposed shift is unlikely to be accepted by Muslims, I would simply ask for the idea to be freely and openly presented to them to decide. To allow for the possibility of open and free debate of such issues among Muslims, it is necessary to maintain complete and unconditional freedom of opinion, expression, and belief. Human beings are not responsible for their decisions and actions unless they have freedom of choice, which cannot be exercised without the ability to present and evaluate all relevant information, to debate and assess different arguments.

This is why I am emphasizing the critical role of constitutionalism and human rights as the framework and safeguards for negotiating the relationship among Islam, the state, and society in the present context of Islamic societies. All of this requires that public authorities maintain law and order, regulate debate and reflection, and adjudicate disagreements in accordance with fair and reasonable principles that are implemented by transparent and accountable institutions. It would therefore follow that securing constitutional governance and protection of human rights is necessary not only for the religious freedom of Muslim and non-Muslim citizens of the present territorial state but for the survival and development of Islam itself. Indeed, freedom of dissent and debate was always essential for the development of Shari'a, because that enabled ideas to emerge and for consensus to evolve around them until they matured into established principles through acceptance and practice by generations of Muslims in a wide variety of settings. Instead of censorship, which is inherently counterproductive for the development of any Islamic doctrine, it is critical to maintain possibilities of innovation and dissent as the only way for religion to remain responsive to the needs of believers.

Throughout this book, I am emphasizing an Islamic perspective to maintain the religious neutrality of the state despite the connectedness of Islam and politics. But an underlying tension regarding concepts like constitutionalism, human rights, and citizenship from this perspective relates to the relationship between their formulations in Western societies and their application to Islamic societies in Africa and Asia. Can such concepts, developed through the experiences of Western societies, be applied in other settings? Yes: I believe this to be not only possible but also necessary, provided that the ideas, assumptions, and institutions associated with these principles are adapted to better fit the local context of different societies.

The application of these principles to Islamic societies is necessary because these societies have continued to live under European models of the territorial state since independence from colonialism. These models of the territorial state are likely to continue as the dominant framework of domestic politics and international relations for the foreseeable future. Even globalizing trends and regional integration represented by such bodies as the European Union and the African Union still operate through the agency of the state, often facing strong resistance from the proponents of traditional notions of national/territorial sovereignty. These realities require the implementation of the principles of constitutionalism, human rights, and citizenship, which have been found to be necessary for regulating the powers of the state and organizing its relationship to individuals and communities under this model. It is therefore desirable to develop these principles as parameters for domestic politics within Islamic societies as well as in their relations with other societies around the world.

However developed or clear at a theoretical level, concepts like constitutionalism, human rights, and citizenship still need to be specified and adapted for local application in a given setting. To be relevant and useful, such theoretical principles must answer questions and concerns arising from the socioeconomic and political context and cultural traditions of each society. It logically follows from this requirement of adaptation of universal principles that the process may or may not work in relation to a specific place at a given point in time. Failures or setbacks in this process are also likely to occur at different points on a continuum, from minor discrepancies regarding practical arrangements for such matters as separation of powers or judicial review to major incompatibility on fundamental or substantial aspects of constitutionalism. A failure to adapt such universal principles to local conditions can also lead to varying degrees of difficulty or ease of correction.

I would therefore recommend focusing on *internal dynamics and processes* to establish and consolidate constitutionalism, human rights, and citizenship within Islamic societies on their own terms and not as a Western imposition. The failures or setbacks we see in present Islamic societies are necessary for the evolution and the establishment of these concepts and are the basis for more successes in the future. The process-and-practice-based approach I am proposing allows for a richer and deeper analysis by requiring us to address the complex social, cultural, and political dynamics within which a range of state and nonstate actors, individuals, and communities, as well as ethnic, social, and religious groups, understand and relate to various concepts and their implementation. Instead of taking an apparent failure as indicative of an inherent defect in society, we should consider the possibility that such an outcome may in fact reflect a weakness in the concept itself or its adaptation to the specific society. It is arrogant and simplistic to assume that any concept or framework is so definitive that there must be something wrong with the facts if they fail to fit the proposed theory.

As emphasized at the beginning of this chapter, the particular relevance of these principles is their critical role as the framework for negotiating the relationship between Islam and the state, on the one hand, and Islam and politics, on the other. The review of the features of the modern state at the beginning of that first section is relevant because of the continuation of the European models of territorial states, whether Muslims constitute the majority or the minority of the population. The brief clarification of the distinction I make between politics and the state is in accordance with my main proposal of separating Islam from the state while maintaining the connection between Islam and politics. As I explained in Chapter 1, the separation of Islam and the state does not mean that Islam is relegated to the purely private domain; Islamic principles can still be proposed for adoption by the state as official public policy or legislation. But such proposals must be supported by civic reason, which means that reasons can be debated among all citizens without reference to religious beliefs. But the practical operation of civic reason requires the safeguards of constitutionalism, human rights, and citizenship.

CHAPTER **4**

India:
State Secularism and
Communal Violence

This chapter examines the tension between the secularism of the Indian state and the realities of communal violence and interfaith relations in current Indian society. This issue is approached with reference to the historical context of the relationship among Islam, the state, and politics, which goes back to at least the eleventh century. The underlying concern is the influence of the relationship between the Indian Muslim community and the state, as well as other religious communities, on legitimizing and securing secularism as a deeply contextual concept and practice that is negotiated over time. This focus raises highly controversial issues, including questions about the religious motivations of rulers in the past, perceptions of self and others among Muslims and Hindus, and the degree of syncretism in Indian social identities. There is disagreement about the theoretical and methodological frameworks of analysis and questions about the availability of independent or verifiable evidence regarding various claims and counterclaims as well as the viability of interpretations about substantive issues. There is an equally rich discussion and strong disagreement regarding the character of Indian state secularism, its Western and indigenous roots, and its failings and successes in postcolonial India. This chapter does not seek to intervene in these specific debates or to assess each scholarly position conclusively, but only to highlight aspects that seem to underlie the legacy of tension between official state secularism and communal relations in present-day India.

There are two lines of inquiry that can be traced through Indian history. The first concerns the relationship between political and religious power in general, including how political and religious authorities have sought to influence society, whether separation or conflation of political and religious authority has been the norm, the consequences of changes in established patterns of the balance of power, and so on. The second line of inquiry relates to the historical relationship among religious communities, particularly Muslims and Hindus, the orientation of the state toward these communities, and how those historical experiences influence current communal tensions. However, the emphasis on communal tension between Hindus and Muslims in this chapter is not intended to overlook the fact of syncretic and overlapping identities, nor to deny the historical realities of coexistence. Reference to some precedents of communal tension also does not imply that Hindus and Muslims have always understood themselves and others in monolithic terms as essentially different peoples. The limited purpose in tracking the history of communal tensions through historical phases is to note the antecedents of the colonial construction of Indian religious identities along such divisive lines and to understand the role of that history in the strained situation of interfaith relations in postcolonial India. The values and sustainable practice of secularism, pluralism, and constitutionalism can be founded only on a clear and pragmatic understanding of historical and current relations and conditions.

It has recently been asserted that "there is broad consensus that there does exist a contemporary 'crisis of secularism' [although] how it is to be interpreted and what, if anything, is to be done about it are matters of vigorous intellectual and political debate" (Needham and Rajan 2007, 1). Addressing such issues is beyond the scope of this book, but as my argument in this chapter will show, responses to this crisis should include an acknowledgment of histories that may not perfectly translate into the model of constitutional secularism but nevertheless provide a basis for values (such as coexistence and tolerance) that are consonant with constitutional secularism. I will return to this theme in the concluding section.

Islam, the State, and Politics in the Precolonial Period

Islam entered the Indian subcontinent, beginning in the eighth century, through conquest, trade, and conversion. The conquest of Sind in northwestern India by Muhammad bin Qasim in 712 CE for the Umayyad dynasty is usually cited as the first contact between Islam and the subcontinent. Muslim Arab traders began settling on the west coast of India but did not propagate Islam, because their chief objectives were economic (Bose and Jalal 1998, 24). The eleventh century saw attacks by Mahmud of Ghazni on northwestern India, including the ransacking of the Hindu temple of

Somnath. In 1192, Muhammad Ghori, a Turk, defeated the Rajput ruler Prithviraj Chauhan. Ghori's victory led to the establishment in 1206 of the Delhi sultanate, which was established primarily in northern India and ruled through various dynasties until 1526.

During the fourteenth century, an Indo-Muslim culture began to emerge, reflecting Turkish-Persian features in the north and Arabic elements in the southern and western coastal regions (Bose and Jalal 1998, 28). Multiple cultural encounters resulted in a distinct Indo-Islamic historical identity, with India as the center of an oceanic culture extending from the Mediterranean to Southeast Asia (Bose and Jalal 1998, 26). When the Delhi sultanate ended, in the early sixteenth century, Babar founded the Mogul Empire, which lasted from 1526 until the mid-eighteenth century, when it began to decline in the face of the rising power of the British East India Company, a precursor of British colonialism. The Delhi sultanate and Mogul Empire periods of so-called Muslim rule reflected a combination of relative autonomy and interdependence between religious and political authority. As the following review will show, that period was largely characterized by coexistence and tolerance in Hindu-Muslim relations, but there is also evidence of Hindu-Muslim as well as intra-Muslim tensions.

The historical or traditional pattern of relationship between religion and political authority in India was one of interdependence. The obligations of the ruler included support of religious institutions and authority and the enforcement of religious conformity. Religious leaders in turn advised the ruler and affirmed the religious legitimacy of his temporal power (Smith 1999, 184). Hindu, Buddhist, Muslim, and Sikh rulers all sought to legitimize state power in terms of religious authority. In the early Hindu polity, religion had the upper hand over political authority, but it began to require state support as new religions emerged in India between 1500 and 500 BCE. While the boundaries between political and religious authority were contested, "the known record suggests a continuous and growing accommodation between religious and state authority founded on the seal of legitimacy and exchanged for protection and favor" (Buultjens 1986, 96–97). The early separation of secular and religious authority was also reflected in the Hindu caste system, which distinguished between individuals ordained by birth to perform different social functions. Such factors seem to have "prevented the formation of strong states with uniformity of religious beliefs; rulers of empires with the widest sway protected diversity" (Mansingh 1991, 298).

The early Arab Muslim rulers of Sind did not radically alter the structures of Indian political authority (Bose and Jalal 1998, 27). Delhi sultans also followed indigenous political traditions, although they introduced some innovations. "The core military and economic institutions of these [Delhi] dynasties were thus not specifically 'Islamic'. The sultans themselves were not religious leaders. Like non-Muslim rulers, they did not gain their authority through their own holiness or sacred learning but through their military and governing skill" (Metcalf and Metcalf 2002, 4). Political expediency prevailed over Islamic orthodoxy from the very beginning, when Muhammad bin Qasim incorporated upper-caste Hindus into his administration, and Turkish rulers of the sultanate, in their time, also needed the help of native populations who were predominantly non-Muslim (Mansingh 1991, 299). While acknowledging allegiance to the caliph and considering their territories part of the territory of Islam *(dar al-Islam),* almost none of the sultans insisted on the application of Shariʿa (Madan 1997, 114). Muslim and Hindu rulers had alliances, as well as conflicts, based on political rather than religious considerations. Subjects professed loyalty to a ruler regardless of his religion, and armies were not based on the ruler's religious affiliation (Mansingh 1991, 299).

In the sultanate, the Hanafi school was the official standard of religious authority and the foundation of justice and religious education (Mujeeb 1967, 58). But Shariʿa was not consistently followed in social life, nor was it the authoritative basis of administration or justice. Shariʿa regulations of commerce were rendered ineffectual because non-Muslims controlled trade, and inheritance rules could not be imposed on the converted Muslim communities, which preferred to follow customary practices. For the majority of Muslims, Shariʿa was "only an object of reverence, not a body of law that was, or could be, enforced" (Mujeeb 1967, 213).

State and religion were for the most part separate, and Shariʿa was not uniformly imposed in matters of criminal law, though it might have happened occasionally at the instigation of the *ulama* (Afif 1891, 211). For example, the institution of consultation *(shura)* was never used to settle matters of political succession, which were decided through war and other strategies (Afif 1891, 48–49). Muslim rulers like Balban (ruled 1266–1286), for instance, did not observe Shariʿa limitations on their own authority as kings (Mujeeb 1967, 73). Balban's primary concern was the welfare of the state, and he often disregarded the provisions of Shariʿa in this respect (Afif 1891, 47–48). Alauddin Khilji also did not believe it possible to establish an Islamic state in India, stating that his actions as ruler were motivated by the good of the state and not whether they were in conformity with Shari'a (Chandra 1997, 77). Yet rulers had to respect the consensus of the *ulama* on doctrinal issues, as they needed their confirmation that the state was governed according to Shari'a (Madan 2004, 102; Hasan 2002, 102). This tension was compounded by disagreements between the *ulama* on many issues. Some pressured the ruler to ban actions of Sufis as un-Islamic. Others were keen to keep the state and/or ruler out of religious matters (Nizami 1958, 23, 47; Hasan 2002, 101–102). There are also examples of relatively greater conflation of religion and state during the sultanate period, in one direction or another. Muhammad bin Tughlaq (ruled 1325–1351) appears to have subordinated religion to political authority. He ordered that some religious authorities be killed for not cooperating with the government (Afif 1891, 491–492). In contrast, his successor, Firuz Tughlaq (ruled 1351–1388), implemented Shari'a with puritanical zeal, including applying it in matters of state finance and taxation (Nizami 1958, 111).

Sharp variations in the relationship between state and religious authorities could be observed during the Mogul Empire, balancing the influence of orthodox *ulama* in state affairs with political considerations, such as enlisting Hindu support through alliances and emphasizing religious tolerance. Akbar, the third Mogul emperor (ruled 1556–1605), combined pre-Islamic Iranian norms of royal authority with Hindu and Muslim traditions. Although hierarchical, the state offered opportunity for individual advancement through merit, and it was inclusive and just. The ruler claimed legitimacy directly from God, not from any specific religion, implying the religious equality of all his subjects (Ali 1978, 41). At the same time, Akbar sought to subordinate religious—specifically Islamic—authority to state power through a manifesto in 1579 in which he declared himself the final arbiter on any matters on which the *ulama* disagreed. Even in this, he was aware of the need to invoke religious authority by having leading *ulama* of the court sign a statement declaring him the caliph and the sultan of Islam, thereby officially severing the symbolic allegiance to the caliphate of the Middle East. Akbar was not necessarily seeking new powers compared to those of earlier rulers; he sought only to formalize the autonomy of his domain through a document that was affirmed by the court *ulama*. Though primarily symbolic, the strategy drew protest from the independent *ulama* and caused rebellions throughout the empire (Mujeeb 1967, 242–243). A different approach was adopted by Aurangzeb during his long reign (1658–1707). While he was also motivated by economic and social factors, Aurangzeb's policies clearly indicated an invocation of religion to justify repressive measures. Public inspectors *(muhtasibs)* in all provinces were entrusted with the task of ensuring conformity to Shari'a. Aurangzeb's reign also saw the resurgence of the orthodox religious establishment under the ruler's patronage, which may be explained in terms of his need for religious legitimacy, since he was viewed as having usurped the throne.

There are conflicting views on the question of conversion and the status of Hindu subjects during Muslim rule (Metcalf and Metcalf 2002, 6–7; Mansingh 1991, 299; Madan 2004, 119). The generalization that can be drawn from the evidence viewed in its totality is that for the most part, the subjects, Hindus or Muslims, of the sultanate and Mogul states were allowed to follow their own customs, though some rulers did not uphold that policy consistently. This reading suggests that from the rule of Muhammad bin Qasim in the eighth century onward, Hindus were largely allowed to follow their own customs as *dhimmis,* or protected subjects. One author quotes the instruction from the caliph to Muhammad bin Qasim regarding the non-Muslim population of Sind: "They have been taken under our protection . . . Permission is given them to worship their gods. Nobody must be forbidden or prevented from following his religion. They may live in their houses in whatever manner they like" (Mansingh 1991, 293). They could drink wine and eat pork, and were granted equal protection of life, including the same monetary compensation for wrongful death or injury as Muslims. If a *dhimmi* could bring a wasteland under cultivation, it became his property, as was the case for Muslims (Khan 1995, 44). Later, in the Mogul era, Akbar emphasized interreligious dialogue and deemed Hindus and Muslims equal subjects of the state. He abolished the pilgrimage tax on Hindus in 1563 and the *jizya* in 1564 and established a temple grant in 1565 (Khan 1997, 85).

It seems that the technical status of Hindus as *dhimmis* was more a concern of the *ulama* than of rulers, and *jizya* collection appears more the exception than the rule, but it is difficult to draw a picture of systematic practice. Under Muhammad bin Qasim, Buddhists and Hindus, as *dhimmis,* had to pay the *jizya* to the ruler; Brahmans were exempt from it, but Firuz Tughlaq extended the tax to them as well (Schimmel 1980, 4–5). Akbar is said to have been intolerant of Hindus early in his life and forcibly converted many to Islam (Khan 1997, 84–85). In the early phase of his rule, Aurangzeb banned the Zoroastrian festival of Nauroz, encouraged conversion, and reimposed the pilgrimage tax on Hindus in addition to the *jizya.* But there were also instances of persecution of particular Muslim groups, such as the Isma'ili Shi'a, *ulama* of the Chishti school, and Mahdawis (Khan 1997, 84, 85).

An important aspect of Hindu-Muslim relations has to do with the sanctity of temples, which continues to incite communal violence to the present day. There is evidence of destruction of temples during the early period of Muslim rule, which was justified in terms of *jihad* and motivated by the wealth of the temples. But temples were contested sites of state authority in India well before the Turkish invasions and the advent of Islam. Attacks on temples were acts intended to demonstrate political power. The Turkish invaders of the tenth and eleventh centuries who attacked temples were thus following an established pattern. It should also be noted that medieval chroniclers often exaggerated incidents of temple destruction to emphasize the religious fervor of rulers (Eaton 2000, 246–281).

On the whole, scholars tend to disagree on the nature and implications of this political history of intercommunal relations. One view asserts that religious authority was invoked to justify the seizure of wealth, to appeal to the religious zeal of soldiers in battle, or to legitimize revolt against established political power (Mansingh 1991, 300, 301). Another scholar presents Hindu-Muslim relations in terms of a compromise between religious orthodoxy and political expediency—of Hindu submission to Muslim political power without an acknowledgment of its legitimacy. There was also tension and contestation among Muslims, as well as between religious authority and secular power (Madan 1997, 111–115).

As stated in Chapter 2, the histories of Islamic societies can be interpreted in different ways, and these issues will remain open to new interpretations and differing conclusions. Probably there were instances of peaceful coexistence as well as some basis for communal tensions, with the practical separation of state power from religious authority as the rule more than the exception. The main point of the preceding brief survey of the Islamic precolonial history of India is to emphasize the contradictions in the relationship between state and religious authorities. While it cannot be said that the precolonial history of India reflects a categorical separation between Islam and the state, that history clearly does not support the claim that the state was "Islamic" or that Shari'a was enforced by the state. But academic consensus about historical events based on scholarly evidence does not necessarily coincide with the way these events are remembered or reconstructed to validate or support various positions in present political discourse. This is the underlying issue for the following sections, first during the colonial period and then after independence.

Islam, the State, and Politics in the Colonial Period, 1750–1947

When the British East India Company took control of various Indian territories in the mid-eighteenth century, it set into motion the transformation of the Mogul Indian state into a European state with territorial sovereignty. The Mogul state ruled through intermediary landholders whose alliance was ensured through coercive power and economic incentives. Its power was never absolute, and resistance to it had been common (Habib 2003, 7). Although the East India Company initially functioned like an Indian state, it gradually reshaped the nature of political authority in India. The decentralized structure of Mogul authority was replaced by a centralized power supported by a strong army, whereby the state took control of administrative and judicial functions. The European model of exclusive sovereignty that was established by the company ranked the claims of the state over the population before the claims of religious, social, and other institutions (Habib 2003, 27, 30). Unlike in the case of European societies, however, this exclusive sovereignty was vested in the colonial administration and not the people of the country, who were deemed to be inferior native subjects. This fundamental contradiction also applied to the way in which the British colonial administration implemented the principle of secularism (in the sense of professed neutrality toward religion) as state policy and the framework for social relations. Thus the precedent for the notion of secularism introduced through colonial rule was neither participatory nor empowering for the vast majority of Indians, as they were designated subjects of British rule and not citizens. This failure may be obvious, because it is inherent to the nature of colonialism, but it should still be noted.

The three main arguments regarding the imposition of secularism and intercommunal relations in the colonial period may be summarized here, before a more detailed elaboration below. First, the colonial state introduced secularism not as a coherent and positive doctrine but rather as a strategy of colonial rule, where the religious neutrality of the state meant noninterference in matters of the religion and customs of the native subjects. In other words, what might be called "secularism in India," from its inception during the colonial period, was not what I would call "Indian secularism," as the sphere of civic reason in which Indians could participate on equal footing with each other or with the colonial rulers. Moreover, the British colonial policy of noninterference in the religious affairs of Indian subjects was based on the identification of religion with the "personal" laws of the community. As will be discussed in the third section, the legacy of separate personal laws and the identification of the right to personal law with religion continue to complicate secularism in postcolonial India.

My second argument is that the colonial construction of Indian history and stereotypes of Hindus and Muslims influenced community relations in the colonial period and later. Ideas of Hindus and Muslims as monolithic groups, of Muslim rulers as invaders who oppressed their Hindu subjects, and of privileged Muslims as outsiders to Indian society took root during British colonial rule. It can be argued that those and related ideas and assumptions came to be reflected in religious-cultural nationalist projects like the Hindu nationalist movement, which defines Hindus as the original inhabitants of India who make up the "Indian nation" and non-Hindu religious minorities as aliens. The counterclaim of the "Muslim nation" can also be traced to these colonial "divide and conquer" policies.

The third argument is that the anticolonial nationalist movement represented a countertradition of relatively inclusive and participatory civic reason in drawing upon secular and religious discourses to bring all communities together in opposition to British colonialism. Unfortunately, anticolonial nationalism failed to transform Indian traditions into a rationale for and foundation of the state prior to independence. On the contrary, independence was marked by the partition of the subcontinent along religious lines into the two states of India and Pakistan. Paradoxically, mainstream Indian nationalism explicitly rejected colonial notions of racial inferiority that assumed Indians were incapable of governing themselves and yet drew upon colonial ideas about Indian identities. Mainstream Indian nationalism at least tolerated, if it did not share, assumptions of Hindu nationalism that interpreted so-called Muslim interests as separate from Indian "national" interests.

Secularism as Colonial Reason, Not Indian Civic Reason

Although the British policy was officially one of "religious neutrality," there were "various kinds of involvements in religious affairs that produced a somewhat confused interpretation of this simple phrase" (Smith 1999, 189).

A primary example of this confusion that has had far-reaching consequences for our purposes here is the colonial construction of separate personal laws for Indian communities fundamentally defined in terms of religion. The colonial administration began the codification of Hindu and Muslim
laws in 1772 and continued through the next century, with emphasis on
certain texts as the authentic "sources" of the law and custom of Hindus and
Muslims, which in fact devalued and retarded those dynamic social systems.
The codification of complex and interdependent traditional systems froze
certain aspects of the status of women, for instance, outside the context of
constantly evolving social and economic relations, which in effect limited or
restricted women's rights (Agnes 1999, 42). The selectivity of the process,
whereby colonial authorities sought the assistance of Hindu and Muslim religious elites in understanding the law, resulted in the "Brahmanization and
Islamization" of customary laws (Agnes 1999, 44). For example, the British
orientalist scholar William Jones (1746–1794) translated the key texts *Al
Sirjjiyah* in 1792 as the *Mohammedan Law of Inheritance* and *Manusmriti* in
1794 as the *Institutes of Hindu Law, or the Ordinances of Manu*. In short, British
colonial administrators reduced centuries of vigorous development of total
ethical, religious, and social systems to fit their own preconceived European
notions of what Muslim and Hindu "law" should be.

Similar policies were pursued through the colonial courts. In 1774 a Supreme Court was established, which was granted jurisdiction over natives
in 1781, but Hindus and Muslims were given the right to follow native custom and law in "personal matters" such as inheritance, marriage, and succession. The confusion about the scope of native and personal laws is clearly
reflected in the conflation of religion and custom, which created the legal
fiction that Hindu and Muslim laws derived from scripture and that Hindus and Muslims were "homogenous communities following uniform laws"
(Agnes 1999, 43). What British colonial officers believed to be "personal"
and "religious" law became synonymous, though such closed categories
would not have made sense for Hindus and Muslims in their precolonial experiences. Thus, I argue, the colonial process of codification rendered an
overdetermined religious identity as the mark of identity itself, defining
what was particular to a community as well as setting its differences from
other communities. What the colonial administrators decided was the realm
of "personal" matters, such as marriage and inheritance, was the repository
of religious identity.

The relationship of marginalized "Untouchable" communities to Hinduism was also complicated by British legislation. The British did not include the term "Untouchable" in the census of 1871–1872, referring to the communities instead as "outcastes" or "semi-Hinduized Aborigines." Most upper-caste Hindus had no particular interest in including Untouchables as official Hindus until 1909, when they wanted to bolster the number of Hindus for electoral purposes against the Muslim minority, who were about to gain separate electorates (Mendelsohn and Vicziany 1998, 28).

Secularism as constructed through the policies and legislation of the colonial administration did not draw upon the *substance* of the political, social, or cultural traditions of the subcontinent. For example, it failed to utilize particular Hindu or Muslim traditions of kingship or recognize syncretic Indian traditions of shared cultural practice across Hindu and Muslim communities that could have provided indigenous notions to support the secular principle. The process by which the colonial principle of secularism was introduced neither included democratic or participatory values nor respected the imperative of Indian civic reason. The few initial representatives of priestly classes, such as Brahmans and Qazis, who were consulted by the colonial administration regarding native laws, were replaced by British orientalist scholars. In other words, the British colonial administration assumed the authority to decide the scope of personal and religious law for Hindus and Muslims, as well as the authority to define religion and to structure the separation of religion from the state. Colonial codification limited the authority of religious institutions in the realm of law—for example, by imposing the structure of English common law—thereby producing so-called Anglo-Hindu law for Hindus and Anglo-Muhammadan law for Muslims. Paradoxically, the colonial construction of an autonomous space for the expression of religious identities undermined the autonomy of religious communities and controlled religion in the name of separating it from the state.

The reactions of the Islamic religious establishment to colonialism were varied, ranging from opposition to acceptance. With the disintegration of the Mogul Empire and the onset of British rule, religious orthodoxy could no longer take the support of political power for granted. In protest against British colonial intrusions into the domain of personal law and interference in Muslim education, the Muslim *ulama* reaffirmed the authority of Shariʿa and their exclusive position as its sole interpreters (Hasan 2002, 102). The reactions of the *ulama* included petitioning the government and establishing centers of religious learning, such as the Nadwat al-ulama and the *makatib* at Deoband. These institutions were generally characterized by conservatism and a rejection of British policies in the spheres of education, law, and religion. All of this has had far-reaching consequences for Indian Muslims up to the present time. Indeed, this history may make it difficult for the Muslim communities of India today to accept notions of secularism or state neutrality regarding religion.

Religion was also mobilized in opposition to colonial rule. For example, in the revolt of 1857, both Hindus and Muslims organized as religious communities and articulated their opposition to the British rulers in religious terms (Ray 2003, 354–355). Shah Abdul Aziz (1746–1824) declared India as *dar al-harb* (territory that is hostile to Islam and Muslims) in *fatwas* issued in the early nineteenth century, which lamented the loss of authority of the imam al-Muslimin, the ruler of Delhi, and the fact of Christian control over the territory. Muslim religious figures, such as Maulana Ahmadullah Shah and Bakht Khan, were also involved in the 1857 mutiny. Orthodox believers attempted a religious mobilization of the Muslim community. Dudu Miyan, the son of Maulana Shariatullah, the founder of the Fara'idi sect, led a peasant revolt against the colonial powers. Such revivalist initiatives did foment an increased political consciousness but could not translate into a broad-based political movement (Mujeeb 1967, 390–399).

At the same time, the orthodox position was complicated by theological debates to prove that the enemy, whether seen as the Mogul emperor or as the East India Company, was a *kafir* (unbeliever) or *mushrik* (polytheist) and whether *jihad* would be legally justified, and whether it was legitimate to form alliances with other religious communities and with Muslims who were perceived as unbelievers. However, the entire blame for inaction should not fall on the Hanafi *ulama*, as their attitudes were mirrored by those of other religious groups, precluding the possibility of united action (Mujeeb 1967, 395–396). Eventually the *ulama* came to accept the fact of British rule, but they continued to preserve their authority over religious tradition (Hasan 2002, 30). Paradoxically, as the acceptance of colonial subjugation was technically justified through theological rationalization, the supreme authority of Shari'a was also emphasized. This largely oppositional position of the orthodox Islamic authorities probably limited the possibility that secularism would be vested with any legitimacy within a theological framework. Colonial emphasis on the image of Muslims and Hindus as opposed and homogeneous communities must have aggravated the situation. The implications of such factors for Hindu-Muslim relations in the colonial and postcolonial period may briefly be clarified as follows.

The Colonial Narrative of Indian History

In the orientalist colonial narrative, cultivated throughout the nineteenth century, Indian history was reduced to three distinct phases: Hindu (ancient), Muslim (medieval), and British (modern). In this reading, ancient India was a glorious Hindu society victimized by barbaric invaders throughout history, from Alexander the Great to Muslim kings. According to this narrative, the despotism of Islamic rule in particular had devastated Hindu India. The British, in contrast, were described as an enlightened force that would rejuvenate Indian society. The widely read *History of British India,* written by James Mill in 1817, was a hegemonic text reflecting this narrative. This view was echoed by other British scholars, such as William Jones, and by the German scholar Max Mueller (1823–1900). Accordingly, the colonial theory described Indian Muslims as culturally alien to India. The notion of a unified Muslim community acting out of singularly "religious" motivation and driven largely by pan-Islamic considerations was also a colonial construction, reinforced by British travelers, missionaries, administrators, and scholars. Islam in this view was unchanging, indeed inimical to change, regressive, and opposed to Western values. All these characteristics were supposedly embodied by all Muslims, who were seen as part of a race and nation (Hasan 2002, 38–39, 41–42). Hindus were described in similarly essentialist terms.

Contrary to this view, while some elite figures, such as Shah Waliullah and Mirza Ghalib, lamented the end of the Mogul Empire, it seems that for the majority of Indian Muslims, neither the achievements of the empire nor its decline were a relevant issue. Most Muslims were willing to work within the framework of the colonial state, which belies colonial stereotypes that endured in British perceptions of Islam and Muslims. At the popular level, there were shared practices among Hindus and Muslims that reflected highly syncretized understandings and expressions of religious-cultural affiliation and close ties between communities. Yet British political decisions and constitutional plans conflated the Mapilla Muslims with the Pathans, the landowning elites of Awadh with the Tamil Muslim merchants, Shi'a and Sunnis, Bohras and Khojas, Deobandis and Barelwis, into a singular, undifferentiated, and fixed image of Indian Islam (Hasan 2002, 40–42).

The idea of a Hindu India ravaged by Islamic invaders would also form the core argument of the Hindu nationalist movement (Hindutva), which stridently emphasized the notion of the Muslim as an outsider in foundational texts. These texts also affirmed the idea of the nation as a religious entity (Panikkar 1999, xi). In *Hindutva—Who Is a Hindu?* (1923), Veer Savarkar, a founder of Hindu nationalism, described Indian Muslims and Christians as aliens in the Hindu nation. In *Six Glorious Epochs of Indian History*, he described Indian political history in terms of foreign invasions and Hindu resistance (Panikkar 1999, xiv–xv). His views were echoed by M. S. Golwalkar in *We or Our Nationhood Defined*, originally published in 1942. Golwalkar held that all those who had migrated to India and their descendants were foreigners and therefore not part of the nation. He asserted that Muslims, Christians, and Parsis should either adopt "the Hindu culture and language" and revert to the Hindu faith or live "wholly subordinated to the Hindu nation," without any rights or privileges (Golwalkar 1945, 52–53).

British colonial rule—specifically, colonial legislation and the administrative classification of Indians into religious categories—is usually cited as the key historical frame for the emergence of communal consciousness among Hindus and Muslims. But it has also been argued that even in the colonial period, "communalism" and "separatism" were temporary phenomena, restricted to certain groups and regions, and even to groups that clashed in religious conflict at one point in time, while most communities lived in amity with each other (Hasan 2002, 215). The role of colonial policies in this regard cannot be denied, but it is also true that ideas of Hindu and Muslim identity, difference, and antagonism were internalized by the communities themselves. The conventional view among scholars of this field is that the last third of the nineteenth century represents the originating moment in the history of communal antagonism, when the scale and frequency of violence between Hindus and Muslims significantly increased. Still, it may be possible to trace the history of Hindu-Muslim tensions to the first half of the nineteenth century or even earlier. One scholar who holds this view argues that syncretic and shared understandings did not preclude the possibility of religious violence in earlier periods (Bayly 1985, 177–203).

Considering all the complex evidence and its conflicting interpretations, we can reasonably conclude that although Hindus and Muslims generally experienced peaceful coexistence, there were tensions between the communities in the colonial period. This was the case regardless of whether these tensions represented continuities from the precolonial period, as described above, or were mostly the outcome of colonial rule. But the more critical point for our purposes here is that the idea of Hindus and Muslims as two separate peoples was shared by Hindu organizations such as the Hindu Mahasabha and Muslim organizations such as the Muslim League. British legislation as well as the politics of the Indian National Congress, the Muslim League, and anticolonial nationalist parties fostered and reinforced the idea that Hindu and Muslim community interests were distinct from each other.

The Complexities of Anticolonial Nationalism

The advent of anticolonial nationalism is conventionally dated to 1885, when the Indian National Congress was founded. The Congress is often regarded as an exemplar of an inclusive model of civic reason, wherein different types of reason, religious and secular, nationalist and pan-Islamic, Hindu and Muslim, were mobilized toward one goal. From this perspective, that framework contained the possibility of being expressed as a *viable* Indian secularism. Anticolonial nationalism had the capacity to generate popular religious and cultural legitimacy for Indian secularism, in contrast to the negative colonial discourse of contradictory religious neutrality. But the nationalist movement was also marked by tensions between the communities, and by the problematic overlap of mainstream Indian anticolonial nationalism with aspects of Hindu nationalism. There were also opposing discourses of Hindu-Muslim relations as understood at the political level by the vanguard of Indian nationalism and the leaders of the Congress and the Muslim League. The failure of the late phase of the anticolonial nationalist movement to develop an inclusive and participatory secular framework not only resulted in the partition of the subcontinent into India and Pakistan, but also has continued to undermine the stability and development of India since independence.

The Khilafat (caliphate) movement of 1919–1924 apparently achieved a level of unity between Hindus and Muslims as well as between secular and religious forces, as a protest against the British decision to carve up the Ottoman Empire after the First World War. Gandhi supported the Khilafat cause, combining it with the nationalist imperative of *swaraj*, or self-rule, in his noncooperation, nonviolent protest against British rule. The supporters of the Khilafat movement argued that pan-Islamism was compatible with nationalism; Indian freedom and the Khilafat cause were seen as inextricably linked, since both Hindus and Muslims were subjugated by British imperial rule. The movement represented a national-level Congress-Khilafat-Muslim League alliance that relied on demonstrations of harmonious interfaith relations, political solidarity between Hindus and Muslims, and the support of peasant unrest. The *ulama* played a crucial role in raising popular support for the cause, providing legitimacy to a movement that would not have been viable under the leadership of Western-educated Muslims. The alliance between the *ulama* and the educated liberal Muslim intelligentsia, such as those associated with the Aligarh Muslim University and the Muslim League, was deliberately cultivated to increase credibility (Hasan 2002, 96–104).

But the Khilafat movement also unleashed other, more divisive forces. At a conference in 1921, some *ulama* contested the necessity for alliance with Hindus and called for greater conformity with Shari'a in the movement's direction (Hasan 2002, 109). Hindu nationalists exploited the movement as an example of the extraterritorial loyalty of Muslims, which by implication compromised their nationalism as Indians (Hasan 2002, 97–98). Some Muslim institutions and leaders issued a call for *jihad* and riots in south India in 1921, which prompted Gandhi to withdraw the civil disobedience movement in opposition to the violence (Hasan 2002, 109–110). Soon after, Mustafa Kemal in Turkey abolished the Ottoman caliphate, which made the issue moot for its Indian supporters. With that, the Indian Khilafat movement lost the focus and symbol of its anticolonial agitation.

The partition is sometimes attributed to the ideas of Saiyid Ahmad Khan and others at Aligarh as the authors of Muslim separatism in the subcontinent, but the emergence of a "communitarian consciousness" was gradual and uneven, given the complexities of the social lives of various Muslim communities as well as differences in doctrinal matters. Historical events such as the partition of Bengal in 1905 and the formation of the All-India Muslim League in 1906 contributed to the partition of India and Pakistan, which was also made imaginable by British legislation providing a structural basis for the two-nation theory. The Morley-Minto reforms of 1909, which granted Muslims separate electorates, legitimized the colonial perspective on Indian society as fundamentally divided on religious grounds. In 1930, Mohammad Iqbal proposed the idea of a Muslim state, one that would be in northwestern regions of India, where the majority of the population was

Muslim. According to one scholar, the key impetus for the creation of Pakistan can be attributed to the critical failure of Congress leadership around the time of the Second World War (Hasan 2002, 197). In Hasan's view, an alliance with the Muslim League and a firm reiteration of Congress's commitment to a "secular and composite nationhood" might have consolidated and unified the efforts of both organizations toward independence. But the policies of the Congress at that time reflected concessions to the Hindu nationalist sympathizers in the right wing of the party. The right wing was wary of increased numbers of Muslim activists joining the party. Hindu nationalist organizations, which were influential among sections of the Congress, were strongly against any Congress-League alliance. The Muslims in the Congress also opposed the alliance, to some extent because of an anxiety to preserve their positions of prominence. In that context, the Muslim League, under Muhammad Ali Jinnah's leadership, was able to gain credibility for its claim to represent the Indian Muslim community (Hasan 2002, 201–203).

The story of the division of the Indian nation should not be seen solely in terms of the Congress-League-British negotiations without reference to other factors, such as the position of the league, shared by the Jamaat-i-Islami and some Deobandi *ulama*, "on Islam, the *Muslim* nation, and the birth of an *Islamic* society" (Hasan 2002, 313, emphasis in original). That position reflected the interests and anxieties of various, largely privileged social classes, such as landowners and professional groups, more than any overwhelming commitment to founding an Islamic society. Another factor to consider is that Jinnah was not by any means representative of many Indian Muslims, and his position did not reflect the multiple perspectives among them. "Pakistan was neither everybody's dream, nor was Jinnah the Quaid [leader] of the socialists and Marxists, the Khudai Khitmatgars, the ulama of Deoband, the Momins, the Shias connected with the Shia Political Conference and scores of Muslim political groups pushed to the periphery and surviving uneasily on the margins of mainstream national and provincial politics" (Hasan 2002, 314). Moreover, groups representing Indian Muslims differed significantly on the question of partition. The Jamiyat-i-ulama-Hind, founded in 1919, strongly opposed partition in the 1940s and was committed to composite nationalism. In contrast, the Jamaat-i-Islami, founded in 1941 by Abul A'la Maududi, dedicated itself to the cause of an Islamic state in Pakistan (Hasan 2002, 369–371). A third factor is that the national boundaries created at partition were meaningless for most Hindus, Muslims, and Sikhs, reflecting "merely the mental images of politicians, lawyers, and intellectuals" (Hasan 2002, 314).

Muslim reactions to the question of a unified India cannot be categorized into the binary of "secular" versus "religious" motivations among separate groups of individuals. It is erroneous to assume that those Muslims who supported a unified India were nonreligious while those who were in favor of partition were religious. Such a simplistic dichotomy is premised on a mistaken reading of the term "nationalist Muslim," in which the "national-ist" aspect is taken to be synonymous with secular disavowal of religion and the "Muslim" aspect of identity. The political actions of both so-called sepa-ratist and so-called nationalist Muslims were motivated by the "interests of religious communities" (Metcalf 1985, 1). Another problematic assumption is the categorization of figures such as Ajmal Khan, Ansari, and Maulana Abul Kalam Azad as "nationalist Muslims," who are treated as an excep-tional category of Muslims, the implication being that their nationalist senti-ment was not shared by Muslims at large. If that is true, then Gandhi and Nehru should be called "nationalist Hindus" (Hasan 2002, 8). Thus the voices of such Muslims leaders as Maulana Azad have been ignored in histo-ries of the Indian subcontinent, whether "imperial," "secular," or "commu-nal." Such misleading narratives portray the events of partition in terms of Hindu and Muslim religious motivations, lending further credence to the idea that religion predominantly shaped the subcontinent's history.

Conversely, it is necessary to understand the relationship between anti-colonial Indian nationalism and Hindu nationalism. The Hindu nationalist organizations did not join hands with the struggle of the Congress. Yet in the broader anticolonial discourse in general, Hindu religious-cultural national-ism was understood as closely connected to mainstream anticolonial na-tionalism. "Hindu interests" were assumed to be identical or at least compat-ible with Indian interests, reflecting a majoritarian reasoning. In contrast, "Muslim interests" were perceived as separate from "national" interests. It seems that Hindus, including some in the Congress, had shared and deeply internalized this assumption since the nineteenth century. As Nehru ob-served in his autobiography, "Many a Congressman was a communalist un-der his national cloak" (1936, 136).

On the Muslim side, too, it cannot be assumed that religious leaders were uniformly in agreement with or supportive of the two-nation theory or the way in which the one or two nations were to be governed after independence. Some Muslim religious leaders, as well as political leaders, were united in proposing the two-nation theory and the call for Pakistan, while others were united in supporting Indian unity and resisting the two-nation proposition. For example, the Dar-ul-Ulum in Deoband, one of the largest Islamic religious schools *(madrasas)* in the world, played a leading role in spearheading India's freedom movement. In contrast, many of the most ardent believers in the one-nation theory *(ummah vahidah)* proposed by the Congress were *ulama* who still imagined an independent India as the way to achieve Shari'a rule. Ironically, among the most enthusiastic supporters of Pakistan were Muslim communists and socialists, especially those affiliated with the Progressive Writers Movement, who were completely opposed to Shari'a rule (Ansari 1990, 189).

In the final analysis, and whatever the reasons may have been, the proponents of the one-nation theory failed to realize their vision. With independence came the partition of the subcontinent and communal violence on an unimaginable scale, with hundreds of thousands, possibly millions, killed in interreligious violence on both sides of the newly created border between India and Pakistan. The legacy of partition has continued to haunt political relations between the two countries as well as majority-minority relations within both states. The shadow of partition also continues to haunt the present status and future prospects of secularism in India, as highlighted in the next section.

Religion, the State, and Politics since Independence

The central issue here is to what extent and in what ways Indian secularism has operated as a principle or foundation of civic reason among different religious communities (not only Muslims) as well as Indian society at large. Relevant questions include whether secularism has been an empowering discourse that has enabled the widest spectrum of Indian citizens across gender, class, religious, regional, and linguistic lines to participate in public discourse. Has the state in practice used secularism in a fair and neutral fashion to genuinely foster an egalitarian culture of civic reason? For the basic propositions of this book, the central question is whether the secularism of the post-independence Indian state has been aware of or incorporated a distinction between Islam and politics and Islam and the state, which may be seen more generally in terms of religion and politics and religion and the state.

To recall the main conclusions of the preceding review, it is clear that the precolonial political traditions of the subcontinent reflected a practical pattern of separation of religion and state, accompanied by a structure where religious and political authority also needed to support each other. The precolonial Indian model, in other words, could have contained the potential for translating into an *Indian secularism* that would have possessed legitimacy within the framework of the cultural and social systems of Hindu, Muslim, and other Indian communities. But the traumatic colonial intrusion substantially undermined that possibility by introducing secularism strictly through the European style of a territorially sovereign state that forcibly replaced indigenous historical structures of political authority. The racial distinction drawn by the colonial rulers between themselves and their Indian subjects also meant that sovereignty in the colonial state was not vested in the Indian people, who were, after all, subjects and not citizens. Secularism, as introduced through the policies of colonial rule, was a negative discourse that was far from being founded on or enabling of participatory civic reason among Indians. Moreover, the policy of purported religious neutrality, ironically, required interference in the religious lives of communities by constructing a realm of "personal law" as synonymous with the religious lives of Indian subjects. Indeed, colonial policy defined Indian communities primarily in religious terms as fundamentally separate and different peoples, thereby undermining the possibilities of Indian secularism founded on shared and equal citizenship in the country.

Communal relations were shaped by colonial perceptions of Indians expressed and implemented in state policies, including the colonialist interpretation of Indian history, which designated Muslims as outsiders to the subcontinent. The idea of Hindus and Muslims as two "nations" was also adopted by Hindu and Muslim organizations, thereby limiting religious-cultural discourses of nationalism within the mainstream Indian anticolonial movement. The relatively more inclusive and participatory anticolonial nationalism at the beginning of the movement represented an alternative version of Indian secularism to that of the British colonial state. In other words, anticolonial nationalism could have provided the basis for an Indian secularism that was more deeply rooted in broader, inclusive Indian cultural and religious values. But strong perceptions of the separate interests of Hindus and Muslims in the politics of the Congress and the Muslim League meant that the emerging Indian state would be divided at the moment of independence. As highlighted earlier, some scholars point to the colonial period as the key historical frame for the emergence of a communal consciousness among Hindu and Muslim communities, while others point to an earlier history of tensions. Whatever the origins or earlier history of intercommunal tensions may have been, the savage interreligious riots and violence between Hindus and Muslims on both sides of the newly created border between India and Pakistan have by far compounded the challenges facing Indian secularism in the postcolonial era.

According to the 1991 census, India had a total population of about 839 million. Hindus numbered 688 million, or 82 percent; Muslims 102 million, or 12 percent; Christians 20 million, or 2.32 percent; Sikhs 16 million, or 1.99 percent; Buddhists 0.77 percent; Jains 0.2 percent; and others about 2 percent. Hindus form the majority community in nearly all states. Muslims are the majority community in one state, Jammu and Kashmir, where they account for 64 percent of the population, and in the Union Territory of Lakshwadeep, where they form 94 percent of the population. They are the main minority in twelve states across India (Madan 2004, 44–45). But this demographic profile is largely the product of the partition of 1947, which has significantly altered the religious composition of various parts of the country through the migration of large numbers of Muslims to Pakistan and Hindus to India. In particular, it seems that nearly the entire professional service-based Muslim middle class migrated to Pakistan (Qureshi 1998, xii). Considering this history and current demographics, and despite the frequent outbursts of violence outlined below, it is still reasonable to conclude that the various religious communities of India have coexisted in relative peace and tolerance. Unfortunately, this seems to have been declining in recent decades.

Although intercommunal relations have been far from ideal, the situation seems to have progressively worsened in the decades since independence. Even at times when such tensions are not openly expressed, relations between the communities have been marked by suspicion, hostility, and a lack of dialogue between various groups. The resurgence of Hindu nationalism since the 1980s and events such as the demolition of the Babri Masjid mosque on December 6, 1992, and its aftermath, as discussed below, have exacerbated the situation. In general, it seems that in recent decades more conservative and rigid notions of religious identity appear to have gained importance among members of all Indian religious communities, whether Hindus, Muslims, or Sikhs. The 1980s also saw the rise of religious militancy among Hindus, Sikhs, and Muslims. Following the assassination of the Indian prime minister Indira Gandhi by her Sikh bodyguards in 1984, parts of

India, especially Delhi, witnessed anti-Sikh riots in which Congress leaders were believed to be complicit. Moreover, traditional caste divisions gained additional importance in undermining intercommunal coexistence in 1990, when an initiative by Prime Minister V. P. Singh to extend the benefits of affirmative action in government educational institutions and jobs to a wider cross-section of Indian society drew strong protest from the largely upper-caste Indian middle classes. Caste stratification became much more apparent and led to Hindu militancy among people who were apprehensive that Hindu votes would be divided.

Aside from the aftermath of partition, Hindu-Muslim relations in India have been marked by periodic violence and riots. Jabalpur experienced communal riots in 1961, Ahmedabad in 1969, and Bhiwandi-Jalgaon in 1970. The end of the 1970s and early 1980s also witnessed a number of major communal riots. Official figures compiled from several sources, including the Home Ministry, indicate the total number of incidents of communal violence between 1954 and 1982 as 6,933 (Brass 1990, 198). As one scholar summarized the situation:

> Between 1982 and 1985, the army was called out as many as 353 times to maintain law and order in different parts of the country. Between 1980 and 1989, India witnessed close to 4,500 communal incidents, in which over 7,000 people lost their lives, almost four times as many deaths of this type as in the 1970s. There has also been a marked increase in the number of districts affected by communal riots, from 61 in 1960 to 250 in 1986–87, out of a total of 403 districts. In 1988 alone, 611 'communal incidents' occurred, of which 55% were in rural areas. More and more incidents in the country have been categorized by the bureaucrats as communally 'hyper-sensitive' (as opposed to merely communally 'sensitive'), rising from 89 in 1971 to 213 in 1988. In 1988 alone, the number of 'hyper-sensitive' districts rose from 82 to well over one hundred. (Upadhyaya 1992, 821–822)

There are various analyses of the reasons for such a drastic situation. One view, for instance, considers the reasons for the difference between Ahmedabad, Hyderabad, and Aligarh and comparative locations that share similar profiles but vary in terms of the occurrence of ethnic violence (Varshney 2002). Comparing Ahmedabad with Surat, Hyderabad with Lucknow, and Aligarh with Calicut (or Kozhikode), this view proposes that where there are strong patterns of civic associational life, the incidence of riots is lower. The notion of associational networks is used in this study to signify stronger networks of civil society among communities rather than informal networks of everyday relations (50–51). Thus, in Calicut, despite an earlier history of violence, including the Mapillah rebellion in the 1920s, Hindus and Muslims are united in terms of combating caste-class subjugation (167). In Lucknow, the local textile economy ties the interests of Hindu businessmen with Hindu nationalist sympathies and with the interests of Muslim workers (203). In Aligarh and Hyderabad, such integrated structures at the level of the local economy do not exist (127–29, 213–15). In Surat, where Hindus and Muslims are joined in both everyday and associational networks, the situation was stable during communal tensions in 1992–1993 where these networks existed, in contrast to the violence in the slums, where such structures were absent (260).

Another scholar has posited that collective Hindu-Muslim violence is not spontaneous and entirely contingent on contextual factors but that such incidents are in fact produced by political events (Brass 2003). In this view, there is no single causal factor that can explain all or the majority of Hindu-Muslim riots and anti-Muslim pogroms in India. But there are "institutionalized riot systems," in which various actors—individuals and groups—play particular functions in riots that are deliberately rehearsed and produced events. The production of riots occurs in the context of competition between political parties and large-scale political mobilizations. This modality of riot production was seen in pre-independent India and continues in independent India.

Other theories can be cited here, but it is not possible or necessary for our purposes to discuss or explain all aspects of communal riots and violence in general. Instead, the object is to highlight the implications of the underlying distrust among communities and the failure of the state to enforce accountability for repeated episodes of large-scale indiscriminate violence, which also tends to create and sustain perceptions of state bias.

We have noted earlier how British colonial rule cultivated and manipulated perceptions of Muslims as outsiders and the role played by Hindu nationalist organizations in perpetuating such perceptions during the struggle for independence. In independent India, especially since the 1980s, with the resurgence of Hindu nationalism, the Sangh Parivar, or family of Hindu nationalist organizations, has dedicated itself to the propagation of the notion of Hindus as the real, original inhabitants of India and Muslims as alien outsiders. The objective of Hindu nationalist historical propaganda is not just to slander Muslims but equally to provoke Hindus into asserting their power, by invoking traditions of Muslim aggression and heroic Hindu resistance. Among the many examples of such efforts to mobilize Hindus to act assertively, the "histories" of the city of Ayodhya that were circulated during the Ram Janmabhumi campaign are particularly revealing of one of the long-term core objectives of the Hindutva movement. Hindu nationalists hold that the Babri Masjid, which was built under Emperor Babar in 1528, was erected on the ruins of a temple at the birthplace of the Hindu god Lord Ram. The "histories" of Ayodhya describe Hindu resistance to the demolition of the temple so the mosque could be built in 1528 and the later efforts to reclaim it. For instance, it is asserted that 174,000 Hindus sacrificed their lives fighting against the Muslims when the temple was first demolished, and that 35,000 Hindus died in the seventy-seven battles fought by Hindus to reclaim the temple (Panikkar 1999, xii–xiii). Demands for the "liberation" of the site from Muslims and the Indian state were made throughout the 1980s, culminating in the destruction of the disputed Babri Masjid at the hands of a Hindu nationalist mob on December 6, 1992, which was followed by bloody Hindu-Muslim riots in the city of Mumbai and elsewhere in India.

Despite its elitism and other flaws, anticolonial nationalism was a generally inclusive phenomenon mobilizing people from diverse social backgrounds toward the goal of independence, but the project of postcolonial nation-building has not been characterized by the same inclusive approach. Intercommunal and intercaste tensions have only been compounded by a low literacy rate and poverty. The Indian state has also failed to address political tensions and to hold those responsible for crimes against minorities accountable to justice (Prasad 1994; Daud and Suresh 1993). One of the most glaring failures in this regard has been the inability to deliver justice to the victims of the 1992–1993 riots that followed the destruction of the Babri Masjid. The Srikrishna Commission was appointed to inquire into the riots of December 1992 and January 1993 in Mumbai. Its mandate included identifying the individuals responsible for criminal acts, including murder, rape, and arson, during the riots and investigating the government's failure to take prompt action to end the violence. The commission's report was categorical in its conclusion that the Shiv Sena, a regional Hindu nationalist party in the state of Maharashtra, and its leaders were responsible for perpetrating organized attacks against Muslims in those Mumbai riots. In 1996, the Shiv Sena government in Maharashtra terminated the commission without taking any action to hold those responsible for the bloodshed, including members of the Mumbai police, accountable for their crimes.

On January 23, 1996, the Maharashtra government also announced that it planned to drop twenty-four cases of incitement and other charges in connection with the riots against Bal Thackeray, the head of the Shiv Sena.

Another failure of the state has been seen in the aftermath of violence against Muslims in 2002 in the Indian state of Gujarat. A train car of the Sabarmati Express, which was carrying a large mob of Hindu nationalist supporters, was allegedly burned by a mob of Muslims at Godhra on February 27, 2002 (Bunsha 2002). Hindu and Muslim eyewitnesses noted that trouble started when members of the Vishva Hindu Parishad (VHP), a Hindu nationalist organization, disembarked from the train and assaulted and harassed Muslim vendors. Retaliation and counter-retaliation followed, resulting in the burning of the train and the death of fifty-nine people (Punwani 2002, 47–51). A systematic attack on Muslims by Hindu mobs followed, resulting in the death of more than 650 Muslims. Urban neighborhoods and villages predominantly inhabited by Muslims were targeted, and Muslims were often burned alive. The anti-Muslim violence amounted to a pogrom, encouraged and supported by the Hindu nationalist Bharatiya Janata Party (BJP) state government in Gujarat and the state police.

In light of this overview, I will now turn to an assessment of the experience of India with secularism. In particular, I am concerned with the implications of the horrendous level of intercommunal violence for the prospects of Indian secularism.

Indian State Secularism and Communal Relations

When the constitution was adopted in 1950 (Panikkar 1999, viii), secularism was considered particularly essential for protecting the rights of religious minorities and reducing religious or cultural conflict of the kind seen in the communal violence in the aftermath of Indian independence (Bhargava 1999, 1). The three basic principles of secularism as articulated in the constitution are "religious freedom," "celebratory neutrality," and "regulatory and reformatory justice" (Dhavan 1999, 48–50). The first principle, religious freedom, is broadly structured to cover all aspects of faith, including but not limited to the right to religious thought and belief and protection against religious discrimination. The second principle seeks to establish a participatory secular state that is neutral in terms of both assistance to and celebration of all religions, without discrimination against any of them. At the same time, the third principle emphasizes social reform that would by definition entail some state interference in religious affairs of communities. While there are permanent tensions within and among these principles, the constitution tries to balance these imperatives in light of the spirit of each of them. The imperative of celebration of all faiths, for example, is intended to operate without partiality toward any one religion. Reform of socially problematic aspects of religion is provided for by the third principle, which may contradict the earlier two principles. Independence of the state from religion is understood by some scholars to mean equidistance from all religions; it may be read as a principled policy that combines the imperatives of both intervention and abstention (Bhargava 1999, 7).

Despite the general affirmation of the value of secularism by Indian constitution-makers, the outcome is unavoidably complex, even contradictory. These complexities derive from the particular history of secularism in India, from its antecedents to its affirmation as a principle of the state at the time of independence. But the fact that Indian secularism is a profoundly contested discourse in its distinctively contextual character does not necessarily mean that it is too exceptional to qualify as true secularism. On the contrary, my argument is that each society's conception and experience of secularism has to be contested and deeply contextual. In accordance with this view, it is clear that the separation between religion and state in India has not been static over time, nor does it simply mirror or echo Western experiences. As an Indian scholar explained:

> [A] widespread misconception exists in India that a unique uncomplicated separation of religion from the state is a feature of all modern, Western societies, and that this separation is conceived in the same manner everywhere, and because consensus on the precise relation between religion and state practice is an incontrovertible fact, the secularity of the state is a settled, stable feature in all Western politics . . . Western secularism, too, is essentially contested, with no agreement on what it entails, the values it seeks to promote, or how best to pursue it . . . ; each country in the West has worked out a particular political compromise rather than implementing a solution uniquely required by the configuration of values embodied in secularism. The separation thesis means different things in the US, in France, in Germany, and is interpreted differently at different times in each place. (Bhargava 1999, 2–3)

The tentative and contested nature of Indian secularism can be appreciated in light of the fact that the word "secular" was not included in the constitution, except incidentally in Article 25(2)(b), until 1976. By the 42nd Amendment of the constitution in 1976, the words "socialist" and "secular" were inserted in the preamble to say that India would be a secular republic. The Statement of Objects and Reasons of the 42nd Constitution Amendment Bill explained that the purpose of inserting the word "secular" was to categorically explain the high ideal of secularism—in other words, to explicitly state what had been implicit in the constitution. Thus it seems that although the value of secularism for the new Indian state was not in doubt at the time of the adoption of the constitution, its precise meaning and implications for Indian society were not settled at that founding moment (Dhavan 1987, 213).

Scholars of India disagree on whether Indian secularism as conceived by Nehru and other nationalist leaders represents a genuinely far-reaching and radical conception of the principle or reflects a misguided utopian idea that was ill-suited for the country (Khilnani 1999; Bhargava 1999). But for our purposes here, it seems that the central deficiency of Nehru's secularism is precisely that it lacked substantive authority, since it did not emerge as a result of negotiations, contestation, and discussion among different religious and secular viewpoints within Indian communities:

> For two or three decades prior to Independence the Congress under Nehru refused to let a secular policy emerge through negotiation between different communitarian voices, by denying at every step in the various conferrings with the British, Jinnah's demand that the Muslim League represent the Muslims, a Sikh leader represent the Sikhs, and a Harijan leader represent the untouchable community. The ground for this denial was simply that as a secular party they could not accept that they did *not* represent *all* these communities. Secularism thus never got the chance to *emerge* out of a creative dialogue between these different communities. It was *sui generis*. (Bilgrami 1998, 395, emphasis in original)

If it had been forged through negotiations and legitimized within communitarian-religious frameworks, secularism would have borne a meaningful relationship to those frameworks. However, given the modality in which it was conceived by Nehru and implemented, Indian secularism could have been no more than a "holding process" (Bilgrami 1999, 396).

For our purposes here, however, the broader issue is whether Indian secularism was the product of contiguous indigenous political traditions that could have provided it, or may still provide it, with the *potential* for popular legitimacy within different social and cultural contexts in Indian society. According to Amartya Sen,

> The long history of heterodoxy has a bearing not only on the development and survival of democracy in India, it has also richly contributed, I would argue, to the emergence of secularism in India, and even to the form that Indian secularism takes, which is not exactly the same as the way secularism is defined in parts of the West. The tolerance of religious diversity is implicitly reflected in India's having served as a shared home—in the chronology of history—for Hindus, Buddhists, Jains, Jews, Christians, Muslims, Parsees, Sikhs, Baha'is and others. (2005, 16–17)

Sen's position may be read as an affirmation that there is a historical basis for and sufficient continuity between Indian traditions of diversity, openness, interfaith dialogue, and present-day secularism in both constitutional form and societal conditions (19). This historical influence manifests itself, Sen argues, in a greater emphasis on *neutrality* as opposed to the more austere secularism of the French model, for example, with its emphasis on *prohibition* of religious symbols (19–20).

Sen's view has been critiqued by Ramachandra Guha, who said that "Sen uses the term 'India' anachronistically; speaking of a time long before its meaning was known or the political and cultural unity it presumes ever exhibited" (2005, 4422). Guha questions the continuity that Sen imputes between Akbar's policies and the way views in the sixteenth century have shaped laws and policies in the present time. "In making these (very large) claims for the relevance to modern politics of ancient history, Sen is at one with the Hindutva camp, except that he differs in who or what to uphold from India's past" (4423).

Another important perspective on Indian secularism is that of Ashis Nandy, whose critique stems from the elitism of Indian secularism and the fact that it privileges the educated middle-class elites. He also finds the imposition of secularism by the state problematic and considers that form of secularism antithetical to religious traditions of tolerance. As I understand his position, the view of secularism he is objecting to is one that is hostile and opposed to religion, one that calls for a separation of religion and politics, not just religion and the state. It is not possible here to discuss Nandy's earlier views and debates with others, but his latest statement should be noted here. He argues that in the decades after independence, secularism played a reasonably positive role, but since then it has become problematic: "It is the record of the ideology after the expansion of political participation and the acceleration of the process of secularization that is dubious" (Nandy 2007, 108). In his view, "Something is drastically wrong with the idea of secularism itself, particularly in societies that do not share the experiences of Europe, do not have sharp interreligious boundaries or church-like structures. These societies have for centuries lived with immense religious diversities and memories of colonial domination. In such societies it matters that the concept of secularism is insufficiently grounded in culture, especially in vernacular culture, that the concept makes no sense to the common run of citizens" (111–112). Unlike those who still affirm the value of the idea of secularism although they are skeptical about its prospects in its present form in India, Nandy sees secularism as having had a reasonably good life and having done some good to the society but now having exhausted its possibilities, so that India needs a "new generation of concepts" (112). His search for alternatives is not motivated by the incompatibility of secularism with Indian culture, which is an important issue, but by "the political nonsustainability of secularism at moments of increasing political participation" (113).

What I take from these debates, as I have outlined earlier in this chapter, is that some elements of the notion of the secular state are to be found in the political traditions of the Indian subcontinent, but other aspects are entirely absent. In view of the need to support the cultural legitimacy of secularism and constitutionalism in every setting, it may be viable and desirable to perceive prior cultural elements as antecedents of and foundations for secularism and constitutionalism. It is neither possible nor necessary to find modern-day political doctrines of secularism fully developed and clearly understood in the past. It may be that Sen has overstated his case and Guha has read too much into what Sen has said. The point for our purposes is whether we can find historical support for an idea, though clearly not in the same form or with the precise implications that that idea has today. In my view, the historical overview presented earlier in this chapter sufficiently confirms the historical antecedents of Indian secularism. Since secularism everywhere is always contextual, contested, and negotiated over time, it is healthy that Indian secularism is now being challenged by scholars like Nandy. In my view, his critique of secularism as simply the separation of religion and the state supports my point about the need to combine that separation with the affirmation and regulation of the relationship of religion to politics.

Notions of individual freedom of religion find a basis in Hindu, Buddhist, and Islamic societies, but the separation of religion and state in the sense that the state should abstain from material support of religion was unknown in Hindu, Buddhist, or Islamic traditions, where royal patronage of religion was part of the obligations of political authority. This aspect of state secularism was introduced into the region with British colonialism, which imposed the European territorial state. In this sense, the development of the whole integrated conception of the secular state can be attributed to Western origins (Smith 1999, 184). But this is only to be expected, because the concept of the colonial and postcolonial state itself was European. The more critical point for our purposes here is that colonial experiences do not negate the existence of broader notions of secularism as a cultural value in Indian society prior to any encounter with the West.

Another relevant factor is that Indian state secularism has a complex relationship with the provision of the Indian constitution that allows different communities to be governed by their personal laws in matters of marriage, divorce, inheritance, and the like. It should first be noted here that this particular feature is a legacy of colonial legislation that equated the domain of personal laws with religious identities and rights. The continuation of this approach by the Indian state after independence generated and sustained a tension between different provisions of the constitution, some guaranteeing equal fundamental rights for all citizens, others entrenching the right to personal laws that include discriminatory provisions. Thus there is a real tension between Article 44 of the constitution, one of the "Directive Principles of State Policy," which calls for the Indian state to strive for a uniform civil code, and Article 26, which grants the right to every religious denomination to manage its own affairs. These tensions within Indian state secularism as defined at independence were different from the British colonial doctrine of supposed neutrality toward religious communities. Indian state secularism was sensitive to the immediate preceding history of interreligious discord and violence and to the possibility of exploitation of religion for political ends.

In other words, Indian secularism was conceived of as a means for ensuring that the state should not itself become an instrument in such exploitation. To this end, Indian secularism did not seek to relegate religion to the private sphere and preserved a role for the state in providing support for religious institutions and organizations (Smith 1999, 216–220). At the same time, however, the substantive content of secularism as a *positive* doctrine in the Indian context was not entirely clarified. Instead, it was subject to contradictory imperatives, such as state-initiated social-religious reform, on the one hand, and the right of collective religious freedom, on the other hand. While state secularism did find some precedents in the political traditions of India, it was not entrenched in those traditions as a coherent doctrine. But it is also probably true that the possibility of satisfactory resolution of such tensions was precluded by the fact of colonial subjugation. The legacy of colonial policies probably also made it difficult for Indian secularism to be grounded in an engagement with religious and community discourses that would have legitimized this principle in the popular consciousness of Indians at large.

In terms of the argument I am making in this book, it seems that Indian state secularism *implicitly* acknowledges that there is a link between religion and politics but does *not* propose or reflect a clear and categorical distinction between this link and the state. In other words, it does not seek to regulate a relationship between the state and politics while ensuring separation between the state and religion. Rather, the lines between these three categories—state, politics, and religion—have been unclear in Indian secularism as it has been applied by the state since independence. As discussed below, the inability of the Indian state to be consistent in practice in its commitment to neutrality toward different religions has led to a blurring of the line between religion and state. This has also meant that secularism as a constitutional principle and social value has operated as one of the foundations of civic reason but has not necessarily always provided all Indian citizens with access to the sphere of civic reason on an inclusive or egalitarian basis.

There are several ways in which Indian state secularism since independence may have been problematic in its contribution to civic reason as well as to ensuring separation of the state and religion. First, it does not provide mechanisms for regulating the role of religion in public life or the relationship between religion and politics. According to one scholar, this may be one of the legacies of Nehru's understanding of religion and morality, as reflected in the initiatives of "social policies for equal rights, a uniform civil code, positive discrimination, spread of education, and removal of superstition" (Mitra 1991, 765). As the first prime minister of independent India, he "set about making a non-issue out of religion from the outset, leading to a paradox that lay at the core of the nascent state. This paradox arose because a secular state that did not provide any formal role for religion in public affairs was superimposed on a society in which religion was a vital interpersonal bond" (Mitra 1991, 755–756).

The failure to clarify and address the role of religion in the public life of Indian society continues to characterize popular and intellectual discourse on secularism. In keeping with Nehru's legacy of viewing religion essentially as an obstacle to modernity, Indian intellectuals have tended to avoid engaging with religion *as* religion in assessing its relationship to secularism. Because they usually perceive religion as a source of primordial communal passions, Indian intellectuals advocate strong state action as a solution for combating communalism, while still invoking the era of Nehru as the ideal age of secularism, despite the state's failure to act in that way. Despite the existence of religion as a political force that is capable of moving millions of people, the democratic political system of the country "does not contain the institutional means to articulate and aggregate demands concerning religious policy, nor does it even provide an adequate political vocabulary to engage in dialogue. When the religious issue gets mentioned at all, it is articulated in a pejorative and polemical manner which only adds further intensity to the problem" (Mitra 1991, 760).

In terms of our analysis, religion has been neither acknowledged nor utilized in any structured manner as a source of public reason in the formal definition of state secularism in India. While this has not led to religion's becoming irrelevant or removed from public life altogether, the lack of mechanisms to regulate its role has resulted in problematic and dangerous forms of religious identity. The situation is further complicated by the inconsistent application of state neutrality with regard to different religious communities and the blurring of the separation of state and religion. While the neutrality of the state requires state institutions to keep equal distance from all religions, that has not been true of the practice of the Indian state, whether in the form of intervention for the purpose of social reform or in public affirmations of the character of the state. Rather, there has been an unequal treatment of communities—for example, Hindu and Muslims—in at least two critical ways.

First, with regard to reformist measures, the Indian state has been more proactive with regard to the Hindu community than with the Muslim community. For example, the Indian state has decreed that Hindu religious institutions should be accessible to members of all castes and classes, as a reform measure to counter the caste-based discrimination that is sanctioned by orthodox Hinduism. Thus, state initiatives in the name of secularism have been more beneficial to vulnerable members of the Hindu community than to vulnerable members of the Muslim community, as illustrated by the issue of women's inheritance. The Hindu Succession Act of 1965 enables Hindu women to inherit a share of their patrimony, but Muslim women do not have a similar right (Thakur 1993, 649). "In enacting this legislation the Indian Parliament took great liberties with the Hindu legal tradition by introducing provisions for divorce, inheritance by daughters, and other revolutionary ideas" (Smith 1999, 227). But this can also be seen as a failure to address similar problems in relation to Muslim communities.

In this light, it seems that the Indian state has interpreted secularism differently for the Hindu community than for the Muslim community. For the Hindu community, the state has often more strongly emphasized the imperative of reform over the imperative of collective religious freedom or freedom of religion. In contrast, it has often chosen to privilege collective religious freedom over reform in the case of the Muslim community. The actions of the Indian state in this regard raise related questions about who represents and speaks for different communities. "The modification of Hindu Law, while painful to the orthodox, has been accepted; after all, the vast majority of legislators were Hindus" (Smith 1999, 227). The implication here is that changes to Hindu law were accepted as legitimate by the majority of Hindus not just because they were enforced by the state but because they were perceived as having been suggested by Hindus, that is, as part of an internal discourse in the community. At the same time, the failure of the predominantly Hindu legislature to address similar issues for Muslims could be seen as a result of either concern about lack of legitimacy among Muslims or indifference. Whether for one of these reasons or some other, the result is a failure to treat different religious communities equally. For example, regarding the administration of Hindu temples through state organizations, "the distinction between the negative function of regulating temple administration to prevent abuses, which the government is empowered to perform, and the positive promotion of Hindu religion, is either not understood or ignored" (Smith 1999, 226). This violates the Indian secularist principles of state neutrality regarding religion and represents a failure of the state to keep equal distance from all religions. It also suggests the problematic consequences of having the Indian state act *as* a Hindu organization, whether that is seen as preferential treatment for Hindus or discrimination against Hindu communities.

Moreover, the Indian state has often treated the views and positions of certain conservative members of Hindu and Muslim communities as synonymous with the community itself. The Indian state has often privileged the "community," conceived in abstract terms, over the individual and his or her rights. Since some members of each community tend to appropriate exclusive control over the collective voice of the community—whether Hindu, Muslim, Sikh, or Christian—some members of those communities do not have equal access to the sphere of civic reason. Thus the claims of individual members of a community as *individuals* are effectively deemed subordinate to the claims of the *community,* or those who claim to speak for the community. In other words, although Indian secularism may contain the potential to empower the individual and all members of all communities in egalitarian fashion, in practice it has been invoked as a principle of affirming group identity over individual identity and has in effect led to discrimination against particular individuals.

The religious neutrality of the state has also been undermined by the political manipulation of religious communities. Following the death of Jawaharlal Nehru, his daughter, Indira Gandhi, became prime minister for a long time, from 1966 to 1977, through increasingly authoritarian measures to retain power (Brass 1990, 40). In 1975, Indira Gandhi declared a state of emergency and officially suspended a range of civil liberties. Despite or perhaps because of that move, the Congress Party lost the 1977 elections to the Janata Party, but the Congress Party came back to power through the 1980 elections. After that victory, the Congress under Indira Gandhi began cultivating communalist politics by using the discontent of the Muslim community to gain Muslims' support, suggesting that Muslims could be safe only by backing the Congress. Both the Congress and the opposition also drew political advantage from incidents of communal violence (Brass 1990, 202). Indira Gandhi was assassinated in 1984 and succeeded by her son, Rajiv Gandhi, as prime minister. In the 1984 elections, the Congress Party pandered to Hindu nationalist and communalist ideologies (Brass 1990, 199). Rajiv Gandhi's government continued the trend toward the communalization of politics by failing to condemn the discriminatory rhetoric of an increasingly militant Hindu right in the late 1980s and early 1990s.

Thus the Indian state increasingly followed a communalized model of politics, cultivating "vote banks" and playing up minority fears while presenting itself in a majoritarian Hindu idiom. Not just the Hindu nationalist BJP, which spearheaded the coalition National Democratic Alliance government from 1999 to 2004, but even the supposedly secular Congress sought to conflate the state with a religious identity. This was done without attempting to alter or amend the secular character of the constitution and of the definition of the state. The appeal to Hindus, whether explicit, in the case of the BJP, or implied, in the case of the Congress, was that the secularism of the Indian state was itself a Hindu value, rooted in the fundamentally Hindu character of Indian society. The corresponding appeal to Muslims and other minorities was that under the leadership of one party, the Indian state would effectively act as a patron to protect their rights. Though lip service has been paid to the constitutional discourse of secularism, Indian politics since the return of Indira Gandhi to power in 1980 has been shaped by the logic of differential treatment of religious communities rather than a discourse of equal citizenship and rights. The dominance of the Congress Party in government since independence has effectively resulted in a compromise of the institutions of the Indian *state*, including secularism, thereby making such principles vulnerable to further erosion by other parties or coalitions in government.

As a result of this communalization of Indian politics, the state has tended to formulate policy responses to sensitive issues in terms of an appeal to "sentiments" of different communities. For all practical purposes, the state has interpreted secularism as granting equal concessions to different communities on matters of religion, instead of keeping an equal distance from all of them. Through this populist strategy the state has not only granted official approval and sanction to conservative and orthodox interpretations of religious identity, but also contributed to a worsening of communal relations and increased hostility between communities. Having set a precedent for the cynical violation of secularism and manipulation of religion, the Indian state has opened a Pandora's box, the consequences of which it is often unable to control. This is clearly illustrated by the action of the state in the Shah Bano controversy.

Shah Bano, a sixty-two-year-old Muslim woman, went to the court in 1985 asking for maintenance from her husband, who had divorced her. The ultimate ruling by the Supreme Court of India was that she had the right to maintenance from her ex-husband under Section 125 of the Criminal Procedure Code, like any other Indian woman. The judgment was not the first granting a divorced Muslim woman maintenance under Section 125, as such judgments had been commonplace for many years. In the course of its judgment, the Supreme Court attempted to justify its ruling on Islamic grounds through an interpretation of some verses of the Qur'an and Sunna but in the process made some controversial remarks. The Supreme Court also invoked the need for a uniform civil code for national integration.

Though some Muslim lawyers and religious leaders supported the Supreme Court judgment, the majority of influential Muslim organizations challenged it as an attack on Islam. For instance, the All India Muslim Personal Law Board (AIMPLB), a party to the case, initiated a campaign challenging the judgment on grounds that it was un-Islamic and violated Muslims' right to follow their personal laws. The AIMPLB also challenged the authority of non-Muslim justices of the Supreme Court to interpret the Qur'an, and this call was headed by conservative Muslim leaders, including those from the Congress Party, which was in power at the time. In the face of the opposition, Shah Bano declined to seek enforcement of the judgment. Parliament, under the Congress prime minister Rajiv Gandhi, passed the Muslim Women (Protection of Rights on Divorce) Act of 1986, which precluded Muslim women from obtaining the benefits of maintenance under the Criminal Procedure Code and limited such relief to the *idda* period of four months provided for by commonly accepted Shari'a principles. The BJP and other Hindu nationalist organizations capitalized on the issue, describing it as yet another instance of the Congress Party and the Indian state pandering to Muslims.

The banning of Salman Rushdie's book *The Satanic Verses* was another instance involving the Muslim community where the Indian state gave higher priority to the logic of collective religious identity than to state neutrality regarding religion, and also favored a conservative interpretation of religious identity. The decision of the Indian state to ban the book represented a tacit acceptance that the offense caused to Muslims by the book was an attack on Muslim identity itself. In banning it, the state violated freedom of expression on the basis of a questionable concession that the existence of the book in India violated Muslims' freedom of religion. The logic of restricting freedom of expression in order to maintain public order encourages threats to create disorder by any group wishing to suppress views and ideas they dislike, while penalizing the victims rather than the perpetrators of disorder. Ironically, the idea that an attack on one's beliefs is an attack on one's identity was used by Hindu nationalists against Muslims in the Babri Masjid situation (Thakur 1993, 651–652). The destruction of the mosque was followed by widespread religious violence and attacks on Muslims. Thus the notion of protecting Hindu sentiments and beliefs was used to justify and mobilize the most destructive violation of the principle of secularism in independent India.

The exploitation of the Babri Masjid controversy by Hindu nationalist parties was effective because the leaders of the Congress Party were also engaged in similar manipulation of the issue. In 1989, for example, Prime Minister Rajiv Gandhi made a campaign speech near Ayodhya, the site of the disputed mosque, where he called for *Ram Rajya* (the rule of the Hindu god Ram) in India. The Congress manifesto for the elections, the judiciary, the government, and other parties, such as the Janata Dal, all reflected similar ambivalence (Mitra 1991, 761). It is relevant for our purposes to contrast the action of the government regarding the Babri Masjid issue in 1949, when it was able to defuse the tension and uphold its own neutrality, with its failure to do so in 1984. The decline in the neutrality of the state between those two dates made it more difficult to resolve the matter through the courts (Mitra 1991, 763). But that situation is understandable, if not predictable:

> The causes behind the inability of the government to continue the doctrine of neutrality in a rigid way are easily understood. Independence brought popular political accountability in place of a distant colonial government ultimately, though not exclusively, based on force. Even more importantly, independence saw the decline of the Muslim proportion in the population from 40 to 14 percent, removing at once the communal balance that the doctrine of neutrality requires for it to be effective. There were other signs of the doctrine fraying at the edges as well. Important concessions intended as temporary measures for the material advancement of the Hindu untouchable castes and tribals were thus made to the hegemonic principle in the .policy of reservation, introducing a certain degree of ambiguity to the state's proclaimed neutrality to all religions. (Mitra 1991, 763–764)

There also seems to be a clear correlation between the erosion of secularism in independent India and the worsening state of communal relations. As issues such as the Shah Bano case and the Babri Masjid dispute get politicized and communalized, the state feels obliged to sacrifice the constitutional principles of secularism for the sake of a political compromise that keeps the peace among communities. Yet that compromise usually exacerbates tensions in communal relations in the long term, since it opens the door for abuse of the neutrality of the state, as well as of the principles of religious freedom and the right to religious expression.

The preceding critical assessment of Indian secularism should not be taken to mean that this principle has completely failed to work in practice or is doomed to failure in the future. Given its limitations during the colonial period and the context of widespread violence following independence and partition in which it was introduced, secularism has indeed managed to provide a working, though unstable, balance for state-religion relations at a critical time in India's history. But assessed against the model of an inclusive discourse of civic reason as defined in Chapter 3, Indian secularism has been limited in several ways. For example, it tends to give higher regard to collective claims in the name of the community than to those of individual members of those communities. It has also favored particular interpretations of religious identity over others, heeded the voices of certain members of the community over others, and subordinated the rights of nonbelievers to those of believers.

As also noted earlier, these shortcomings of Indian secularism are accompanied by a lack of theoretical clarification and constitutional expression regarding the public role of religion. This has continued to be true even as religion has come to play a more contested, controversial, and very visible role in the public domain in India. That theoretical failure has meant that the state has dealt with the public role of religion in an arbitrary and opportunistic manner. It can be argued that defining the public role of religion more categorically might have prevented some of the problems of Indian secularism highlighted earlier. But it may also be true that the ambiguity of Indian secularism has provided flexibility and possibilities for implementing it in a diversity of ways to secure and sustain its legitimacy among different communities. In the final analysis, any critique of Indian secularism should aim to strengthen the theory and guide the practice rather than call for abandoning the principle itself.

Legitimizing Secularism among Indian Communities

The underlying objective of this chapter is to understand how the historical and current relationship of the Indian Muslim community to the state and to other religious communities is likely to influence the legitimacy and sustainability of Indian secularism as a deeply contextual concept and practice that is negotiated over time. This objective has been sought in the preceding discussion by exposing persistent tensions in these multiple relationships and their shifting contexts during various phases of Indian history up to the present. In particular, the Indian experience reveals the complexity of the tension between state neutrality regarding religion and the need to regulate and mediate the role of religion in public life.

One general conclusion from this analysis of the Indian case is the need to clarify the relationship among religion, the state, and politics beyond mere assertions of secularism and neutrality. In other words, there is a need for a process that enhances and promotes the legitimacy of secularism among different religious traditions, rather than simply assuming that the value of secularism is self-evident or will be readily appreciated among all communities. The outcomes of such negotiation between secularism and religious, cultural, and ethical frameworks cannot be predicted and will vary depending on the factors and actors involved. The outcomes themselves may also be subject to contestation and evolution, but the crucial point is that the process has to be deliberately initiated and promoted and cannot happen on its own. Multiple strategies and paradigms to enhance the space of civic reason between the secular and the religious can be used by civic actors and opinion leaders to legitimize this process and work with it in addressing issues of public concern.

The imperative of state neutrality regarding all religions does not preclude the state's role in fostering *internal* dialogue and debate within communities and dialogue *across* communities about secularism and other issues of general concern. To play this role effectively, the state should promote an understanding and practice of secularism that gives higher priority to *citizenship* than to vague notions of *collective group identity* that are vulnerable to abuse and manipulation by some elite in the name of the community. A related point is that the Indian state needs to emphasize a discourse of *individual rights,* that is, to insist categorically that the principle of freedom of religion or religious expression belongs to individual citizens. This does not mean that there is no place for collective or community rights and concerns, but that they should be allowed to evolve through the agency of individual members of the community. Accordingly, the Indian state should not accept the claims of self-appointed representatives of religious or cultural communities that they are the authentic voices of the community. It is not possible to elaborate on the complex issues of individual and collective identity and rights, except to emphasize the synergy and interdependence of the two, whereby it is the individual person who makes choices and acts on them, but she or he always does so within the framework of the community. The objective of these and other guidelines for state policy and practice is to provide and ensure the much-needed basis for secularism as a sphere of civic reason in Indian society that is empowering of minorities, of different communities, and of men and women.

Another general conclusion I wish to emphasize relates to the need for legitimization of secularism within various religions' frameworks. I do believe that Indian secularism, for all its flaws, can provide the space and flexibility for state commitment to secularism along the lines described above. As noted earlier, the obligation of the state to protect the rights and promote the interests of its citizens may require it to facilitate and encourage citizens to participate in the debate and process of reform, without imposing its own view of what that reform should be (Bilgrami 1999, 380–417; Chatterjee 1999, 345–379). The role of the state here is to promote the widest possible consensus among individual citizens and communities about the values of secularism, pluralism, constitutionalism, and human rights. Whether and to what extent this may undermine the neutrality of the state regarding religion will remain the subject of debate and disagreement (Bilgrami 1999, 411). This is what I have referred to earlier as the contextual negotiation of secularism to balance the state's neutrality with the state's obligation to protect the rights of individual citizens within their communities. But these principles and their mediation also need to be legitimized through internal discourse in communities. To this end, different communities and the state should draw upon indigenous traditions and historical experiences. The legitimacy and sustainability of Indian secularism needs somehow to tap the consciousness of Indian citizens and communities, including recollections of relevant precolonial conceptions and historical experiences. Assuming that to be true, the question is whether and how that can be done today, when some of those resources have been obstructed by the colonial intrusion into almost all parts of the subcontinent. Can traditional Indian values and institutions be relevant and effective in a radically transformed world that is shaped by Eurocentric conceptions of sovereignty, secularism, and power relations?

One aspect of the difficulty is that recollections of ideas and the meaning of institutions and relationships of the precolonial past are filtered through the lenses of European notions of what counts as history and how to interpret it. Another aspect is that possibilities of implementing policies emerging from such recollections are inhibited by ways in which the world today is organized and operated on the basis of European knowledge and understanding. To achieve continuity of historical experiences in the process of building constitutionalism over time, as discussed in Chapter 3, Indians need to reconnect to their precolonial past as if colonialism and its aftermath never happened. But since colonialism and its aftermath did happen, the challenge here is to the imagination of Indians to see and act on what might have happened, and to seek ways to read their own history in the most positive light possible. The nature and operation of this process are what I call "retrieving the irretrievable and imagining the unimaginable" (An-Na'im 2006, chap. 2).

I am not suggesting that Indians should strive to retrieve an "imaginary" history of complete and perfect secularism in a golden age of the precolonial past. Rather, I am advocating that they should seek to clarify, adapt, and implement what they "remember" to have been (and what may still continue to be, in one form or another, today) their indigenous conceptions and institutions of sovereignty, secularism, and rights. Indians should be able to seek to retrieve, rejuvenate, and develop such conceptions and institutions, regardless of whether or not they can verify and validate their recollections, and their relevance and utility, in terms of Eurocentric historiography and epistemology. However, the retrieval project I am suggesting emphasizes a critical examination of that historical experience, instead of the blind sentimental assertion of recollections of ideas and institutions. This project should also include the adaptation of historical notions of sovereignty, secularism, and accountability to present realities by imagining how they might have evolved *as if* they were never interrupted by colonial intrusion.

Significant change always occurs over time, by building on both the successes and the failures of continuing struggles and the influence of a variety of factors and forces operating and interacting in the daily lives of individuals and communities. But this does not mean that it is unnecessary to question the conceptual assumptions and direction of the processes of cultural change required in order to legitimize secularism in Indian communities. Indeed, as suggested earlier, a reconceptualization of secularism may be necessary to accelerate or redirect the processes of change in accordance with the accumulated wisdom of the communities and their leaders. Tentative proposals of reconceptualization may and should be made, evaluated and accepted or rejected, and tried in practice; they may work or fail to work. This would be particularly valuable when existing assumptions and directions for action do not seem to be working well enough for one reason or another. Toward this end, the history of anticolonial nationalism, as well as the legacies of figures such as Gandhi and Maulana Abul Kalam Azad, whose viewpoints can be interpreted as a simultaneous commitment to religion and secularism that does not privilege one over the other, can also be utilized as rich resources for such a project of "retrieving the irretrievable and imagining the unimaginable."

A related initiative is for the Indian state to regulate its own definition of secularism, to acknowledge the role of religion more clearly rather than continue to promote the fallacy that religion plays no role in public life or politics. At least one structural reason that Indian secularism has been compromised might be that the role of religion in public and political life is unregulated in the constitution and hence susceptible to abuse. But legislative reform for a constitutional amendment to redefine the scope of secularism should be undertaken with caution and should itself be based on civic reason in the most inclusive possible manner.

Initiatives of these sorts will enable the legitimacy of Indian secularism to be rearticulated on multiple grounds. A secularism that is subject to negotiation and embedded in state and society in this fashion might divest secularism of its negative connotations as antireligious or an alien Western imposition. It will also redefine secularism as a project of society and a basis for social reason rather than solely or primarily a project of the state. When understood and practiced in this way, secularism will succeed in protecting the rights, reflecting the voices, and respecting the agency of individuals and groups, of the genders, of diversity of ethnicity and linguistic or religious communities, of belief and nonbelief, and of diversity of views among and across believers and nonbelievers. In light of the initiatives described above, we may also imagine a model of Indian secularism made up of Islamic secularism, Hindu secularism, Sikh secularism, Christian secularism, and so on. In this model, each and all of these contextual secularisms would legitimize the constitutional separation of religion and state, while the state in turn would regulate the role of religion in public life. This paradigm can rejuvenate and revitalize Indian secularism as well as enrich the religious lives of communities, while at the same time leading to a more harmonious state of interfaith relations.

CHAPTER 5

Turkey:
Contradictions of
Authoritarian Secularism

The end of World War I marked the collapse of the Ottoman Empire and the drastic reduction of its territory. Mustafa Kemal soon led a successful revolution against the remnants of the old Ottoman government, and in 1922 a new republic was established. It instituted a series of rapid reforms aimed at thoroughly transforming Turkish political and social life by secularizing and westernizing the country and by strictly limiting—as well as controlling—the role of religion and religious institutions. Kemal's party, the People's Republican Party (CHP), ruled Turkey until the beginning of the multiparty system in the mid-twentieth century. A series of military coups or actions (in 1960, 1971, 1980, and 1997), often instigated in part by what the army saw as a threat to the secular nature of the government, led to a rather authoritarian style of democracy in Turkey. Dissenting voices, especially those of religious or ethnic groups, have been suppressed. More recent events, however, like the election of the secular pro-Islamic Justice and Development Party (AKP) and the decision to pursue full membership in the European Union (EU), may indicate improvement in the quality of democratic governance and protection of human rights for all segments of Turkish society. But it remains to be seen whether this positive trend will continue.

The following discussion of the experiences of Turkey is limited to certain aspects that are particularly relevant to the proposed theory of Islam, the state, and society and does not claim to present a comprehensive study of those experiences. The object here is to clarify and illustrate the contradictions of the imposition of secularism by the state, what I call authoritarian secularism, without giving sufficient attention to promoting the legitimacy of this principle among the population at large. In terms of the main propositions presented earlier, the problem occurs when authoritarian regimes seek to promote secularism as a separation of religion from the state without being able or willing to address the connectedness of religion and politics. In applying this analysis to Turkey in this chapter, I do not mean to suggest that this is true of that country alone, but only to illustrate a problem that is already present or can easily arise in other settings. Authoritarian secularism has been a hallmark of several countries of the region, from Ba'ath Party dictatorship in Iraq and Syria and Arab nationalism in Egypt under Nasser to the French model of Tunisia under Bourguiba and Marxist Algeria under the FLN.

Using the case of Turkey to make this point does not imply that there were no efforts to promote secularism in the popular culture of that country or that the connection between Islam and politics was completely and effectively terminated by state secularism. Indeed, Turkey's long and rich Ottoman experience can be seen as an illustration of how secularism can mediate the separation of Islam and the state, on the one hand, and connect Islam and politics, on the other. This process has evolved through customary (örfi) law as well as enacted state law (kanun) under European influence since the eighteenth century. The hallmark of the Ottoman system was the strong and authoritarian secular power of the state, which ruled over a highly pluralistic population made up of diverse religious and ethnic communities with varying degrees of autonomy. At the same time, the moral and political authority of Islamic religious authorities and leaders of the minority communities throughout the empire served as a check on the authoritarianism of the sultan-caliph and his officials. While the authoritarian nature of the state survived the revolution that established today's Republic of Turkey, the role of religious authorities and leaders of minority communities has been officially suppressed in the name of secularism and Turkish nationalism. Still, negotiations of secularism continued into the republican era, though under drastically different conditions, and have apparently come to a more constructive engagement in the late 1990s and early 2000s, as I will briefly explain later.

The Islamic identity of Turkey is rooted in its culture, tradition, and the religious affiliation of the vast majority of its population, while the secular nature of the state is entrenched in its constitution, which makes ten references to "secular" or "secularism." As I will briefly explain later in this chapter, any perceived threats to Kemalist republican secularism have been met with great hostility by state authorities, including the military. But it is also clear that strong tensions persist regarding the role of Islam in public life. The underlying question for this chapter is whether republican authoritarianism succeeded in achieving its purported objectives of secular constitutional governance, and at what cost. In terms of the proposed theory, my contention is that acknowledging and regulating the role of Islam in the public domain is critical for diminishing the contradictions of authoritarian secularism. In other words, the desirable objective of separation of Islam and the state is, in my view, defeated by the failure of the state to respect the legitimate role of Islam in public life.

To explore the contradictions of attempting to impose secularism through authoritarian power, I begin by looking at the roots of the present-day system, since the Ottoman Empire negotiated secularism among diverse religious and ethnic communities spread across vast regions. The dynamism of the pragmatic Ottoman system illustrates how Islamic societies evolve in response to internal change as well as external factors. There is also both continuity and change in how the ideas of secularism, pluralism, and citizenship were negotiated from the empire to the republic, through Atatürk's reforms and subsequent developments. But the real or perceived dilemmas of that more ideological and authoritarian republican *laïcité* (*laiklik* in Turkish) highlighted in the second part of this chapter may lead to its eventual transformation into more coherent secularism as proposed in this book. Although the outcome remains to be seen, it seems that the vicious cycle of the politics of mutual apprehension can be mediated through external as well as internal factors and developments, as indicated by the most recent developments. As I will emphasize in conclusion, however, the outcome of this process is significant for the prospects of secularism throughout the Muslim world.

Pragmatic Ottoman Secularism

The Ottoman Empire began as a principality in northwestern Anatolia and expanded rapidly after establishing its independence from the waning Seljuk Empire of the eleventh century. The Ottomans took over Constantinople from the Byzantine Empire in 1453, renamed it Istanbul as their new capital, and conquered Syria, Egypt, and western Arabia in 1516–1517. Having reached the height of its military and political power by the sixteenth century, the Ottoman Empire began to be challenged by the rising Western powers at the time of Sultan Murad IV (ruled 1623–1640). Military defeats in Europe and the Indian Ocean at the hands of European states with their superior technology were seen as consequences of the deviation from the ancient world order *(nizam-ı alem)*. Ottoman intellectuals seeking to find causes for the decline of the empire focused on what they viewed as cultural and religious decay, deviation from tradition, and moral corruption. This is a familiar theme in Islamic history, as can be seen, for instance, in the work of Nizam al-Mülk (died 1092) (Hourani 1991, 209). Many commentators of the seventeenth century argued that the solution for the weakness of the Ottoman army and state was to be found in "returning to the ancient law" *(kanun-u kadim)*, the customs and traditions of high Islamic and Turkish culture (İpşirli 2001, 220) and proposed reforms in the state and education from this perspective (Kafi 1989). By the beginning of the eighteenth century, however, the call to return to the Golden Age was replaced by calls for a "new order" *(nizam-ı cedid)*. Rather than continue to focus on internal affairs, the Ottoman state began for the first time to examine Western culture and civilization carefully, sending ambassadors to some of the important European capitals to report on developments there (Unat 1968). Despite the different orientation of these reform movements, both can be seen as responding to the same underlying need for adaptation to changing conditions.

Thus recent and present debates among Muslims over the proper role and scope of religion find parallels in the history of the Ottoman Empire. In 1656, for example, according to Katib Çelebi's book *The Balance of Truth (Mizanu'l-Hakk fi İhtiyarı'l-Ehakk)*, some of the most divisive debates revolved around theological, moral, mystical, and legal issues. In their time and context, those debates can be seen as reflecting liberal versus strict interpretations of Shari'a. Some *ulama*, headed by Sheikhulislam Ebussuud Efendi, held that singing, dancing, whirling, smoking tobacco, drinking coffee, shaking hands, bowing for reverence, establishing cash foundations, and accepting money for religious teaching and services were permissible under Shari'a within the confines of some religious restrictions. Other *ulama*, headed first by Birgili Mehmet Efendi and later by Qadizade, asserted that these were completely unlawful in Islam. Moreover, such differences sometimes generated conflicts among the masses, which had to be controlled with great difficulty by the sultan's security forces (Çelebi 1957).

Traditionally, Ottoman society was divided between the ruling elite *(askeriyye)* and their subjects *(raiyye)* (Yediyıldız 2001, 491–558). The ruling elite, who were exempt from paying taxes because of their services to the state, consisted of four subgroups: (1) the palace (the household of the sultan), (2) the military elite *(seyfiyye)*, (3) learned scholars employed by the empire *('Ilmiyye)*, who were part of the *ulama*, and (4) the scribal/bureau-cratic elite *(kalemiyye)*. Within the rest of society there were various (some-times overlapping) subgroups, including Sufi orders; *ulama* outside the ap-paratus of the state, including those engaged with charitable foundations *(awqaf)*; guilds of artisans and communities of artists; and non-Muslim com-munities *(millets)*. Such social groups existed outside the state hierarchy in various degrees of relative autonomy. It is important to note that these subgroups overlapped and interacted, and the occasional ordinary conflicts occurred among them. Throughout Ottoman history, the state tried increas-ingly to integrate these groups within its authority structure and to harmo-nize their relations through what today might be called checks and balances.

In contrast, the *ulama* perceived themselves as a community of scholars who exercised moral authority over the generality of the population *(avâm,* or commoners) and even over the ruling elite. The *ulama*, including to a lim-ited extent those employed by the state, tried not only to maintain auton-omy from the state but also to assert their authority over it, because they saw themselves as representing God's word and Shari'a. However, this asser-tion of the superiority of religious authority was constantly contested by the ruling elite, who also sought to assert their worldly power and superiority over the *ulama*. These competing views of power and authority were re-flected in the balance between the sultan and the sheikhulislam, who was the head of the *ulama* and generally seen as equal to the grand vizier, the highest-ranking "civil" state official. The sheikhulislam was appointed by royal warrant, while accession to the Ottoman throne depended in turn on a *fatwa* from the sheikhulislam. The tension between these two authorities can be seen in the fact that the sultans appointed and deposed the shei-khulislam, while the latter sometimes sanctioned the dethroning of the sul-tan through a *fatwa*. But in issuing that sort of *fatwa,* the sheikhulislam would have been acting as party to the *coups de palace*, not on his own inde-pendent initiative (Uzunçarşılı 1984, 192; Dursun 1989, 329).

It should be emphasized, however, that Islam was not the only religion in the Ottoman Empire, and Muslims constituted only a minority in some parts of its territories. The religious composition of various regions and the empire as a whole also varied over time, in response to a variety of factors and developments (Yediyıldız 2001, 518–520). While it is not possible to dis-cuss those demographics here, it is important for our purposes to briefly re-view the ways in which the Ottoman state dealt with this religious diversity through the communal-autonomy system of different religious communities, or *millets* (Ortaylı 1986, 997).

The status and rights of individual persons were based on their *millet*, with the greatest rights accorded to Sunni Muslims; non-Sunni Muslims enjoyed lower status. From a formal point of view, the status and rights of all Christian and Jewish Ottoman subjects, as People of the Book, were supposed to be governed by the *dhimma* system. They were allowed to keep and practice their religion within prescribed limitations but were not supposed to serve in the army, ride horses or carry arms, hold high-ranking office, or be active in public political life in general. Members of these communities were required to dress in a distinctive style, pay a special tax *(jizya)*, and live in segregated communities, especially in the cities. However, these rules were not strictly enforced in practice. Some were employed in important and sensitive positions as ambassadors and governors and were exempt from the *jizya* and dress requirements (Eryılmaz 1990; Gülsoy 1999; Krikorian 1978).

Christian and Jewish communities were also subjected to symbolic restrictions, such as the prohibition on the public performance of religious rituals in Muslim areas or housing restrictions to signify the inferiority of *dhimmi* communities and their members. However, some of the administrative measures taken by the Ottoman state, such as the relocation of Christian and Jewish communities from the provinces to Istanbul and the limitation of their residence to specific neighborhoods, were motivated primarily by the economic interest of the state or were a result of social conditions. Forced relocations were also sometimes imposed as individual or collective punishment (Kenanoğlu 2004, 325; Üçok 1986, 574–579). Requirements of dress code and visible signs of identity were also part of a general Ottoman policy of segregation by class, profession, and ethnoreligious identity that were not limited to *dhimmi* status as such (Mardin 2001, 90–91).

The internal and external relationships of each *dhimmi* community were regulated primarily by its own leaders, subject to the overriding jurisdiction of the Ottoman state. These communities were segregated on grounds of religion and sect, so that Gregorian Armenians, Protestants, and Catholics were considered to be different religious communities and lived in separate neighborhoods, with their own churches and schools, under their respective legal jurisdictions (Ortaylı 1986, 997). The Greek Orthodox Church enjoyed the highest level of autonomy and prestige in the *millet* structure, with the patriarchate in Istanbul serving as the religious, judicial, and financial headquarters of all Greek Orthodox communities throughout the empire. The Synod Council of the Patriarchate, consisting of archbishops and high-ranking priests, controlled both religious and secular (worldly) affairs, including censorship of all books written in Greek on any subject. The Armenian patriarchate also enjoyed significant autonomy in the religious, administrative, and judicial affairs of its community, though with less prestige than its Greek counterpart.

Jews were an important part of the Ottoman *millet* system, especially as their population gradually increased by immigration from Hungary (1376) and France (1394), as well as from Spain and Italy throughout the fifteenth century (Ortaylı 1986, 1001). Jews did not have a clerical hierarchy like that of Christians, however, and the representative role of the grand rabbi of Istanbul was not officially confirmed until 1835. Though the whole Jewish community in the Ottoman Empire was considered a single *millet*, Jews organized themselves in separate communities *(kahals)* according to their previous origins and cultural affiliations, each with its own contacts with the Ottoman state. Each *kahal* was responsible for collecting taxes and delivering the required proportions to the Ottoman treasury, spending money for community activities, regulating kosher food services, and punishing offenders. Each local Jewish community had its own synagogue, rabbi, teacher, school, hospital, and cemetery, and many of them had judicial councils called *Bet Din*, headed by a rabbi chosen by the community (Shaw 1991, 48–61).

The Ottoman Legal System

The Ottoman legal system was decentralized, diverse, and dynamic, to cope with the wide religious, ethnic, and cultural diversity of the population. Building on the legal traditions of preceding Islamic empires, the Ottomans developed a dynamic system of law *(kanun-u Osmani)*, which consisted of three parts: (1) Shariʿa, (2) *kanun* (including customary law, called *örf*), and (3) minority legal regimes applicable to non-Muslim *millets*. The principles of Shariʿa followed by the Ottoman state were primarily of the Hanafi school of Islamic jurisprudence. While local judges were generally permitted to follow other schools of Islamic jurisprudence, the official use of the Hanafi school by the state made it highly influential throughout the Ottoman Empire, including areas where other schools of Islamic jurisprudence had been followed traditionally. Even within the jurisdiction of the Hanafi school, there was leeway for judges to adopt views from other schools or to send a case to a different judge from another school (Aydın 2001, 459–464; Imber 2002, 218–220).

The courts were official institutions that operated under the authority of the central government in Istanbul, which appointed and paid all judges and generally ensured the enforcement of their judgments. This relationship between the central government and judges allowed state officials to decide the geographical and subject-matter jurisdiction of judges whom they authorized to apply Shari'a principles. Consequently, those judges' decisions were officially accepted and backed by the coercive power of the state. The courts could also endorse a ruling made by an arbiter or mediator agreed upon by the parties (*sulh* decree), which was then entered in the official records of the court and enforced by state officials. The ruling of a judge applying Shari'a principles was generally final and binding, but a party who did not accept the decision was allowed to apply for a second hearing of the case by the court of the sultan *(divan),* as the ultimate appellate court.

Kanun was legislation enacted by the sultan in his authority as supreme ruler *(wali-ıl-amr)*. It was usually derived from custom and therefore varied accordingly from one region to another throughout the empire. This legislative authority of the sultan was presumably sanctioned by Shari'a itself to regulate matters not covered by its own principles, such as the structure of state institutions, the imposition of taxes that are not required under Shari'a, and certain punishments. *Kanun* legislation was supposed to be of limited duration, usually expiring when the sultan who had enacted it died or was dethroned, unless reenacted by the new sultan. It is reported that the first *kanun* was made by Osman Ghazi, the founder of the Ottoman state, to impose a market tax called *baj* in Bursa, which was continued by his descendants (Aydın 2001, 440). The corpus of *kanun* evolved slowly over time, as sultans preserved the legacy of their predecessors, and began to be systematized first under Sultan Mehmed II and then by Sultan Süleyman II, who came to be known as Kanuni for his efforts to bring coherence and consistency to this body of law (İnalcık 2000; Aziz Efendi 1985; Müezzinzade 1962).

The third part of the Ottoman legal system was the law and administration of justice according to the authorities of each non-Muslim religious community, as noted earlier. Thus a member of those communities would have been born, married, divorced, and buried according to the religious and customary law of his or her community, which also governed a wide range of other legal matters, including economic and social relations. It was possible for a church community to try to sentence an offender to prison and then deliver him to Ottoman authorities for the execution of the verdict. But Shariʿa and the *kanun* of the Ottoman state had overriding jurisdiction in criminal law and other matters beyond the issues assigned to the communal jurisdiction of *dhimmi* communities. In addition to the jurisdiction of state courts in disputes involving a Muslim party, which were always under the jurisdiction of the Shariʿa courts, members of *dhimmi* communities sometimes preferred to go to those courts if they expected a more favorable outcome there than was likely before their own authorities. For instance, it was easier for Christian and Jewish women to obtain divorce from Shariʿa courts and take the decree to their communal authorities to enforce than to secure that outcome directly before their communal authorities (Çiçek 2001, 31–48).

While the legal autonomy of non-Muslim communities within the Ottoman Empire was strong and extensive in comparison to that in other parts of the world during that period of history, it was also subject to a number of important limitations. The sultan's power to appoint or dismiss a *millet*'s religious and community leaders ensured that those in positions of authority within the community were loyal (or at least not disloyal) to the Ottoman ruler. The possibility of access to Islamic courts for individual persons, even if not actually exercised, may have served as a limitation on the power of the minority ecclesiastical or Jewish courts. The possibility of exercising that option may have provided individual members of those communities with some redress if they felt aggrieved by their own leaders, but it should also be noted that that would have happened at the discretion of the Islamic sovereign and his officials.

The systematic usage of *kanun*, along with Shariʿa, by the Ottomans reflected a long tradition of state authority as the lawmaker, which can be traced back to the pre-Islamic Turkish culture that some historians argue underlies Turkey's modern secularism (Fleischer 1986; İnalcık 2000, 27–48). It is not possible to discuss here the rationale for evoking nostalgic investment in pre-Islamic tradition and whether it has achieved or can achieve its desired objectives. The point for our purposes is simply that the ancient and continuous systematic use of *kanun* was due to the fact that Shariʿa does not address certain areas that are indispensable for the administration of the state. These areas were left open to public-policy considerations according to the changing needs of society as determined by state officials, without being bound by the methodology of Shariʿa *(usul al-fiqh)*. Moreover, as state officials determined whether Shari'a applied, the whole process was political and secular, not religious.

Historians debate whether Shari'a and *kanun* constituted two separate and distinct types of law, one religious and the other secular. Those who contend that *kanun* was separate and secular see it as a Turkish invention that provides a historic explanation for Turkey's transition to secularism in the twentieth century. Others, however, argue that *kanun* has always been part of the Islamic legal tradition and was authorized and envisioned by Shari'a scholars from the beginning. They also note that the Ottomans themselves did not see any contradiction between Shari'a and *kanun*. Although promulgated by the sultan, the texts of *kanun* were generally drafted by the sultan's private secretary *(nişancı)*, who would be from the *ulama* and well versed in Shari'a, in consultation with the sultan and other authorities, particularly the sheikhulislam (Aydın 2001, 441). *Kanun* texts were also accepted by the *ulama*, who viewed them as a necessary basis for the political authority that was a prerequisite to the implementation of Shari'a (İnalcık 2000, 44).

In view of the significant change in the nature of the territorial postcolonial state, as emphasized earlier, I would draw a different conclusion from the debate about the relationship of Shari'a and *kanun* in the modern context. From my perspective, all law or legislation that is enforced through state institutions is secular, even when drawn from or based on Shari'a principles. Since it is not possible to enforce all the various interpretations of Shari'a by different scholars because of strong disagreements among and within the schools, enforcement through state institutions will necessarily have to be selective among competing views. Moreover, whatever principles of Shari'a are enforced, the actual enforcement happens through the political will of the state and not by virtue of their being Shari'a principles as such. The fact that the Ottoman state appointed the judges, who were supposed to apply the Hanafi school (while actively allowing the views of other schools in some locations), paid the judges' salaries, determined the scope of their jurisdiction, and enforced their judgments confirms that relevant Shari'a principles were enforced through the political will of the state. This is true regardless of whether *kanun* was independent of Shari'a.

Decline and Transformation

The classical Ottoman legal system outlined above began to face serious challenges as the economic and cultural foundations of the empire gradually changed over time. For example, by the late sixteenth and early seventeenth centuries, a cash-based economy and system of taxation replaced the previous system of in-kind taxation (Akdağ 1963; Griswold 1983; Faroqhi et al. 1994, 413–471). Another significant socioeconomic change was the increasing migration of peasants away from agricultural life and into urban areas (Faroqhi 1995, 91–113; Faroqhi et al. 1994, 435–438). Consequently, the structures and institutions of the Ottoman state also began to evolve and undergo significant reform during the seventeenth and eighteenth centuries. The office of the grand vizier, for instance, was moved outside the palace and began to take responsibility for day-to-day affairs of the country that were beyond the immediate control of the sultan. That change marked the end of traditional dynastic absolutism and the formation of a more independent administration with new, specialized bureaucratic organs and institutions of the state (Findley 1980, 49–58).

The social configurations and institutions of the *ulama* class also saw significant change during this period. A growing urban population meant that increasing numbers of *ulama*, many of them at high levels, were coming from the merchant class. Families began sending their children to *madrasas* not just to learn but to gain certification for future employment as part of the state's elite *ulama*. By the second half of the seventeenth century, this growing elite began to display the characteristics of an entrenched aristocracy, with inherited positions and a monopoly over the religious endowments *(awqaf)* (Abou El-Haj 1988, 17–30). The role and importance of the elite *ulama* within the government gradually declined, however, with the growing modernization of the Ottoman state. The traditional administrative, political, and ideological roles and positions of the *ulama* were increasingly taken over by secular bureaucrats (Findley 1980, 61–66).

The *millet* system began to dissolve in the nineteenth century because of pressure from Western powers, which gained technological, military, and economic ascendance over the weakening Ottoman Empire. A series of treaties, called "capitulations," granted European countries certain economic and diplomatic privileges while doing business in the Ottoman Empire and gave them greater rights to control and influence *dhimmi* communities in the name of "protecting" them. The privileges available to certain *dhimmi* groups under the capitulations influenced many individuals to convert; Armenian and Orthodox Christians, for example, sometimes converted to Roman Catholicism in order to take advantage of benefits available to Catholics under capitulations to France. This resulted in fierce competition among the various religious and church groups and led the Ottoman state to ban non-Muslims from changing their religious affiliation. By allying themselves and doing business with Western countries, the *dhimmi* populations became economically stronger than ever. This newfound strength began to assert itself in the form of nationalist movements, which not only became widespread among the *dhimmi* communities but spread to include ethnic Muslim groups such as Arabs and Albanians.

As the economic and military strength of the Ottoman Empire declined through such socioeconomic, political, and demographic changes, a consensus emerged about the need for reform. Every real or perceived problem in the Ottoman military, government, legal, or economic systems was seen as contributing to the empire's military defeats, thereby adding fuel to the reform movement. Although, or perhaps because, European powers were viewed as a threat to Islam and the empire, the Ottomans were convinced that they needed to adopt the scientific and technological progress that was the source of the superior power of Western countries in order to overcome that threat. The lack of legal standardization across the empire, which had been seen as expedient flexibility in the past, came to be viewed as an impediment to trade and economic development, while the capitulations enabled the Western powers to impinge on Ottoman sovereignty. An internal debate ensued between those who supported the adoption of a Western-style legal system as necessary for the survival of the empire and those who considered that position treason to Islamic and Turkish traditions. Some of those who agreed that legal reform was needed argued that it could be done through an evolutionary process based on Shari'a law and Ottoman culture.

In response to these external and internal pressures, the Ottoman Empire underwent a process of intense legal reform beginning in the mid-nineteenth century and lasting until the formation of the republic in the 1920s. The first clear step in this process, which became known as the Tanzimat (reorganization), was an 1839 edict called *Hatti-i Sharif* of Gülhane, which for the first time officially affirmed the legal equality of all non-Muslim and Muslim subjects of the sultan, although it specifically referred to Shari'a as the law of the empire (Küçük 1986, 1007–1024). Demands by European powers for additional reforms led to the Ottoman Reformation Edict of 1856, which abolished the poll tax on *dhimmis (jizya)*, prohibited derogatory treatment of or reference to *dhimmi* communities and their members, extended military service to non-Muslims, and reaffirmed their equal status. Moreover, this edict did not make any reference to Islamic principles.

These changes severely restricted the authority of the religious elites among non-Muslim communities and led to increased alienation and division along religious and ethnic lines instead of uniting the population as equal citizens of the same state (Küçük 1986, 1018).

Another key step in the reform process was the promulgation of the Mejelle, the first codification of Shari'a, which combined Islamic legal principles with a Western organizational system. These codes, which were prepared by a commission of scholars, judges, and political leaders, were enacted into law between 1869 and 1876. They began with a codification of general principles of Shari'a *(kulliyyat)* followed by legal principles of transactions *(mu'amalat)*, which included sales and contracts. The Mejelle gave priority to matters of commercial law, most likely because this was the area where standardization and codification of law were required by the rise of capitalism and increasing economic relations with the European states. In addition, the Ottoman state adopted a number of statutes that were closely modeled on European codes, including the Royal Commercial Law of 1850, the Royal Penal Code of 1851, and the Procedural Law of 1880. Moreover, the first Ottoman constitution, which was enacted in 1876, provided for various aspects of the modern principles of equality before the law and nondiscrimination on grounds of religion. Those principles were consolidated by subsequent constitutional development during the rest of the Ottoman era and further entrenched under the republic after 1923.

The educational system was reformed along corresponding lines. In traditional Ottoman society, *madrasas* had a virtual monopoly over education, and their graduates became high-ranking officials not only among the *ulama* elite but among the military and bureaucratic elites as well. A growing number of secular schools and their graduates began to challenge the dominance of that system and the *ulama* who controlled it. The mounting complexity and specialization of the law also led to the establishment of a number of institutions of legal education outside the traditional system (Aydın 2001, 458). On the other hand, the Ottomans also sought to reform the traditional system itself, and opened a modern *madrasa* (Dar'ül-Hilafeti'l-Aliyye Medreseleri) in 1914.

Legal reforms extended to opening specialized courts, like the commercial courts in 1864. Following European models, new courts consisting of a panel of judges were introduced for the first time, and an appellate court was also established during that period. A Ministry of Justice was established in 1868 to serve as the sole authority in the field of administration of justice.

While the goal was to standardize and centralize administration of the law under this ministry, the reality was a proliferation of the types and number of courts within the Ottoman state. As a result, there were Islamic Shariʿa courts, courts for non-Muslims, specialized courts, panel courts, and consular courts run by foreign powers under the capitulations. There were efforts to unify these court systems—for instance, to close the consular courts, which were seen as impinging on Ottoman sovereignty, end separate courts for non-Muslims, and place all personal-status issues under the jurisdiction of the Shariʿa court system. But such measures encountered great resistance, both internally and externally (Aydın 2001, 485–486).

Debate about the role of secularism began in the Ottoman Empire after the enactment of the first constitution in 1876. It is beyond the scope of this book to provide detailed discussion of those debates, but it is important briefly to note their wider context, which included the competing perspectives and interests of different groups and generations of reformers. The context was partly set by the fact that the Ottoman state began to promote a Western-oriented bureaucratic class by sending young men to France for education after 1789. Those students returned to serve as a distinct group of statesmen *(pashas),* who were the architects of Tanzimat reforms, including the new educational system (Zürcher 2004; Weismann and Zachs 2005). As the Tanzimat approach prevailed over the first generation of Ottomans to acquire a Western education within the Ottoman Empire, this educated generation was marginalized within the system, unable to find jobs in the bureaucracy. As a result, the young Ottomans became harshly critical of the Tanzimat mentality and turned their energies to alternative avenues, such as civil-society-based critiques of the state—for example, through the *Tercüman-ı Ahval (Interpreter of the Times),* the first privately owned newspaper of the empire, established in 1860. The young Ottomans also began to reevaluate approaches to Shariʿa in relation to new understandings of equality and justice. In contrast to the Tanzimat bureaucracy, the young Ottomans embraced their Ottoman and Islamic identities while also claiming to be more progressive than the best-educated *pasha* of the period.

In that context, the leading ideologue of the Young Turks, Ziya Gökalp, tried to develop a secular model for the Ottoman Empire based on a perspective of combining the best aspects of Islamic and Turkish tradition with Western modernity. As a sociologist, he sought to combine Western sociology with Islamic *fiqh* in a new discipline he called the "science of the social roots of the law" *(içtimaî usul-ü fıkıh),* in which sociologists and *ulama* would cooperate to modernize Shari'a (Gökalp 1959, 196–199; Heyd 1950, 87–88). Said Halim Pasha, grand vizier, social thinker, and political scientist, opposed Ziya Gökalp's eclecticism and called for the modernization of *fiqh* by using its internal mechanisms. İsmail Hakkı, another modernist scholar, also called for the modernization of *usul al-fiqh* through internal revival (Berkes 1964, 349–360, 490–495).

These developments in the last decades of the Ottoman Empire have been interpreted in different ways. From one perspective, they are seen as having resulted in a fragmented legal and judicial system that failed to meet the needs of Ottoman society. The wholesale adoption of European codes and legal structures was also criticized by some for not yielding the expected outcomes because they failed to take into account the cultural structure of Ottoman society. In addition, this line of thinking argues, the patchwork integration of Western legal norms destroyed the legal unity of the previous Ottoman system and arguably, by increasing its dependence on Western law, "prepared the ground for the wholesale acceptance of it in the future" (Aydın 2001, 484). A counterview maintains that although the Ottoman reform efforts never coalesced into a coherent and unified legal system, they nonetheless can be seen as a primarily evolutionary approach to legal reform and an attempt to revitalize Shari'a and the Ottoman legal system through a synthesis of Islamic and Western legal traditions and cultures. Late Ottoman movements toward constitutionalism and pluralism may have been strongly influenced by the demands and examples of the European powers, but they were still grounded in Islamic principles. Some modern Turkish historians and sociologists argue that these efforts would have culminated in a modern legal system that they would regard as authentically Islamic. But that process, this view holds, was abruptly aborted by the Young Turks' revolutionary shift toward westernized secular law and culture (Tanpınar 1985; Ülken 1979; Mardin 1962 and 1989). It seems to me that there is some validity to both positions, but what is more significant from my perspective is that such debates are indeed taking place along lines of analysis and assessment similar to the one I am proposing in this book.

Ideological Republican Secularism

The victory of Mustafa Kemal's army in August 1922 marked the end of the Turkish war of liberation and the creation of the republic. Under Kemal's leadership, the new republic began a series of rapid and radical reforms aimed at turning Turkey into a modern secular state. Following the French model of *laïcité,* Kemalists sought to restrict the role of religion to that of a private belief system strictly outside the public sphere. This new ideology was implemented through a series of laws and policies between 1922 and 1935. Major reforms included the abolition of the caliphate, the closing of traditional *madrasas,* and the abolition of the religious courts in 1924. During the following year, the regime abolished Sufi orders, prohibited the wearing of the Ottoman head cover for men *(fez),* discouraged the veiling of women, and adopted the Gregorian calendar as the sole official calendar. In 1926 a new civil code based on the Swiss model was adopted, thereby breaking the link with Shari'a as well as introducing civil marriage and divorce laws. In 1928 the state was declared secular, Islam was abandoned as the official religion of the state, and a new Latinized Turkish alphabet was adopted. Sunday was established as a weekly legal holiday in 1935 (Jacoby 2004, 80).

However, the Kemalist form of secularism was designed to enable the state to control religion rather than simply remove it from the public sphere. One important step in that direction was to control the *ulama* and Sufi orders through such measures as the Law of the Unification of Education, which closed all *madrasas* and placed all education in the hands of the Ministry of Education. The *ulama* were banned from wearing their traditional robes (and the *fez* and turban), and they were no longer allowed to use titles such as *alim* and *sheikh,* which implied Islamic religious authority. The 1928 adoption of the Roman alphabet and banning of the teaching of Arabic and Persian sought to sever cultural and intellectual ties both to the Ottoman past and to the modern Muslim world (Berkes 1964, 477).

Such measures meant that the *ulama* no longer had a significant role to play in society. The knowledge they specialized in and represented was seen as a relic of the past and a drag on the state's efforts to bring modernity to Turkish society. Their opportunities for employment using their traditional knowledge and education were limited to mosques and other religious institutes. Since those institutions were also controlled and financed by the state, the independence of the *ulama* was effectively stifled. This old intellectual class was replaced by a new one that sought to break the ties of the past and create a nation with a new secular culture. For example, the Turkish History Institute interpreted Turkish history, while the Turkish Language Institute remolded the Turkish language (Lewis 2002).

Convinced that modernizing and westernizing Turkey were in the country's best interest, the Kemalists' goal was to educate the population and lead them—even force them, if necessary—into a secular and modern society. Kemal's charisma and position as the "savior" and "father" of the nation after his victory in the war of liberation were used to promote popular perceptions of him as infallible, benevolent, and overpowering. Any questioning or criticism of or dissent from Kemalist reforms was (and often still is) considered treason to the country. Any measure or policy that was held by the state as a feature of modern civilization had to be adopted as rapidly as possible, and only rarely was any further deliberation or justification deemed either necessary or desirable. State institutions tended to implement such policies first, and then intellectuals and journalists were supposed to seek to establish the rationale behind them retroactively. Fear that political opposition or critical thinking could derail these new reforms meant that anyone who disagreed with or questioned them from any ideological or other perspective had to be silenced or forced into exile.

One of the most controversial issues that confronted the new republic was the abolition of the caliphate. Although the Turkish Grand National Assembly (GNA) abolished the sultanate in 1922, it initially kept the office of the caliphate and appointed a member of the Ottoman dynasty as the new caliph. Many people, including leading Turkish nationalists such as Ziya Gökalp, supported the separation of the sultanate and caliphate and advocated a caliphate that would have no role in national politics. Instead, the new caliph was envisioned as the spiritual leader of the global Muslim community *(Umma)*—in essence, the Muslim equivalent of the pope. This approach, its proponents argued, would actually strengthen the caliphate by expanding its power internationally as the basis of a new era of Muslim unity, while the Turkish state would benefit from being the protector of the caliphate (Gökalp 1922a, 1–6; Gökalp, 1922b, 1–5).

Others, including Mustafa Kemal himself, saw the continuing presence of a caliph as a mere historical relic that threatened the national sovereignty of the newly established republic (Alpkaya 1998, 199). This group challenged the vision of the caliph as an international religious leader as an impossible reinvention of the office and concept of the caliphate. To those holding this view, the caliphate was not a truly Islamic institution but a mere "decoration" of the old sultanate government. They neither accepted the possibility of redefining the caliphate in its Islamic sense nor believed such redefinition to be desirable, considering it a meaningless dream that the new republic could not afford (Nadi 1955, 38–40).

It is relevant for our purposes that those seeking to abolish the caliphate sought to justify their views through religious as well as political arguments. Seyyid Bey, the minister of justice, published pamphlets and spoke on the floor of the assembly. He argued that neither the Qur'an nor the Sunna contained any details about the caliphate, which proved that the office was not a religious institution but rather worldly and political. The Qur'an, Seyyid Bey observed, contained only two points about the proper system of government: consultation *(meshverret)* and obedience to authority *(ulû'l emr)*. Islam did not therefore insist on any one particular form of government, and any form of government that followed these principles could be legitimate. Consequently, not only was there no obstacle in Shari'a to a parliamentary government, but in modern times it was the only form of government that could legitimately realize the Islamic requirements of consultation and the rule of law. In his view, the traditional general overriding authority of the caliph *(Wilaya al 'Amma)* meant responsibility over public affairs that was based on a contract of agency *(aqd-î Wakâlet)*, whereby the caliph was the agent of the nation and his power directly derived from the state's will and choice. According to Seyyid Bey, any caliphate that was not established through the free choice of the Islamic community at large *(Umma)* was illegitimate under Shari'a. He therefore concluded that there had been no legitimate caliph after the death of Ali, the fourth caliph, since after that time the caliphate began to be taken over by force rather than the free will of the *Umma* (Seyyid Bey 1923, 27–28).

Debates about the abolition of the caliphate were accompanied by debates over abolishing Shari'a and religious endowments and the need to reform the educational system by bringing *madrasas* under the Ministry of Education. While these proposals were all passed by the GNA, some of its members expressed strong concerns about attempts to make religion simply a matter of "the hereafter," arguing that religion would always affect politics. Other members went even further, maintaining that Islam was different from Christianity and could not be separated from worldly matters, as was the case with religion in European nations (Alpkaya 1998, 231).

These early parliamentary debates no doubt contributed to the legitimacy of the Kemalist reforms at the beginning. But after they were launched, those reforms were deemed by the state to be beyond questioning, and it has become a crime to criticize Atatürk or the six principles of Kemalism (republicanism, nationalism, populism, statism, secularism, and revolutionism) as the immutable and eternal foundations of the modern regime. All intellectuals are required to subscribe openly to the official state ideology as expressed in those principles, which also form the substance of the required curriculum in high schools and in every department or faculty in the universities, regardless of field of study. Students are required to take courses repeatedly to internalize the principles of Atatürk and uphold his revolutionary legacy. Any debate about laicism must begin by reconfirming commitment to the principles of Atatürk as the best model for Turkey, one that can never be questioned or changed.

Given these constraints, limitations, and legal restrictions, free public debate on the issue of laicism and its problems has been very difficult in Turkey. Consequently, the expression of discontent with present practices goes undocumented. What is clear is that the overwhelming majority of the Turkish population apparently supports a secular system of governance. Public complaints tend to focus on the government's authoritarian and heavy-handed practices and human rights violations rather than challenge the secular system itself. Some Turkish historians are impressed by the depth and diversity of the debate on religion and politics that took place toward the end of the Ottoman era, in the late nineteenth and early twentieth centuries, and express dismay at the superficiality of the discourse during the twentieth century and today (Mahçupyan 2005). But there is no effort to engage in similar debate to reaffirm Turkish secularism, let alone question any of the assumptions and objectives of the founders of the republic or the policies of the present Turkish state in the name of upholding the republican principle.

Real or Perceived Dilemmas

As indicated earlier, a broader discussion of the experiences of Turkey since the transition to republican secularism in the 1920s is beyond the scope of this book. Instead I will consider the question of whether Kemalist republican authoritarianism has succeeded in achieving its declared objectives, and at what cost. The various specific issues examined in this section may help clarify the dilemma of balancing the separation of Islam and the state with acknowledging and regulating the role of Islam in politics. The underlying point of this review is that the republican Turkish state has sought to suppress or control the role of Islam instead of regulating and negotiating that role within a democratic constitutional framework, as proposed in Chapter 3. But the perceived need of the Turkish state to suppress or control the public role of Islam is itself based on an acknowledgment of the powerful influence of religion, though not in the positive sense I am proposing. As I will emphasize later, Turkish secular political parties, as well as the state, still have to accept and engage the reality of the political role of Islam.

Although any reference to Islam as the religion of the state was eliminated in 1928 and the republican view of secularism was reaffirmed in the 1937 amendments of the 1924 constitution, the ruling party, the CHP, had to confront the political reality of Islam when multiparty politics was restored in 1946. The CHP had to revise its militant disregard of Islam when the party leaders realized that their emerging rival, the Democratic Party, was attracting religious conservatives. Some CHP members of Parliament also felt that secularist reforms went too far by creating a moral or ethical vacuum in the socialization of youth (Mardin 2001, 120–122). In response, the CHP reintroduced elective religious education classes in schools, opened schools to train imams and preachers, and established the School of Divinity at Ankara University. At the same time, however, the ruling party added Article 163 to the criminal law to punish "religious propaganda against the secular state" (Zürcher 1998, 339). For its part, the Democratic Party continued to affirm its commitment to secularism as the founding principle of the state while it sought to develop political support for itself among Islamic groups like Nur Cemaati, led by Bediüzzaman Said Nursi. The military coup of 1960 marked the end of this alliance, presumably because of the concerns of some army generals that Said Nursi was seeking to establish a theocratic state in Turkey (Mardin 2001, 122–123). It therefore may be relevant to consider the political role of the army in promoting and sustaining a view of secularism that excludes any possibility of Islamic politics in the country.

The Role of the Army

The Turkish Armed Forces (TSK) has probably been the strongest supporter of Kemalist secularism and the most effective enforcer of its tenets. The Kemalists not only gained power through the army, but their CHP party, which dominated Turkish politics until the end of one-party rule, also used the army to advance its specific ideology of modernization, westernization, and secularism. It also used mandatory military service to indoctrinate young men throughout the country, many of whom were leaving their villages for the first time in their lives, into Kemalist ideology. Army conscripts and recruits received ideological training in history, government, and religion, as well as education in geography, mathematics, and agriculture. The army also engaged in "village solidarity" projects, using soldiers as manpower to build schools, canals, and mosques and to meet the agricultural needs of villagers. After the work was done, the army commander would present the village with a flag and a statue of Atatürk as symbols of an enduring relationship between the village population and the modernist regime, via the army (Şen 1997, 19–27).

This use of the army to serve the political and ideological goals of the Kemalist government shaped the way the Turkish army viewed itself, primarily as the protector of the state from any perceived internal threat, such as political Islam, sectarianism, or Kurdish nationalism, rather than as a national defense force against external attack (Cizre 1999, 57–79). This politicization of the armed forces has been reflected in the series of actual and threatened military coups that have retarded the country's constitutional development. The 1961 constitution enacted by the military regime then in control created the National Security Council (MGK). The council's role supposedly is limited to making recommendations to the government and providing support and coordination in national security matters. In reality, the MGK has provided the army with a platform for sharing state authority with the civilian politicians. With each subsequent coup (in 1971 and 1980), the MGK became a stronger and more autonomous political entity, firmly controlled by the military. By emphasizing and strengthening the role of the MGK, the 1982 constitution severely restricted public debate on certain political and social issues in the name of protecting national security (Bayramoğlu 2004, 59–118; İnsel 1997, 15–18).

The army's role as the guardian of Kemalist secularism was dramatically illustrated by the events of February 28, 1997, when the army, acting through the MGK, forced the resignation of Prime Minister Necmettin Erbakan and his Islamist Welfare Party (RP). This intervention was based on a regulation passed a month earlier enabling the MGK to take control from the parliamentary government in times of "crisis," which were broadly defined to include not only war and natural disasters but also internal social movements (İnsel 1997, 16). In addition to forcing a change in government at the end of February 1997, the MGK demanded stronger measures against Islamist movements and stronger control over religious charitable foundations and schools. The February 28 military intervention attracted substantial support from the Turkish media and public, who generally blamed the Welfare Party for provoking the coup. This apparently confirms the view that the modern urban classes in Turkey regard the army as the guardian of secularism against the threat of Islamic fundamentalism.

It is therefore ironic that pressure to restrain the military from interfering in the democratic politics of the country did not come from the westernized secular Turkish elite, as one would expect. Instead, restrictions on the MGK came about as part of the recent constitutional reform undertaken by the Turkish state to facilitate the country's membership in the European Union, as outlined in the last section of this chapter. It is too early to predict accurately how the army leaders will react to these new restrictions on their powers, especially if faced with what they perceive to be a threat to the secular status quo. But it is also clear that secularism is too deeply entrenched in Turkey to be dependent on protection by the army. For my purposes here, the contradiction of authoritarian secularism in Turkey is that the political role of the army has undermined secularism instead of protecting or promoting it. The popular perception that the army is the guardian of secularism weakens the legitimacy of secularism and violates its foundation on constitutional democratic government.

State Control of Religion and Religious Education

In furtherance of its policy of maintaining a tight grip on religion, the republican state has continued many of the Ottoman practices of recognition, support, and control of religious institutions and practice, both Muslim and non-Muslim. National identity cards issued by the state currently require that every citizen specify an affiliation with one of the four religious communities officially recognized pursuant to the Lausanne Treaty of 1923: Muslims, Armenian Orthodox Christians, Greek Orthodox Christians, and Jews. It is relevant to note how the quest for membership in the European Union appears to be forcing change in this policy. The Third Report on Turkey of the European Commission Against Racism and Intolerance, adopted on June 25, 2004, recommended that the Turkish government remove religious affiliation from identity cards and ensure protection for the rights of minority religious groups under the Lausanne Treaty.

The majority of Muslims are Sunni, although there are a small number of Shiʿa and a substantial Alevi minority that is estimated to include between 5 and 12 million people. This wide disparity is noted here because it emphasizes the political sensitivity and contradictions of official and popular attitudes regarding religion. The government does not treat Alevis as a separate religious group, though that is the view among the majority of the Sunni population. While other religious groups exist in Turkey, including various Christian denominations, Baha'is, and Yezidis, they are not officially recog-

nized, and their members are generally listed as "Muslim" on their identification cards. Turkish law also bans Sufi orders *(tarikats)* and Sufi lodges
(cemaats), although this ban is not strictly enforced and many remain active
and widespread. Moreover, only the government may designate a place of
worship, and religious services may take place only in areas so designated.

Article 136 of the constitution established the Department of Religious
Affairs (Diyanet), with the general charge to "exercise its duties prescribed
in its particular law, in accordance with the principles of secularism, removed from all political views and ideas, and aiming at national solidarity
and integrity." This department is responsible for regulating and operating
Turkey's approximately 75,000 registered mosques and their imams, who
are considered civil servants. The policies and activities of the department
usually reflect Sunni Muslim doctrines and do not allocate funds to support
Alevi or Shi'a mosques or imams, but those communities are generally free
to do so themselves through private funds. Another government agency, the
General Directorate for Foundations (Vakıflar Genel Müdürlüğü), regulates
Muslim charitable foundations, as well as some activities of non-Muslim
religious groups, churches, synagogues, and religious properties (Yılmaz
2005; Küçükcan 2003, 501–504). These organs are the primary means by
which the Turkish state controls the religious life of Muslims throughout the
country.

Another tension inherent in the Kemalist view of secularism is in the field
of religious instruction or education. From the beginning, the Kemalist state
took complete control over religious education in the country, placing it under the Ministry of Education. The state took religious education out of the
hands of the *ulama* in order to use the modernist, centralized national education system to create a new nation with a secular identity and ethical system (Akşit 1991, 161). During the one-party rule of the CHP, the state provided only very limited religious educational opportunities. But with the rise
of multiparty democracy, the new regime established Imam and Preacher
Schools, which were renamed Imam and Preacher High Schools (IPHS) in
the 1970s and redesigned to allow graduates to be able to continue on
to university on equal footing with graduates of secular high schools. The
number of these schools grew considerably, and enrollment rose steadily
during the 1970s under coalition governments, which included the Islamist
MSP party. These schools continued to grow slowly after the 1980 military
coup, but the interest of Turkish Islamists in these schools generated suspicion among secularists.

The military intervention of February 1997 led to reform of the educational system to make the IPHS system substantially less appealing for many students. A law enacted in August 1997 makes eight years of secular education compulsory for all students and mandates primary and secondary school instruction in "religious culture and moral education" under state supervision and control. This law permits other religious education and instruction to be given with the consent of the student on request of his or her legal representatives if the student is a minor. The content of religious instruction is strictly controlled by the state and based on Sunni Muslim doctrine. It is criticized by many Sunni Turks as inadequate, while non-Sunni Muslims object to it because it ignores their religious beliefs. Members of recognized religious minority groups may be exempted from this Islamic religious instruction upon request, as required by the terms of the 1923 Lausanne Treaty, which formed the basis of the republican era. Members of unrecognized religious groups are not exempted legally, although they are often exempted in practice.

After completing eight years of primary and secondary education, students may continue on to a secular high school or an IPHS. IPHS schools are classified as vocational, and while graduates of these schools are permitted to attend university, the 1997 legislation subjects them to an automatic reduction in their entrance exam grades if they enroll in a university program unrelated to religion. Although some parents still send their children to IPHS schools for more extensive religious education—not with the goal of having them become imams or religious officials—the disadvantage these students face in being accepted at the university level tends to discourage enrollment. On the other hand, scholarships and free board offered by many IPHS schools continue to make them attractive to poor students and to girls from conservative families who would not send their daughters to a secular high school.

The future of the IPHS system and the broader question of the proper place for religious education in general are matters of considerable debate in Turkey. Some argue that the main role of the IPHS schools is to teach religion rather than train religious professionals, and call for lifting the automatic reduction that disadvantages IPHS students in university entrance examinations. But an attempt in 2004 by the Justice and Development Party (AKP) government to fulfill its campaign promise to revise the law was highly criticized in the media and in academic circles and was vetoed by the president of the republic. Secularists generally support the policy of limiting the function of the IPHS schools to the training of religious workers. This approach allows the state to maintain firm control over all religious instruction, and of related career prospects, because the state first trains religious workers such as imams and teachers of religion in state schools and then employs these graduates in mosques and schools, where they are civil servants receiving their salaries from the secular state (Çakır, Bozan, and Talu 2004).

A third approach advocates easing the divide between IPHS and secular schools by offering elective religious classes in regular high schools. This raises a host of issues, however, regarding not only the content of such classes but also the risk that students are likely to be pressured into taking these "elective" classes. In addition, religious conservatives worry that allowing religious classes in secular high schools would further weaken enrollment in IPHS schools, while secularists fear that such classes would turn secular schools into new IPHS schools. Finally, proponents of a fourth approach argue that a secular government has no business providing religious education in any venue and that all religious education should be privatized. But others view the total privatization of religious education with suspicion because they fear it would give too much freedom to Islamic fundamentalists, who might use such opportunities to promote their own views and recruit students.

It is of course not possible or appropriate here to attempt to assess or evaluate these and other positions regarding the issues of religious education. My purpose is simply to note the variety of views and the way in which the various arguments indicate the underlying tensions within society and in the relationship between religion and the state. The critical question in terms of the thesis of this book is how to safeguard the framework of constitutionalism and human rights and promote and facilitate civic reason in negotiating and mediating such unavoidable disagreements regarding public policy. As emphasized earlier, I am concerned with securing the space for negotiation of such issues through civic reason and in local contexts.

The Ban on Headscarves

Among all the contradictions of authoritarian secularism in Turkey, the issue of women's headscarves has become the most controversial and symbolic subject of the 1990s and early 2000s. The disproportionate, if not absurd, extent of the symbolic significance of the issue is clearly illustrated by the secularist-Islamist confrontation over the candidacy of Abdullah Gül for the presidency of Turkey in April–August 2007 (Associated Press 2007). Strong opposition by the Kemalist People's Republican Party and the army cited the fact that Gül's wife wears a headscarf as confirmation of their suspicion that he cannot be trusted to uphold secularism as mandated by the constitution. It is neither possible nor necessary for our purposes here to discuss all aspects of the headscarf issue and related developments at the Turkish and European levels. Instead, I will highlight some aspects and recent developments in terms of the dilemma facing the secular state in Turkey, namely, how to deal with the growing political power of Islamists without resorting to authoritarian tactics to continue the suppression of this movement.

The majority of women who cover their heads in public wear a traditional headscarf used by lower- and middle-class urban and rural women since the founding of the republic, without objection by the government or public controversy. But a new type of head cover, similar to that adopted throughout the Muslim world since the 1980s, has come to be associated with the rise of the Islamic movement in Turkey and elsewhere. In contrast to the traditional Turkish headscarf, this style completely covers a woman's neck and shoulders. Turkish women choose to cover their heads for a variety of reasons, including custom, modesty, religious observance, and/or as a sign of political affiliation. The question for our purposes is whether the state is able to negotiate the apparent dilemma of respecting the personal-choice and religious-freedom aspects of wearing the scarf while regulating the political role of religion.

Beginning in the early 1980s, students were required to abide by the same dress code as civil servants. While this code would prevent women from wearing jeans or miniskirts to school, it became in effect a prohibition against the headscarf. The code was amended to authorize reprimanding students who appeared "in anachronistic clothing" (Official Gazette 1987). When the Motherland Party (ANAP), then in power, amended the regulation to allow women who covered their hair for religious reasons to attend university, that move was challenged by President Kenan Evren, the leader of the 1980 military coup. The case was brought before the Constitutional Court, which found the proposed law unconstitutional. The court later found a second, more general law, designed to allow freedom of dress in the universities, to be constitutional, but its decision specifically excluded headscarves as "religious symbols," which were not allowed within the "public sphere," including universities. This interpretation of the law was criticized by many and ignored in practice (Tuna 2006).

In practice, restrictions on headscarves were gradually eased, and the matter stayed largely out of public debate until the 1997 military intervention, when the issue was used as an argument against the Islamist Welfare Party (RP), which was being forced out of power. In its 1998 decision banning the RP as a political party, the Constitutional Court raised the unrelated issue of headscarves and said that they should be banned from universities. Although this statement should not have had legal effect because it was unrelated to the matter before the court, the authorities invoked it to prevent students wearing headscarves from registering, attending classes, or even entering university campuses or buildings (Tuna 2006).

The headscarf ban was rapidly extended to apply to greater numbers of situations. The Council of Higher Education prohibited headscarves in university housing, and women wearing headscarves were not allowed to come onto university property even as visitors. The headscarf was also banned in high schools, including the IPHS schools, which are run by the government, and among state employees in general, although many of these had held the same job for years while wearing a headscarf without any difficulties. Even a woman who tried to wear a wig instead of a headscarf to cover her hair and another who wore a scarf to cover her bald head while she was receiving medical treatment for cancer were dismissed from their teaching positions (Tuna 2006). In 1999, Merve Kavakçı was elected to Parliament from the Islamist Virtue Party (VP) and attempted to attend the swearing-in ceremony wearing a headscarf. An angry protest led by the secular Democratic Left Party forced her to leave without being sworn in. Kavakçı was later deprived of her seat on the previously unknown ground that she had failed to disclose that she was also a citizen of the United States, and the VP was banned on the ground that it was the focus of antisecular activities (Öktem 2002).

Moreover, any resistance to the ban on the headscarf or questioning of its legality by teachers, administrators, and even judges was met with pressure and retaliation by the state authorities. University employees who refused to implement the ban were dismissed from their jobs on unrelated charges, and judges who questioned the lawfulness of the ban or the dismissal of employees in such cases were removed from those cases and sometimes transferred to other courts. Meanwhile, judges who actively supported the ban were assigned to courts where these cases were heard (Tuna 2006). Judges who ruled that the ban had no legal ground or that employees had been dismissed without cause often faced government retaliation, finding themselves subjected to investigation or transferred. Investigations might sometimes include examinations of the judge's social life and family. One judge, for example, received a letter of investigation noting that he listened to religious recordings, hosted men and women in different rooms in his private home, and had a wife who covered her head. In other cases, civil servants were dismissed or denied promotion on suspicion of "Islamist" or "anti-state" activities (*Mazlumder* 2004). With the election of the pro-Islamic AKP in 2002, the headscarf debate turned into a protocol crisis. The reaction to the wife of Bülent Arınç, the president of the Grand National Assembly, wearing a headscarf at an official diplomatic ceremony in November 2002 triggered a strong reaction in the press and throughout the government. President Sezer, a staunch Kemalist, gave a speech a few days later stating that the headscarf was a personal choice that was permissible in private. However, he emphasized that Turkish society was ruled by law, not by religion and custom, and cited the Constitutional Court's earlier description of the headscarf as a "religious symbol" that should be prohibited in the "public sphere."

Regardless of the merit of the issue as such, or the validity or reasonableness of the positions of various actors, this vehement and highly publicized controversy over the headscarf reflects a deeper confusion and ambivalence about the relationship between the secular state and religion. Secularists in Turkey see the headscarf as a political statement against Turkey's secular government, the tip of the iceberg of Islamic fundamentalism. Some of the most vehement opponents, such as Kenan Evren, who first instituted the ban in the 1980s, trace the rise of political Islam in Turkey—symbolized by the number of women wearing the Islamic headscarf—to countries such as Iran, which they accuse of seeking to export Shari'a to Turkey. But the persistence of the issue clearly shows that significant numbers of Turkish citizens continue to take strong and deeply entrenched positions on both sides of the controversy. It also seems clear that popular opposition to the expansive ban played a part in the election of the pro-Islamic AKP in 2002. Yet the AKP still had to move very slowly and cautiously on the issue to avoid a hostile reaction from the secularist establishment or the military. For example, an "amnesty" law that would pardon 240,000 women expelled from universities since 2000 was approved in the Turkish Parliament in March 2005, overriding an earlier veto of the law by President Sezer (*Al-Jazeera* 2005). Why should an "amnesty" be needed if there was no legal basis for the ban in the first place?

Both critics and supporters of the headscarf ban claim that Turkey's constitution supports their position on the subject. Critics of the ban, including the AKP, claim that it violates the religious freedom of women and the principles of equal opportunity in education and employment. Supporters of the ban, including Mustafa Bumin, the head of the Constitutional Court, claim that any attempt to change the law to allow women to wear headscarves in the universities or civil service violates the constitution and that a constitutional amendment is required if the ban is to be lifted (Turkish Press Review 2005). A literal or narrow reading of the relevant provisions of the Turkish constitution seems to support this latter view. Article 24 of the Turkish constitution does not speak of "freedom of religion" as such, but of "freedom of . . . religious belief and conviction . . . Acts of worship, religious services, and ceremonies shall be conducted freely, provided that they do not violate the provisions of Article 14." There is no explicit reference to freedom to display a "religious symbol," which is how the headscarf issue has come to be framed.

It can be argued that a woman's sincere belief that a headscarf is a religious requirement should be protected as a matter of "religious conviction" under Article 24, but all religious freedom in Turkey is subject to limitation. Article 14, which Article 24 specifically refers to as a limit on religious freedom, states: "None of the rights and freedoms embodied in the Constitution shall be exercised with the aim of violating the indivisible integrity of the state with its territory and nation, and endangering the existence of the democratic and secular order of the Turkish Republic based upon human rights." It is this vague language about "endangering the existence of the democratic and secular order" that has been so successfully used to support the ban, in spite of the lack of any law or regulation explicitly prohibiting the headscarf as such. Moreover, Article 24 itself places limits on freedom of religion, stating: "No one shall be allowed to exploit or abuse religion or religious feelings, or things held sacred by religion, in any manner whatsoever, for the purpose of personal or political influence." Supporters of the ban argue that since wearing a headscarf is a symbol of political Islam, allowing it would be the first step on a slippery slope leading secular Turkey toward a "legal order of the state [based] on religious tenets." Hence, wearing the headscarf is an exploitation or abuse of religion that must be prohibited under Article 24. Other potential constitutional arguments against the ban on the headscarf, such as the right to education (Article 42), the right to work (Article 49), and equal rights for women (Article 10), are also subject to the broad limitation regarding dangers to the "secular order" under Article 14. Arguments based on these other articles have so far been ineffectual in the Turkish Constitutional Court.

While it may be true that Turkey's candidacy for membership in the European Union will improve the human rights situation in the country in general, as noted earlier, it does not seem to bring a satisfactory resolution of the headscarf issue. In *Leyla Şahin* v. *Turkey*, the European Court of Human Rights unanimously held that the Turkish ban on the headscarf does not violate Article 9 of the European Convention on Human Rights (freedom of thought, conscience, and religion); and no separate question arose under Articles 8 (right to respect for private and family life), 10 (freedom of expression), and 14 (prohibition of discrimination) taken together with Article 9 of the convention and Article 2 of Protocol No. 1 (right to education). The court upheld the ban as primarily pursuing the legitimate aims of protecting the rights and freedoms of others and of protecting public order.

The primary issue in the headscarf debate has been how to distinguish between the "public sphere," from which the Constitutional Court says headscarves must be banned, and the "private sphere," in which they are permitted. According to the court, since the public sphere should be secular and neutral, offering equal protections and equal service for all, public workers should not be allowed to carry religious or ideological signs that might indicate their beliefs or attitudes. This distinction is clearly important, and while the religious and ideological neutrality of the state must be upheld, the practical difficulty lies in defining the terms and maintaining consistency in the application of these principles. Some Turkish commentators have noted, for example, that students or teachers have not been banned from campus or investigated for wearing an Atatürk pin or other insignia, which are clearly ideological symbols (İnsel 2002). This unequal treatment of religious and ideological symbols raises the issue of whether the state is truly neutral. If the rationale is that the neutrality of the state requires it to assure citizens that they will receive equal treatment at the hands of officials, this requirement is violated as much by allowing an official to wear the ideological insignia of Atatürk (which is associated with the CHP as a political organization) as it is by allowing a woman to wear a headscarf.

Failure to provide authoritative and clear definitions of the terms "public sphere" and "private sphere" also raises the risk of arbitrary and unfair extension of the ban to other places. In November 2003, for example, a judge ordered that a woman defendant wearing a headscarf be removed from the courtroom, saying that she had "no right to be [wearing that] in a public area—a courthouse." In another case, a judge in Tuzla asked a female employee who was complaining about being dismissed for wearing a headscarf to leave the courtroom unless she took off her headscarf. There are also reports that women have been refused treatment at state medical facilities because they were wearing headscarves (Tuna 2006). Potentially even public transportation could be deemed a "public area" from which women wearing headscarves could be banned (Sellars 2004).

Some Turkish opinion leaders and academics have suggested that one way to ease the headscarf ban would be to distinguish between public-service providers and public-service recipients. This approach agrees with the prevailing argument that it is important that the state—as represented through public-service providers—maintain its neutrality and treat all citizens equally. Therefore it is right and proper that public-service providers remain free of all symbols that might indicate their ideological or religious beliefs. In contrast, however, citizens—the public-service recipients—are guaranteed freedom of religion and conscience, thought, and opinion and therefore have the right to carry symbols of their beliefs and ideology. According to this approach, a university student is a public-service recipient, who should be allowed the choice of whether to wear a headscarf, while a university instructor is a public-service provider and may not wear any ideological or religious symbol. Likewise, a patient is a public-service recipient, who should have the right to medical care regardless of his or her appearance, while a doctor is a public-service provider (İnsel 2004). While this approach would certainly reduce the scope of the ban in the short term by allowing students and other citizens to wear headscarves or other symbols even within the public arena of a university, it does not resolve the question of what happens after graduation. A female student would be allowed to cover her head while a student at a university, as a public-service recipient, but if she seeks employment in that same university, she becomes a public-service provider, representing the state, and therefore must remove her headscarf.

Others who support the complete removal of the ban argue that all citizens, including those employed by the state and acting as public-service providers, have a constitutional right to wear religious and ideological symbols. Under this approach, government neutrality and fairness to all public-service recipients is entrusted to the "goodwill" of the public-service provider (İnsel 2004). Thus a university professor should be allowed to wear a headscarf if she chooses, and students should trust her goodwill and professional integrity to guarantee that she will not discriminate among her students who wear secular or religious symbols. Questions facing this approach include whether it should apply to all religious or ideological symbols in every situation or case, or be considered on a case-by-case basis to assess the risks of bias and/or its consequences. Another question is whether it is fair or realistic to expect people to trust those in positions of authority over them without some verifiable safeguard and accountability for abuse.

Whichever view one may prefer, the underlying question is how to guarantee the neutrality or goodwill of either the state or its representatives. To ban both public-service providers and recipients from wearing symbols in the public sphere only removes one type of *visible* source of concern about potential bias by concealing differences in religion or ideology. But that does not eliminate such biases or guarantee that public-service providers will not act on their biases once they detect, or even suspect, such differences with the service recipient. The question is about the true meaning of the neutrality of the state and how to ensure its observance in practice. In my view, the answer lies in the constant mediation of such dilemmas within the framework of constitutionalism, citizenship, and human rights, as discussed in Chapter 3, rather than in categorical rulings on such issues as the role of the army, religious education, and headscarves. From this perspective, the debate outlined above can be seen as an illustration of the working of civic reason, regardless of what we might think of the outcome at any point in time, provided the integrity and dynamism of the process is maintained. It may be helpful to offer some reflections on this example of civic reason without presuming to judge its outcome.

The fact that a style of women's dress has become so loaded with political significance reflects the much larger Turkish dilemma of negotiating a balance between religion and the state. While all religious and ideological symbols can be banned from the public sphere in theory, the high visibility of headscarves means that women are disproportionately deprived of their rights to education and to work. The headscarf ban has deprived hundreds of thousands of women of educational and professional opportunities. With education controlled by the state, girls and women who cover their heads and cannot afford to pursue their education abroad are deprived of any opportunity for higher education, as the headscarf ban applies even to the religious Imam and Preacher High Schools and the schools of theology. Women wearing headscarves also find their employment options extremely limited, as the ban effectively shuts them out of any job that requires them to be present in the "public sphere," even if they are not state employees. For instance, the Turkish Bar Association launched an investigation against three female lawyers for wearing headscarves in the Ankara courthouse building (*Hürriyet* 2003).

Such paradoxical situations also show the fragility of women's rights even after decades of secularism. Despite the authoritarian and aggressive drive to secularize and modernize the whole country, Turkish society remains highly conservative, especially when it comes to the role of women. It is probably true that such conservative views are more prevalent among supporters of Islamic parties (Çarkoğlu and Toprak 2000). But it is also clear to me that education and economic development can play a critical role in promoting all human rights, including the rights of women to equality and human dignity. By limiting women's access to education and employment, especially for those who come from conservative or lower-class backgrounds and are thus more likely to wear headscarves, the ban is probably counterproductive. Instead of encouraging and supporting women with headscarves to receive education and thereby secure employment and economic independence, secularists are undermining their purported objective of securing greater freedom and social development for all citizens.

In my view, the purpose and rationale of secularism is to enhance religious pluralism and individual freedom of choice regarding whether or not to observe Islamic precepts. It is wrong to coerce women to cover themselves by enshrining religious obligations in state legislation, thereby depriving them of the fundamental principle of individual and personal responsibility toward God. But it is equally wrong for the state to present women with the difficult and degrading choice between upholding their religious beliefs and losing their rights to education, employment, and personal autonomy in general. This view does not assume that state intervention is the only or primary limitation on freedom of choice for women—or men, for that matter—because pressure from one's family or community can be even more oppressive and inhibiting. Those other sources of violation of the rights and freedoms of the individual must be addressed through appropriate means, including Islamic reform and popular educational initiatives, as I proposed earlier. A clear understanding of secularism as a negotiation between the religious neutrality of the state and the public role of religion is critically important for the legitimate objectives and rationale of both religion and the state.

The Challenges and Prospects of Islamic Politics

The particular relevance of the headscarf debate and the problematic role of the army were dramatically illustrated by the crisis over the candidacy of Abdullah Gül for the presidency of Turkey in April 2007, as highlighted below. My objective in reviewing the various positions on the headscarf issue and their implications is to emphasize that secularism is a negotiation process that can be conducted through civic reason and its safeguards, as explained earlier. It is obviously not possible to predict the outcome of this process with certainty, especially regarding a particular issue, like the Gül controversy, or in terms of a specific time frame. It is reasonable to expect the best policy to emerge through public debate and contestation of the alleged rationale or justification for one view or another. The question I am raising is about the process of negotiating not only what constitutes good policy and how to implement it, but also how to adapt and change policy when it becomes clear that it is not as good in practice as it may have sounded in theory. Moreover, such negotiations are not purely internal to the particular country. In this case, the Turkish state and society have tended to be significantly influenced by Europe, from Ottoman reforms in the nineteenth century and republicanism in the twentieth century to membership in the European Union by the early twenty-first century. The fact that the government of an Islamist party may be the one that brings Turkey into the European Union may provide the impetus for the reconciliation of Kemalist authoritarian secularism with constitutionalism and human rights protection. It may be helpful to recall the context and antecedents of the most recent developments before concluding with some reflections on the prospects of the emerging possibility of Islamic politics within Turkish secularism.

Turkey's demographics alone are sufficient to emphasize the importance of its coming to grips with what I argue is the intimate connection between religion and politics. Muslims constitute 97 percent of the population of Turkey, including a sizable Alevi minority and smaller Shi'a minority. But the official statistic is given as 99 percent, because the Turkish government includes those citizens whose actual religions are not recognized by the state, such as Protestant Christians and Baha'is. While a large majority of the country's Muslims describe themselves as devout believers, they also continue to support a secular state where the role of religion is relegated to private life. At the same time, 21.2 percent of the population claim to support a religious state based on Shari'a, although there is little consensus on what that means (Çarkoğlu and Toprak 2000). It is therefore clear, on the one hand, that despite strong discontent with authoritarian practices in the name of Kemalist ideology, secularism has been firmly established in Turkey and is not openly opposed by any major political party or group (Ahmad 2003, 182). On the other hand, the meaning and implications of secularism continue to be contested among competing perspectives. Corresponding ambivalence can also be found among those who support the enforcement of Shari'a to promote the ideals of justice and to combat moral degeneration and economic corruption but who do not agree on what that objective means and how to realize it in practice (White 2002, 201–226).

The rise of political Islam began in the 1970s with a movement called the National View (Milli Görüş) and the National Order Party (MNP), which was established in 1970 by Necmeddin Erbakan, an independent member of Parliament for the city of Konya. The MNP was soon disbanded by the Constitutional Court on the grounds that it was opposed to republican *laïcité*. When its successor, the Milli Sellamet Partisi (MSP), founded in 1973, was also closed down following the 1980 military coup, the Welfare Party (RP) took its place. The RP found a following among those who felt that they had been left behind by the economic changes of the 1980s and 1990s. While the formation of a customs union with the EU and the emergence of new markets in the territories of the former Soviet Union translated into enormous wealth for some segments of the Turkish population, others suffered from those developments. Privatization and inflation hurt the less educated and lower-middle classes, and waves of immigration from rural areas to the cities exacerbated unemployment problems and made the gap between rich and poor more visible.

In this economic and social climate, the emphasis that the RP placed on the alleviation of poverty, justice, and equality attracted a growing following in urban areas, well beyond its original rural base in central Anatolia. As the media visibility and popularity of RP leaders grew, the beards and headscarves of the Islamist leaders became controversial—symbols of Islamic identity for some Turks and political provocation and a threat to the secular status quo for others. A "war of symbols" ensued, as a countermarket developed to enable secular Turks to emphasize their Kemalist identity. Western-style women's clothing was advertised as "contemporary" or "standard," and posters, stickers, greeting cards, and pins bearing Atatürk's likeness suddenly grew in popularity in 1994, when the Islamist RP won elections of local authorities and municipalities. Thus symbols of political and ideological identity became a major source of tension and contestation (Navaro-Yasin 2002, 229–258).

Recent political developments in Turkey illustrate the ongoing tension between secularists and Islamists, while public opinion seems to favor a mediation rather than a separation of religion and politics. A study by the Pew Forum on Religion and Public Life notes that Turks hold ambivalent, "strong but contradictory feelings" about the role Islam should play in public life. Not all that surprisingly, citizens also seem to be choosing a freer, more prosperous Turkey.

> In a June 2006 survey, 44% of Turks said they believed democracy could work in their country, a decline from the number in 2005 (48%) and 2003 (50%). And about half the population (47%) thinks religion's role in national political life has grown in recent years. Of those who believe religion is taking on greater importance, 50% say that the development is bad for the country; 39% say it is good. Yet most Turks cite Islam as a central part of their identity. A 43%-plurality of Turks identify themselves first as Muslim rather than by nationality, and another 27% identify themselves equally as Muslim and Turk. (Ruby 2007)

The political backdrop of the most recent developments includes the efforts of the secularists in April 2007 to block the election of the candidate of the AKP, Abdullah Gül, to the presidency at the expiration of the term of Ahmet Necdet Sezer. The secularists oppose Gül's Islamic roots and commitments, citing the fact that his wife wears a headscarf as an indication of the advent of an Islamic state that will impose Shari'a on the country. The prospect of AKP control of both Parliament and the presidency led to large secularist protests and threats by the secularist army. Opposition party members in Parliament boycotted the presidential vote, thus denying the AKP the quorum necessary to elect Gül. In the face of such opposition, Gül initially withdrew his candidacy, and Sezer remained the acting president, even though his term had officially expired. Hoping to strengthen his hand with a political mandate, Prime Minister Recep Tayyip Erdoğan called for early parliamentary elections. The AKP swept the election of July 2007, winning 47 percent of the popular vote, though losing a few actual seats because of a more united opposition. The prime minister then proposed Gül again as the AKP's presidential candidate, and this time Gül was elected president, on August 28, 2007.

It seems clear to me that the struggle in Turkey is between two views of secularism, one totalitarian and the other probably more democratic, and not between advocates of theocracy and secularism. In April 2007 the opposition led by the CHP and the army tried to frame the issue as a desperate defense of the secular state against the secret designs of the AKP to establish an Islamic state to enforce Shariʿa. But the results of the general elections in July 2007 indicate that the people did not believe that charge. The AKP also seems to have succeeded because of its promise to deliver membership in the European Union, significantly improve economic conditions, provide universal health care according to EU standards, and build modern roads all over Anatolia.

Given the moderate political approach of the AKP in its five years as the ruling party and its strong pursuit of Turkey's membership in the European Union, secularist fears seem largely unfounded. At the same time, as the AKP gains more power, it must be careful that its pro-Islamic policies do not compromise the secular state and the space of civic reason. The AKP's greatest strength may be in its successful efforts to move away from the authoritarian political model that has defined modern, secular Turkey. In particular, the AKP has catalyzed widespread economic growth by opening up the economy. While the opposition has framed the recent confrontation as Islam versus secularism, the appeal of freedom and economic prosperity should not be underrated. The recent AKP victory was quite likely a referendum on Turkey's democratic and economic future rather than on the status of Islam in the country.

It will therefore be disastrous for the country if the army intervenes to nullify the people's democratic choice. It will be equally destructive if the newly fortified AKP vindicates the apprehensions of its opponents about the party's commitment to the secular state. On the other hand, if the AKP can continue to open up the political space to religious voices while holding resolutely to a separation of Islam and the state and increasingly embracing the principles of human rights, constitutionalism, and citizenship, that may address the apprehensions of the opposition and establish Turkey as a model of the ideas discussed in this book. Even with the most recent confrontation, political developments since the late 1990s offer promising indications of a growing mutual tolerance and accommodation between the two sides of the debate. The AKP is perhaps a model of a workable compromise in Turkey insofar as it is an officially secular party working within the secular state and system and demonstrating what seems to be a genuine commitment to constitutionalism and human rights for all citizens, while maintaining a pro-Islamic stance that allows it clearly and openly to use its members' religious convictions about public-policy issues as a guide to political actions. This is a relatively new development, and there are clear, well-grounded fears and uncertainties on both sides. Turkish secularists may see the explicit secularism of the AKP and the religious public in general as a tactical move *(taqiyya)* to hide their real hostility to secularism and their intention to dismantle the secular state. Secularists fear that once Islamists gain enough power, this secular mask will drop away and the real intention to establish an Islamic state to enforce Shari'a will emerge (Kösebalaban 2005).

On the other side, religious Muslims look at the country's history of military coups and bans against political parties associated with Islam and worry that their ability to participate in politics may come to a sudden end. They are concerned that their Islamic orientation will be used as an excuse by the army or courts to remove them from the public forum. These concerns are heightened by the fear that the European Union, whose members are uncertain about the possible inclusion of a Muslim country, might support a crackdown on parties or ideas associated with Islam. They point to the EU court's decision to uphold the headscarf ban as an example.

From the perspective of the secular state proposed in this book, the Turkish experience calls for clarification of an underlying tension and contradiction. The Kemalist view of secularism that is still dominant in Turkey is based upon complete state control of religion. It regulates religious education and religious practice, controls the finances of the mosques, puts imams on the government payroll, and dictates men's and especially women's dress codes at school and work. This model is profoundly problematic, in my view, because it seeks to control and manipulate the role of Islam in public policy and politics in the name of secularism while denying citizens who take Islam as a foundational force in their lives the right and opportunity to live by their own convictions. This model is also profoundly paradoxical because it cannot pursue its control of religion and religious institutions without violating human rights. In other words, the model necessarily undermines constitutionalism and human rights in the name of upholding these principles.

Those who support the status quo try to present this cleavage in Turkish politics as a clash between the forces of secularism and those of Islamic fundamentalism, although the advocates of change and democracy come from a broad range of backgrounds and ideologies, with Islamist politicians and liberal-minded secular leftists allied in calling for greater freedoms. The defenders of the status quo tend to cast their opponents as Islamists and themselves as the guardians of secularism, raising the threat of Islamic fundamentalism and the imposition of Shariʿa in an attempt to intimidate and confuse the citizens of the country into submission to authoritarianism. As indicated earlier, the National Security Council has long considered the possibility of the Turkish government's falling into the hands of those who may impose Shariʿa as the number-one threat to the nation, warranting the restriction of constitutional rights, especially those associated with freedom of religion (Jacoby 2004, 150). This fear of Shariʿa has been grossly exaggerated for political purposes, in my view, as there is no major group or party in Turkey that threatens, or even questions, the secular nature of the Turkish state. The broader national consensus from a very wide variety of perspectives is clearly in favor of a religion-friendly secular democracy, similar to what prevails in Europe and North America.

It is also relevant to consider the role of European influence on the Turkish experience, in shaping Kemalist conceptions of republican secularism in the 1920s as well as influencing the prospects of its transformation in the early 2000s. The preference of the majority of the population for genuine and sustainable constitutional democracy and respect for human rights is clearly reflected in their strong support for European Union membership, which is seen as a powerful safeguard against sliding back into Kemalist and/ or military authoritarianism. On the other hand, those who oppose Turkey's membership in the EU generally oppose democratic reforms and changes in the status quo (Selçuk 2000). But as the decision of the European Court of Human Rights on the headscarf issue cited earlier shows, the role of Europe can be as ambiguous and contradictory now as it was a century ago. European ambivalence is also reflected in its perception of Turkey as a Muslim country, despite decades of heavy-handed and authoritarian efforts by the Turkish government and army to secularize and westernize the country and alienate its population from Islamic culture. Many Europeans oppose Turkey's EU membership on precisely this ground, arguing that the cultural homogeneity of Europe will be lost if Turks are accepted (Howe 2000, 1–10).

Turkey's current model of secularism, which survives by keeping a tight hold on religious practice, controlling religious education, and restricting religious freedom, is causing constant and widespread discontent in a large majority of the population. Minority religious views, such as those of Alevi and Shiʿa citizens, are stifled. People who choose to be actively religious are shut out of public life and denied basic rights of education and work. Yet the recent election of the moderate, pro-Islamic AKP and the push toward EU membership indicate that the vast majority of Turks, while supporting a secular government, desire a more moderate and democratic approach to religious freedom, one that will allow them to freely incorporate Islam and their Muslim identity into both their public and private lives. This latest development is encouraging for the prospects of integrating a positive view of Islamic politics into the Turkish understanding and practice of secularism. This will not be easy, and it will certainly not be a final and conclusive solution for all problems. Instead, I see this new trend as a positive step in the direction of negotiating public policy and legislation among competing perspectives. The possibility of Islamic politics is necessary in Turkey in order to give significant numbers of citizens, collectively and individually, access to a fair process of civic reason, as discussed in earlier chapters. I will thus conclude with a brief review of this positive development and how it would enhance, rather than diminish or threaten, secularism in Turkey.

Both sides of the debate tend to emphasize their own apprehensions about the intentions of their opponents and discount the concerns of the other side as unfounded or exaggerated, and it is neither possible nor necessary for our purposes here to adjudicate this polemical politics. Instead, I emphasize that the most recent developments in the country can show both sides that reconciliation of what they once viewed as two extremes is not only possible but desirable. Even if the Islamists are using commitment to a secular democratic form of government only for tactical reasons, working within the secular system will actually change the party itself, and its members will come to have a more pragmatic view of the advantages of the secular system. If the leaders of the AKP or another Islamist political party are able to address the core concerns of their constituencies, then they will realize that secularism does not have to mean the complete exclusion of Islam from politics, and that in fact a secular state is a better vehicle for furthering their political beliefs than an "Islamic" state would be. Conversely, if the CHP and other secularists can continue to enjoy the protection of constitutional safeguards and compete for power through the democratic process, they will come to appreciate the benefits of a negotiated national consensus on the issues.

The current role of Islam in Turkish political discourse, while still very limited, may also enable the secular state to realize that there is room in a secular society for many different types of voices, including those informed by religious beliefs. Secularism in Turkey may therefore be transformed, becoming less authoritarian and rigid, giving greater freedom to religion and religious institutions, and creating space in which to accommodate a variety of voices. The ability of Turkey to strike a balance among secularism, human rights, Islam, and constitutional rights that will work for all its citizens is not only of great importance to Turkey itself but will also play an important role in informing this debate throughout the Muslim world. If Turkey is able to show that a secular regime can still find a place for religious discourse and human rights for all, then it will go a long way toward rehabilitating the term "secular" among Muslims everywhere. Likewise, if Turkey is able to show that it can allow an Islamic political voice to be heard while maintaining a secular government and constitutional rights for all, it will reassure secularists throughout the world that Islam has a place in political discourse.

Finally, it is important to emphasize that Turkey is closely watched and analyzed throughout the Muslim world as a test case for the views and apprehensions of all sides to the debate. For instance, I was in Indonesia for four weeks in July and August 2007 to launch a version of this book in the Indonesian language *(Islam dan Negara Sekular: Menegosiasikan Masa Depan Syariah)*. The case of Turkey was raised by those discussing the book and by the general audience at every book launching in five cities. It was also discussed at seminars, public lectures, and media interviews. Paradoxically, the crisis over the candidacy of Abdullah Gül was cited as a vindication of mutual apprehensions similar to those of Turkish protagonists: Indonesian Islamists cited that situation as proof that secularism is inherently and permanently hostile to religion, while secularists cited the same events as justification for their opposition to any role for Islam in politic. I tried to argue to all sides that these developments support my call for making the distinction between state and politics, whereby the unavoidable connectedness of Islam and politics is regulated to ensure and safeguard the institutional separation of Islam and the state. I also tried to explain that the persistent crisis of Turkish secularism also supports my call for mediating the relationship among Islam, the state, and politics and constantly negotiating the role of Shari'a in public life, instead of trying to impose a categorical resolution. I should note, however, that most of those debating my views were reacting to their own preconceived notions of what I "must be" saying, regardless of what I was actually saying. Paradoxically, Indonesian Muslims were taking positions based on the experiences of their own country and society and on fixed interpretations of what they believe to be happening in Turkey, halfway across the world.

CHAPTER 6

Indonesia:
Realities of Diversity and
Prospects of Pluralism

It may be helpful to begin this chapter on the dynamics of diversity and pluralism in Indonesia with an overview of the country's recent history and context. The present state of Indonesia is a product of the struggle against Dutch colonialism. While there was earlier localized resistance to colonial rule in various parts of the archipelago, the initiative for wider opposition to Dutch rule emerged with the rise of Sarekat Islam in 1917, but this mass political movement broke up over ideological and political differences by the late 1920s, and the initiative shifted to the nationalists as the authors of the idea of Indonesia. With the establishment of the Indonesian Nationalist Party (PNI) in 1927, Sukarno emerged as a leading advocate of Indonesian unity, independence, and the separation of state and religion. But Muslim parties and movements returned with another wave of political activism from around 1930 up to the mid-1950s, so that when Sukarno and Muhammad Atta declared independence on August 17, 1945, three days after the Japanese surrender in World War II, Muslim parties were part of the new Indonesian coalition government (Lapidus 2002, 666–668). But the Netherlands did not concede independence for the country as a whole until 1950, and held on to what is now West Papua until 1963. Sukarno was elected president under the 1950 constitution, but stable government was difficult to achieve because of divisions among political parties before and after the country's first nationwide election in 1955.

For our purposes, we should note the opposing positions regarding Islam and the state. The nationalist leaders supported a secular state based on Pancasila, the five principles of the state philosophy, namely, monotheism, humanitarianism, national unity, representative democracy by consensus, and social justice. Some Muslim groups called for an Islamic state *(negara Islam),* and others sought a compromise position, suggesting that the pream-

223

ble of the constitution affirm the obligation of the state to apply Shari'a among Muslims (the so-called seven words clause). In the first constitution, known as the Jakarta Charter of 1945, the nationalists prevailed on both counts, affirming the Pancasila principles and excluding the clause some Muslims wanted, but this issue has remained controversial up to the present time (Salim and Azra 2003, 1). Moreover, a combination of factors, including unsuccessful rebellions in Sumatra, Sulawesi, West Java, and other islands beginning in 1958, and the failure of the constituent assembly to agree on a new constitution, enabled Sukarno in 1959 unilaterally to revive the provisional 1945 constitution, which gave him broad presidential powers. He then used these to impose an authoritarian regime in what he called "guided democracy." He also moved closer to Asian communist states and the Indonesian Communist Party (PKI), in contrast to his earlier foreign policy of refusing to take sides in the cold war.

When the PKI attempted a military coup in October 1965, Major General Suharto was able to establish control over Jakarta. Violence swept throughout Indonesia in the aftermath of the coup attempt, and hundreds of thousands of alleged communists and their sympathizers were killed. In March 1967, the Provisional People's Consultative Assembly (MPRS) named General Suharto acting president, and Sukarno was forced into virtual house arrest until his death, in 1970.

Under what President Suharto called the "New Order" (Orde Baru), he established economic rehabilitation and development as the primary goals of his administration, and in 1968 the People's Assembly formally elected him president for a full five-year term. He was subsequently reelected to successive five-year terms in 1973, 1978, 1983, 1988, 1993, and 1998. But a combination of economic factors, including the Asian financial and economic crisis of 1997 and falling prices for oil and gas and other commodity exports, forced him to resign in May 1998, three months after the MPR had selected him for a seventh term (Lapidus 2002, 674). In June 1999, Indonesia held its first free national, provincial, and subprovincial elections since 1955. The *Reformasi* era following Suharto's resignation also led to a strengthening of democratic processes, including a regional autonomy program, and the first direct presidential election, in 2004. Although relations among different religious and ethnic groups are largely harmonious today, acute sectarian discontent and violence remain problems in some areas.

The premise of this chapter is that diversity is about religious, ethnic, and other forms of demographic variety and difference, while pluralism is the value system, attitudes, institutions, and processes that can translate that diversity into sustainable social cohesion, political stability, and economic development. Part of this premise is that the phenomenon of diversity is a permanent feature of all human societies everywhere, manifested in different forms and dynamics among them over time. In other words, diversity is factual or empirical, and pluralism is an ideology and system that accepts diversity as a positive value and facilitates constant negotiations and adjustments among varieties of difference without seeking or expecting to terminate any or all of them permanently. For instance, the existence of difference over matters of religion or belief is a permanent feature of every society; pluralism is the orientation or system that is based on genuine acceptance of this empirical fact in organizing relationships among different religious and belief communities, rather than on the desire to fuse them all into one or eliminate any of them. Human beings can always choose to uphold the ideology of pluralism and engage in negotiations and adjustments among different communities of believers. To recall my earlier emphasis on the critical role of human agency, it is people, and not abstract notions like "state" or "nation," who shape and work with their own differences, thereby realizing genuine and sustainable pluralism. By the same token, people may fail to accept and negotiate their differences or to realize pluralism, but such failure is not final or conclusive. Since every failure holds a new possibility of success in the future, the question should always be what people can do to achieve the transformation of the permanent realities of difference into sustainable pluralism.

Indonesia is probably one of the most diverse countries in the world today in almost every sense of this term. The geography and diversity of the archipelago is likely to continue to present fundamental challenges for the possibility of applying the nation-state model. As noted earlier, this model is problematic because it is often taken to mean imposing an artificial uniformity to achieve an ideal unity that is usually based on the preferences of the ruling elite or dominant group among the population. This can happen under a so-called secular or religious state, even under the guise of pluralism, which is the underlying concern of this chapter. The idea of Indonesia as a unified country was invented in the late 1920s by the leaders of the struggle for independence from Dutch colonial rule, who claimed to unite some 17,000 islands into a single, coherent nation. Residents of the inhabited islands belong to a very large number of racial and ethnic groups, speak numerous languages, and identify with almost as many religious and cultural traditions. But we are concerned here only with religious diversity in relation to religious pluralism as a normative and institutional system, from an Islamic point of view.

There are several theories about the advent of Islam in Nusantara (now known as Indonesia) and the numerous routes and agents of the varied processes of Islamization, whether directly from southern Arabia or via India, by professional preachers or Sufi masters (Azra 2004, 2–19). For our limited purposes here, various scholarly positions can be reconciled by accepting that initial limited and superficial contacts with Muslims from Arabia, Persia, and India probably date back to the eighth century, but large-scale, sustained, and systematic Islamization began to happen much later—as recently as the eighteenth or nineteenth century, according to some scholars (Mudzhar 2003, 4–9). There is more agreement, it seems, on the view that Islamization happened in peaceful ways, though there were instances of Muslim rulers using force to convert surrounding peoples to Islam. Intensive trade relations with the central regions of the Islamic world and Arab migration, especially from Hadramaut and Yemen, also contributed to the process. However, by its very nature, Islamization was neither uniform nor comprehensive, as it tended to depend on location, time frame, and circumstances, such as the nature and resilience of preexisting cultural and religious traditions. For example, coastal areas, with their maritime culture and cosmopolitan lifestyle, were more receptive than the interior areas, with a secluded peasant culture.

Among the factors that prompted large-scale conversion in the fourteenth century was the simultaneous decline of Hindu/Buddhist kingdoms in Nusantara, such as Majapahit, Sriwijaya, and Sunda, and the rise of Islamic kingdoms, such as Aceh Darussalam, Malaka, Demak, Cirebon, and Ternate (Azra 2002, 18–19). It is reasonable to accept that the process was not only very gradual but also synchronistic, as the majority of Islamic preachers in the archipelago, especially the nine Sufi saints *(wali songo)* of Java, were willing to accommodate preexisting beliefs and practices instead of insisting on prophetic exclusiveness. In many cases, Muslim preachers are reported to have attracted many people to Islam by asserting its superior supernatural powers (Azra 2002, 21). As happened elsewhere in the Muslim world, the "purification" of the faith from "un-Islamic superstitions" became the subject of reformist movements in Indonesia, such as the Padri movement in the first half of the nineteenth century, which was influenced by the Wahhabi theology of the Hanbali school, and more recently the Muhammadiyah movement, which was founded in 1912 (Mudzhar 2003, 10–14).

It is also relevant to note that such factors as scattered territory, diverse populations, and reliance on trade with distant peoples probably contributed to making the inhabitants of the archipelago traditionally receptive to external cultural influence. Islam adapted well to these factors by accommodating local traditions, norms, and institutional elements whenever they were believed to be consistent with fundamental Islamic principles. This approach is traditionally accepted as the Sunna of the Prophet himself and was systematically applied by the first generations of Muslims through their initial expansive thrust into Iraq, Persia, Egypt, and North Africa. Applying this approach in Nusantara, Muslim scholars were able to freely use *adat* (local customs, social habits, or practices, especially those relating to juridical or legal rulings) in their decisions and deliberations. As *adat* for each community changed over time, so did Islamic adaptability and the gradual processes of integration. Both *adat* and Shari'a are said to have been treated as applicable legal systems among local Islamic communities (Lukito 1998, 27–49; Lukito 2003). But it seems reasonable to assume that the integration of Islam into the daily lives of believers, as well as their sociocultural institutions and political relations, are better understood in terms of a wide spectrum, from the most thoroughly Islamized to the nominally Islamic. This assumption seems to be both commonly accepted and sufficient for our purposes here, though the precise role of various factors in the dynamics of Islamization in specific communities over time may need further examination.

Regarding religious diversity in particular, it is difficult to classify many Indonesians as belonging to one particular religion, let alone a uniform or monolithic understanding and practice of that religion. It is therefore not helpful to assert that the country now has the largest Muslim population in the world, because the Muslims of Indonesia subscribe to a wide range of understandings and practices of Islam, some of which may not be recognized as Islamic at all by some Muslims in other parts of the world. At the same time, it is true that the clear majority of the population does identify as Muslim in their indigenous understandings of Islam, which have traditionally been pluralistic and tolerant of difference. It is also true that there has been a trend toward a more puritanical, "Wahhabi" view of Islam that seeks to challenge earlier, more tolerant attitudes and practices and impose an artificial religious uniformity.

In terms of the thesis and argument of this book in general, I am concerned in this chapter with the role of an internal Islamic discourse in the potential or possible transformation of these realities of diversity into genuine and sustainable pluralism. In other words, I am focusing only on Islamic discourse within the country, as influenced by other internal and external factors, without attempting to discuss ethnic, linguistic, or other forms of diversity. But I am raising the question of how pluralism can be realized and sustained, rather than simply presenting a purportedly neutral analysis of its failures or limitations in the Indonesian context. The proactive approach I am proposing is certainly subject to questions about the feasibility and desirability of the artificial uniformity of the nation-state model: in what sense should one be seeking to consolidate pluralism, and within which frameworks?

As with the discussions of India and Turkey in the preceding chapters, the following discussion of Indonesia is intended merely to illustrate relevant aspects of the general theory presented earlier, without claiming to be exhaustive or comprehensive in this regard. Even to the extent that relevant issues are identified and examined, I realize that they can be approached from a range of helpful perspectives. With these and other caveats in mind, the following discussion is organized as follows. The first two sections present a historical overview of the relevant issues as well as a demographic profile to demonstrate the religious diversity of Indonesia. Both of these aspects constitute the background and context of the present debate about the relationship among Islam, the state, and society. Aspects of that debate in the provinces, as well as among elites at the center, will then be highlighted, before I conclude with an assessment of the present situation in Indonesia in relation to the general theory and framework presented in this book.

The Background and Context of the Current Debate

It should be recalled that the underlying theme we are concerned with is whether Indonesia should be established as an Islamic state that enforces Shariʿa as positive legislation and official policy or as a religiously neutral state that respects and facilitates the right of Muslims in their various communities to live in accordance with their religious beliefs and culture. In terms of the thesis of this book, the first option is incoherent and untenable; the second is precisely the purpose of secularism, as discussed earlier, which is the separation of Islam and the state but also the regulation of the relationship between Islam and politics. From this perspective, the following review will focus on the antecedents of and recent developments regarding the debate around legal enforcement of Shariʿa by the state in the postcolonial era. In this review, I will not discuss whether Shariʿa was enforced by the state in precolonial times and during colonial rule, because that is not, strictly speaking, relevant to the subject of this book. As noted from the beginning, the relationship among Islam, the state, and politics in present Islamic societies now operates in the context of a totally different kind of state and administration, namely, one shaped by global economic and political systems, than the kind that prevailed during the precolonial era.

The antecedents of the present debate about the enforcement of Shari'a by the state can be traced back to Islamic resistance movements in the nineteenth century, but the issue could not have been contemplated in relation to Nusantara/Indonesia as a whole at that time, simply because even the idea of this united entity did not exist until the late 1920s. It should also be noted that there was no united entity under Dutch colonial rule, either. Nevertheless, this recent "national" phase remains connected in the consciousness of Muslims to earlier regional movements and experiences, which enables the proponents of an Islamic state to invoke those historical models in support of their present claims. In this sense, there is continuity from the early stages of the Islamization of Nusantara through Dutch colonialism, the struggle for the independence of a united Indonesia, and the post-independence period up to the present. At the same time, the issue of Islamization changed significantly after independence was declared in 1945, because of the drastically transformed national and global context. But it may be helpful to briefly review the pre-independence background of the Shari'a debate.

Contestations of the outcome of the "founding moment" in 1945 continued after independence and constituted the partial rationale for separatist initiatives, like that of Darul Islam's so-called Islamic state in West Java, from 1948 to 1962, and similar developments in South Sulawesi and Aceh. At the Constituent Assembly following the 1955 elections under the provisional constitution of 1950, the Islamists launched another challenge to the Pancasila model of the state. Since neither side managed to get the two-thirds majority vote needed to have its proposal adopted, President Sukarno dissolved the Constituent Assembly by decree on July 5, 1959, and returned the country to the 1945 constitution. It is probably true that Sukarno had other motives for that move, since the 1945 constitution granted the president extensive powers and was vague on the limitations of the office (Mudzhar 2003, 18n28). But the point remains that the deadlock of the Constituent Assembly provided him with the opportunity, perhaps the pretext, to diminish the prospects of constitutional democracy in Indonesia. The impact became much more drastic during the three decades of Suharto's subsequent dictatorship, established under the guise of "guided democracy" initiated by Sukarno.

Another relevant development to be noted here is the emergence of Islamic reform among Indonesian scholars like Hasbi Ash Shiddieqy and Hazairin, both of whom died in 1975. Shiddieqy proposed the concept of "*fiqh* Indonesia" starting in the early 1940s, but his ideas received little attention from Indonesian intellectuals at the time. As he continued to develop this position over the following three decades, Shiddieqy emphasized the need to shift from varieties of traditional *fiqh*, which do not take into account the unique characteristics of the Indonesian Muslim community. He called for an Indonesian *fiqh* that is based on fundamental Shari'a sources and methodology but rooted in the specific values of the local community. In 1951, Hazairin was the first to propose the establishment of a new Islamic school of thought *(madhhab)* that would reflect the specific features of Indonesian history and respond to the needs of society, instead of relying exclusively on the traditional Shafi'i school, which prevails among the majority of Indonesians. Both scholars emphasized the Indonesian *adat* system, but Hazairin called for the rejuvenation of the Shafi'i school in accordance with local conditions, while Shiddieqy urged using all schools of Islamic jurisprudence as sources for the formulation of Indonesian *fiqh*. These two positions can be seen as confirming the coexistence and interdependence of Shari'a and *adat* among Indonesians. These ideas and their underlying rationale continue to be reflected in state policies, such as the promulgation of the Code of Islamic Courts (1989), the presidential decree of 1991 on the compilation of Islamic law, and the establishment of so-called Islamic banking services.

In general, it seems that efforts to facilitate dialogue between *adat* and Shari'a were supported by a wide consensus, with Islamic scholars striving to develop interpretations of Shari'a in favor of reconciliation of the two systems. This view also tends to perceive efforts to contrast these systems as politically motivated or unappreciative of their doctrinal consistency (Lukito 2003; Lukito 1998). But the role of political factors in these issues should not be dismissed as irrelevant or illegitimate, as such factors can influence this relationship one way or the other at an underlying structural level, even when not explicitly acknowledged. This can be seen, for example, in the development of the Kompilasi Hukum Islam (Compilation of Islamic Law), the Undang-Undang Peradilan Agama (UU No. 7, 1989), and the Bank Muamalat Indonesia and other banks that applied Shari'a principles during the New Order. This process was viewed with great suspicion by some segments of the Indonesian population, who perceived it as undermining the Jakarta Charter. In particular, those who opposed the developments saw them as state sponsorship of Shari'a principles, in accordance with the formula that was rejected in 1945 for favoring Muslims, as noted earlier. Others attempted to discount such apprehensions, arguing that the foundation of the Indonesian state under the Pancasila was beyond question. But the question is precisely whether this foundation is being challenged.

With the downfall of the Orde Baru regime in 1998, controversy about the Jakarta Charter and the role of Shari'a in the state reemerged. Broadly speaking, there are currently two types of Islamic movements involved in the debate about state enforcement of Shari'a. Those who support an active role for the state in enforcing Shari'a include Dewan Dakwah Islamiyah Indonesia (DDII), Komite Indonesia untuk Solidaritas Dunia Islam (KISDI), Majelis Mujahidin Indonesia (MMI), Front Pembela Islam (FPI), Laskar Jihad, Hizbut Tahrir Indonesia (HTI), and others. Those opposed to such a role for the state are primarily Muhammadiyah, Nahdlatul Ulama, and such Islamic nongovernmental organizations as Paramadina, Jaringan Islam Liberal, and others. But the structural changes introduced by the regional autonomy policies in 1999 have added to the complexity of the situation by enabling communities to implement some Shari'a principles at the local or regional level regardless of the position of the national government (Salim 2003, 222–228). Such initiatives are viewed with suspicion by the opponents of an Islamic state, who are worried that state sponsorship of these activities may culminate in the reinstatement of the seven words clause, holding that the state should have "the obligation to apply Shari'a for its adherents," which was omitted from the Jakarta Charter of 1945. These worries may seem premature or exaggerated insofar as the recent initiatives for the enforcement of Shari'a are supposed to be implemented through the Pancasila-based state and not by seeking to transform it into an Islamic state. But in addition to concern about the progressive realization of the Islamists' strategy, apprehensions are also driven by the ambiguity of the basic claim itself: what does an Islamic state and the enforcement of Shari'a mean, and what are the consequences for all Indonesian citizens? As I have suggested earlier in this book and will briefly discuss later in this chapter, any effort to enforce Shari'a is problematic, because it means imposing the rulers' view of Shari'a on Muslims as well as non-Muslims.

This persistent controversy emphasizes the complexity of the issues. On the one hand, those supporting policies such as the compilation of Islamic family law and the establishment of Islamic banking see them as the necessary fulfillment of the state's obligation to regulate such matters for Muslims, for whom these are said to be matters of religious belief. On the other hand, this is precisely the issue for the opponents of such measures: how can it be claimed that the state does not favor Islam or Muslims when it openly sponsors programs that seek to promote some Shari'a principles as a matter of state policy? What is seen by some as a necessary systematic organization of Shari'a principles regarding family law or banking, so that they can be applied by state courts, is objectionable to others for the same reason: why should state courts enforce any religious law at all? This tension of course goes deeper into the process and rationale by which Muslims were persuaded to accept Orde Baru policies (for example, family planning programs) that were perceived by some as a violation of Shari'a. Initial resistance to that foundation of the state was overcome for some by an Islamic rationale of "what cannot be achieved in its totality should not be totally abandoned" *(Mâ lâ yudraku kulluhu lâ yutraku kulluhu)*. But that rationale also assumes or requires that at least some of the objectives or purposes of an Islamic state should be achieved by the Pancasila state. As will be briefly explained later, the Islamists of the founding stage and its subsequent generations endured the amendment of the Jakarta Charter and the Pancasila principles without abandoning their own objectives. Indeed, it is probably true that the Islamists of today are trying to transform the state to fit their own model, as they have done in Iran and Sudan and are attempting to do elsewhere.

In conclusion of this first section, we should recall that the basic premise of this study is that while Shari'a is binding on Muslims everywhere, its observation has always been voluntary—a matter of personal conviction. What is at issue is whether this obligation is to be enforced through the coercive authority of the state or whether the state should be neutral regarding all religions, precisely in order to ensure and protect the right and ability of all citizens to live in accordance with their religious and other beliefs. The position I am advocating, religious neutrality of the state, is reinforced by the realities of religious diversity in Indonesia, even among Muslims, as can be seen from the following brief review.

The Realities of Religious Diversity in the Archipelago

Although Indonesia is not a religious state today, religion has been an important aspect in the establishment of the country. The five principles on which the state was founded in 1945 are belief in one supreme God, humanitarianism, nationalism expressed in the unity of Indonesia, consultative democracy, and social justice. Article 29 (1) of the 1945 constitution provides that "the state shall be based upon the belief in the One and Only God." But although Article 29 (2) provides that "the state guarantees all persons the freedom of worship, each according to his/her own religion or belief," this freedom of religion is limited in practice to six officially recognized religions: Islam, Catholicism, Protestantism, Hinduism, Buddhism, and Confucianism (Departemen Agama Republik Indonesia 1998, 105). This limitation, along with other aspects of the ambiguous and uncertain status of freedom of religion in Indonesia, is particularly troubling in view of the religious diversity of the population highlighted in this section.

According to the census results released by the Central Body for Statistics in 2003, 177 million Indonesians are Muslims and 23 million are identified as adherents of other recognized religions (Catholic, Protestant, Hindu, Confucian, and Buddhist) (Departemen Agama Republik Indonesia 2005). Indonesians who live in remote areas of the country also practice so-called local religions, which existed before any of the now officially recognized religions came to the region. These local religions tend to share some similar patterns and concepts with other "Austronesian religions" (Fox 1995). To integrate these remote communities, officially called "isolated people," the Indonesian state established a special body under the Ministry of Social Welfare, which has so far identified 919,570 people as belonging to these communities all over the country (Direktorat 2005). As can be seen from the following brief examples, Indonesian local religions share with the official religions a belief in God as well as similar social norms and patterns, yet they do not fit the official categories. Indonesian Islam also defies clear or simple classification.

Indigenous Religions

The Badui of western Java, a community numbering around 6,000, live in small settlements in Banten Province. Claiming to be the original inhabitants of West Java, the Badui believe in a god *(Batara Tunggal)* with indivisible power and force that is prevalent everywhere and may be personified as a man who is both wise and sacred. They also have several sacred places and megalithic sites that are associated with ancestors. One of the sites is regarded as the center of the universe. The Badui observe a set of norms and rules established by their ancestors, who entrusted their community with preserving the well-being of the center of the world. They are thus required to ensure that "the mountain may not be destroyed, the valley may not be damaged, the prohibition may not be violated, the ancestral injunction may not be changed, what is long may not be cut short, what is short may not be lengthened" (Garna 1998, 76–77).

In eastern Java, around Bromo Mountain, the Tengger people, numbering around 50,000, make up the only Javanese community that still preserves non-Islamic priestly traditions directly descended from the Sivaism (Shivaism) of the Majapahit Hindu kingdom. Their religious ceremonies include offering ritual meals at the peak of Bromo Mountain to honor their ancestors and offering food and animal sacrifices to the spirit of the still-active volcano (Hefner 1998, 78). As a result of intensive interaction with the Balinese, the Tengger people have gradually come to accept that their religion is closely related to Balinese Hinduism (Hefner 1989, 265–266).

The Batak Toba people in North Sumatra, numbering about 6,000, identify with the Parmalim religion, including belief in God, and conduct an annual feast to express their gratitude to him. Like other local religions, Parmalim teachings emphasize the importance of maintaining nature, such as the obligation to plant a tree upon cutting one down. The Siberut islanders, who live in the Mentawai Archipelago to the west of Sumatra (no population estimates are available), believe that everything—humans, animals, plants, and objects—has a soul. Since nonhuman entities are social partners, they must agree to being used by humans. Actions that are incompatible with the nature of the nonhuman entity's being used by humans are not permitted, and failure to obey such taboos sets the entity against the person (Schefold 1998, 72). The Dayak, a large ethnic group of about 600,000 people and 405 subethnic groups, are the native people of Kalimantan, the third largest island of Indonesia. They believe in one god, worship their ancestors, and uphold an obligation to protect nature. They believe that they are required to serve three powerful deities: God as the highest element, who creates all the creatures; the guardian spirit of the earth; and the ancestors.

The religion of the Wana of the Central Sulawesi still retains its ancient forms although it has adopted some elements of the new, now official religions, such as the use of Arabic phrases from Muslim prayers. The religious policies of the Indonesian state have also pressured younger Wana to convert to the recognized religions. As happened elsewhere in Indonesia, those who live in the interior have converted to Christianity, while people in coastal areas are now associated with Islam. As a result of such pressures, the Wana people have adopted some of the practices and food prohibitions of the recognized religions, but they have adjusted those elements to their ancient traditions and religious identity (Atkinson 1998, 88–89).

Some ethnic groups that live in Sumba, a rocky coral island in eastern Indonesia, and collectively number about 500,000, have retained their ancestral religion and managed to resist conversion to either Christianity or Islam. Their religion includes belief in the spirits of the dead, sacred places, heirloom objects, and the instruments used to communicate with the invisible world. Important invocations are sung to a standing drum, whose spirit travels with the priest's voice to the "upper world." The highest deities are never addressed directly but are approached through a series of intermediaries. Each boundary or barrier—the village gates, the steps to a house, the stone foundation of the ancestral tombs—is guarded by a pair of spirits, one female and one male, who must be named and propitiated as speakers advance on their imaginary journey to the source of misfortune (Hoskins 1998, 90).

The Asmat, an ethnic group numbering about 65,000 who live in the province of Papua in eastern Indonesia, believe that life and death are inextricably connected. Although it is accepted that everyone dies, the Asmat do not recognize that death can occur for natural reasons. Whether a person dies of old age, sickness, or an accident, it is always deemed to be the result of enemy action, which weakens the body and spirit through the use of supernatural power until the person eventually dies. They believe that unless the victims of such enemy actions are avenged, their souls will cause misfortune for the living (Jay 1998, 96–97).

This sort of belief system is clearly problematic for keeping the peace within such communities and in their relations with others, challenging or undermining the role of the state in keeping law and order. An approach to pluralism as affirmative acceptance of difference within and among communities, as advanced in this chapter, must include attention to ways of mediating or regulating competing rights and interests. In this instance, the issues can be seen in terms of freedom of religion and the requirements of social peace and political stability. Since keeping the peace and protecting people's lives and property are necessary for the possibility of social life, they should have priority over religious beliefs or cultural practices, such as the Asmats' requirement for vengeance. But it should also be noted that the state is not a neutral arbiter. Those who act in the name of the state have their own interests and biases, even when they are acting with the best of intentions for promoting the public good, which is often unlikely.

While the state of Indonesia does not acknowledge the wide variety of local religions and emerging sects, it avoids the difficulty in practice by deem-
ing people to be believers in one supreme God. This presumption of belief in
God, as one of the five principles on which the state was founded, was introduced by the Decree of the People's Consultative Assembly of the Republic
of Indonesia (Tap MPR RI No. IV/MPR/1978). This decree has been repealed
by the Decree of MPR No.I/MPR/2003, but discriminatory practices continue. In administrative terms, Indonesians who are deemed to exist beyond
the realm of recognized religions are not subject to the Ministry of Religion.
Instead, the administration of those tribal communities is vested in the Ministry of Education and Culture (now the Ministry of National Education).
The ministry exercises its control over unrecognized religions through some
246 organizations. Some of these religions have been dissolved or are no
longer organized at all. Many of them are prohibited, such as the Karuhun
religion, outlawed by the attorney general of West Java Province in 1982.
Some local religions or new sects are established as modern associations. Adherents of the Karuhun religion organized themselves into PACKU (the Association of People of Karuhun), but some local religions are neither organized by the ministry nor represented by an association. Some of the serious
consequences of these restrictive and confusing state policies include forcing
the adherents of local religions to choose one of the officially recognized religions for their national identity cards (Saidi 2004, 197–346).

Furthermore, since their own religious rituals regarding marriage and
death are outlawed, they have to conduct such ceremonies in accordance
with one of the recognized religions. If an adherent of a local religion wants
to get married and chooses to be a Muslim for that purpose, he must go to
the Religious Affairs Office. If he elects to be married as a believer in any of
the other recognized religions, he must do so at the Civil Administration
Office. The legal status and consequences of his marriage will therefore be
governed by the law applicable to the religion he elected to identify with,
though that may not be consistent with his own religious beliefs at all. In addition, instead of recognizing tribal religions as distinct and independent, the
state has been pressuring their adherents to integrate into one of the official
religions, especially Hinduism. This seems to be true of the Kaharingan of
the Ngaju in Kalimantan, the Alukta of Toraja (Sulawesi), the Pelbegu of
Batak, and the Towani of Bugis (Fox 1995, 522).

To maximize the monitoring of these local religions and to anticipate the
emergence of new sects, the government established an institution called

Bakor Pakem (Coordinative Council for Monitoring Sects and Beliefs in the Society) under the office of the attorney general (Departemen Agama Republik Indonesia 1998, 110–112). In addition to monitoring the existence of some syncretic practices, Bakor also persecutes new or emerging sects that are considered by established religious authority to be deviant or heretical. For example, Bakor successfully brought the Ahmadiyya sect before the courts to be declared a deviant Islamic sect, and the attorney general issued a ban on this religious group in 1989. Other groups deemed to be deviant sects have likewise been banned (Aqsha, van der Meij, and Meuleman 1995, 443–464). Adherents of local religions are also subjected to Islamic and Christian missionary campaigns. As noted earlier, for instance, the Tengger people have been pressured since the 1930s by local *ulama*, particularly of the Nahdlatul Ulama organization, to modify some of their traditional religious practices. The Tengger people are also pressured to purify their local Hindu beliefs and convert to the officially recognized Hindu Parisada. Similarly, Christian missionaries have been striving to convert the Nias, the Batak Angkola, and the Toba in North Sumatra and the Sa'dan of Toraja in South Sulawesi (Hefner 1989, 247–265).

Syncretic Islam

As a result of the gradual and peaceful process by which Islam spread throughout Southeast Asia, it tended to adjust to and incorporate some elements of preexisting local cultures (Madjid 2000, 2–10). The mutual influence among Islam and local cultures and religions varies from one part of Indonesia to another, and there are no reliable data on this issue. But it is possible to consider the membership of major Islamic organizations—Nahdlatul Ulama, Muhammadiyah, and Persatuan Islam (Islamic Union)—as indicators of the demographics of orthodox Muslims. For example, Nahdlatul Ulama claims to have about 35 million members all over Indonesia, whereas Muhammadiyah has about 20 million. There are also some smaller but significant Muslim organizations, such as al-Irsyad, Muslimin Indonesia, Hizbut Tahrir, Majelis Mujahadin, and so forth. The existence of these various organizations itself confirms the fact that there is no agreement among those who identify as orthodox Muslims about what that means. It is also reasonable to assume that some members of these various Islamic organizations still retain some of their pre-Islamic cultural or religious values and institutions, as illustrated by the following examples.

While having formally converted to Islam, the Sasak people, who live on Lombok Island in West Nusa Tenggara Province, retain elements of their Sasak-Boda animist religion (Budiwanti 2000). Their version of Islam is called Islam Wetu Telu (literally, "three times Islam") and is differentiated from orthodox views (Islam Lima Waktu; literally, "five times Islam") (Budiwanti 2000, 33). This contrast in the name indicates that Islam Wetu Telu adherents perform the Muslim prayer three times a day, while orthodox Muslims pray five times a day, but there are other differences. According to Wetu Telu adherents, their religion is based on the cosmology accepted by the Sasak people, a worldview based on three stages of human life (birth, life, and death), not just on a difference in the number of daily prayers. In their system of belief, the ancestors are very important and always involved in every religious performance. For instance, Wetu Telu adherents pay the Islamic religious tax *(zakat)* on behalf of those who are dead as well as those who are alive, and they celebrate numerous religious ceremonies, both Islamic and non-Islamic. Many of the Sasak, it seems, do not feel obliged to pray five times or fast during Ramadan, because those religious obligations are binding only on *kiyai* (religious preachers), who enjoy a very special position in the Sasak community (Budiwanti 2000, 159).

The Amma Towa community (also known as the Kajang people) of Bulukumba, South Sulawesi, have their own ways of practicing Islamic teachings. They recite the Islamic confession of faith and perform male circumcision *(khitan)* as Islamic requirements, but the majority of them do not feel obliged to perform prayers five times a day. They also believe that the obligation to make the pilgrimage to Mecca *(hajj)* can be fulfilled by sacrificing two cows and providing a ton of rice to the village. For Amma Towa, the basic teachings of *Pasang ri Kajang* (an important message from the ancestors of the Kajang community) are more important than the Qur'an and Sunna of the Prophet of Islam. This message from the ancestors—which they believe to be divine teachings transmitted from one generation to another to regulate behavior toward God, man, and nature—is enforced by the community. Anyone who violates one of the principles or rules is to be punished by death, corporal punishment, or exile from the local region (*GATRA Weekly* 2003, 52–55).

In Tasikmalaya West Java, the Kampung Naga people identify themselves as Muslims but believe that the obligation to pray five times only applies on Friday. They also maintain that their ritual of Hajat Sasih, which they conduct on the tenth day of Dzulhijjah, is the way to perform the obligation of pilgrimage to Mecca. Like other tribal communities, Kampung Naga people highly respect their ancestors and perform rituals for that purpose (SundaNet 2005).

Kejawen (Javanese Muslims) preserve their ancient local traditions without being classified as backward or isolated people. For instance, celebrations of the Prophet's birthday in the Sultanate Ngayogyakarta (in Yogyakarta) include the ritual of purifying weapons such as *keris*. Elements of ancient Hindu, Buddhist, and animist traditions have been integrated into Islamic beliefs in this part of Indonesia. For some of the Kejawen, spiritual quality is much more significant than observance of ritual practices prescribed by Shari'a (Mulder 2001, 2, 5). Classic Javanese literature contains aspects of Hindu and Buddhist mysticism as well as Islamic Sufi thought, such as the idea of the unity of existence *(wahdatul wujud)*. This Sufi principle is also represented as the unity between the subject and his master, which facilitates the concept of the king as God's representative in this world (Simuh 2002, 141, 156, 157). Islamic and local cultures also mix harmoniously in shadow-puppet performances, like the story of *wayang*, which was utilized by the *wali songo* (the nine saints) to spread and propagate Islam in Java, using the legendary Hindu epics the Mahabharata and the Ramayana (Simuh 2002, 131).

The rich religious diversity of Indonesia is difficult to summarize in this limited space. For our purposes here, however, it should be emphasized that the traditions of religious coexistence and mutual influence are probably being undermined by forced assimilation into dominant religions in recent years. The synergistic mixing of Islamic and Hindu religious identity among Islam Wetu Telu, Ammatowa Kajang, and Islam Kampung Naga is being threatened by efforts to "purify" Islam—efforts supported by state officials and funded by international and local Islamic organizations (Budiwanti 2000, 285–305). These trends, as well as countercurrents of resistance by local communities, are part of the wider debate in Indonesia about the establishment of an Islamic state and the state enforcement of Shari'a.

In view of the preceding review of religious diversity, I find it remarkable that the demand for state enforcement of Shari'a is sometimes claimed to be the valid democratic choice of the clear majority of Indonesians. This claim is false, because democracy is rule by the majority provided that the rights of the minority, even of one person, are respected. Furthermore, the claim is simplistic and misleading, because there is significant diversity among the Muslims of Indonesia, including those who are calling for an Islamic state.

Several Islamic parties have competed among themselves and against so-called secularist parties in all general elections since independence. It is also clear that the combined percentage of the vote Islamic parties received each time has always been far below the percentage of Muslims in the total population of the country (88 percent). According to an Indonesian scholar working with various sources, the six Islamic parties that participated in the 1955 general elections received a combined total of 45 percent of the vote. The highest percentage achieved by any one of them—20 percent, for the Masyumi Party—was equal to that of the secularist Indonesian National-ist Party. Four Islamic parties competed in the 1971 general elections, realiz-ing a combined total of 20 percent of the national vote. The same four Is-lamic parties united to form the PPP for the 1977 general elections and still received only 27.5 percent of the national vote. The percentage achieved by the PPP was 26 in 1982, 15 in 1987, and 22 in 1997 (Mudzhar 2003, 20–21). The extraordinary circumstances of the 1999 general elections (follow-ing the resignation of President Suharto), in which forty-eight parties com-peted, make it harder to characterize the parties as secular or Islamic in or-der to determine the total percentage of the vote for each side (Mudzhar 2003, 21–31). But it is still reasonable to conclude that the general elections of 1999, as well as those of 2004, support the view that Islamic parties com-pete against each other and that their total combined percentage of the vote falls far below that of Muslims in the population at large.

Views from the Provinces

To gain some sense of the debates on issues of Islam, the state, and society in different parts of Indonesia, I requested that the Institute for Islamic and So-cial Studies (LKiS), based in Yogyakarta, organize and conduct a series of focus-group discussions (FGD) in seven locations. In view of the scale and com-plex demographic diversity of Indonesia, the LKiS process could not possibly be representative of such debates throughout the country. Even at the level and locations at which FGDs were convened, many aspects of the process could have been done in different ways. Discussions were held in Bahasa In-donesian to enhance effective participation, but the findings were commu-nicated to me in English, which adds to risks of distortion or misrepresenta-tion. Nonetheless, for my modest and limited purpose of "listening in" for reflections, critique, and suggestions regarding the thesis and analysis of this book, this process was successful and most helpful. This assessment is primarily based on my confidence in LKiS and its ability to conduct a credible and productive series of FGDs in collaboration with appropriate local partners, to secure the effective participation of significant local actors, and to report on the whole process accurately.

LKiS is a nongovernmental organization (NGO). Initially its activities were limited to discussion groups among Muslim students from traditionalist backgrounds. Since the 1980s, the group has organized informal meetings to discuss various problems related to the authoritarianism of the New Order, especially its tendency to manipulate Islam as the source of political legitimacy, and has explored ways to promote democratic values. In September 1993 the group formally institutionalized itself as an NGO working to promote democratic values and disseminate tolerant and transformative Islamic thought through public discussion, the publication of books and weekly bulletins, and other strategies of public-policy advocacy. For example, between 1997 and 2003, LKiS conducted a training program to disseminate human rights values from innovative Islamic perspectives in many *pesantrens* (traditional Islamic boarding schools) in various regencies of Java as well as Aceh, Mataram, and Makassar. The organization also conducted a "Pilot Project for Transformative and Tolerant Muslim Society" to test the practical utility and sustainability of some of the strategies of social transformation developed at the institute and to construct a workable model for future application. The organization's mission, methodology, popular credibility, and ability to reach and work with an extensive network of grassroots organizations and groups, as well as the high level of commitment and motivation among its leaders and staff and its impressive record of achievements, all made it an excellent choice for the sort of process I had in mind.

To enable all participants in the FGDs for this study to exchange views as freely as possible, without concern about the presence of an outsider, it was agreed that I would not participate in the direct implementation or deliberations of any of these FGDs. My role was limited to providing LKiS with a brief paper on the concept and methodology of the general study and its main themes and issues, which they translated into Indonesian and distributed to all participants in advance of each FGD. I also discussed general plans and objectives of the meetings with the LKiS staff charged with implementing them at local sites during a visit to Yogyakarta in June 2004. We agreed on the selection of locations to reflect a good cross-section of opinions and experiences around the main issues and themes of the study. The timing, selection of participants, logistical arrangements, and facilitation of the discussions at each meeting were all left to the discretion of LKiS, in collaboration with local partners in each location. This process was fully consistent with the concept and objectives of this study as a whole, because LKiS and I share a similar ideological orientation and commitment to the protection of human rights, people-centered development, and social justice. Having taken the initiative in 1994 to publish an Indonesian translation of my book *Toward an Islamic Reformation* (1990) and distribute thousands of copies of it throughout the country, the organization knows and generally agrees with my views on Islamic reform and my approach to sustainable social transformation. For my part, in view of the mission, methods, and record of achievement outlined above, I have full confidence in the organization's ability to deliver the highest-quality social research on precisely the sort of issues with which I am concerned.

As agreed, LKiS organized and conducted FGDs in seven selected locations between August and October of 2004, as summarized below. All meetings were organized by M. Jadul Maula, the director of LKiS. Lutfi Rahman, the organization's program officer for advocacy and networks, assisted in the selection of participants and the logistical arrangements. Jadul Maula also served as the facilitator of discussions in all seven meetings, thereby enhancing continuing and comparative reflection. FGDs were convened at Tasikmalaya, West Java, on August 3; Kudus, Central Java, on August 15; Pamekasan, East Java, on August 23; Banjarmasin, South Borneo, on September 7; Banda Aceh, Sumatra, on September 21; Mataram, West Nusa Tenggara, on October 7; and finally at Padang, West Sumatra, on October 13. An average of fifteen participants at each meeting (for a total of more than one hundred) discussed the issues for some four to six hours and formulated their own conclusions. The LKiS facilitator and staff prepared a general report, as well as detailed reports of each FGD, first in Bahasa Indonesian, to get the most accurate record possible, and then in English. I also asked colleagues who are fluent in both Indonesian and English to review both versions to ensure the accuracy and comprehensiveness of the translation.

According to LKiS reports, these meetings went very well according to plans, but there were some problems and limitations. For instance, some invited participants canceled at the last minute, which did not permit time to replace them with due regard to operational criteria. In some cases, a local personality or spokesperson for a group or organization arrived unexpectedly, and it was difficult to turn such a person away without compromising the credibility of the process with charges of exclusivity or censorship. Because of such factors, the precise balance and representativeness of some groups were not always what the organizers desired. The organizers' efforts to ensure significant and effective participation by women were unsuccessful, as there were only one or two women in five of the meetings, three in one, and four in the seventh meeting. In general, the profile of participants in all FGDs can be summarized as follows: 25 percent from Islamic organizations, such as Nahdlatul Ulama, Muhammadiyah, Majelis Mujahidin, Hizbut Tahrir Indonesia, and Persis; 20 percent academics and researchers from regional universities; 10 percent *ulama* from the *pesantren*; 13 percent activists from local nongovernmental organizations; 10 percent from Islamic political parties, such as the PKS (Welfare Justice Party), the PBB (Star and Crescent Party), and the PKB (National Awakening Party); 7 percent Christian clergy; 7 percent government officials and members of the elected legislative body; and 8 percent other local personalities, such as social or cultural activists and university student leaders.

The general format and process of each FGD can be described as follows. After the local organizers of the meeting and the designated LKiS facilitator explained the nature, process, and objectives of the meeting, all participants introduced themselves to the group. As explained in the detailed reports on each FGD, these initial introductions related the issues to be discussed to local debates and concerns, which were familiar to the local organizer as well as to the LKiS coordinator, rather than to abstract matters or debates around Jakarta and other urban centers. After that opening stage, the facilitator provided a more detailed introduction of topics for discussion and reviewed the concept paper and terms of reference which had been distributed in advance to all participants. The floor was then opened for all participants to express their opinions, report their experiences, and react to one another. Throughout the proceedings, the facilitator continued to clarify the issues, raise questions, and encourage participants to speak out as necessary or appropriate. Before the closing of each session, he reviewed the discussion and summarized the various views and conclusions. All participants were then encouraged to clarify or respond to the facilitator's review and summary before the meeting was concluded. Detailed records of the whole process have been kept by LKiS in Yogyakarta, and I keep an extensive report in English, but what follows are the reflections and conclusions of Jadul Maula, the facilitator of all the discussions.

These discussions should be understood against the background of the

Indonesian state's repeated failures to achieve the total enforcement of Shari'a, as outlined in the first section of this chapter. The advocates of total enforcement are now trying to achieve at least some of their objectives through the regional autonomy policy introduced in 1999, after the fall of the Suharto regime, which enables local government authorities to respond to the aspirations of communities through local regulations *(peraturan daerah)*. But popular responses to these initiatives have been very mixed among and within the provinces and districts, and tend to change over time. Any given issue has different implications for different communities and groups, depending on historical associations, socioeconomic status, ideological orientation, and political interests. The results are often unpredictable and sometimes unexpected or surprising. The experiences of local committees for the enforcement of Shari'a indicate that the members often do not know each other, and when they conduct "comparative" studies in other towns, they tend to be disappointed with the experiences of others. They conclude that their own experience must be the "most authentic," despite their knowledge of its limitations.

This analysis and assessment seems to be well demonstrated by the FGDs in all seven locations, reflecting a wide variety of experiences about Islam, society, and the state among different constituencies within the same location. For example, when the local government of Tasikmalaya issued local regulations based on assumptions about the self-image of the town as a profoundly Islamic community and home for numerous *pesantrens,* the local population, including *pesantren* communities, reacted with marked skepticism and resistance. Acehnese take great pride in their strong identification with Islam since it first came to this archipelago and in their continued intensive demographic, religious, cultural, and economic relations with the Middle Eastern and South Asian Islamic communities, earning their region the nickname Veranda of Mecca *(Serambi Mekkah)*. Yet they are not only resisting the formal enforcement of Shari'a by local government authorities but also expressing ambivalence about the principle itself. In Mataram, where Hindus constitute at least half the population, local enforcement of Shari'a has generated strong tensions.

Participants at the FGD in Kudus, a town known for its long history of Islamic identity, including experiences of so-called Islamic rule, provided a most insightful and instructive set of remarks that may help clarify the ambiguity of the notion of the enforcement of Shari'a. The facilitator observed that the participants seemed to differentiate between Shari'a with a capital

"S" as opposed to what they regarded as "shariʿa" with a small "s," which referred to both Islamic jurisprudence *(fiqh)* and state legislation *(qanun)*. This characterization may be summarized as follows:

- Shariʿa with a capital "S" is used to refer to the totality of God's detailed guidance for humanity. This vision of Shariʿa is believed to be eternal and universal, but it is to be derived from the totality of God's signs *(ayat)*, which are conveyed in the material world, as well as in the Qurʾan.

- Shariʿa with a small "s," which is *fiqh,* is the product of the human law-making process *(tashriʿ)*, or *ijtihad* (juridical reasoning by Islamic scholars according to the traditional methodology of Islamic jurisprudence, *usul al-fiqh*). However strongly believed to be valid and binding, the product of this process is always merely speculative conjecture *(dzanny ad-salalah)* and necessarily temporary and transient. Although *fiqh* purports to regulate human behavior *(ahkam al-mukallafin)*, there is always flexibility and freedom for each human being *(mukallaf)* to choose among a range of options *(aqwal al-ulama)* without fear of committing an offense or sin that warrants punishment.

- *Qanun* is the product of legislation by the authorities of the state *(taqnin)*, which means that it is always a political decision that is enforced through the coercive authority of the state to punish violators. For the process of legislation to be good and valid, it should be based on *ijtihad* (juridical reasoning) that reflects both religious-juridical and sociological considerations *(fiqhiyyah wa ijtimaʿiyyah)*, which are the product of the inclusive participation of all citizens through public debates.

The views expressed during the FGDs should be seen as overlapping perspectives along a spectrum rather than rigid dichotomies. Any classification, like "moderate" or "extremist," can be misleading, but it can be used in broad comparative terms, provided it is not understood as setting rigid or absolute categories. Along the spectrum, it is possible to identify views that perceive Shariʿa as a standard and universal principle from God for all humankind, which should operate in the best interest of human beings, as illustrated by the example of the Prophet and his Companions *(sahaba)*. Those holding this view believe that the state can be used as the instrument for striving to achieve the legitimate and feasible enforcement of Shariʿa, but there is no obligation to establish an Islamic state. Shariʿa can be enforced gradually within the national republican framework. Another view is that

Islam is the religion of God, which must be enforced in its totality, including its whole social/economic/political system, without compromise or accommodation between the secular and Islamic systems. If possible, the secular system should immediately be replaced by the Islamic system through whatever means are available to Muslims, including violent armed struggle. But if Muslims are not strong enough, they should prepare and seek to establish their own separate Islamic system, through a clandestine movement if necessary. A third perspective refuses to accept that the enforcement of Shari'a would improve the present corrupt and oppressive system of government and administration. This view regards the advocates of Shari'a enforcement as promoting a merely normative-moralist claim that obscures the true nature of Islam as represented by its principles of compassion and justice for all of humanity *(rahmatan lilalamien)*. Efforts should therefore be focused on replacing the existing oppressive structure and system, not on the enforcement of Shari'a.

Some participants in the various FDGs insisted that religion should be the private concern of believers, not enforced through the state, which is the expression of pluralistic common objectives and programs for the totality of the population, equally and without discrimination. But others presented a "transformative" perspective, perceiving Islam as consisting of ethical socioreligious principles that are always in dialectical interaction with existing social and political systems, rather than a standard and eternally fixed sociopolitical system as such. As ethical principles, Islam can influence human consciousness and understanding as well as public policy. This transformative approach is critical of the fact that the way a public agenda is introduced and implemented by the existing state or political system does not fairly represent the aspirations of all the citizenry because it has been dominated by large capitalist interests.

A similar range of views can be found regarding citizenship. Some participants could not even comprehend the idea, because their point of departure was the total enforcement of Shari'a as the immediate command of God, rather than the "modern state," which they saw merely as camouflage for secularism. From this perspective, all human beings can be divided into only two groups, believers and nonbelievers. In contrast, other participants clearly understood the idea of citizenship and sought to translate it into practical actions.

Secularism, whether as a concept or as an operational system, was observed by almost all the participants in the seven FGDs to be a construct and experience of Western societies designed to subordinate religion. In Muslim experiences, secularism is perceived as something that has been enforced by colonialism and its aftermath. From this perspective, participants seemed not to understand the effort to redefine secularism attempted in this book and therefore rejected it in their respective ways. Those holding "extremist" or "moderate" views refused to engage in an effort to redefine the concept or the term "secularism" and did not give a reason for their position. Others seemed to be willing to accept the redefinition of the concept but saw it as difficult for the majority of Muslims to accept. Some could accept the redefinition in principle, recognizing that it has already been implemented by Muslims, but still preferred to use alternative terms like "symbiosis of religion and state" or "transformative Shari'a." In addition, some participants regarded the "redefinition" approach as the wrong strategic entry point for promoting reform among Muslims. They proposed instead raising other objectives, such as the empowerment of civil society *(masyarakat Madani* or *mujtama al-madani),* which they felt would be more acceptable to Muslims.

Discourse at the Center

In addition to my earlier reservations about the elusive notion of the "nation," especially in a country like Indonesia, I hesitate to call this section "national discourse," because that term may indicate a more inclusive scope than is probably the case. At the same time, the purpose of this discourse is to examine and propose solutions for foundational questions facing the country as a whole and which are thus supposedly accessible to all Indonesians, not just participants and audiences in Jakarta and other urban or intellectual centers. Calling this "discourse at the center" may also be objectionable, but I use it here to indicate a broader scope than local discourses, while realizing that this phrase does not include every point of view.

The history of the Indonesian state, both in the period leading up to independence and in the decades following it, reveals that the relationship among Islam, the state, and society was—and continues to be—a central concern of lawmakers and politicians, as well as of intellectuals and reformers across the spectrum of political and ideological orientations. To what extent the debates have been widely inclusive of all segments of society and Indonesian civil society is a more complicated issue. In Indonesia, as in other countries, intellectual elites with various, sometimes conflicting perspectives and objectives have usually claimed to speak on behalf of the nation or country as a whole. Some intellectual movements, like that of the late Nurcholish Madjid or those undertaken by Islamic organizations like Nahdlatul Ulama, have a *relatively* wider degree of civil-society participation. In including these and other social movements and individual intellectuals, I am not suggesting that any of these initiatives necessarily represent a broad-based consensus that holds across Indonesian society in all its diversity. Rather, the purpose is to present a sampling of views and positions regarding the nature of the state and its relationship to Islam and society that have been expressed at a broader level or have sought to reach and influence Indonesians throughout the country.

The substantive and symbolic role of Islam in the struggle for Indonesian independence has been a key factor in the contestations over defining the relationship among Islam, the state, and society in the postcolonial context. As with anticolonial movements elsewhere, there are competing nationalist narratives of Indonesian independence. The Syarikat Islam, founded in 1911, utilized Islam as an overarching and unifying structure in mobilizing nationalist consciousness (Mudzhar 2003, 15–16). When the concept of Indies nationalism was proposed by the National Congress of All Netherlands India in 1922, some leaders, like Omar Said Tjokroaminoto and Mohammad Natsir, sought to legitimate this emergent nationalism as essentially Islamic in character. In contrast, "secular nationalists," such as Sukarno and Sutomo, located that nationalism in religiously neutral terms and histories. From the late 1920s onward, the vision of the latter group has dominated, but the former ideology, which calls for an Islamic state, has not withered away.

The controversy over the removal of the clause that the state should "apply Shari'a to its adherents" from the Jakarta Charter and Pancasila, as explained earlier, has continued throughout the postcolonial political history of the Indonesian state. It has been a pivotal issue and rallying point for Islamist challenges to the Pancasila model, as well as a pretext for the state authority to consolidate its power at the cost of democracy. For example, a strong challenge to the Pancasila model was launched by S. M. Kartosuwirjo, whose movement for an independent Islamic state in West Java lasted from 1948 to 1962. Other religious secessionist movements, like those in South Sulawesi and Aceh, also mobilized Islam and the idea of the Islamic state for ideological and political objectives. On the other side, the failed Islamist challenge to the Pancasila model following the elections in 1955 allowed Sukarno to return the country to the 1945 constitution instead of the 1950 provisional constitution, under whose aegis the elections had been held. The contest over Islam and the state has contributed to damaging some aspects of constitutional democracy, not only at the early stages of Indonesia's history but also subsequently, during Orde Baru and to the present.

At the historical moment of independence, law itself was an object and arena of contention, deeply implicated in the debate about the identity of the new state and the role of Islam in it. The colonial court system that discriminated between indigenous Indonesians and Europeans was abolished at independence, but there was no major change in the content of the law when Indonesia transitioned from a colonial to a sovereign state, with many laws adopted from the colonial system (Lukito 2003, 17). During the early phase of independence, Indonesian leaders sought the unification of law to reinforce the unity of the nation. This imperative was reflected in efforts to create a national legal system, which were accompanied by the dismantling of customary courts. However, creating a uniform body of law was difficult because of the pluralistic nature of Indonesian society. Thus in the early postcolonial state, as in the colonial period, different categories of law applied to different classes, colonial law intermingled with religious and traditional beliefs, and exponents of *adat* law continued to practice colonial law. Indeed, beyond Java, the project of centralization and unification of law often led to violent uprisings (Lukito 2003, 19–20).

Pluralist and uniformist groups differed about traditional *adat* laws, while secular nationalists and Muslim nationalists differed about Islamic law (Lukito 2003, 18–19). The uniformists, who viewed *adat* law as backward and antimodern, argued that a uniform legal system reflecting the unity of Indonesia was a necessary condition for Indonesian modernity. The pluralists, who viewed *adat* as an embodiment of Indonesian identity and national pride, opined that a pluralist legal system attuned to diverse social conditions was more genuinely reflective of Indonesian society (Lukito 2003, 22). In contrast to *adat*, Islamic law was not affected by the unification of law, because it was powerful on the national scale and not only locally (Lukito 2003, 25).

But this does not mean that Islamic law has not been affected by developments since independence; there have been particular modes of state intervention and regulation in the domain of Islam. These state initiatives also point to the crucial, if often implicit, question of who has the authority to represent Islam and on what basis that authority is constructed. Religious courts were brought under the Ministry of Religion in 1946. In 1948, it was decreed that religious courts would be amalgamated into regular courts and cases with Muslim litigants that required resolution under Islamic law would be handled by Muslim judges. This law was never put into effect by the Indonesian government, and religious courts continued to function as before. Yet this policy reflected the government's position of subordinating Islamic courts to regular courts (Lukito 2003, 25). Moreover, the majority of judges and officials in the Department of Justice and civil courts radically differed from judges in Islamic courts in their conception of law. Legal officials at the ministry and judges of civil courts were largely graduates of Dutch law schools with westernized understandings of the law, while those who served in Islamic courts had been trained in traditional Islamic institutions that subscribed to the classical Shafi'i school of Islamic jurisprudence and possessed limited judicial knowledge (Lukito 2003, 26). Judges take the oath in the name of Allah and swear to "be faithful to and defend and apply the Pancasila as the basis and ideology of the state, [and] the Constitution of 1945" (Hooker and Lindsey 2003, 42). The Pancasila is constantly used as a reference point in judicial decisions as a matter of implementing state policy.

As a consequence of state control of religious courts, the state intervenes in what may be considered the private domain. The *Kompilasi*, "a guide to applicable laws for judges within the jurisdiction of the Institutions of the Religious Justice in solving cases submitted to them," is binding law in Indonesia (Hooker and Lindsey 2003, 46). Family-law matters are treated accordingly as "enforceable state civil law," and from the perspective of the government, the *Kompilasi* now possesses "the force and status of Islamic doctrine" (Hooker and Lindsey 2003, 46). According to some scholars, as a result of state intervention in the domain of religion, "the Islamic religion in Indonesia—at least insofar as it relates to the legal system—is the subject of almost total state executive control. Ultimate authority rests there, not in revelation. At the practical level, the *shari'ah* is now thoroughly 'reformed,' indeed trivialised, in the *Kompilasi*" (Hooker and Lindsey 2003, 50).

Concurrently with state action and initiatives in the post-independence era, movements such as the Muhammadiyah and Nahdlatul Ulama reflected important developments in theological and doctrinal Islam that would gain currency in Indonesian society. The former, with an urban merchant following, emphasized a purification of Islam divested of all syncretism, while the latter established itself among rural populations and emphasized a commingling of traditional and syncretic Islamic practices. As noted earlier, scholars like Hasbi Ash Shiddieqy and Hazairin proposed reformist frameworks, articulating a redefined role for Islam. Shiddieqy, for example, writing in the 1940s, called for a specifically Indonesian *fiqh*, as opposed to traditional *fiqh*, that would be predicated on fundamental Shari'a sources and methodology but rooted in the specific values of the local community. In 1951, as noted, Hazairin proposed the establishment of a new Islamic school of thought *(madhhab)* rooted in Indonesian history and sensitive to Indonesian needs, as an alternative to the traditional Shafi'i school predominantly followed by Indonesians. Both these scholars, in their different ways, emphasized the rejuvenation of *adat* in a reformulated Islam adapted to Indonesian culture and society. The 1970s and 1980s also witnessed a range of Islamic reform movements that took varying positions on the relationship between religion and the state.

The constant negotiation over the role of Islam and the recalibration of the Islam-state-society equation in different phases of postcolonial Indonesian political history thus derive from a number of intertwined factors. Islamist organizations have not uniformly been opposed to the state and its policies; indeed, they vary in their policies, politics, and ideological standpoints. Movements that call for more categorical affirmation of separation of religion and state have also emphasized a simultaneous rejuvenation of Islam in civil society. While noting the complex dynamics of these developments, we can see this scenario for the purpose of analysis in terms of a dialectical relationship among state and nonstate actors. On the one hand, the state—more specifically, various regimes or governments—has sought to respond to nonstate movements and initiatives by incorporating the ideas of the latter into state policy. For instance, the ideas of Shiddieqy and Hazairin and their underlying rationale continue to be reflected in state policies, like the promulgation of the Code of Islamic Courts (1989) and the Presidential Decree of 1991 on the compilation of Islamic law. The state itself has also taken a more proactive role in Islamizing institutions, perhaps to counter the growing legitimacy of Islamist movements. On the other hand, the nonstate movements—whether revivalist or modernist, whether eventually seeking state power or not—have critiqued and reacted to state policies while proposing alternative understandings of Islam and seeking to build community support. This dialectic has both shaped and been shaped by the relationship between Islam, politics, and the state in postcolonial Indonesia.

Post-independence Islamic intellectualism was relatively strong among some activists in some Islamic student organizations, such as Himpunan Mahasiswa Islam (HMI, Islamic University Student Association), formed in

1947 (Effendy 1995, 105). Some of the younger figures among these activists were Djohan Effendy, Manshur Hamid, Ahmad Wahib, and Dawam Rahardjo. They reasserted several important propositions and packaged these into a new religious-political perspective on the relationship between Islam and the state (Effendy 1995, 106). First, in their view, there is no clearcut evidence that the Qur'an and Sunna oblige Muslims to establish an Islamic state. Second, they recognized that Islam does not contain a set of sociopolitical principles or an ideology. Third, since Islam is conceived as timeless and universal, Muslims' understanding of it should not be confined to a formal and legal sense of it drawn from a specific time or place. Fourth, they strongly believed that only Allah possesses the absolute truth. Thus it is virtually impossible for mankind to grasp the absolute reality of Islam (Effendy 1995, 106–107).

Islamic reform in Indonesia in the 1950s meant not only a move away from previous forms of worship but also attempts to Islamize political and economic institutions, including calls for an Islamic state and the implementation of the Jakarta Charter. This situation came to a head in 1965 with attacks on Indonesian Communist Party members by the military and Muslim organizations, some of whom called these actions *jihad* to recapture the Indonesian nation from those they regarded as secularists and atheists (Hefner 1995, 35). With subsequent restrictions placed on political Islam, Muslims were divided in their support for the government, which for its part was apprehensive about the politicization of religion. Since the political environment at the time made mass mobilization around these issues difficult, some leaders turned their attention to social and educational reform programs. Scholars like Nurcholish Madjid, Dawam Rahardjo, Djohan Effendy, and Abdurrahman Wahid saw these reform programs as the focus of pluralistic Islam and a rejection of the idea of an Islamic state (Hefner 1995, 37).

Under Suharto, the New Order regime rejected the rehabilitation of the Masyumi political party. Masyumi leaders who supported an Islamic state against the Jakarta Charter during the Old Order of the Sukarno period were also prevented from any involvement in politics. The New Order regime formed a coalition with two parties that worked closely with Golongan Karya (Golkar), the governing party under Suharto. The Islamic parties formed the Partai Persatuan Pembangunan (PPP), and the nationalist and Christian parties formed the Partai Demokrasi Indonesia. During the New Order period, Mochtar Kusumaatmadja argued for a selective unification of the law, under which "the areas most immediately connected with the cultural and spiritual life of the people should be left undisturbed, while in other neutral areas regulated by the social intercourse of modern imperatives the government could benefit from imported legal concepts" (Lukito 2003, 24). This model contributed to law being used as a vehicle for modernization, which was in effect a governmental tool of social control under the New Order regime. The pluralist group lost out, while nationalist arguments gathered strength and *adat* law began to fade (Lukito 2003, 24).

In the immediate aftermath of September 1965, following the coup by which Suharto took power, Muslim political parties found themselves marginalized as Suharto weakened their influence. The Muslim leaders split into two groups to deal with this situation. They agreed not to challenge the state directly but instead to appeal to the community *(dakwah)*. However, the groups disagreed about long-term political goals. The first group, the Masyumi, defined themselves as modernists and included Mohammad Natsir and Anwar Harjono. They saw *dakwah* as important in its own right but also considered it essential to build mass support to allow for the capture of the state (Hefner 2002, 142). The decline of the Muslim business class meant that this group directed its efforts toward the urban poor and lower-middle classes, a less educated social segment.

The second group was made up of young modernists, Muslim students and youth organizations associated with the "renewal" movement of Nurcholish Madjid, Dawam Rahardjo, Aswab Mahasin, and Munawir Sjadzali. Young and well-educated, from a nonparty background, they were skeptical about what they called the "mythology of the Islamic state" and rejected "the assertion that state power was the best way to advance Muslim interests" (Hefner 2002, 143). In contrast to the older group's view of a distant golden age of Islam, the young modernists focused on the uniqueness of Indonesian history and its ethnoreligious pluralism and disagreed with the tendency to confuse idealized Arab culture with Islam itself (Hefner 2002, 143). They familiarized themselves with the discourses of democracy and human rights. Arguing against the creation of a centralized state with control over politics and culture, they advocated "the creation of a Muslim 'civil society' capable of counterbalancing the power of the state and promoting a public culture of pluralism, participation, and social justice" (Hefner 2002, 144).

As intellectual projects, Islamic reform movements were deeply engaged with questions of the role of Islam in state and society. According to Nurcholish Madjid's movement for theological renewal, Indonesian Muslims were unable to differentiate between transcendental values and temporal values. In his view, these two sets of values were often reversed among Muslims of Indonesia: transcendental values were conceived to be temporal and vice versa. As a result, "Islam is [viewed as] equal in value to tradition; and becoming Islamic is comparable to being traditionalist" (Effendy 1995, 108). In his response to this confusion, Madjid proposed that Muslims should naturally perceive the world and its temporal affairs as they are. Viewing the world and its objects in a sacred or transcendental manner can be considered to be theologically contradictory to the very notion of Islamic monotheism (Effendy 1995, 108). Madjid maintained that there is nothing sacred about the matter of an Islamic state, Islamic political parties, or an Islamic ideology, which means that Muslims should be able to "secularize" or "desacralize" their perceptions of these worldly issues. In light of this, he introduced the phrase *"Islam Yes, Partai Islam No"* (Islam Yes, Islamic Party No) (Effendy 1995, 108–109).

The religious-political project of Munawir Sjadzali that emerged in the 1970s also contributed greatly to the development of a new political meaning of Islam. From this perspective, the substantive values of political Islam were identified as justice, consultation, and egalitarianism. This understanding was also congruent with the increasing exposure of young Muslim intellectuals and activists to modern education and economic development (Effendy 1995, 116–117). The participants in the new movement questioned the overall strategy, tactics, and goals of political Islam as defined by the older elites. Many of them even directly challenged the notion of Islam as an ideology and the idea that the state could be an extension (or integral part) of Islam (Effendy 1995, 104).

The late 1970s and early 1980s saw an unexpected Islamic revival in Indonesia as young Indonesians searched for new forms of public participation at a time when other arenas for social and political debate and association had been closed down by the Suharto regime. Muslim associations managed to circumvent the state and influence public policy. State regulation of religion—specifically its recognition of only five religions—caused a decline in syncretic Islamic traditions, and many Muslims adopted a more pious profession of Islam (Hefner 2002, 145–146). With assistance from the Department of Religion, the Muslim community carried out a cultural and religious revival, including increasing the number of mosques, improving Islamic educational institutions, and reversing the decline in piety that had resulted from the politicization of Islam under the Old Order government (Hefner

1995, 37). Ironically, the authoritarian nature of the New Order state induced Islamic activists of that period to incorporate democratic, pluralistic, and civil-societal values into their interpretation of Islam.

Whatever the reasons may have been, Muslims began seeking to deepen their understandings of Islam by attending seminars and public forums, in particular those held by the Paramadina Foundation, with Nurcholish Madjid. At these forums, which included campus discussion groups, a number of academics, including Harun Nasution, introduced their students to Western and Middle Eastern modernist thought (Hooker 2004, 233). In the early 1980s, the young modernist group was joined by Nahdlatul Ulama. Despite their traditionalist orientation, the Nahdlatul Ulama recognized the importance of democratizing and pluralizing their organizational culture. Therefore, civil Muslim politics was developing in both modernist and traditionalist circles, focusing on the creation not of an Islamic state but of Muslim civil society with Islamic values of justice, freedom, and acceptance of difference (Hefner 2002, 144–145). In 1990, the ICMI (Association of Indonesian Muslim Intellectuals) was founded, supported by Suharto and led by B. J. Habibie. The organization has a diverse membership, and there has been speculation about the political manipulation of ICMI by the state (Hooker 2004, 234).

In the 1980s, the Suharto government adopted an attitude of political accommodation toward a number of interests of the Islamic community, which influenced the relationship between Islam and the state in Indonesia. Such accommodation included enactment of laws on education, including a clause that every state school must provide religious lessons to its students; establishment of the religious judiciary and the compilation of Islamic law; the establishment of an organ to regulate Islamic charity; and permission for female students to wear the veil in state schools.

The debate over religious courts continued in the 1980s and "was indicative of the bias that existed against the position of Islam in the state" (Lukito 2003, 27). There are conflicting assessments of the quality and impact of Islamic courts (Hooker and Lindsey 2003, 56). Many Muslims agreed that Islamic law was important in the Indonesian lawmaking process but that it was not dependent on the existence of Islamic law courts. Islamic law could be applied in regular courts. Others argued that Islamic courts were essential so that secular lawyers could not meddle in sacred law (Lukito 2003, 27).

Under Law No. 7 of 1989, all religious courts were given a uniform name, and religious court jurisdiction was expanded to include all Muslim family-law matters, namely marriage, divorce, repudiation, inheritance, bequest, gift, and endowment *(waqf)*. With that law, religious courts came to have equal status with civil courts: "As long as they continue to fulfill the requirements of any modern court, their status, in relation to other judicial bodies in Indonesia, cannot be undermined" (Lukito 2003, 28). But non-Muslim and nationalist groups strongly opposed this law as an attempt to revive the Shari'a clause omitted from the Jakarta Charter in 1945—a back-door way of establishing an Islamic state.

Suharto's turn to Islam in the early 1990s reflected his awareness of the strength of the Islamic resurgence and the calls for democratization by Muslim youth. Some of his measures were welcomed by both conservative and democratic Muslims, many of whom became his supporters. The senior modernists even supported Suharto in 1997, denouncing the opposition as secularist and anti-Islamic. They saw external opposition to Suharto as opposition to Indonesia, because both were Muslim. The senior modernists also emphasized statist rather than civil Islam (Hefner 2002, 147).

The period following the downfall of the Suharto regime saw the resurgence of a number of old issues pertaining to the relationship among Islam, the state, and society and the role of Islam in the new Indonesia. Many Islamic parties, including the PPP and the PBB, participated in the 1999 elections. These parties raised the issue of the Jakarta Charter in the annual session of the People's Consultative Council (MPR). During debate on the amendment to the 1945 constitution, they tried to reenact the famous clause that obligated the state to apply Shari'a for its adherents, but their efforts failed because all other factions in the MPR rejected it.

During this post-Suharto period, a number of regions in Indonesia have demanded the formal enforcement of Shari'a. Aside from Aceh, which was given special autonomy, including the right to implement Shari'a, provinces such as South Sulawesi and a number of others have indicated their increasing desire to apply Shari'a. The reformation era has also provided an opportunity for the growth of hard-line Islamic movements, such as Laskar Jihad, Front Pembela Islam, Hizbut Tahrir Indonesia, and Kongres Mujahidin Indonesia. These groups demand the enforcement of Shari'a in Indonesia, and a number of them are inclined to use violence in expressing their aspiration to carry out the function of "morality police" *(amar ma'ruf nahi munkar)*.

In the new era of political and social liberalization after the fall of Suharto, the *Reformasi* movement focused on the importance of good governance and democracy. NGOs and Muslim civil-society organizations proliferated, and previously undercover Muslim groups operated more openly. This openness resulted in many books, articles, television discussions, and public lectures. In 2001 there were discussions about "liberal Islam"—about "its meaning, its contribution to the contemporary expression of Islam, its relevance for Indonesia, its place in the life of individual Muslims" (Hooker 2004, 235). These discussions were carried to the community through a variety of media, including an Internet mailing list and a book called *Wajah Liberal Islam di Indonesia (The Face of Liberal Islam in Indonesia)*. These developments indicate a vibrant civil society in which the role of Islam in state and society is being debated. As Madjid noted, many Indonesian Muslims are aware that "it is wrong to make generalizations about other communities, and that it is imperative to seek cooperation with like-minded people or with people with the same commitment to the betterment of human life" (1994, 76). Civil-society organizations like the Liberal Islam Network have been deeply engaged in promoting a pluralistic and liberal version of Islam, although they have met with criticism from other voices.

It seems clear that the relationship of Islam, the state, and society in Indonesia remains controversial, often symbolic or serving as a proxy for other social and political issues. Various parties to the debate seem to be more concerned with opposing what they assume or understand to be the positions of their presumed protagonists than with clarifying their own position. That is, groups are better known for what they oppose than for what they propose regarding the role of Shari'a in the state. It is also clear that although Islam has never been a state religion, Islamic discourse has influenced and has been influenced by policies of the state. The difficulty is in identifying the exact nature and implications of the influence of Islamic discourse, because of profound ambivalence on the issues even with the same groups. There is much talk about Islam and Shari'a but little clarity about what these things mean or how they should concretely affect state policies and legislation. For instance, the government allowed the application of Shari'a in Aceh as part of the autonomy package (Law No. 18 of 2000), but that did not lead to consistent policy, owing to lack of agreement between Acehnese leaders about what the application of Shari'a means (Hooker and Lindsey 2003, 33). At the same time, with the decline in the credibility of the Pancasila since the fall of Suharto, the door has been opened for Islamic parties to play a larger role in the Indonesian state (Hooker and Lindsey 2003, 33, 34). Widespread ambivalence among Indonesians has serious implications for the peaceful survival and development of the country as a whole, perhaps because of the illusive mirage of categorical answers, whether of total separation or complete fusion of Islam and the state.

Before considering more reflections on the general thesis and analysis of this book as a whole, we may find it helpful to note some of the serious implications of this persistent ambivalence, which can be briefly illustrated with reference to its implications for citizenship. The debate on citizenship in modern Indonesia is inextricably linked first to the idea of the modern state itself and second to the Pancasila, since that is the framework that specifies the basis of belonging to the Indonesian state. It does not appear that any Islamist groups completely and categorically reject the idea of the modern state itself. But the key difference between those who call for an Islamic state and those who advocate stronger separation of Islam and the state is that the advocates of an Islamic state seek to define *the state itself as an instrument of religion,* while this claim is resisted by other Islamic reform and renewal movements as well as by those described as secularist since the Jakarta Charter. Islamist and nationalist groups also differ over the sufficiency of the Pancasila in reflecting the character and serving the needs of Indonesian society. These respective positions are directly related to the issue of citizenship.

As outlined in the earlier sections of this chapter, the debate over citizenship and the Pancasila has resurfaced periodically since the independence of Indonesia. For example, it was particularly prominent in the parliamentary session after the first election in 1955, and the inconclusive resolution of the matter was used by Sukarno to revert to the earlier 1945 constitution. After the fall of the Suharto regime at the end of the 1990s, the issue once again became a subject of debate, this time with wider participation among social forces. During various stages of this cyclical debate, Islamic reformist intellectuals emphasized both the secular character of the state and, to an extent, the particularity of the modern notion of the state as a condition for citizenship. Sjadzali, for example, sees the current form and structure of the state as the best imaginable model and believes it should therefore be the final goal for Indonesian Muslims. In his view, Indonesia is gradually evolving as a "religious state," in the sense of being a state that is concerned with the implementation and development of religious values, without having to become a "theocratic" state, which is constitutionally based on certain formal religious institutions (Effendy 1995, 115, 116). I would also recall here the strong position of public intellectuals like the late Nurcholish Madjid, who firmly criticized the idea of the Islamic state. He emphasized the virtues of tolerance and pluralism and pointed to clear precedents of these values in Islamic history, though not expressed in terms of modern concepts, which are new to all religions. To him, Islam is always "adaptable to the environment of any culture of its adherents, anywhere and at any time" (1994, 70).

It can be argued that the Pancasila is, in several fundamental respects, a powerful and enabling framework for defining Indonesian citizenship along secular and nonreligious grounds; it embodies and promotes commitments to social and religious pluralism and tolerance, all of which contribute to an ethos of inclusive citizenship. Madjid, for instance, argued that "Pancasila is the one and only ideology to guide Indonesian people in their activities at national, political and community levels" (1994, 59). He noted that Adam Malik, the former vice president of Indonesia, saw the Pancasila as similar in spirit to the "Constitution of Medina" created by the Prophet, as a formula for a state based on social and religious pluralism (64).

The Pancasila model as a framework for citizenship can also be criticized on several grounds, such as its degree of inclusiveness and the methods by which its legitimacy was sustained. Sukarno and his colleagues created the Pancasila as a modus vivendi between secular nationalism and the Islamic state, but it was accepted only after further "Islamicization." For example, the first principle, "belief in God," was changed to "belief in one supreme God"; the third principle, originally "nationalism," was changed to "unity of Indonesia," because nationalism was challenged as inconsistent with Islamic universalism; and the fourth principle, "democracy under the guidance of wisdom through the deliberation of the people's representatives," refers to "wisdom through deliberation," a *hikmah* ascribed to the Prophet Muhammad (Madjid 1994, 57). Thus Islamic legitimacy was sought for the Pancasila even by secular nationalists like Sukarno, but it was sought *within* those principles that defined the state structure and not outside the realm of the state.

However, in its emphasis on the belief in one supreme God, Pancasila limits nontheistic rationales for citizenship and belonging. Moreover, in recognizing only five main religions, the Pancasila attempts to impose artificial and narrow uniformity among highly diverse Indonesian identities, seeking to force some four hundred ethnic and language groups into five categories of religion. This clearly violates the equal citizenship of Indonesians who wish to be identified by different terms. It should also be noted here that the Pancasila model itself was enforced and affirmed by a coercive nondemocratic state—for example, when the Suharto regime decreed in 1983 that the Pancasila should be the basis of all political parties. Such negative associations have certainly contributed to the diminished legitimacy of the Pancasila model in the post-Suharto era.

Initial resistance to the Pancasila and citizenship was overcome for some through an Islamic rationale of "what cannot be achieved in its totality should not be totally abandoned." But that rationale also assumes that some of the objectives or purposes of an Islamic state should be achieved by or through the Pancasila state itself. From this perspective, the proposal to reintroduce the clause about Shari'a that was excluded from the Jakarta Charter is an assertion of Indonesian identity as essentially Muslim and a construction of Indonesian history as essentially "Islamic." In this way, citizenship of the modern state is subsumed under a more overarching rationale of an exclusively Islamic identity. Although advocates of this view often make the point that Shari'a will apply only to Muslim citizens, the recent experiences of countries like Sudan and Nigeria clearly show this to be both unworkable in a modern state in its global context and necessarily discriminatory against non-Muslim citizens. In terms of the thesis and analysis of this book in general, the question is what the Islamic nature of the state means for citizenship. As we have seen earlier, especially in Chapter 2, there is no agreement among Muslims about what this vague concept means, and any definition that includes the enforcement of Shari'a by the state is problematic for Muslims as well as non-Muslims, as discussed in Chapter 3.

However, it is also clear from the review of debates in the provinces earlier in this chapter that most Indonesian Muslims find the term "secularism" objectionable because of its negative associations with European colonialism and current Western imposition. As I have argued throughout this book, secularism should be defined as the neutrality of the state regarding all religions, as a framework for regulating the political role of religion and not the means for excluding religion from the public domain. I will now conclude by summarizing how the information and analysis presented in this chapter support this view.

False Dichotomies and Unnecessary Dilemmas

The basic conclusion of this chapter is that debates over the relationship among Islam, the state, and society in Indonesia tend to create false dichotomies and raise unnecessary dilemmas. It is misleading to imagine a sharp dichotomy between an Islamic and a secular state, because the state is by definition a secular political institution, especially in the present context of Islamic societies. But as emphasized from the beginning, secularism does not mean the exclusion of Islam from public life or the relegation of its role to the purely personal and private domain. The appropriate balance can be achieved through the institutional separation of Islam from the state, with regulation of the political role of Islam, whereby Muslims can propose some Shariʿa principles for adoption as public policy or enactment into legislation, provided that it is done in accordance with civic reason and subject to constitutional and human rights safeguards, which are necessary for Muslim as well as non-Muslim citizens. If this approach is taken, then it becomes unnecessary to choose between an Islamic state that enforces Shariʿa and a secular state that completely rejects Shariʿa. As explained earlier, the view of an Islamic state to enforce Shariʿa is based on a false claim, because any Shariʿa principle that is enforced by the state only represents the view of the ruling elite and becomes the political will of the state rather than the religious law of Muslims. Conversely, a secular state that completely excludes religion from public policy and legislation is also based on a false claim, because Islam, or any religion for that matter, cannot be separated from politics. I am recalling the argument made in detail throughout this book in order to apply it to the case of Indonesia, rather than attempting a comprehensive summary of all its elements.

It may be helpful to note here that it is not possible to separate religion from custom or culture in the historical or contemporary experiences of Indonesian communities, because people do not experience life in terms of such abstract analytical categories. As noted earlier, Dutch colonial policy regarding law reflected a diverse range of arrangements between *adat* and Shariʿa across diverse contexts, reflecting a combination of local culture and contingencies of immediate politics as well as long-term objectives of the colonial administration. But if secularism is seen in terms of coexistence, tolerance, and pluralistic cultural traditions, then the realities of Indonesian society were certainly consistent with secularism as defined in this book. This is true even if we acknowledge the fact that the Dutch colonial administration probably advocated secularism more for its own ends than from any necessary commitment to the Indonesian populace. The conception of a secular state in the history of Indonesian communities was an empirical fact of both the precolonial and colonial periods, though it was not articulated or expressed as a coherent social ideology. This history, I am suggesting, supports the call of this chapter for promoting the demographic fact of diversity and transforming it into a proactive affirmation of pluralism as an ideology. Although Indonesian communities were indeed pluralistic in the past, that pragmatic reality should be consolidated into a clear national ideology in accordance with the nature of the postcolonial state.

The contestation over secularism in the pre-independence era and its legacy for later developments took the form of polemics between two factions, namely the so-called secular nationalists, or religion-neutral nationalists, and the Islamic nationalists, about the relationship of Islam and nationalism. The debates continued through the nationalist struggle, from the time of the demand for an Indonesian parliament through the preparations for independence. As noted earlier, a key moment in this debate, indeed a founding moment for the independent and modern Indonesian state, was the removal of the clause obligating the state to implement Shari'a for its Muslim citizens from the Pancasila. Without that move, Indonesia could not have come into existence as an independent united country or enjoyed any level of political stability and economic development after independence. Yet the debate continued in the Consultative Assembly before it was dissolved in 1959 and during the Orde Baru. The preceding review of discourse in the provinces and at the center clearly shows that the nature of Indonesian secularism and the position of Islam remain highly debated and contested to the present day. In my view, this is healthy and necessary and should continue into the future. The challenge is how to guide and promote this process in constructive ways instead of wasting time and energy on futile quests for the illusion of an Islamic state or a notion of secularism that is hostile to or exclusive of religion.

At independence, secularism and the separation of state and religion were defined through the Pancasila. It is important to note here that the Pancasila does not include the word "secularism," or categorically call for separation of religion and politics, or insist that the state should have no religion. Rather, these imperatives can be achieved through the fact that the Pancasila refrains from endorsing one religion as privileged by the state and creates a commitment to an egalitarian and pluralistic society. However, by officially recognizing five religions, the Indonesian state limits and structures the range of religious identities that citizens can have. The dominant view of the Pancasila as the basis of the Indonesian state categorically specifies a place for the believer in any of the five recognized religions, but not necessarily for the nonbeliever. This view includes secular believers in its model of citizenship but has no place for secular nonbelievers. As Madjid ob served, while the Pancasila operates as the national and community-level framework in Indonesia, "individually [Indonesians] can, and are in fact encouraged to, profess their personal world-outlooks as expressed in religions" (1994, 59).

The debate over secularism and its role in the Indonesian state and society was influenced earlier by Sukarno's vision of the state-religion relationship as expressed in his writings, as well as by a critique of his writings by Muhammad Natsir, an advocate of a greater role for Islam in the Indonesian state. In an article whose title can be translated as "Why Turkey Separated Religion from the State," Sukarno approvingly quotes Atatürk's statement "I set Islam free from the state because I want Islam to become a strong religion, and I set the state free from Islam because I want the state to become a strong institution" (1965a, 406). Explaining the statement, Sukarno argued that when religion was independent of the state, it would become self-reliant; that the interests of religion and the state were not identical; and that with the intermingling of state and religion, religious authorities would curtail the freedom of the state to make decisions. For example, he understood Atatürk to have emphasized the value of economic reasoning, as opposed to the conservative, fatalistic theology that had a hold on Turkish society. A religiously rooted fatalism among Turkish people had led to economic crises and promoted a passive outlook toward life, since it justified the status quo as God's will and not as the outcome of human action or inaction. Sukarno also saw Atatürk as opposed to the antidevelopment movement and as believing that *darwishes* or Sufis were responsible for Turkey's poor economic situation and for the negative mindset and lack of initiative shown by the people. For Sukarno, these conditions deviated from the ultimate principles of Islamic teachings.

In another article, the title of which translates as "I Am Not Dynamic Enough," Sukarno responded to criticisms of his first article (1965b). Here again he emphasized the separation of religion and state. He argued that democracy would be ineffectual if one particular religion formed the basis of the state system, since it would undermine the solidarity between Muslims and non-Muslims, the latter being opposed to the implementation of Shari'a. Sukarno was also apprehensive about conflict between members of Indonesian society if different segments of the population held different views about state authority (450, 452). He also proposed that Muslims should seek to benefit through the institution of the House of Representatives in a democratic system. In his view, Muslim representatives could introduce Islamic values by enacting regulations without formalizing such initiatives in the structure of an Islamic state. If the state formalized Islam, people would not be automatically willing to comply with Shariʿa rules, but if the spirit of Islam infused the life of the state, Muslim aspirations would automatically be accommodated (452–453).

In several articles, Muhammad Natsir offers a critique of Sukarno's views as expressed in the latter's writing. In one article, Natsir argued that Sukarno was captivated by the Turkish model and questioned Sukarno's claim that there was the necessary consensus among *ulama* that the integration of state and religion was lacking in Indonesia (1973a, 434). In another article, Natsir emphasized that in the election of a representative, such as a president or *khalifah,* the most important qualification is the candidate's understanding of and compliance with the behavior, rights, and duties of a ruler as regulated by the Qurʾan and Sunna (1973b, 437). He also disputed Sukarno's argument that the separation of the state and religion does not matter as long as parliamentary members embrace and absorb religious values in their daily life, as a result of which their decisions will reflect their religious spirit. According to Natsir, Islam is not simply an external element to be accommodated by the state; rather, the state itself should be an instrument of implementing religious rules. He asserted that Parliament could play only a limited role in solving problems; that Parliament's duty was to enforce law, not to determine principles of law, because those were unchangeable; and that parliamentary decisions themselves were influenced by political context. While contending that democracy was a good system, Natsir argued that it could result in what he called "party-cracy" *(partai-cratie)* or "crony-cracy" *(kliek-cratie),* which defeats the purpose and rationale of democratic government.

I am referring to that debate here not only as representative of two competing positions—what I call false dichotomies and unnecessary dilemmas—but also to highlight a way of mediating and reconciling such polarized positions as represented by such Islamic intellectuals as Nurcholish Madjid and Muhammad Natsir. As government initiatives after the ascendancy of Suharto in 1965 marginalized the role of Muslim groups, the issue of the modernization of Indonesian Islam gained importance. In particular, the situation raised the question of whether the modernization of Islam required "secularization" (Hefner 1995, 36). Islamic secularists like Madjid called for the "renewal" of Islam and argued that the politicization of Islam undermined piety and "confused a profane preoccupation with a sacred one."

They also held that since there is nothing in scripture to indicate that Muslims must create an Islamic state, mundane goals should not be confused with sacred ones, and Muslims should respond to and live with Indonesia's pluralism (Hefner 1995, 36).

In my view, the framework proposed by Nurcholish Madjid offers a good Islamic alternative to the vision of Natsir. Madjid also proposed some elements of liberalization in Islamic teachings, such as secularization, intellectual freedom, the idea of progress, and open attitude (1998). As he defined it, secularization is the ability to distinguish between transcendental and temporal values. This secularization is also intended to develop an understanding that humans are God's vice-regents in this world; they are given the freedom to choose and decide for themselves and at the same time have to bear responsibility for their actions before God.

It is true that Nurcholish Madjid and his colleagues have been accused of trying to transform Islam into a "spiritual personalist ethical system" (Hefner 1995, 36). For example, H. M. Rasjidi, an Indonesian Muslim scholar and former minister of religious affairs of Indonesia, saw Madjid's notion of secularization as inseparable from Western secularization (1972, 14). On the contrary, Madjid and his colleagues "rejected the ideology of *secularism,* with its privatization of religion, while supporting *secularization,* construed as the desacralization of things wrongly sacralized" (Hefner 1995, 36). Yet their opponents insisted that Islam is a "total way of life," providing norms of how law and society should be organized; therefore, secularization means abandoning the social and ethical totality demanded by Islam (Hefner 1995, 37).

It seems that the resistance to secularism may be at least in part a hostility to the term itself, with its associations with colonial rule and connotations of antipathy to religion. After the fall of the Suharto regime, the debate has also developed in new directions, beyond the framework of the Pancasila, to issues of the autonomy of various regions and the emergence of political, social, and cultural groups that were denied a voice during the Orde Baru. On the one hand, groups like the Liberal Islam Network and the magazine *Syir'ah* attempt to offer and develop a more inclusive and self-critical Islamic discourse that encompasses the value of secularism. On the other hand, there are also voices like Hartono Ahmad Jaiz and the magazine *Sabili,* which call for narrower and more exclusive interpretations of Islam and Shari'a which are not consistent with a secular state as a framework for pluralism and constitutionalism.

But the varied positions in the debate cannot just be reduced to those op-posed to or in favor of the term "secularism." Rather, there is a range of views about the relationship of Islam and the state that lie between the ex-tremes of total fusion and total separation, perhaps itself pointing to the di-verse understandings of secularism in Indonesia. In the final analysis, what is critically important is to keep the debate itself alive and constructive. It is profoundly problematic for Indonesia as a whole if either the Islamic state model or the secular state model is implemented in any way that diminishes the possibilities of debate and adaptation. Examples of these negative ten-dencies can be cited from the post-independence history of Indonesia, in-cluding recent so-called *fatwas* that brand concepts like pluralism and secu-larism as anti-Islamic. Constructive debate must avoid such inflammatory accusations and focus on substantive and mutually respectful arguments.

CHAPTER **7**

Conclusion: Negotiating the Future of Shariʿa

The framework proposed in this book provides the normative and institutional parameters and safeguards for the negotiation and mediation of the role of Shariʿa among Muslims and non-Muslims now and in the future. By negotiation and mediation I mean to emphasize that there is no categorical and permanent resolution of the paradox of how to secure the religious neutrality of the state within the reality of the connectedness of Islam and politics. The conception of the secular state I am proposing offers an alternative vision to perceptions of secularism and the secular state that many Muslims find objectionable. Instead of sharp dichotomies between religion and secularism that relegate Islam to the purely personal and private domain, I call for balancing the two by separating Islam from the state and regulating the role of religion in politics. This view combines continuity of histories of the secular realm in Islamic societies with reform and adaptation of these traditions to offer future possibilities for these societies. In particular, I argue that there is nothing "un-Islamic" about the concept of a secular state as the necessary medium for negotiating the organic and legitimate role of Islam in public life. The Qurʾan addresses Muslims as individuals and community, without even mentioning the idea of a state, let alone prescribing a particular form for it. It is also clear that the Qurʾan does not prescribe a particular form of government. As early Muslim leaders immediately recognized, however, some form of political organization is clearly necessary for keeping the peace and organizing the affairs of the community. This idea can be supported and legitimated from an Islamic perspective, since it is necessary for social life anywhere.

But whatever Muslims devise as a state to serve these vital purposes will necessarily be a human construction, which is inherently secular and not Islamic as such. The same is true about the system of government that will

267

rule through state institutions. The question for the future of Shariʿa is how to devise a state and a system of government, which are inherently secular, that can best serve the purposes of Shariʿa for Muslims as individuals and communities. Moreover, since Muslims must always coexist and collaborate with other communities, at local, national, regional, and global levels, non-Muslims are equally concerned about the states and governments they share with Muslims. Indeed, interdependence and cooperation among different human communities is explicitly stipulated in the Qurʾan (49:13). I will return later to the implications of this view for the audiences of this book.

My purpose is to affirm that the secular state, as defined in this book, is more consistent with the inherent nature of Shariʿa and the history of Islamic societies than are false and counterproductive assertions of a so-called Islamic state or the alleged enforcement of Shariʿa as state law. This view of the secular state neither depoliticizes Islam nor relegates it to the private domain. My proposal is opposed to domineering visions of a universal history and future in which the "enlightened West" is leading all of humanity to the secularization of the world, in which the secularity of the state is the logical outcome. In the conception of secularism I am proposing, the influence of religion in the public domain is open to negotiation and contingent upon the free exercise of the human agency of all citizens, believers and unbelievers alike.

As a Muslim, I need a secular state in order to live in accordance with Shariʿa out of my own genuine conviction and free choice, personally and in community with other Muslims, which is the only valid and legitimate way of being a Muslim. Belief in Islam, or any other religion, logically requires the possibility of disbelief, because belief has no value if it is coerced. If I am unable to disbelieve, I will not be able to believe. Maintaining institutional separation between Islam and the state while regulating the permanent connection of Islam and politics is a necessary condition for achieving the positive role of Shariʿa now and in the future.

In this final chapter, I will discuss and further elaborate some aspects of this proposed framework for the future of Shariʿa, including my emphasis on a process-based model of negotiated secularism and the rehabilitation of religion in public life. I will also examine the distinction between secularism and secularization, and illustrate how it is relevant to my particular concern with the future of Shariʿa rather than its history. Since this proposal for a positive role for Shariʿa involves multiple audiences and levels of discourse, I will begin with some reflections on aspects of the scope and methodology of this framework.

My primary audience is Muslims everywhere, but that is neither a monolithic, exceptional, nor static category of readers. Muslim intellectuals and professionals, who tend to be the ruling elite and opinion-makers in their societies, are largely shaped by European-style education, which enables them to appreciate philosophical concepts and terms that may not be known to those educated in the traditional Islamic schools *(madrasas)*. Thus, even if this book were addressed exclusively to Muslims, that would still be a diverse and dynamic group. Ironically, Western media and some scholars tend to take an "orientalist" view of Islam and Muslims that is based on a narrow view of traditional interpretations of Shariʿa and medieval scholarship. Conversely, the views of liberal, Western-educated Muslims are assumed to be unauthentic and their values unrepresentative of "real" Islam. In this way, Western media and public opinion call upon Muslims to "modernize" and adhere to universal values of constitutionalism and human rights. Yet those who do that are dismissed in Western public discourse as "westernized" and not sufficiently Muslim, a view shared by traditional conservative Muslims. Part of the argument I am making in this book is that Muslims can be liberal in their own right, from an Islamic perspective, without having to satisfy preconceived notions of how they ought to be "sufficiently Muslim," whether in Western or conservative Islamic discourse.

In view of this concept of the state and the critical role of civic reason, the future of Shariʿa cannot be secured without due regard for the interests and concerns of those who are not Muslim; they must also be included in my intended audience, though not in the same way as Muslims. Focusing on a particular audience would mean selecting a certain methodology of argumentation and choosing terms and concepts that resonate with the intended readers. Since no audience lives in isolation from other human beings near and far, my mode of argumentation and choice of terms and concepts should also be comprehensible for non-Muslims. The issue is complicated by the fact that audiences tend to overlap, and terms and concepts have varieties of shades of meaning and implications for different readers. Some of the terms and concepts I use in this book, like "Shariʿa," "secularism," and "citizenship," evoke a range of meanings and associations among any group of readers.

It is true that my primary objective is to persuade Muslims to support and promote the proposed conception of the dynamic relationship among Islam, the state, and politics. To this end, I have attempted throughout this book to support these propositions from an Islamic perspective, as explained in Chapter 1. Since this subject should be a matter of general concern because of its implications for human dignity and social justice at home and abroad, I am also calling on non-Muslims to participate in debating these issues in relation to public policy and state law. Muslims are also encouraged to participate in debates among other religious communities in relation to public policy and state law. Such debates regarding all relevant religious traditions should of course be conducted with civility, mutual respect, and discretion. They should also focus on matters of public policy and law and avoid questions of religious doctrine and ritual practices. These standards may often be difficult to maintain in practice, but consensus about the propriety, manner, and limits of internal debate and interreligious dialogue will evolve over time.

Part of this inclusive approach is the consideration of concepts and arguments from broader comparative perspectives, including Western political and legal theories and experiences, all as part of the civic reasoning process proposed in this book. The point here is not only that including non-Muslims in an Islamic discourse regarding public policy is expedient or tactical, but also that this is the way it has been done throughout Islamic history and should continue to be done in the future. It is neither possible nor desirable, in my view, to identify and deploy purely "Islamic" arguments, to the exclusion of non-Islamic arguments, as if the two forms of discourse can evolve in isolation or be separated from each other. The spectacular spread of Islam, which was sustained for a thousand years, has partly been the result of its ability to adapt to local conditions and adopt preexisting sociopolitical institutions and cultural practices. The philosophical and jurisprudential foundations of early Islamic social and political institutions evolved through active debate with Jewish, Christian, Greek, Indian, Persian, and Roman traditions during the seventh through ninth centuries. Moreover, Islamic discourse continued to adopt, adapt, and negotiate with preexisting religious and cultural traditions as Islam spread into central and Southeast Asia and sub-Saharan Africa over the following centuries.

These processes continued through the encounter with European colonialism from the sixteenth century up to the present. This phase is particularly important for the argument I am making in this book, because of the continuing and multifaceted impact of European colonialism and Western hegemony generally over Islamic societies and communities. As discussed in

Chapters 1 and 3 and illustrated with the cases of India, Turkey, and Indonesia, the adoption of European models of the state and positivist conceptions of law require the incorporation of corresponding concepts and principles of secularism, constitutionalism, human rights, and citizenship. This does not mean total and unquestioning incorporation of all things Western, but that Islamic societies are neither uniform nor exceptional. Indian Muslims, for instance, probably have more in common with their Hindu neighbors than they do with Nigerian or Senegalese Muslims. I am not suggesting that being Muslim is irrelevant, or that there are no differences between religious communities. My point is that Muslims and their societies are neither superior nor inferior simply because of their religious beliefs. This balancing of the normality and the specificity of Islamic societies is also relevant to some terms and concepts used in this book, in relation to their counterparts in Western experiences.

Any conception of the secular state is always deeply historical and contextual everywhere. Each of the Western systems that are commonly accepted today as secular evolved its own deeply contextual definition out of its own historical experience. Upon close examination of American, British, Italian, French, Swedish, Spanish, or any other Western European experience, we find that it is unique and specific to the history and context of the country. Whatever common features can be found among these systems are the product of comparative analysis in hindsight and not the result of the uniformity of preconceived models that were deliberately applied to produce specific results. Indeed, the meaning and implications of secularism in each of those situations are contested and contingent, varying over time, sometimes in different parts of the same country. As illustrated by continuing controversy over school prayers and public displays of religious symbols in the United States and religious education in France and Germany, secularism can have different connotations in different Western societies, sometimes across parts of the same society or over time.

These reflections apply to other central concepts and terms I have incorporated in my argument in this book, such as "constitutionalism," "civil society," and "civic reason." In all of these and other relevant ideas, there is a dialectic relationship between the local, deeply contextual experience of various societies and universal norms or principles that can be extrapolated from those experiences. There is no abstract or preconceived universally agreed-upon blueprint of what constitutionalism, citizenship, civil society, and civic reason must mean. Whatever generalizations we can make about these and related ideas are based on comparative reflection upon actual experiences, after the fact and over long periods of time. No society or region of the world has the power or authority to define these concepts for others, though all societies can and do learn from each other's experiences, even when that is not realized or acknowledged. The balance of power and differences in resources, which are currently still in favor of Western over non-Western societies, may make it harder to appreciate these realities of the autonomy and interdependence of human societies. The point may be clearer when we consider the longer range of human history, and it can also be observed in our daily experiences of resisting coercive imposition while accepting friendly and respectful efforts to influence our views or behavior.

In this light, any relevant idea and argument in the debate about a secular state, constitutionalism, democracy, and so forth in Islamic settings should not be reduced to misleading and untenable dichotomies of "Western" versus "non-Western" concepts and institutions. These debates in any part of the world are about the achievement of shared visions of human dignity and social justice under similar conditions in the present local and global context. There is also a long history of exchange of ideas and experiences among a wide variety of religious and cultural communities, regardless of perceptions of internal or external origins or pedigree of those influences. While elites or ideologues may assert a fundamental difference between "them" and "us," there has always been profound dialogue and exchange across ancient and medieval civilizations and into the colonial and postcolonial era. There are and will be in the future some who will insist on the them-and-us dichotomy; indeed, confrontation and hostility tend to beget the same in response.

Focusing on such extreme positions on both sides can only lead to a senseless spiral of mutual violence and destruction. Instead of dwelling on parochial justifications of concepts and institutions deemed to be Western, or overlooking the unequal histories in which they were introduced to Islamic societies, I deliberately choose to seek mediation of conflict and cultural legitimization of concepts and institutions like constitutionalism, human rights, and secularism that are necessary for the realization of self-determination by all human beings everywhere (An-Na'im 2006). The greater challenge for Muslims in the future is not in living with the West but in living with ourselves, and securing human dignity and well-being for all. In my view, the human encounter is so deep and multifaceted everywhere, across religious, cultural, philosophical, and ideological boundaries, that we can always find evidence of cooperation and service as well as of insult and injury by the other. For our purposes here, what is problematic is the claim that the origins or legacies of ideas, discourses, and institutions completely determine their meaning or impact in any and all contexts.

Despite the deep inequalities inflicted by colonialism and its varieties of violence, the West has been understood, received, resisted, and reworked in a number of ways by non-Western peoples. As explained by Ashis Nandy, one mode of engagement in colonial India was to locate the West as an aspect of an internal debate within the traditions of Indian society. From this perspective, the West is constructed to "make sense to the non-West in terms of the non-West's experience of suffering." This victims' construction of the West was different from the strategies of those who sought to "beat the West at its own game," which was another logic of engagement by colonized Indians (Nandy 1983, xiii). Such alternative constructions of the West confirm that "victims" should not only be seen as victims, nor do they necessarily see themselves as victims. Non-Western societies cannot simply be viewed as "the other" in relation to the West. They define themselves on their own terms, although the West may well be one of the elements in that definition. "India is not non-West; it is India" (Nandy 1983, 73). Postcolonial societies already have their own understanding of and experience with the institutions and concepts that are commonly called Western. Many of these theories deviate from the accepted paradigms of academic knowledge and can be seen as an implicit critique of the West. The point is neither to tame that dissent nor to accept or reject Western knowledge uncritically, but to foster a creative and productive engagement between the various perspectives. Indeed, concepts and institutions like secularism, constitutionalism, and human rights are already an important part of the postcolonial history of non-Western societies and are already subject to vibrant and ongoing evaluation and debate, regardless of what Western societies do or fail to do with these ideas.

In addition to affirming the human agency of non-Western societies in appropriating whatever concepts and institutions they find useful, I am opposed to what might be called a cultural/ideological counteroffensive from within those societies. This dimension reflects an anxiety on the part of Islamic reformers to develop a complete countermodel of modernity from what they believe to be an exclusively Islamic framework, to match that of the West. The outcome, it seems to me, tends to be a limited and static understanding of Islam and an inadequate model of modernity. This anxiety about the West paradoxically reflects an obsession with the West, while seeking to deny the value of anything Western. This is what Boroujerdi, an Iranian scholar, calls "orientalism in reverse" and "nativism" (1996, 10, 14, 19). "Orientalism in reverse is a discourse used by 'oriental' intellectuals and political elites to lay claim to, recapture, and finally appropriate their 'true' and 'authentic' identity. This self-appropriation is almost invariably presented as a counterknowledge to Europe's oriental narrative" (11–12). Ironically, orientalism in reverse shares foundational assumptions with the Western orientalist discourse it seeks to challenge. Itself a product of colonialism, orientalism in reverse valorizes the West in constructing it as the reference point for defining the self, betraying "the infatuation with the dominating other (the West) . . . Even in their newly acquired capacity as speakers, authors, and actors the 'Orientals' continue to be overdetermined by the occidental listener, text, and audience" (12–13). The key difference between orientalism and orientalism in reverse is that the latter "is more concerned with representing (or 'big brothering') *its own domestic constituency* than with understanding and dominating the exotic other" (13; emphasis added). Orientalism in reverse in Islamic discourse seeks to intimidate and dominate Muslims, rather than liberate them by confronting the orientalism of the West.

As I see it, the challenge is to transcend this logic of opposition that is obsessed with what it seeks to oppose, to reach a proactive logic beyond the dichotomy of West and non-West. From this perspective, I have freely discussed whatever concepts, institutions, and discourses that I found relevant and useful for my argument, instead of avoiding any of these simply on the grounds that they are Western. In the final analysis, all aspects of the proposal presented in this book are premised on my belief in the possibilities of human solidarity in response to our shared human vulnerability to the dangers and risks to life and livelihood. In our present interconnected and globalized world, we must not underestimate the powerful possibilities of solidarity and dialogue across societies and civilizations, which can contribute to greater mutual understanding and celebration of both differences and commonalities.

Islam, the State, and Society

My core proposition for the future of Shari'a rests on the separation of Islam and the state, accompanied by the nurture and regulation of the organic relationship between Islam and politics. It is not possible, nor desirable in my view, for people of any society to keep their religious beliefs, commitments, and concerns out of their political choices and decisions. Recognizing and regulating the role of religion as a legitimate source of guidance for political decisions is healthier and more practical than forcing religious reasoning into the domain of fugitive politics. It is also necessary, I believe, to challenge the superiority of an abstract notion of a purely secular rationale to a religious rationale, where the latter is presumed to be a less valid form of argument. The model of secularism I am proposing does not in any way accord less value to religious modes of being in the world, thinking, or arguing than to nonreligious modes. It is also premised on the belief that the categories of understanding that people employ in their everyday lives cannot neatly be parsed into the secular (as nonreligious) and the religious. My main point here is well made by Ashis Nandy in rejecting a view of secularism that excludes religion from politics:

> If you are seriously committed to democracy, you cannot in the long run stop people from bringing their entire self into politics. For no one consistently divides one's religious and political selves in the way the theory of secularism demands. That's not psychologically feasible. There is no empirical evidence—in psychiatry, psychoanalysis, or psychology—that a healthy, normal person can constantly live with a divided social and ethical self. At crucial moments, he or she has to bring his or her deepest beliefs into public life, to reduce cognitive dissonance. (2006, 103–104)

This is why I distinguish between Islam and the state, on the one hand, and Islam and politics, on the other, to insist on institutional separation in the first relationship and to encourage continued connectedness in the second. Securing institutional separation of Islam and the state is necessary for affirming and encouraging the interaction between Islam and politics. Indeed, as I have argued elsewhere, secularism and religion require each other in fundamental and deep ways (An-Naʿim 2005). Some of this interdependence may be highlighted as follows.

On the one hand, the internal transformation of religions is critical for the survival of religious traditions and the legitimacy of religious experience. Every orthodox precept that believers take for granted today began as a heresy from the perspective of some other orthodox doctrine and may well continue to be considered heretical by some believers. The separation of religion and state is necessary for securing the legal and political space in which this transformation can happen, as and when necessary. Without a secular state that enables freedom of belief and expression, there is no possibility of development (which is to say life) within the doctrine of any religion, and no possibility of peace within or between religious communities. The secular state also secures effective possibilities for preventing an exclusivist and authoritarian religious group from threatening the essential interests of any segment of the population. I speak of possibilities because the secular state will not itself achieve these objectives. Neither will the internal transformation and rejuvenation of a religious tradition happen without the human agency of believers; nor will protection against religious authoritarianism materialize in practice without the active engagement of citizens. But the secular state is essential for these possibilities to arise and remain accessible.

On the other hand, secularism needs to be subjected to a drastic limitation of its normative claims and scope if it is to achieve its own purpose, which is the safeguarding of political pluralism in heterogeneous societies. In other words, secularism is able to unite diverse communities of belief and practice into one political community precisely because the moral claims it makes are limited and thus unlikely to be the source of serious disagreement among citizens. In other words, the secular state is a necessary framework for negotiating ethical differences among citizens, but not for adjudicating and resolving such differences. Consequently, secularism cannot by itself justify for believers some of its own components, like constitutionalism, human rights, and citizenship. It may be necessary, indeed, to seek a religious justification for the principle of secularism itself, which is what I am trying to do in this book. For the moral underpinnings of these doctrines and their institutional expression, believers may need to refer to their own religious convictions. I am not saying that this is always necessary for all believers everywhere, but I do believe it is necessary to keep this possibility open at least for Muslims.

This symbiotic relationship of religion and secularism may be summarized in the following way. Secularism needs religion to provide a widely accepted source of moral guidance for the political community, as well as to help satisfy and discipline the needs of believers within that community. Religion needs secularism to mediate relations among different communities (whether religious or antireligious or nonreligious) that share the same political space. In other words, the vital function of the secular state in regulating the public role of religion itself requires religious legitimization for believers, which is unlikely unless traditional understandings of religion are open to transformative reinterpretation. For that to happen, however, we need the safeguards of secularism, constitutionalism, human rights, and citizenship.

None of this is to suggest or imply that the religious convictions of the majority of the population should be imposed on the minority, or on dissidents within the religious community itself, except by their own free and voluntary acceptance through civic reason. This limitation on the power and rights of the majority is what I am referring to as safeguards of secularism, constitutionalism, human rights, and citizenship. These concepts and institutions may overlap in many ways, but each of them is essential in its own right and for purposes that cannot be served by the others, as discussed in Chapter 3. For instance, the democratic principle of majority rule is effectuated through state institutions but cannot mean that a particular political majority is allowed to take over the institutions of the state to the exclusion of other political forces in the country. This is the point of the distinction made in Chapter 3 between the state and politics. Moreover, the agreement of the totality of the population cannot override the human rights of a single citizen, even if those rights are not asserted in practice. This is why fundamental rights should be entrenched against constitutional amendment, even if approved by the entire population.

It is important here to emphasize what my proposal does not claim to cover or purport to do. This proposal does not advocate a programmatic model for *how* specific Shari'a principles should be reformulated in particular societies or across societies. I do believe that Islamic reform is necessary for the legitimacy and coherence of the proposed model among Muslims. I personally believe in a particular reform methodology, but I do not insist on it as a prerequisite for the proposed framework and can fully accept any reform methodology that can achieve the desired objective. Far from claiming to prescribe the meaning of Shari'a or what its principles should be, I am seeking only to secure conditions under which I can present my views on Islamic reform and debate those presented by others, subject to the safeguards of civic reason.

I am also not claiming to conclusively resolve long-standing debates about the nature of democracy, secularism, constitutionalism, and related matters. I do call for a rethinking of secularism, in particular for greater acceptance of a role for Islam in public life. But that is in no way a claim to conclusively resolve controversies about issues of public policy like abortion or religious education in state schools. In the case of India, for instance, I am not suggesting that the state or the judiciary should redefine the scope of Muslim personal law once and for all by reinterpreting specific Shari'a principles in a particular manner. Rather, my objective is to offer a framework for negotiating a way to balance the need of Muslims for Islamic legitimacy of personal or family law with respect for the human rights and fully equal citizenship of women.

In essence, the proposed framework seeks to establish a sustainable and legitimate theoretical and institutional structure for an ongoing process, where perceptions of Shari'a and its interaction with principles of constitutionalism, secularism, and democratic governance can be negotiated and debated among different interlocutors in various societies. In all societies, Western or non-Western, constitutionalism, democracy, and the relationship between the state, religion, and politics are highly contextual formations that are premised on contingent sociological and historical conditions and entrenched through specific norms of cultural legitimacy. The model proposed here combines the regulation of the relationship between Islam and politics with the separation of Islam and the state as the necessary medium for negotiating the relevance of Shari'a to public policy and law. In this gradual and tentative process of consensus-building through civic reason, various combinations of persons and groups may agree on one issue but disagree on another, and consensus-building efforts on any particular topic may fail or succeed, but none of that will be permanent and conclusive. Whatever happens to be the *substantive* outcome on any issue at any point in time is made, and can change, as the product of a process of civic reasoning based on the voluntary and free participation of all citizens. For this process to continue and thrive, it is imperative that no particular view of Shari'a is coercively imposed in the name of Islam, because that would inhibit free debate and contestation.

What about the free choice and religious conviction of Muslims who believe in the idea of an Islamic state to enforce Shari'a through the state's institutions? Does the proposed framework deprive them of the right to live in accordance with their own religious obligation? Are these Muslims required to abdicate, or at the very least suspend, this belief when entering the realm of civic reason? To be clear on the point, these Muslims are of course completely free to observe Shari'a principles in their own personal lives, provided that that does not violate the rights of others. What is at issue is the claim of some Muslims to impose their beliefs on others, a claim of a right to violate the rights of others. This is the core claim that I have most strongly sought to challenge from an Islamic point of view throughout various parts of this book. I will now try to summarize my objections to this core claim.

At a most fundamental level, the separation of Islam and the state is necessary for any possibility of belief, as well as for its legitimacy and value over time. By protecting my freedom to disbelieve, a secular state, as defined in this book, is necessary for my freedom to believe, which is the only way belief has any meaning and consequences. The claim of some Muslims to have the religious right and obligation to enforce Shari'a through state institutions must be forcefully blocked because it constitutes an immediate and total repudiation of the right of all citizens to believe in Islam or another religion or opinion. Paradoxically, the belief of some Muslims in the obligation to enforce Shari'a through state institutions repudiates their own ability to hold and advocate that view. Even those who believe in an Islamic state to enforce Shari'a need the freedom to hold and advocate that view, which will be lost to them if they achieve their objective, because the individual Muslims who control the institutions of the state will decide what Shari'a means and how to implement it.

To elaborate briefly, once Shari'a is invoked as Shari'a and its binding force on all citizens is predicated on this fact, the domain of civic reason will be lost, because conversation, debate, and negotiation among interlocutors can no longer take place on equal footing. The essence of civic reason is that the significance of reasons cannot be separated from their rationale, and that the rationale for reasons must be framed in terms that are applicable and accessible to all. Civic reason also requires recognizing that the means are as important as the ends. But when the rationale of Shari'a principles is that they are simply what some believe to be the will and command of God, all other rationales are effectively silenced. It is true that people disagree about reasons and their rationales, but such differences would be beyond debate and contestation among citizens if they were presented as a transcendental and absolutist claim of an individual's religion. A Muslim who is arguing that charging interest (riba) should be illegal because it is prohibited in Shari'a (haram) may be able to present some general policy rationale to support the argument that other citizens can debate, accept, or reject without passing judgment on the religious belief of that Muslim. But if the religious prohibition itself is the rationale, there is nothing left to debate with other citizens. At the same time, a Muslim citizen will not be completely free to choose to observe this religious prohibition out of genuine conviction, but rather will be compelled to comply in obedience to the coercive authority of the state.

The point to emphasize here is that any claim to have established an Islamic state or that the state is Shari'a is in fact a false claim. As discussed in Chapters 1 and 2, the notion of requiring an Islamic state to enforce Shari'a is a dangerous illusion: the state is a political institution that cannot be Islamic. There has never been agreement among Muslims on what "Islamic" means in this context. No state has ever been acknowledged by Muslims as a valid example of the concept. In the present modern context, the idea of an Islamic state is inherently inconsistent with the premise of constitutionalism and is not viable in practice. No state can successfully operate on the totality of what Muslims accept as Shari'a principles. I am making this point so categorically here in an effort to preempt claims that past failures of any "experiment," like those of Pakistan or Sudan, were the result only of bad implementation and not of flaws in the model of an Islamic state itself. The historical reality is that there has never been an Islamic state, from the state of Abu Bakr, the first caliph in Medina, to Iran, Saudi Arabia, and any other state that claims to be Islamic today. This obvious reality is due to the incoherence of the idea itself and the practical impossibility of realizing it, not simply to bad experiments that can be rectified in the future.

From a historical perspective, the polity of Medina during the time of the Prophet is of course an inspiring model of the sort of values Muslims should strive for in self-governance, transparency, and accountability. But that experience should not be discussed as an example of an Islamic state that Muslims can replicate after the death of the Prophet. Unless there is another prophet (and Muslims do not accept that possibility), that first polity or state cannot be replicated anywhere. For the rest of Islamic history, the state has always been a political, not religious, institution, though it has not, of course, fit the model of the secular state as defined here. As described in Chapter 2, the historical experience of Islamic societies in general has been one of differentiation of religious and political authorities. Rulers sought the support of Islamic scholars and religious leaders to legitimize their political authority, but religious authorities could not provide that legitimization if they were seen to be too closely identified with the state. In other words, the distinction between the state and religious institutions was historically both necessary and difficult to maintain in practice for both sides. This ambivalence meant that most political regimes in Islamic history fell in between these two polar models. They never achieved the complete conflation or convergence of Islam and the state according to the ideal of the Prophet, yet they always claimed or sought to be closer to it than to its polar opposite, complete separation between religious and political authority. The way to clarify and mediate that historical ambivalence, I have argued in this book, is to distinguish between the state and politics, so that Islamic religious authority is separate from the institutions of the state while being legitimately active in the political life of the community.

Conversely, it is imperative for the success of the framework described above that the state does not itself become partisan to any specific position in the negotiation of the role of Islam and Shari'a in the community. This is what I referred to earlier as the religious neutrality of the state as an objective, precisely because complete neutrality is impossible for human beings to achieve. It should also be noted here that since the state and its institutions are not human agents, any action taken in the name of the state is in fact the action of the officials who control and operate the relevant organs of the state. This reality only emphasizes the imperative of neutrality of all state institutions and actors on matters of religious doctrine and practice in the community. The state should not intervene in the processes of civic reasoning, whether to support a secular or a religious rationale, except to uphold constitutional and other safeguards of free and fair debate and contestation. In other words, the role of state institutions should be limited to protecting civic reasoning and adjudicating disputes according to established constitutional and judicial criteria and processes.

Since, as noted earlier, those who rule through state institutions cannot be completely neutral, the objective is to promote the neutrality of the state through a variety of safeguards to ensure political and legal accountability. This critical and delicate role of the state is the reason that the distinction between "state" and "politics" is both necessary and difficult to maintain. As discussed earlier, the purpose of this distinction is to safeguard the integrity and continuity of state institutions, like the civil service and educational and health-care systems, and protect them from manipulation by an elected government, especially when it enjoys strong political support. The fact that this distinction will not be a permanently settled boundary in any society, as various political actors strive for greater power, confirms its critical importance for the proper functioning of state institutions and the political process in general. Since it cannot be entrusted to competing political actors, the distinction between the state and politics requires the proper functioning of constitutionalism, human rights, and citizenship as the essential framework for civic reasoning, as discussed in Chapter 3.

The value of protecting the possibility of dissent and difference can be appreciated in terms of the relationship of heresy to the authenticity and rejuvenation of religious life. Obviously, many heresies simply perish and disappear, but there is no orthodoxy that was not a heresy when it started. From this perspective, every religious community should safeguard the psychological and social as well as political possibility of heresy and disagreement among its members, because that is the best indicator of the honesty and authenticity of the beliefs and practice within that community. Believers must always remain within their religious community completely voluntarily or leave by their complete free choice—there is simply no human or religious value in coerced religious belief or practice.

All the principles and processes outlined above are intended to protect and promote free and honest compliance with Shariʿa by Muslims, which is the only way to be a Muslim at all. From my perspective, secularism, constitutionalism, human rights, and related concepts and institutions can all be rendered in the service of honest fidelity to Shariʿa and genuine compliance with its commands. This is what I mean when I say that I need a secular state to be a Muslim. I am neither suggesting that Shariʿa is inherently incompatible with constitutionalism, human rights, or democracy nor calling for it to be subordinated to these principles. In my view, it is counterproductive to see the issue as one of Shariʿa *versus* constitutionalism, human rights, or democracy. On the one hand, as I have argued earlier and elsewhere (An-Naʿim 1990), the legitimacy of these principles varies according to the cultural, religious, and philosophical belief or orientation of the individual. For Muslims, that will probably include belief in the compatibility of the principles with Shariʿa as the normative system of Islam, which is the product of a long and complex process of interpretation and contextual practice. But if all of this is true, it may be asked, why am I opposing the enforcement of Shariʿa as state law and policy?

There are at least two levels of response to this question. At one level, it is clear that there is no uniform and settled understanding of Shariʿa among Muslims that can be enforced by the state. This is true even within the same school of Sunni or Shiʿa jurisprudence, let alone across different schools and sects. It should also be emphasized at this level that since every understanding of Shariʿa, even if universal among Muslims, is a human interpretation, none should be enforced as state law in the name of Shari'a or Islam as such. At another level, because Shari'a is always the product of human interpretation of divine sources, any interpretation of it will reflect the human limitations of those who are interpreting it, despite the divinity of the sources they are working with. From this perspective, Shari'a will always remain open to reinterpretation and evolution, in response to the constantly changing needs of Islamic societies and communities in different times and places.

The gradual decline of Islamic civilizations and their consequent domination by European colonial powers over the past three centuries contributed to the growing rigidity, overdetermination, and trivialization of Shari'a among Muslims. Ironically, Muslims and others often blame Shari'a and Islam in general for the backwardness and underdevelopment of Islamic societies. This view is both inaccurate and unproductive. Since Shari'a and Islam are not independent entities that can do anything on their own, the decline of Islamic societies must be the consequence of what Muslims do or fail to do. To blame Shari'a or Islam is not productive because to do so shifts responsibility and the ability to change away from Muslims to abstract notions. If the problem is with Shari'a itself, then we have to wait for Shari'a to solve it, but if it is the failure of Muslims to correct what is wrong with their understanding of Shari'a, then it is their responsibility to correct that and implement it in practice.

From this perspective, I am proposing reinterpretation of specific aspects of historical interpretations of Shari'a, namely, male guardianship of women (*qawama*), sovereignty of Muslims over non-Muslims (*dhimma*), and violently aggressive *jihad*. Even if these principles of Shari'a are not enacted as state law and policy as such, their moral and emotional impact on Muslims will severely undermine the ethos of constitutionalism, human rights, and citizenship. Given the social and moral authority of Shari'a for Muslims, these principles are likely to translate into discrimination against women and non-Muslims, and to legitimize such discrimination with or without the endorsement of the state. Even if state officials were to intervene to stop discrimination against women and non-Muslims through the coercive and disciplinary power of the state apparatus, such intervention is likely to be seen as a violation of Shari'a. Moreover, the risk of this "popular" resistance to state action against discrimination can be cited by state officials to justify their failure to act. The persistence of these attitudes about gender and interreligious relations and about political violence more generally can also motivate private persons to act on them directly to enforce their personal views of Shariʿa while claiming to be acting in the interests of Islam against an "irreligious" or "heretical" state.

As indicated earlier, the model of the secular state presented in this book is not contingent on acceptance of a particular Islamic reform methodology, but I do believe that the need for reform cannot be denied. One Islamic methodology that I find to be appropriate for achieving the necessary degree of reform is that proposed by Ustadh Mahmoud Mohamed Taha (Taha 1987). This book is not about issues of Islamic reform, which I have discussed in detail elsewhere (An-Naʿim 1990), but it may be helpful to note its main premise and methodology of juridical reasoning *(ijtihad)*. As Ustadh Taha explained, the earlier universal message of Islam of peaceful propagation and nondiscrimination was contained in parts of the Qurʾan that were revealed in Mecca (610–622). But when the Prophet migrated with his few persecuted followers to Medina in 622, the Qurʾan had to provide for the concrete needs of the emerging community, which had to struggle for survival in an extremely harsh and violent environment. In this light, it is clear that traditional Shariʿa principles of *qawama, dhimma,* and violently aggressive *jihad* were in fact concessions to the social and economic realities of the time and not the message Islam intended for humanity at large into the indefinite future. Since those principles were developed by early Muslim jurists applying their own methodology of interpretation, which was not sanctioned as such in the Qurʾan or Sunna of the Prophet, different conclusions can be drawn by applying a new methodology. This analysis, I believe, provides a coherent and systematic methodology of interpretation of the totality of the Qurʾan and Sunna, in contrast to the arbitrary selectivity of some other modern scholars, who fail to explain what happens to the verses they choose to overlook. But since this or any other approach to Islamic reform must be implemented in the concrete context of present Islamic societies, a brief clarification of this situation may be useful here. Whatever future Shariʿa may have, it must evolve out of its recent past and current status.

Colonial Transformation and Postcolonial Inhibitions

As discussed earlier in this book, it is grossly misleading to speak of the enforcement of Shariʿa by the state in Islamic history, because the notions of state and law had very different meanings from our understanding of these institutions in the postcolonial era. During the first three centuries of Islamic history, various aspects of Shari'a, such as the sciences of jurisprudence *(fiqh)*, the Qur'an, the Sunna, and theology *(kalam)*, were developed by independent scholars working outside the framework of the state. Since those fields constituted the substance and methodology of the education of rulers and their officials, Shari'a principles would have influenced the administration of justice. But Shari'a could not have been enforced by the state in the modern sense of systematic enactment of a legal system, simply because the state lacked the authority to enact Shari'a. That authority was vested in *ulama,* who enjoyed the confidence of their communities. The imperial states of the time neither had the centralized political power of the modern state nor attempted to provide comprehensive administration of justice.

It is therefore incorrect to speak of the legal and public-policy role of Shari'a as something that Muslims used to have and should reenact now that they have achieved political independence from colonial rule. On the one hand, it is not possible to return to the precolonial era, because of the drastic transformation of Islamic societies and their state formations. All Muslims now live under territorial (nation-) states, which are characterized by "a centralized and bureaucratically organized administrative and legal order run by an administrative staff, binding authority over what occurs within its area of jurisdiction, a territorial basis and a monopoly of the use of force" (Gill 2003, 2–3). On the other hand, the formation and development of Shari'a by independent scholars outside the framework of the state defies codification and centralized enforcement by the European model of the state which Muslims inherited from colonial rule. As discussed earlier, the enforcement of Shari'a as state law is inconsistent with its nature, because enactment requires selection of some views over others, whereas that choice is the right and responsibility of each Muslim as a matter of religious conviction. That is why the founding scholars of Shari'a objected to the adoption of their views by the state and did not claim the exhaustive authority to determine the Shari'a ruling on any issue for all Muslims (Weiss 1998, 120–122).

That tradition of early Islamic scholars was indeed pious and intellectually honest, and it provided valuable flexibility in local legal practices under highly decentralized imperial states. But when it is considered in relation to modern legal systems, the obvious question is, how and by whom can reasonable and legitimate differences of opinion among schools and scholars of Shari'a be settled in order to determine what is the law to be applied by state courts and other authorities? The basic dilemma here can be explained as follows. On the one hand, there is the paramount importance of a minimum degree of certainty in the determination and enforcement of state law for any society. The nature and role of state law in the modern state also requires the interaction of a multitude of actors and complex factors which cannot possibly be contained by an Islamic religious rationale. A religious rationale is key for the binding force of Shari'a norms for Muslims, yet given the diversity of opinions among Muslim jurists, whatever the state elects to enforce as law is bound to be deemed an invalid interpretation of Islamic sources by some of the Muslim citizens of that state. The imperatives of certainty and uniformity in national legislation are now stronger than they used to be, not only because of the growing complexity of the role of the state at the domestic and national levels, but also because of the global interdependence of all peoples and their states.

Moreover, it is not possible to reverse the colonial transformation of the administration of justice, which effectively displaced the institutional and methodological conditions under which Shari'a operated in the past (Hallaq 2004). As openly secular state courts applying European codes began to take over civil and criminal matters during the colonial era and after independence in the vast majority of Islamic countries, the domain of Shari'a became progressively limited to the family-law field. But even in this field, the state continues to regulate the relevance of Shari'a as part of broader legal and political systems of government and social organization (Coulson 1964, 218–225). However, an earlier, related development during the Ottoman Empire was the patronage of the Hanafi school, which eventually resulted in the codification of that school by the mid-nineteenth century. That was the first ever codification of Shari'a principles, which marked a significant shift to European models of the state and administration of justice and away from traditional approaches to the role of Shari'a in these fields. The symbolic significance of the Ottoman "capitulations" to European powers, which culminated in the abolition of the caliphate by 1924, marked the irreversible shift to European models of the state and its legal system, which came to prevail throughout the Muslim world.

European colonialism was spectacularly successful not only in its scale and scope but in transforming the global economic and trade system as well as the political and legal institutions of the colonized societies. The question for our purposes here is what impact these new realities had on the relevance and application of Shari'a among Muslims. This question is of course not new. During the era of the imperial states of the past, there was tension between these new institutional developments and the need for the daily administration of justice to be legitimized in terms of Shariʿa principles, which paradoxically required the state to respect the autonomy of scholars, because that was necessary in order for them to legitimize the authority of the state. Rulers were supposed to safeguard and promote Shariʿa without claiming or appearing to create or control it (Imber 1997, 25). That traditional tension has continued into the modern era, in which Shariʿa remains the religious law of the community of believers, independent of the authority of the state, while the state seeks to enlist the legitimizing power of Shariʿa in support of its political authority. This ambivalence persists because Muslims are neither able to repudiate the religious authority of Shariʿa nor willing to give it complete control over their lives, because it does not provide for all the substantive and procedural requirements of a comprehensive and practicable modern legal system (Gerber 1999, 29). These qualities came to be more effectively provided for by European colonial administrations throughout the Muslim world by the late nineteenth century. While this process unfolded in different ways among Islamic societies, the experience of the late Ottoman Empire has probably had the most far-reaching consequences.

The concessions made by the Ottoman Empire to European powers during the nineteenth century set the model for the adoption of Western codes and systems of administration of justice. Ottoman imperial edicts justified the changes in the name of strengthening the state and preserving Islam and emphasized the need to ensure equality among Ottoman subjects, thereby laying the foundation for the adoption of the European model of the state and its legal system. The Ottoman *Majallah* was promulgated over a ten-year period (1867–1877) to codify the rules of contract and tort according to the Hanafi school, combining European form with Shariʿa content. It also included some provisions drawn from sources other than the Hanafi school, thereby expanding the possibilities of "acceptable" selectivity from within the Islamic tradition. The principle of selectivity *(takhayur)* among equally legitimate doctrines of Shariʿa was already accepted in theory, as noted earlier, but not in practice in terms of legislation of general application. By applying it through the institutions of the state, the *Majallah* opened the door for more wide-reaching subsequent reforms, despite its initially limited purpose.

Those reforms had the paradoxical outcome of making the entire corpus of Shariʿa principles more available and accessible to judges and policymakers by transforming their nature and role through formal selectivity and adaptation so they could be incorporated into modern legislation. Shari'a principles began to be drafted and enacted into statutes that were premised on European legal structures and concepts. This was often done by mixing some general or partial principles or views from one school of Islamic jurisprudence with those derived from other schools, without due regard for the methodological basis or conceptual coherence of any of the schools whose authority was invoked. Another aspect of the paradox is that the emerging synthesis of the Islamic and European legal traditions also exposed the impossibility of the direct and systematic application of traditional Shari'a principles in the modern context.

The legal and political consequences of these developments were intensified by the significant impact of European colonialism and global Western influence in the fields of general education and professional training of state officials, business leaders, and other influential social and economic actors. Changes in educational institutions not only dislodged traditional Islamic education but also introduced a range of secular subjects that tended to create a different worldview and expertise among young generations of Muslims. Moreover, the monopoly of Islamic scholars on intellectual leadership in societies that had extremely low literacy rates has been drastically eroded by the fast growth of mass literacy and increasing higher education in secular sciences and the arts. Thus not only did Shari'a scholars lose their historical monopoly on knowledge of the sacred sources of Shari'a, but traditional interpretations of those sources are no longer viewed as sacred or unquestionable by ordinary lay Muslims. Regarding legal education in particular, the first generations of lawyers and jurists had advanced training in European and North American universities and returned to teach subsequent generations or to hold senior judicial office.

More generally, the establishment of European model states for all Islamic societies, as part of a global system based on the same model, has radically transformed political, economic, and social relations throughout the Muslim world. By retaining these models at home and participating in them abroad after independence, Islamic societies have become bound by the national and international obligations of membership in a world community of states. While there are clear differences in the level of their social development and political stability, all Islamic societies today live under national constitutional regimes (including countries that have no written constitution, such as Saudi Arabia and the Persian Gulf states) and legal systems that require respect for certain minimum rights of equality and nondiscrimination for all their citizens. Even where national constitutions and legal systems fail to expressly acknowledge and effectively provide for these obligations, a minimum degree of practical compliance is ensured by the present realities of international relations. These changes are simply irreversible, though their full implications are not sufficiently developed or observed in practice.

Another aspect of this modernization process has been the fossilization and distortion of the role of Shari'a in various Islamic societies, which began with the construction of static formations of identities and traditions by colonial administrators for their administrative convenience. Ironically, that colonial legacy has been perpetuated and reinforced as the logic of the state after independence and has resulted in devastating consequences for the integrity and dynamism of Shari'a. For example, the colonial codification of Hindu and Muslim laws in India, which privileged certain textual aspects of complex and interdependent traditional systems, froze some aspects of the status of women outside the context of constantly evolving social and economic relations (Agnes 1999, 42). The construction of personal law conflated religion and custom, thereby creating the legal fictions that Hindu and Muslim laws derived from scripture and that Hindus and Muslims were "homogenous communities following uniform laws" (Agnes 1999, 43). In Turkey, the history of the republic reveals another mode of fossilizing Shari'a through state control of Islam in order to keep it out of politics and the public sphere altogether. Implemented through a series of laws passed between 1922 and 1935, the model of Kemalist secularism controls and regulates all *public* aspects of Islam in Turkish life, thereby demarcating the private realm as the authentic domain of religious belief and commitment.

To summarize, whenever the state has been used to enforce Shari'a, the outcome has been a highly selective set of principles in total isolation from their legitimate methodological sources. Frozen in this manner, Shari'a has become a reified symbol of communal identity and a zone of contestation of political authority. In addition to being open to political manipulation, this appropriation of Shari'a by the state has made seizing the state itself the primary objective of those who advocate coercive enforcement of Shari'a through state institutions. Whether they succeed or not, that quest makes Shari'a the symbol of despotic and authoritarian rule among the population at large. At the same time, the creative and liberating possibilities of Shari'a are stunted and constrained by the bureaucratic inertia of state institutions.

Restoring the Liberating Role of Shari'a

For Muslims, Shari'a should be known and experienced as a source of liberation and self-realization, not a heavy burden of oppressive restriction and harsh punishments. No action or omission is valid from a Shari'a perspective unless it is completely voluntary, and there is no religious merit in coercive compliance. It is from this perspective that I hold the proposed framework to be necessary for restoring and securing the liberating role of Shari'a. The two legs of the proposed model are the institutional separation of Islam and the state, on the one hand, and regulation of the public and political role of Islam, on the other. As emphasized from the start, this framework does not preclude the application of some principles of Shari'a through state institutions, provided it is supported by civic reasons that the generality of the population can debate and accept or reject without reference to religious belief. Moreover, like all matters of public policy and legislation, the operation through state institutions of what some may believe to be Shari'a principles must be subject to constitutional and human rights safeguards. To be clear on this point, all citizens are free to observe their own religious or philosophical beliefs, provided that that does not violate the rights of others. But if Muslims or other believers wish to use state institutions to enforce any principle or rule that they believe to be decreed by their religion, they must show it to be consistent with constitutional and human rights safeguards and persuade other citizens through civic reasoning.

This combination of institutional separation and regulation of the political role of Islam is necessary to protect Shari'a from manipulation by ruling elites, and thereby enables it to play a stronger and more legitimate role in the public life of Islamic societies. Having originated and operated outside the framework of the state from the start, Shari'a can best be rejuvenated in the same way, in accordance with its genuine and necessary nature as the voluntary obligation of Muslims, which cannot be coerced. Shari'a values can provide a strong basis for a powerful and positive critique of political oppression and effective accountability for economic exploitation and social injustice, and it can support responsible environmental policies. Whatever social good the advocates of an Islamic state seek to achieve can be realized only when the necessary policies and strategies are launched and sustained from within civil society and liberated from the inhibitions and limitations of bureaucratic state institutions.

To advance this vision for the future of Shari'a, it is also necessary to appreciate and try to redress the serious apprehension of many Muslims that the proposed model will necessarily result in the secularization of society itself and diminish the role of Islam in public life. In my view, this apprehension is grossly exaggerated, as believers will always find ways of expressing their convictions through the political process and in social relations. As discussed earlier, if religious belief and piety are declining in any society, they cannot be restored through coercion or inducement through state institutions. To the contrary, state intervention in matters of religious belief and practice is deeply corrupting, by breeding hypocrisy *(nifaq)*, which is repeatedly and categorically condemned in the Qurʾan. It is also destructive of the efficacy and legitimacy of the state by entrenching religious discrimination and introducing vague and subjective factors in public administration.

It may also be helpful here to clarify the purpose of or rationale for insisting on a public role for Islam in present-day Islamic societies. The term "Shariʿa" is often used in public discourse as if it is synonymous with Islam itself, as the totality of the obligations of Muslims both in the private, personal religious sense and in social, political, and legal norms and institutions. In fact, Shariʿa is only the door and passageway into being Muslim and does not exhaust the possibilities of human knowledge and lived experience of Islam. There is therefore much more to Islam than Shariʿa, though knowing and complying with the dictates of Shariʿa are the way to realize Islam as the principle of monotheism *(tawhid)* in the daily lives of Muslims. It should also be emphasized that any conception of Shariʿa is necessarily and always derived from human interpretation of the Qurʾan and Sunna, reflecting what fallible human beings are able to comprehend and seek to comply with given the limitations of their own specific historical context. For me as a Muslim, it is clear that no conception of Shariʿa can ever be the perfect or eternal representation of the divine command, simply because of the limitations of human comprehension and experience. It is equally clear, however, that human comprehension and experience are the only way the Qurʾan and Sunna of the Prophet can be present in our lives and have their transformative impact on our attitudes and behavior.

There may well be good reasons for the anxiety of some Muslims about the secularization of their societies in the sense of declining religious conviction and piety, but that cannot be redressed by state intervention in the religious life of individual persons and their communities. The best response to this must be at the voluntary civil-society level, not through state institutions. Expecting the state to enhance religious belief and piety assumes that the officials and bureaucrats who operate the various institutions at least share the faith we wish to promote, if not that they are able to inspire others to higher levels of piety. Hypocrisy and corruption are the inevitable consequences of making subjective factors like religious faith and piety criteria for appointment and promotion in bureaucratic positions. The same will be true of the work of state bureaucracies that are charged with promoting religiosity or morality among the public at large.

It is ironic that leading scholars of the call for an Islamic state, like Abul A'la al-Maududi and Sayyid Qutb, advocated a Soviet/fascist model of the totalitarian state, which is supposed to transform society in the image of the ruling party (Maududi 1980; Shepherd 1996). The fundamental defect of the idea of the Islamic state is that the logic of the invocation of religious or moral authority can very easily be inverted, so that instead of regulating political power by religious authority, religion itself becomes subordinated to power through the powerful technologies of the modern state apparatus. It is also impossible to distinguish cynical invocations of religion for political power from well-intentioned initiatives. As I have argued, the state by definition is an *amoral* institution and cannot possess or embody its own autonomous morality. Moral judgments and responsibility can be attributed to human beings, not to abstract institutions. To call the state Islamic can only shield the human beings who act through the apparatus of the state from responsibility for their actions.

As comparative reflection on the experiences of Islamic and other societies readily reveals, the public role of religion is being constantly negotiated and renegotiated among different actors. Since this process is deeply contextual, however, the complex role of religion in the political life of any society should be understood on its own epistemological, political, and cultural terms. Using words such as "secularism" and "secularization" may be helpful in distinguishing different approaches to the public role of religion, but such words cannot substitute for deeply contextual analysis of each situation on its own terms. There is simply no universal definition of secularism as separation of religion and the state, or of secularization as the diminishing role of religion in public life. Each society's experience with either or both is specific to that society and its religion(s), and cannot be transplanted or applied to another society. For our purposes here in particular, the separation of Islam and the state is required for the active and legitimate negotiation of the public role of Islam *in each society according to its own context*. Thus the model of the secular state I am calling for is in fact an *enabling* discourse for *promoting* the role of Islam in public life. But as I have also repeatedly emphasized, this process of negotiation is subject to constitutional and human rights safeguards for the role of civic reason in setting public policy and legislation. A minimal secularism of separation of religion and the state is the precondition for a negotiated, richer, and deeper secularism, the substance of which will include religious discourse and which will necessarily be specific to each society in its historical context.

In the final analysis, I submit, the state can serve the ideals of an Islamic society for social justice, peace, goodness, and virtue by enabling and facilitating their realization through civic discourse and the fabric of political life. The proposed religious neutrality of the state is indeed required for the future development of Shariʿa itself. As emphasized earlier, consensus *(ijmaʿ)* is the most foundational source and methodology of Shariʿa. It is through the consensus of successive generations of Muslims that we have come to accept the text of the Qurʾan to be the accurate representation of divine revelation as received by the Prophet more than fourteen hundred years ago. The authenticity of the Sunna as an accurate representation of what the Prophet said or approved is also established through consensus. Whatever is accepted by any group of Muslims as being part of Shariʿa is established by virtue of their consensus, simply because there is no pope or other human person or group with the authority to establish any principle of Shariʿa. These and other vital functions of consensus among Muslims would be completely corrupted and distorted if state officials and bureaucrats were allowed to control or manipulate debate and disputation among Muslims. As noted earlier, since every orthodoxy started as a heresy, we must protect, indeed celebrate, the possibility of heresy in order to ensure the relevance and future development of Shariʿa. For every heresy we suppress, we miss the possibility of an idea or principle that future generations of Muslims may wish to establish as part of their orthodox Islam. I say that no human being should have that power to control what others may wish to believe or disbelieve. That is why I believe that Shariʿa will not have any future for me as a Muslim if some Muslims are allowed to prescribe for me what can or cannot be part of my religious experience in the name of a so-called Islamic state. There are many legitimate functions for the state, like keeping the peace, adjudicating disputes, and providing essential services, but its authority cannot and should not extend to determining what is or is not Shariʿa.

References

Abd al-Raziq, Ali. 1925. *al-Islam wa-usul al-hukm, bahth fi al-Khilafah wa al-hukumah fi al-Islam* (Islam and the Principles of Government). Cairo: Matbaat Misr.

Abou El Fadl, Khaled. 2001. *Rebellion and Violence in Islamic Law.* New York: Cambridge University Press.

Abou El-Haj, Rifat. 1988. "The Ottoman Nashiatname as a Discourse over 'Morality.'" In Abdeljelil Temimi, ed., *Mélanges, Professeur Robert Mantran.* Tunis: Zaghouan.

Afif, Shams Siraj. 1891. *Tarikh-i-Firoz Shahi.* Written by Shams Siraj Afif, completed by Ziauddin Barani (Persian text). Calcutta: Asia Book Society.

Agnes, Flavia. 1999. *Law and Gender Inequality: The Politics of Women's Rights in India.* New Delhi: Oxford University Press.

Ahmad, Aziz. 1970. "India and Pakistan." In P. M. Holt, Ann K. S. Lambton, and Bernard Lewis, eds., *The Cambridge History of Islam,* vol. 2, 97–119. Cambridge, Eng.: Cambridge University Press.

Ahmad, Feroz. 2003. *Turkey: The Quest for Identity.* New York: Oneworld.

Akdağ, Mustafa. 1963. *Celali İsyanlari* (Celali Rebellion). Ankara: Ankara Üniversitesi Dil ve Tarih-Coğrafya Fakültesi Basımevi.

Akiba, Okon. 2004. "Constitutional Government and the Future of Constitutionalism in Africa." In Okon Akiba, ed., *Constitutionalism and Society in Africa,* 3–22. Burlington, Vt.: Ashgate.

Akşit, Bahattin. 1991. "Islamic Education in Turkey: Medrese Reform in Late Ottoman Times and Imam Hatip Schools in the Republic." In Richard Tapper, ed., *Islam in Modern Turkey,* 145–170. London: I. B. Tauris.

Ali, Ausaf. 2000. "Contrast between Western and Islamic Political Theory. In *Modern Muslim Thought,* vol. 1. Karachi: Royal.

Ali, M. Athar. 1978. "Towards a Reinterpretation of the Mughal Empire." *Journal of the Royal Asiatic Society of Great Britain and Ireland:* 38–49.

Al-Jazeera. 2005. "Turkey Approves Headscarf Amnesty." Mar. 16, 2005. http://English.aljazeera.net/English/Archive/Archive?ArchiveID=10376. Accessed Aug. 31, 2007.

Alpkaya, Faruk. 1998. *Türkiye Cumhuriyeti'nin Kuruluşu: 1923–1924* (Foundation of the Turkish Republic 1923–1924). Istanbul: İletişim.

Al-Samarʿi, Nuʿman Abd al-Razid. 1968. *Ahkam al-Murtad fi al-Shariʿa al-Islamyia* (Rules Applicable to Apostates in Islamic Shariʿa). Beirut: al-Dar al-Arabiya.

Anderson, Norman. 1976. *Law Reform in the Muslim World.* London: Athlone.

An-Naʿim, Abdullahi Ahmed. 1986. "The Islamic Law of Apostasy and Its Modern Applicability: A Case from the Sudan." *Religion* 16: 197–223.

———. 1990. *Toward an Islamic Reformation: Civil Liberties, Human Rights, and International Law.* Syracuse, N.Y.: Syracuse University Press.

———. 1996. "Islamic Foundations of Religious Human Rights." In John Witte, Jr., and Johan D. van der Vyver, eds., *Religious Human Rights in Global Perspectives: Religious Perspectives,* 337–359. The Hague: Martinus Nijhoff.

———. 2001. "Human Rights in the Arab World: A Regional Perspective." *Human Rights Quarterly* 23(3): 701–732.

———. 2003. "Introduction: Expanding Legal Protection of Human Rights in African Context." In Abdullahi Ahmed An-Naʿim, ed., *Human Rights under African Constitutions: Realizing the Promise for Ourselves,* 1–28. Philadelphia: University of Pennsylvania Press.

———. 2005. "The Interdependence of Religion, Secularism, and Human Rights: Prospects for Islamic Societies." *Common Knowledge* 11(1): 56–80.

———. 2006. *African Constitutionalism and the Role of Islam.* Philadelphia: University of Pennsylvania Press.

An-Naʿim, Abdullahi Ahmed, and Francis Deng. 1997. "Self-determination and Unity: The Case of Sudan." *Law and Society* 18: 199–223.

Ansari, Khizar Humayun. 1990. *The Emergence of Socialist Thought among North Indian Muslims, 1917–1947.* Lahore: Book Traders.

Aqsha, Darul, Dick van der Meij, and Hendrik Meuleman. 1995. *Islam in Indonesia: A Survey of Events and Developments from 1988 to March 1993.* Jakarta: INIS.

Arjomand, Said Amir. 1984. *The Shadow of God and the Hidden Imam.* Chicago: University of Chicago Press.

Asad, Muhammad. 1961. *Principles of State and Government in Islam.* Berkeley: University of California Press.

Associated Press. 2007. "Turkey's Prime Minister Warns against Interfering in Democracy." *International Herald Tribune,* Aug. 14. http://www.iht.com/articles/ap/2007/08/15/europe/EU-POL-Turkey-Presidency.php. Accessed Aug. 19, 2007.

Atkinson, Janet. 1998. "Wana: Engaging the Unseen." In James J. Fox, ed., *Indonesian Heritage: Religion and Ritual,* 88–89. Singapore: Archipelago.

Aydın, M. Akif. 2001. "The Ottoman Legal System." In Ekmeleddin İhsanoğlu, ed., *History of Ottoman State, Society, and Civilisation,* vol. 2, 431–489. Istanbul: IRCICA.

Ayoub, Mahmoud. 2004. "Dhimmah in Qur'an and Hadith." In Robert Hoyland, ed., *Muslims and Others in Early Muslim Society,* 25–35. Trowbridge, Eng.: Ashgate.

Aziz Efendi. 1985. *Kanunname-i Sultani li-Aziz Efendi* (Aziz Efendi's Book of Sultanic

Laws and Regulations). Trans. Rhoads Murphey, ed. Şinasi Tekin. Cambridge, Mass.: Harvard University Press.

Azra, Azyumardi. 2002. *Jaringan Global dan Lokal Islam Nusantara* (Global Network and Local Islam in Nusantara). Bandung: Mizan.

———. 2004. *Jaringan Ulama Timur Tengah dan Kepulauan Nusantara Abad XVII & VIII, Akar Pembaruan Islam Indonesia, Edisi Revisi* (The Origins of Islamic Reformism in Southeast Asia, Networks of Malay-Indonesian and Middle Eastern [Ulama] in the Seventeenth and Eighteenth Centuries, rev. ed.). Jakarta: Kencana.

Baehr, Peter, Cees Flintermand, and Mignon Senders. 1999. Introduction. In *Innovation and Inspiration: Fifty Years of the Universal Declaration of Human Rights*, 1–6. Amsterdam: Royal Netherlands Academy of Arts and Sciences.

Bauer, Joanne, and Daniel Bell, eds. 1999. *Human Rights in East Asia*. New York: Cambridge University Press.

Bayly, C. A. 1985. "The Pre-History of Communalism? Religious Conflict in India, 1700–1860." *Modern Asian Studies* 19: 177–203.

Bayramoğlu, Ali. 2004. "Asker ve Siyaset" (Army and Politics). In Ahmet İnsel, Ali Bayramoğlu, and Ömer Laçiner, eds., *Bir Zümre, Bir Parti: Türkiye'de Ordu* (A Class, A Party: Army in Turkey). Istanbul: Birikim Yayinlari.

Berkes, Niyazi. 1964. *The Development of Secularism in Turkey*. Montreal: McGill University Press.

Berkey, Jonathan. 2004. "The Muhtasibs of Cairo under the Mamluks: Toward an Understanding of an Islamic Institution." In Michael Winter and Amalia Levanoni, eds., *The Mamluks in Egyptian and Syrian Politics and Society*, 245–276. Leiden: Brill.

Bhargava, Rajeev, ed. 1999. *Secularism and Its Critics*. New Delhi: Oxford University Press.

Bilgrami, Akeel. 1998. "Secularism, Nationalism, and Modernity." In Rajeev Bhargava, ed., *Secularism and Its Critics*, 380–417. New Delhi: Oxford University Press.

Boroujerdi, Mehrzad. 1996. *Iranian Intellectuals and the West: The Tormented Triumph of Nativism*. Syracuse, N.Y.: Syracuse University Press.

Bose, Sugata, and Ayesha Jalal. 1998. *Modern South Asia: History, Culture, Political Economy*. New York: Routledge.

Brass, Paul R. 1990. "The Politics of India since Independence." In *The New Cambridge History of India*, vol. 1. Cambridge, Eng.: Cambridge University Press.

———. 2003. *The Production of Hindu-Muslim Violence in Contemporary India*. New Delhi: Oxford University Press.

Brems, Eva. 2001. *Human Rights: Universality and Diversity*. The Hague: Kluwer Law International.

Budiwanti, Erni. 2000. *Islam Sasak: Wetu Telu versus Waktu Lima*. Yogyakarta: LKiS.

Bunsha, Dionne. 2002. "The Facts from Godhra." *Frontline*, Aug. 2. http://www.frontlineonnet.com/fl1915/19150110.htm. Accessed July 2005.

Buultjens, Ralph. 1986. "India: Religion, Political Legitimacy, and the Secular State." *Annals of the American Academy of Political and Social Science* 483: 93–109.

Çakır, Ruşen, İrfan Bozan, and Balkan Talu. 2004. *İmam-Hatip Liseleri:Efsaneler ve Gerçekler* (Imam-Preacher High Schools: Legends and Facts). Istanbul: TESEV. Available at http://www.tesev.org.tr/etkinlik/1-4.pdf.

Çarkoğlu, Ali, and Binnaz Toprak. 2000. *Religion, Society, and Politics in Turkey.* Istanbul: TESEV. Available at http://www.tesev.org.tr/eng/project/TESEV_search.pdf.

Case No. 1989/1, Judgment No. 1989/12, Constitutional Court of Turkey. Available at http://www.anayasa.gov.tr/eskisite/KARARLAR/IPTALITIRAZ/K1989/K1989-12.htm.

Cassese, Antonio. 1995. *Self-determination of Peoples: A Legal Reappraisal.* Cambridge, Eng.: Cambridge University Press.

Chandra, Satish. 1997. *Medieval India: From Sultanat to the Mughals. Part One: Delhi Sultanat* (1206–1526). New Delhi: Har-Anand.

Chatterjee, Partha. 1999. "Secularism and Toleration." In Rajeev Bhargava, ed., *Secularism and Its Critics,* 345–379. Delhi: Oxford University Press.

Çiçek, Kemal. 2001. "Cemaat Mahkemesinden Kadı Mahkemesine Zımmilerin Yargı Tercihi" (The Judicial Preference of *Dhimmis* between the Community Courts and Qadi Courts). In Kemal Çiçek, ed., *Pax Ottomana: Studies in Memoriam of Prof. Nejat Göyünç,* 31–50. Haarlem: SOTA/Ankara: Yeni Türkiye.

Cizre, Ümit. 1999. "Türk Ordusunun Siyasi Özerkliği" (The Anatomy of the Turkish Army's Political Autonomy). In *Muktedirlerin Siyaseti: Merkez Sağ-Ordu-İslamcilik* (The Politics of the Empowered: Central Right-Army-Islamism), 57–79. Istanbul: İletişim.

Coulson, Noel J. 1957. "The State and the Individual in Islamic Law." *International and Comparative Law Quarterly* 6: 49–60.

―――. 1964. *A History of Islamic Law.* Edinburgh: University of Edinburgh Press.

Crone, Patricia, and Martin Hinds. 1986. *God's Caliph: Religious Authority in the First Centuries of Islam.* London: Cambridge University Press.

Daftary, Farhad. 1990. *The Ismai'ilis: Their History and Doctrines.* New York: Cambridge University Press.

Daud, S. M., and H. Suresh. 1993. *The People's Verdict.* Bombay: Indian Human Rights Commission.

Deng, Francis M. 1995. *War of Visions.* Washington, D.C.: Brookings Institution.

Departemen Agama Republik Indonesia (Ministry of Religious Affairs of the Republic of Indonesia). 1998. *Himpunan Peraturan Perundang-undangan Kehidupan Beragama seri E* (Compilation of Laws about Religious Life, vol. E). Jakarta: Sekretariat Jenderal Departemen Agama.

―――. 2005. *Number of Population by Religion Year 2005.* Available at http://www.depag.go.id/dt_penduduk.php. Accessed Apr. 17, 2005.

Dhavan, Rajeev. 1987. "Religious Freedom in India." *American Journal of Comparative Law* 35: 209–254.

―――. 1999. "The Road to Xanadu: India's Quest for Secularism." In K. N. Panikkar, *The Concerned Indian's Guide to Communalism,* 34–75. New Delhi: Viking.

Direktorat Pemberdayaan Komunitas Adat Terpencil, Direktorat Jenderal Pemberdayaan Sosial Departemen Sosial Republik Indonesia (Directorate for the Empowerment of the Isolated Adat Communities, General Directorate for Social Empowerment, Department of Social Affairs of the Republic of Indonesia). *Pemetaan Sosial komunitas Adat Terpencil Nasional* (Social Mapping of the Isolated Adat Communities Nationwide). http://www.katcenter.info/pemetaan/ petannasional php?level+1. Accessed Apr. 19, 2005.

Doi, A. Rahman I. 1981. *Non-Muslims under the Shari'ah (Islamic Law)*. Lahore: Kazi.

Donner, Fred. 1981. *The Early Islamic Conquests*. Princeton, N.J.: Princeton University Press.

Drinan, Robert F. 2001. *The Mobilization of Shame: A World View of Human Rights*. New Haven, Conn.: Yale University Press.

Dursun, Davut. 1989. *Osmanlı Devletinde Siyaset ve Din* (Religion and Politics in the Ottoman State). Istanbul: İşaret Yayınları.

Eaton, Richard M. 2000. "Temple Desecration and Indo-Muslim States." In David Gilmartin and Bruce B. Lawrence, eds., *Beyond Turk and Hindu: Rethinking Religious Identities in Islamicate South Asia*, 246–281. Gainesville: University Press of Florida.

Effendy, Bahtiar. 1995. "Islam and the State in Indonesia: Munawir Sjadzali and the Development of a New Theological Underpinning of Political Islam." *Studia Islamika* 2: 101–121.

Ephrat, Daphna. 2002. "Religious Leadership and Associations in the Public Sphere of Seljuk Baghdad." In M. Hoexter, S. Eisenstadt, and N. Levitzion, eds., *The Public Sphere in Muslim Societies*, 31–48. Albany: State University of New York Press.

Eryılmaz, Bilal. 1990. *Osmanlı Devletinde Gayri Müslim Tebaanın Yönetimi* (The Governance of the Non-Muslim Subjects in the Ottoman State). Istanbul: Risale Yay.

Faroqhi, Suraiya. 1995. "Politics and Socio-economic Change in the Ottoman Empire of the Later Sixteenth Century." In Metin Kunt and Christine Woodhead, eds., *Suleyman the Magnificent and His Age: The Ottoman Empire in the Early Modern World*, 91–113. London: Longman.

Faroqhi, Suraiya, Bruce McGowan, Donald Quataert, and Sevket Pamuk. 1994. *An Economic and Social History of the Ottoman Empire*, vol. 2. Cambridge, Eng.: Cambridge University Press.

Faruki, Kemal. 1971. *The Evolution of Islamic Constitutional Theory and Practice from 610 to 1926*. Karachi: National Publication House.

Fernandes, Leonor. 1987. "Mamluk Politics and Education: The Evidence from Two Fourteenth-Century Waqfiyya." *Annals Islamiques* 23: 104–105.

Findley, Carter Vaughn. 1980. *Bureaucratic Reform in the Ottoman Empire: The Sublime Porte, 1789–1922*. Princeton, N.J.: Princeton University Press.

Fleischer, Cornell. 1986. *Bureaucrat and Intellectual in the Ottoman Empire: The Historian Mustafa Ali (1541–1600)*. Princeton, N.J.: Princeton University Press.

Fox, James J. 1995. "Southeast Asian Religions: Insular Cultures." In Mircea Eliade, ed., *Encyclopedia of Religion*, vol. 13, 523–526. New York: Macmillan.

Franklin, D., and M. Baun, eds. 1995. *Political Culture and Constitutionalism: A Comparative Approach*. New York: M. E. Sharpe.

Frenkel, Yehoshua. 1999. "Political and Social Aspects of Islamic Religious Endowments: Saladin in Cairo (1169–73) and Jerusalem (1187–93)." *Bulletin of the School of Oriental and African Studies, University of London* 62: 1–20.

Garna, Yudistra. 1998. "Badui: The Centre of the World." In James J. Fox, ed., *Indonesian Heritage: Religion and Ritual*, 76–77. Singapore: Archipelago.

GATRA Weekly. 2003. Laporan Khusus: "Pesan Suci Tuntunan Leluhur" (Special Report: "The Sacred Messages of the Ancestors"). Nov. 21–Dec. 6, 52–55.

Gerber, Haim. 1999. *Islamic Law and Culture 1600–1840*. Leiden: Brill.

Ghazali, Abu Hamid Muhammad. 1968. *Al-tibr al-Masbuk fi Nasa'ih al-Muluk* (The Minted Gold Filings in Admonishing Kings). Cairo: Maktbat al-Kulyat al-Azharia.

Gibb, H.A.R., and J. H. Kramers, eds. 1991. *Shorter Encyclopaedia of Islam*, 3d ed. Leiden: Brill.

Gill, Graeme. 2003. *The Nature and Development of the Modern State*. New York: Palgrave Macmillan.

Gökalp, Ziya. 1922a. "The Real Meaning of the Caliphate." *Küçük Mecmua* (Minor Magazine) 24 (Nov. 27): 1–6.

———. 1922b. "Functions of the Caliphate." *Küçük Mecmua* (Minor Magazine) 26 (Dec. 11): 1–5.

———. 1959. *Turkish Nationalism and Western Civilization: Selected Essays*. Trans. and ed. Niyazi Berkes. New York: Columbia University Press.

Golwalkar, M. S. 1945. *We or Our Nationhood Defined*, 3d ed. Nagpur: Bharat.

Griswold, William J. 1983. *Political Unrest and Rebellion in Anatolia 1000–1020/1591–1611*. Berlin: Klaus Schwarz-Verlag.

Guha, Ramachandra. 2005. "Arguments with Sen" [book review]. *Economic and Political Weekly* 40, no. 41 (Oct. 8): 4420–4425.

Gülsoy, Ufuk. 1999. *Osmanlı Gayrimüslimlerinin Askerlik Serüveni* (The Military Role of Ottoman Non-Muslims). Istanbul: Simurg Yay.

Habermas, Jurgen. 1995. "Reconciliation through the Public Use of Reason: Remarks on John Rawls' Political Liberalism." *Journal of Philosophy* 92 (Mar.): 109–131.

Habib, Irfan. 2003. Introduction. In P. J. Marshall, ed., *The Eighteenth Century in Indian History. Evolution or Revolution?* New Delhi: Oxford University Press.

Haji, Amin. 1988. "Institutions of Justice in Fatimid Egypt (358–567/969–1171)." In Aziz Al-Azmeh, ed., *Islamic Law: Social and Historical Contexts*, 198–214. New York: Routledge.

Hallaq, Wael B. 1984. "Was the Gate of Ijtihad Closed?" *International Journal of Middle East Studies* 16: 3–41.

———. 2004. "Can the Shari'a Be Restored?" In Yvonne Haddad and Barbara Freyer Stowasser, eds., *Islamic Law and the Challenges of Modernity*, 21–54. Walnut Creek, Calif.: AltaMira.

Hamidullah, Muhammad. 1968. *Muslim Conduct of State,* rev. 5th ed. Lahore: Sh. M. Ashraf.

Hasan, Mushirul. 2002. *Islam in the Subcontinent: Muslims in a Plural Society.* New Delhi: Manohar.

Heater, Derek. 2004. *A Brief History of Citizenship.* Edinburgh: Edinburgh University Press.

Hefner, Robert W. 1989. *Hindu Javanese: Tengger Tradition and Islam.* Princeton, N.J.: Princeton University Press.

————. 1995. "Modernity and the Challenge of Pluralism: Some Indonesian Lessons." *Studia Islamika* 2: 21–45.

————. 1998. "Tengger, the Hindu Javanese." In James J. Fox, ed., *Indonesian Heritage: Religion and Ritual,* 78–79. Singapore: Archipelago.

————. 2002. "Varieties of Muslim Politics: Civil vs. Statist Islam." In Fu'ad Jabali and Jamhari Makruf, eds., *Islam in Indonesia: Islamic Studies and Social Transformation,* 36–151. Montreal: Indonesian-Canada Higher Education Project.

Henkin, Louis. 1994. "A New Birth of Constitutionalism: Genetic Influences and Genetic Defects." In Michel Rosenfeld, ed., *Constitutionalism, Identity, Differences, and Legitimacy,* 39–53. Durham, N.C.: Duke University Press.

Heyd, Uriel. 1950. *Foundations of Turkish Nationalism: The Life and Teachings of Ziya Gökalp.* London: Luzac.

Hodgson, Marshall G. S. 1974. *The Venture of Islam: Conscience and History in a World Civilization,* vols. 1 and 2. Chicago: University of Chicago Press.

Hoexter, Miriam. 2002. "The Waqf and the Public Sphere." In M. Hoexter, S. Eisenstadt, and N. Levitzion, eds., *The Public Sphere in Muslim Societies,* 119–138. Albany: State University of New York Press.

Hooker, M. B., and Tim Lindsey. 2003. "Public Faces of *Shari'ah* in Contemporary Indonesia: Towards a National *Madhhab.*" *Studia Islamika* 10: 23–64.

Hooker, Virginia. 2004. "Developing Islamic Arguments for Change through 'Liberal Islam.'" In Virginia Hooker and Amin Saikal, eds., *Islamic Perspectives on the New Millennium,* 231–251. Singapore: ISEAS.

Hoskins, Janet. 1998. "Sumba: The Presence of the Marapu." In James J. Fox, ed., *Indonesian Heritage: Religion and Ritual,* 90–91. Singapore: Archipelago.

Hourani, Albert. 1991. *A History of the Arab Peoples.* Cambridge, Mass.: Belknap/Harvard University Press.

Howe, Marvine. 2000. *Turkey: A Nation Divided over Islam's Revival.* Boulder, Colo.: Westview.

Hürriyet. 2003. "Baro'dan Türbanlı Avukat Soruşturması" (The Bar Prosecutes Lawyers with Headcovers), July 22. http://webarsiv.hurriyet.com.tr/2003/07/22/320160.asp. Accessed Aug. 31, 2007.

Ibn Qaym al-Jawzeyyah. 1985. *Al-Turuq al-Hukmiah fi al-Siyyassah al-Shar'iyyah* (Methods of Government in Islamic Politics). Cairo: Dar al-Madani.

Ibn Rushd (Averroës). n.d. *Bidayat al-Mugjtahid* (Primer on the Law and Wisdom), vol. 2. Cairo: Dar al-Fikr al-Arabic.

————. 2001. *Fasl al-Maqa bayn al-Shar'a wa al-Hikmah min Itsal.* Trans. by Charles E. Butterworth as *The Book of the Decisive Treatise Determining the Connection between the Law and Wisdom.* Provo, Utah: Brigham Young University Press.

Ibn Taymiyyah. 1983. *Al-ssiyassah al-shar'iyyah fi islah al-Ra'i wa al-Ra'iyyah* (Islamic Politics in Conducting the Affairs of the Ruler and the Ruled). Beirut: Dar al-Afaq al-Jadeedah.

Ilesanmi, Simeon O. 2001. "Constitutional Treatment of Religion and the Politics of Human Rights in Nigeria." *African Affairs* 100: 529–554.

Imber, Colin. 1997. *Ebu's-Su'ud: The Islamic Legal Tradition.* Stanford, Calif.: Stanford University Press.

————. 2002. *The Ottoman Empire 1300–1650: The Structure of Power.* New York: Palgrave Macmillan.

İnalcık, Halil. 2000. *Osmanlı'da Devlet, Hukuk, Adâlet* (State, Law, and Justice in the Ottoman Empire). Istanbul: Eren.

İnsel, Ahmet. 1997. "MGK Hükümetleri ve Kesintisiz Darbe Rejimi" (MGK Governments and a Regime of Continuous Coups). *Birikim Monthly* 96 (Apr.): 15–18.

————. 2002. "Kamu Alanına Hükmetme Savaşı (Hegemony War on the Public Sphere). *Radikal 2 Weekly,* Dec. 1.

————. 2004. Interview with Ahmet İnsel, conducted by radio presenters Omer Madra and Evrim Altug, for *Açik Gazete* (Open Paper), Açık Site-Açık Radio, July 14. Transcript available at http://www.acikradyo.com.tr/default.aspx?_mv=prn&aid=7238.

İpşirli, Mehmet. 2001. "Ottoman State Organization." In Ekmeleddin İhsanoğlu, ed., *History of Ottoman State, Society, and Civilization,* vol. 1, 133–284. Istanbul: IRCICA.

Irwin, Robert. 1986. *The Middle East in the Middle Ages: The Early Mamluk Sultanate 1250–1382.* London: Croom Helm.

Jackson, Sherman. 1995. "The Primacy of Domestic Politics: Ibn Bint al-Aazz and the Establishment of Four Chief Judgeships in Mamluk Egypt." *Journal of the American Oriental Society* 115, no. 1 (Jan.–Mar.): 52–65.

Jacoby, Tim. 2004. *Social Power and the Turkish State.* London: Frank Cass.

Jafri, Syed H. M. 2000. *The Origins and Early Development of Shi'a Islam.* Oxford, Eng.: Oxford University Press.

Jay, Sian. 1998. "Asmat: Cycles of Revenge." In James J. Fox, ed., *Indonesian Heritage: Religion and Ritual,* 96–98. Singapore: Archipelago.

Jok, Jok Madut. 2001. *War and Slavery in Sudan.* Philadelphia: University of Pennsylvania Press.

Kafi, Hasan. 1989. *Usulü'l-Hikem fi Nizami'l-Alem* (The Roots of the Secrets about the Regulations of God in the Universe)(prepared for publication by M. İpşirli). *İstanbul Üniversitesi Edebiyat Fakültesi Tarih Ensitüsü Dergisi (TED)* (Istanbul University Faculty of Letters, the Review of the Institute of History). Istanbul.

Katib Çelebi. 1957. *The Balance of Truth.* Trans. C. L. Lewis. London: Allen and Unwin.

Kenanoğlu, M. Macit. 2004. *Osmanlı Millet Sistemi: Mit ve Gerçek* (Ottoman Millet System: The Myth and the Reality). Istanbul: Klasik.

Khadduri, Majid. 1955. *War and Peace in the Law of Islam.* Baltimore: Johns Hopkins University Press.

Khadduri, Majid. 1966. *The Islamic Law of Nations: Shaybani's Siyar.* Baltimore: Johns Hopkins University Press.

Khan, Iqtidar Alam. 1997. "Akbar's Personality Traits and World Outlook—A Critical Appraisal." In Irfan Habib, ed., *Akbar and His India,* 79–96. Delhi: Oxford University Press.

Khan, Maimul Ahsan. 2003. *Human Rights in the Muslim World.* Durham, N.C.: Carolina Academic Press.

Khan, M. Ifzal-ur-Rahman. 1995. "The Attitude of the Delhi Sultans Towards Non-Muslims: Some Observations." *Islamic Culture* 69, no. 2: 41–56.

Khilnani, Sunil. 1999. *The Idea of India.* New Delhi: Penguin.

Kister, M. J. 1986. "The Massacre of the Banū Qurayza: A Reexamination of a Tradition." *Jerusalem Studies in Arabic and Islam* 8: 61–96.

Kösebalaban, Hasan. 2005. "The Impact of Globalization on Islamic Political Identity: The Case of Turkey." *World Affairs* (June 22): 27–37.

Krikorian, Mesrob K. 1978. *Armenians in the Service of the Ottoman Empire 1860–1908.* London: Routledge and Kegan Paul.

Küçük, Cevdet. 1986. "Ottoman Millet System and Tanzimat." In *Tanzimat'tan Cumhuriyet'e Türkiye Ansiklopedisi* (The Encyclopedia of Turkey from Tanzimat to the Republic), vol. 4, 1007–1024. Istanbul: İletişim.

Küçükcan, Talip. 2003. "State, Islam, and Religious Liberty in Modern Turkey: Reconfiguration of Religion in the Public Sphere." *Brigham Young University Law Review*: 475–507.

Lambton, Ann K. S. 1985. *State and Government in Medieval Islam.* Oxford, Eng.: Oxford University Press.

Lapidus, Ira M. 1967. *Muslim Cities in the Later Middle Ages.* Cambridge, Mass.: Harvard University Press.

———. 1975. "The Separation of State and Religion in the Development of Early Islamic Society." *International Journal of Middle East Studies* 6: 363–385.

———. 1996. "State and Religion in Islamic Societies." *Past and Present* 151 (May): 3–27.

———. 2002. *A History of Islamic Societies,* 2d ed. Cambridge, Eng.: Cambridge University Press.

Lev, Yaacov. 1988. "The Fatimid Imposition of Ismaʿilism on Egypt (358–386/969–996)." *Zeitschrift der Deutschen Morgenandischen Gesellschaft* 138: 313–325.

———. 1991. *State and Society in Fatimid Egypt.* Leiden: Brill.

Lewis, Geoffrey. 2002. *The Turkish Language Reform: A Catastrophic Success.* Oxford, Eng.: Oxford University Press.

Little, Donald P. 1986a. "The Historical and Historiographical Signficance of the Detention of Ibn Taymiyya." In *History and Historiography of the Mamluks.* London: Variorum Reprints.

———. 1986b. "Religion under the Mamluks." In *History and Historiography of the Mamluks.* London: Variorum Reprints.

Lukito, Ratno. 1998. *Pergumulan antara Hukum Islam dan Adat di Indonesia* (The Struggle between Islamic and Customary Law in Indonesia). Jakarta: INIS.

———. 2003. "Law and Politics in Post-Independence Indonesia: A Case Study of Religious and Adat Courts." In Arskal Salim and Azyumardi Azra, eds., *Shari'a and Politics in Modern Indonesia,* 17–32. Singapore: ISEAS.

Madan, T. N. 1997. *Modern Myths, Locked Minds: Secularism and Fundamentalism in India.* New Delhi: Oxford University Press.

———. 2004. "Religions of India: Plurality and Pluralism." In Jamal Malik and Helmut Reifeld, eds., *Religious Pluralism in South Asia and Europe.* New Delhi: Oxford University Press.

Madelung, Wilfred. 1997. *The Succession to Muhammad.* Cambridge, Eng.: Cambridge University Press.

Madjid, Nurcholish. 1994. "Islamic Roots of Modern Pluralism, Indonesian Experience." *Studia Islamika* 1: 55–79.

———. 1998. "The Necessity of Renewing Islamic Thought." In Charles Kurzman, ed., *Liberal Islam: A Source Book,* 284–294. Oxford, Eng.: Oxford University Press.

———. 2000. "Islam in Indonesia: A Move from the Periphery to the Center." *Kultur* 1: 1–16.

Mahçupyan, Etyen. 2005. "Laiklik ve Hazımsızlık" (Laicism and Intolerance/Lack of Internalization). *Zaman,* June 20. http://www.zaman.com.tr/webapp-tr/yazar.do?yazino=184643. Accessed Aug. 31, 2007.

Makdisi, George. 1981. *The Rise of Colleges: Institutions of Learning in Islam and the West.* Edinburgh: Edinburgh University Press.

Mansingh, Surjit. 1991. "State and Religion in South Asia: Some Reflections." *South Asia Journal* 4, no. 3: 293–311.

Mardin, Şerif. 1962. *The Genesis of Young Ottoman Thought: A Study in the Modernization of Turkish Political Ideas.* Princeton, N.J.: Princeton University Press.

———. 1989. *Religion and Social Change in Modern Turkey: The Case of Bediüzaman Said Nursi.* Albany: State University of New York Press.

———. 2001. *Türkiye'de Din ve Siyaset Makaleler 3* (Religion and Politics in Turkey, Articles vol. 3), 8th ed. Istanbul: İletişim.

Maududi, Abul A'la. 1979. *Purdah and the Status of Woman in Islam.* Trans. and ed. Al-Ash'ari. Lahore: Islamic Publications.

———. 1980. *Human Rights in Islam,* 2d ed. Leicester, Eng.: Islamic Foundation.

Mazlumder. 2004. "Din Özgürlüğü ve 'Bize Özgü' Laiklik" (Religious Freedom and "Our Kind of" Secularism), Aug. 1. http://www.mazlumder.org/ana.php?konu=makale&id=209&lang=tr. Accessed Aug. 31, 2007.

McCarthy, Thomas. 1994. "Kantian Constructivism and Reconstructivism: Rawls and Habermas in Dialogue." *Ethics* 105 (Oct.): 44–63.

McHugh, J. T. 2002. *Comparative Constitutional Traditions.* New York: Peter Lang.

Mendelsohn, Oliver, and Marika Vicziany. 1998. *The Untouchables: Subordination, Poverty, and the State in Modern India.* Cambridge, Eng.: Cambridge University Press.

Mernissi, Fatima. 1991. *Women in Islam: An Historical and Theological Enquiry.* Trans. Mary Jo Lackland. Oxford, Eng.: Basil Blackwell.

Metcalf, Barbara D. 1985. "Nationalist Muslims in British India: The Case of Hakim Ajmal Khan." *Modern Asian Studies* 19: 1–28.

Metcalf, Barbara D., and Thomas R. Metcalf. 2002. *A Concise History of India.* Cambridge, Eng.: Cambridge University Press.

Mitra, Subrata Kumar. 1991. "Desecularising the State: Religion and Politics in India after Independence." *Comparative Studies in Society and History* 33: 755–777.

Morony, Michael G. 2004. "Religious Communities in Late Sassanian and Early Muslim Iraq." In Robert Hoyland, ed., *Muslims and Others in Early Islamic Societies*, 1–23. Trowbridge, Eng.: Ashgate.

Mudzhar, Mohammad Atho. 2003. *Islam and Islamic Law in Indonesia: A Socio-Historical Approach.* Jakarta: Office of Religious Research and Development and Training, Ministry of Religious Affairs.

Müezzinzade Manisalı Ayn Ali Efendi. 1962. *Osmanlı Devleti Arazi Kanunları: Kanunname-i Al-i Osman* (Ottoman State Land Law: Code of Ottoman State). Ed. Hadiye Tuncer. Ankara: Tarım Bakanlığı.

Mujeeb, M. 1967. *The Indian Muslims.* Montreal: McGill University Press.

Mulder, Niels. 2001. *Mistisme Jawa* (Javanese Mysticism). Yogyakarta: LKiS.

Nadi, Yunus. 1955. *Birinci Büyük Millet Meclisi* (First Grand National Assembly). Istanbul: Sel Yayinlari.

Nandy, Ashis. 1983. *The Intimate Enemy: Loss and Recovery of Self under Colonialism.* Delhi: Oxford University Press.

———. 2006. *Talking India: Ashis Nandy in Conversation with Ramin Jahanbegloo.* New Delhi: Oxford University Press.

———. 2007. "Closing the Debate on Secularism: A Personal Statement." In Anuradha Dingwaney Needham and Rajeswari Sunder Rajan, eds., *The Crisis of Secularism in India*, 107–117. Durham, N.C.: Duke University Press.

Natsir, Muhammad. 1973a. "Persatuan Agama dengan Negara" (The Unity of Religion and State). In *Capita Selecta*, 429–435. Jakarta: Bulan Bintang.

———. 1973b. "Mungkinkah Quran Mengatur Negara" (Is It Possible for the Qur'an to Rule the State?). In *Capita Selecta*, 447–450. Jakarta: Bulan Bintang.

Navaro-Yasin, Yael. 2002. "The Identity Market: Merchandise, Islamism, Laïcité." In Deniz Kandiyoti and Ayse Saktanber, eds., *Kültür Fragmanları: Türkiye'de Gündelik Hayat* (Culture Fragments: Daily Life in Turkey). Istanbul: Metis.

Needham, Anuradha Dingwaney, and Rajeswari Sunder Rajan. 2007. Introduction. In A. D. Needham and R. S. Rajan, eds., *The Crisis of Secularism in India*, 1–42. Durham, N.C.: Duke University Press.

Nehru, Jawaharlal. 1936. *An Autobiography: With Musings on Recent Events in India.* London: John Lane.

Newby, Gordon D. 2002. *A Concise Encyclopaedia of Islam.* Oxford, Eng.: Oneworld.

Nielson, Jørgen. 1985. *Secular Justice in an Islamic State: Mazalim under the Bahri Mamluks 662/1264–789/1387.* Leiden: Nederlands Historisch-Archaeologisch Istituut te Istanbul.

Nizami, Khaliq Ahmad. 1958. *Salatin-i-Delhi Ke Mazhabi Rujnahat* (Religious Orientation of the Rulers of the Delhi Sultanate). Delhi: Nadwatul-Musannifin.

Official Gazette, Jan. 8, 1987 (19335) (removed by amendment, Dec. 18, 1989 [20386]).

Öktem, Niyazi. 2002. "Religion in Turkey." *Brigham Young Law Review:* 371–403.

Ortaylı, İlber. 1986. "Osmanlı İmparatorlugu'nda Millet" (Millet in the Ottoman Empire). In *Tanzimat'tan Cumhuriyet'e Türkiye Ansiklopedisi* (The Encyclopedia of Turkey from Tanzimat to the Republic), vol. 4, 996–1000. Istanbul: İletişim.

Panikkar, K. N. 1999. "Introduction: Defining the Nation as Hindu." In K. N. Panikkar, ed., *The Concerned Indian's Guide to Communalism.* New Delhi: Viking.

Parvin, Manoucher, and Maurie Sommer. 1980. "Dar al-Islam: The Evolution of Muslim Territoriality and Its Implications for Conflict Resolution in the Middle East. *International Journal of Middle East Studies* 11, no. 1 (February): 1–21.

Pennock, J. Roland, and John W. Chapman, eds. 1979. *Constitutionalism.* New York: New York University Press.

Petry, Carl. 1981. *The Civilian Elite of Cairo in the Later Middle Ages.* Princeton, N.J.: Princeton University Press.

Piscatori, James. 1986. *Islam in a World of Nation-States.* Cambridge, Eng.: Cambridge University Press.

Poggi, Gianfranco. 1990. *The State: Its Nature, Development, and Prospects.* Stanford, Calif.: Stanford University Press.

Prasad, Kamala, et al. 1994. *Report of the Inquiry Commission.* New Delhi: Citizens' Tribunal on Ayodhya.

Punwani, Jyoti. 2002. "The Carnage at Godhra." In Siddharth Varadarajan, ed., *Gujarat, the Making of a Tragedy.* New Delhi: Penguin.

Qureshi, I. H. 1970. "Muslim India Before the Mughals." In P. M. Holt, Ann K. S. Lambton, and Bernard Lewis, eds., *The Cambridge History of Islam,* vol. 2, 3–34. Cambridge, Eng.: Cambridge University Press.

Qureshi, M. Hashim. 1998. Introduction. In M. Hashim Qureshi, ed., *Muslims in India since Independence: A Regional Perspective.* New Delhi: Institute of Objective Studies.

Rahman, Shaikh Abdur. 1972. *Punishment of Apostasy in Islam.* Lahore: Institute of Islamic Culture.

Rasjidi, H. M. 1972. *Koreksi terhadap Drs.Nurcholish Madjid tentang Sekularisasi* (A Correction to Drs. Nurcholish Madjid on Secularism). Jakarta: Bulan Bintang.

Rawls, John. 2003. *Political Liberalism,* expanded ed. New York: Columbia University Press.

Ray, Rajat Kanta. 2003. *The Felt Community: Commonalty and Mentality before the Emergence of Indian Nationalism.* New Delhi: Oxford University Press.

Rizvi, S.A.A. 1970. "The Breakdown of Traditional Society." In P. M. Holt, Ann K. S. Lambton, and Bernard Lewis, eds., *The Cambridge History of Islam,* vol. 2, 67–96. Cambridge, Eng.: Cambridge University Press.

Rosenbaum, Alan S. 1988. Introduction. In *Constitutionalism: The Philosophical Dimension,* 1–6. Westport, Conn.: Greenwood.

Ruby, Robert. 2007. "Can Secular Democracy Survive in Turkey?" Pew Forum on Religion & Public Life, Pew Research Center, May 4. http://pewresearch.org/pubs/470/can-secular-democracy-survive-in-turkey. Accessed Aug. 19, 2007.

Sabra, Adam. 2000. *Poverty and Charity in Medieval Islam: Mamluk Egypt, 1250–1517.* Cambridge, Eng.: Cambridge University Press.

Saeed, Abdullah, and Hassan Saeed. 2004. *Freedom of Religion, Apostasy, and Islam.* Burlington, Vt.: Ashgate.

Safran, William. 1990. "The Influence of American Constitutionalism in Postwar Europe: The Bonn Republic Basic Law and the Constitution of the Fifth French Republic." In George Athan Billias, ed., *American Constitutionalism Abroad,* 91–109. Westport, Conn.: Greenwood.

Saidi, Anas, ed. 2004. *Menekuk Agama, Membangun Tahta: Kebijakan Agama Orde Baru* (To Fold Religion, to Build the Throne: The New Order Policies on Religions). Jakarta: Desentara.

Salim, Arskal. 2003. "Epilogue: *Shari'a* in Indonesia's Current Transition: An Update." In Arskal Salim and Azyumardi Azra, eds., *Shari'a and Politics in Modern Indonesia,* 213–232. Singapore: ISEAS.

Salim, Arskal, and Azyumardi Azra. 2003. "Introduction: The State and *Shari'a* in the Perspective of Indonesian Legal Politics." In Arskal Salim and Azyumardi Azra, eds., *Shari'a and Politics in Modern Indonesia,* 1–16. Singapore: ISEAS.

Sanders, Paula. 1994. *Ritual, Politics, and the City in Fatimid Cairo.* Albany: State University of New York Press.

Savarkar, V. D. [1923] 1989. *Hindutva—Who Is a Hindu?* 6th ed. Bombay: Veer Savarkar Prakashan.

Schefold, Reimar. 1998. "Siberut: Souls in Fragile Harmony." In James J. Fox, ed., *Indonesian Heritage: Religion and Ritual,* 72–73. Singapore: Archipelago.

Schimmel, Annemarie. 1980. *Islam in the Indian Subcontinent.* Leiden: Brill.

Selçuk, Sami. 2000. *Longing for Democracy.* Ankara: Yeni Türkiye.

Sellars, Serpil Karacan. 2004. "Tug-of-War Over Islamic Headscarf . . . in Turkey." Panos London Online, Mar. 5. http://www.panos.org.uk/newsfeatures/featuredetails.asp?id=1186. Accessed Aug. 31, 2007.

Sen, Amartya. 2005. *The Argumentative Indian: Writings on Indian History, Culture, and Identity.* New York: Farrar, Straus and Giroux.

Şen, Serdar. 1997. "Türkiye'yi Anlamak ya da Geçmişten Geleceğe Silahlı Kuvvetler" (Understanding Turkey or the Armed Forces from the Past to the Future). *Birikim Monthly* 96 (Apr.): 19–27.

Seyyid Bey. 1923. *Hilafet ve Hakimiyet-i Milliye* (The Caliphate and National Sovereignty). Ankara.

Shaw, Stanford J. 1991. *Jews of the Ottoman Empire and the Turkish Republic.* New York: New York University Press.

Shepard, William E. 1996. *Sayyid Qutb and Islamic Activism: A Translation and Critical Analysis of Social Justice in Islam.* Leiden: Brill.

Shoshan, Boaz. 1981. "Fatimid Grain Policy and the Post of the Muhtasib." *International Journal of Middle East Studies* 13: 181–189.

Simuh. 2002. *Sufisme Jawa.* Yogyakarta: Bentang.

Smith, D. E. 1999. "India as a Secular State." In Rajeev Bhargava, ed., *Secularism and Its Critics.* Delhi: Oxford University Press.

Sukarno. 1965a. "Apa Sebab Turki Memisah Agama dari Negara?" (Why Did Turkey Separate Religion from State?). In *Dibawah Bendera Revolusi* (Under the Banner of Revolution), 403–445. Jakarta: Panitya Penerbit Dibawah Bendera Revolusi.

———. 1965b. "Saya Kurang Dinamis" (I Am Not Dynamic Enough). In *Dibawah Bendera Revolusi* (Under the Banner of Revolution), 447–455. Jakarta: Panitya Penerbit Dibawah Bendera Revolusi.

SundaNet. 2005. http://www.sundanet.com/artikel.php?id=249. Accessed Apr. 12, 2005.

Taha, Mahmoud Mohamed. 1987. *The Second Message of Islam*. Syracuse, N.Y.: Syracuse University Press.

Tanpınar, Ahmet Hamdi. 1985. *Türk Edebiyatı Tarihi: 19. Asır* (History of Turkish Literature: The 19th Century). Istanbul: Çağlayan Kitabevi.

Thakur, Ramesh. 1993. "Ayodhya and the Politics of Indian Secularism: A Double-Standards Discourse." *Asian Survey* 33: 645–664.

Tuna, Hüsnü. 2006. "The Scope and the Consequences of the Ban on Head Scarf in Turkey." *Lawyers Association, Report 3*. Warsaw, OSCE Human Dimension Implementation Meeting, Oct. 2–13. http://www.osce.org/documents/odihr/2006/10/21317_en.pdf. Accessed Aug. 31, 2007.

Turkish Press Review. 2005. "Bumin Voices Opposition to Lifting Ban on Headscarves in State Institutions." http://www.byegm.goc.tr/yayinlarimiz/chr/ing2005/04/05x04x26.htm#%200. Accessed Aug. 31, 2007.

Üçok, Coşkun. 1986. "Law in the Ottoman State before Tanzimat." In *Tanzimat'tan Cumhuriyet'e Türkiye Ansiklopedisi* (The Encyclopedia of Turkey from Tanzimat to the Republic), vol. 2, 574–579. Istanbul: İletişim.

Ülken, Hilmi Ziya. 1979. *Türkiye'de Çağdaş Düşünce Tarihi* (History of Modern Thought in Turkey). Istanbul: Ülken Yayınları.

Unat, Faik Reşit. 1968. *Osmanlı Sefirleri ve Sefaretnameleri* (Ottoman Ambassadors and Ambassador-Reports). Ankara: Türk Tarih Kurumu.

Upadhyaya, Prakash Chandra. 1992. "The Politics of Indian Secularism." *Modern Asian Studies* 26: 815–853.

Uzunçarşılı, İsmail H. 1984. *Osmanlı Devletinin İlmiye Teşkilâtı* (The Institution of *Ulama* in the Ottoman State). Ankara: Türk Tarih Kurumu.

Varshney, Ashutosh. 2002. *Ethnic Conflict and Civic Life: Hindus and Muslims in India*. New Haven, Conn.: Yale University Press.

Walker, Paul. 1997. "Fatimid Institutions of Learning." *Journal of the American Research Center in Egypt* 34: 197–200.

Weismann, Itzchak, and Fruma Zachs, eds. 2005. *Ottoman Reform and Muslim Regeneration*. London: I. B. Tauris.

Weiss, Bernard. 1998. *The Spirit of Islamic Law*. Athens, Ga.: University of Georgia Press.

White, Jenny. 2002. "The Dilemma of Islamism." In Deniz Kandiyoti and Ayse Saktanber, eds., *Kültür Fragmanları: Türkiye'de Gündelik Hayat* (Culture Fragments: Daily Life in Turkey). Istanbul: Metis.

Yediyıldız, Bahaeddin. 2001. "Ottoman Society." In Ekmeleddin İhsanoğlu, ed., *History of the Ottoman State, Society, and Civilisation*, vol. 1, 491–557. Istanbul: IRCICA.

Yılmaz, İhsan. 2005. "State, Law, Civil Society, and Islam in Contemporary Turkey." *Muslim World* 95 (July): 385–411.

Yusuf, Abu. 1963. *Kitab al-kharaj* (Book of *al-kharaj* Tax). Cairo: al-Matbaʿa al-Salafiyya.

Zaman, Muhammad Qasim. 1997. *Religion and Politics under the Early ʿAbbasids: The Emergence of the Proto-Sunni Elite*. Leiden: Brill.

Zürcher, Erik Jan. 1998. *Modernleşen Türkiye'nin Tarihi* (The History of Modernizing Turkey). Istanbul: İletişim.

———. 2004. *Turkey: A Modern History*. London: I. B. Tauris.

Index